METAMORPHOSES

ADVISORY EDITOR: BETTY RADICE

PUBLIUS OVIDUS NASO was born in 43 B.C. at Sulmo
(Sulmona) in central Italy. He was sent to Rome to attend the
schools of famous rhetoricians but, realizing that his talent lay
with poetry rather than politics, he began instead to cultivate
the acquaintance of literary Romans and to enjoy the smart
witty Roman society of which he soon became a leading
member. His first published work was *Amores*, a collection of
short love poems; then followed *Heroides*, verse-letters
supposedly written by deserted ladies to their former lovers,
Ars Amatoria, a handbook on love, *Remedia Amoris*, and
Metamorphoses. Ovid was working on *Fasti*, a poem on the
Roman calendar, when in A.D. 8 the Emperor Augustus
expelled him for some unknown offence to Tomis on the
Black Sea. He continued to write, notably *Tristia* and *Epistulae
ex Ponto*, and always spoke longingly of Rome. He died, still
in exile, in A.D. 17.

MARY M. INNES is a graduate of Glasgow and Oxford
Universities. She taught for some time in the Universities of
Belfast and Aberdeen and has since spent over twenty years
proving to schoolgirls that the classical languages can and
should be enjoyed. She has now retired to a Scottish University
town.

THE
Metamorphoses
OF OVID

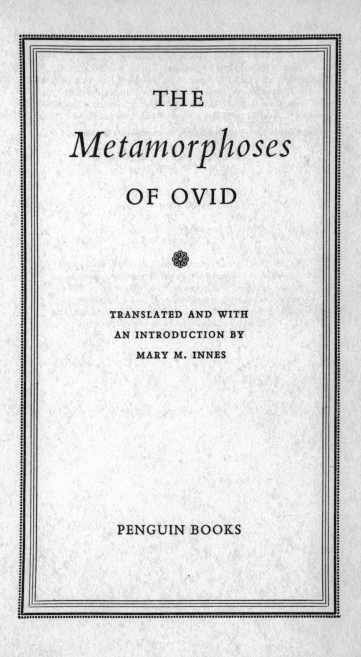

TRANSLATED AND WITH
AN INTRODUCTION BY
MARY M. INNES

PENGUIN BOOKS

PENGUIN BOOKS

Published by the Penguin Group
Penguin Books Ltd, 27 Wrights Lane, London W8 5TZ, England
Penguin Books USA Inc., 375 Hudson Street, New York, New York 10014, USA
Penguin Books Australia Ltd, Ringwood, Victoria, Australia
Penguin Books Canada Ltd, 10 Alcorn Avenue, Toronto, Ontario, Canada M4V 3B2
Penguin Books (NZ) Ltd, 182–190 Wairau Road, Auckland 10, New Zealand

Penguin Books Ltd, Registered Offices: Harmondsworth, Middlesex, England

This translation first published 1955
33 35 37 39 40 38 36 34

Printed in England by Clays Ltd, St Ives plc
Set in Monotype Bembo

CONTENTS

❋

CONTENTS

CONTENTS

CONTENTS

INTRODUCTION

❁

AMONG all the writings of Latin authors, few have appealed
to a wider public or had more effect on later literature than the
Metamorphoses of Ovid. In this work, the poet has gathered together a
rich assortment of tales, which have one element in common: they all
deal with transformations. He tells us of chaos changed into ordered
harmony, of animals turned to stone, of men and women who become
trees or animals, stones or stars. With this slender unity of theme, he
has produced a poem of fifteen books, which holds the reader's atten-
tion to the end. The telling of stories must have been one of the earliest
forms of entertainment, but it has lost none of its fascination, and in
the *Metamorphoses* Ovid reveals himself as a prince of story-tellers.
The tales he has to offer are not new: he has collected them from the
pages of the Greek poets whose works formed an essential part of the
education of every Roman, from previous anthologies of Greek
myths, from Latin folk-lore, and even from further afield, from
Babylon and the East. But he has infused new life into the old stories,
retailing them with the inimitable grace and practised ease of one who
knows well how to hold his audience. The result is a treasure-house of
myth and legend, which was read with delight in his own day, and has
continued to charm succeeding generations, providing a source from
which the whole of western European literature has derived inspira-
tion. And yet this poem, coloured with rhetoric, it is true, but full of
the freshness and charm of a world newly born, is the work of one
who was, at the same time, among the most sophisticated of Latin
writers.

I. OVID'S LIFE AND WORKS

Ovid was born at Sulmo, about ninety miles east of Rome, in the year 43 B.C. He is himself the best source of information concerning his life and times, for he liked nothing better than talking about himself, and counted himself lucky to live when and where he did. His father intended him to pursue a career of public office, and so he was brought to Rome, with his brother, and there attended the schools of well-known teachers of rhetoric. But he quickly realized that the life designed for him was wholly unsuited to his tastes, and that any fame he might win would be derived from poetry. He lacked the earnest application necessary to make a success of a political career whereas poetry, as he tells us himself, flowed from his lips of its own accord. He therefore began to cultivate the acquaintance of literary men in Rome and, at the same time, to enjoy the pleasures of the city. He was soon acknowledged as a leading member of its gay and witty society. Augustus had at last brought peace to his troubled country, and the younger citizens, at any rate, freed from anxiety and to a large extent from any responsibilities, were ready to make the most of the pleasurable opportunities that offered. Magnificent new buildings were being built to enhance the appearance of the city, shows and entertainments were lavishly provided for the people's amusement. Meanwhile the literary salons of Messala and Maecenas encouraged young writers to exercise their talents, free from any mundane cares. There was plenty of scope for a talented young poet to enjoy himself, and Ovid did so to the full. But, in the midst of his gay social life, he retained a deep respect for his fellow poets and, though he only saw the great Virgil, was proud to count himself the friend of Horace and Propertius.

His first published works were the *Amores*, a collection of shorter poems, weaving different variations on the basic theme suggested by the title. They followed closely in the tradition set by earlier elegiac poets, though the sincerity of Ovid's passion for the lady Corinna, and even her existence, may be doubted. Numerous allusions in the poems show him to be, as one would expect, already widely acquainted with mythology, and ready to embellish his verses with reminiscences of the classical tales. It is in the *Heroides*, however, which followed soon after, that he first uses stories of earlier, legendary, lovers as material for his own poetry, giving a new vitality to the ancient myths. These letters in verse, supposedly written by deserted ladies to the lovers who have abandoned them, led naturally to his next production, the *Ars Amatoria*, a handbook on the subject of love. Whatever criticisms it may have aroused, the *Art of Love*, as it is usually called, does undoubtedly convey a fascinating picture of contemporary Rome, and the daily life of its gay pleasure-loving society. In the course of this poem, Ovid occasionally digresses from his main theme to tell at length one of the old myths which has some relevance to his argument, or has been suggested to him by the context. In these passages his skill as a story-teller is already clearly revealed: they stand out from the rest as delightful cameos, instinct with a freshness and sympathy that contrasts notably with the polished cynicism of the rest. The pleasure which he obviously derived from relating the stories of Daedalus and Icarus, Cephalus and Procris, Theseus and Ariadne, all of which are retold in the *Metamorphoses*, may well have suggested the idea of a longer poem in which he could exercise his narrative gift on such themes exclusively. In any case, the *Art of Love* was a tour-de-force which could not be repeated: he published the *Remedies of Love*, to provide an antidote for his own prescriptions, but after that it was necessary to find some other medium for his restless genius.

It was probably at this time that he experimented in a more ambitious field, and composed his tragedy, the *Medea*, which was highly praised in antiquity, but has unfortunately not survived. It would have been interesting to compare it with the treatment of the same theme in the *Metamorphoses*. But, however successful it was, Ovid apparently decided against continuing in this branch of literature.

His next production was the *Metamorphoses* itself. For this he abandoned the elegiac couplet, and employed the hexameter line throughout. From its metre and its length – fifteen books in all – it can claim to be regarded as Ovid's essay in epic verse, and it is so regarded by Quintilian. Others have denied its right to be considered as an epic, for it can scarcely be said to possess the underlying unity that should characterize such verse. However, thanks to Ovid's unfailing dexterity, the work is so cleverly constructed that the reader is led on from one story to the next, without being conscious of any lack of cohesion. The poem has a certain chronological framework, beginning with the transformation of chaos into an ordered universe, then ranging at length through Greek mythology to the Trojan war and the escape of Aeneas to Italy. This leads to a synopsis of early Roman kings and so, with rather a rapid bound, to the transformation of Julius Caesar into a star, for the greater glory of his adopted son, the emperor Augustus with whose praises the poem ends.

But it was in vain that Ovid paid his tribute to Augustus. Before the *Metamorphoses* had received its final polish, while the *Fasti*, a poem on the Roman calendar, was only half-done (for he had characteristically begun on this before the completion of his previous work) Ovid was suddenly expelled from Rome, on some charge that was never made explicit, and ordered to live a life of exile at Tomis on the Black Sea coast. We have the poet's word for it that he had been guilty only of an indiscretion, not a crime, but for the rest we can only speculate. In a final burst of melodrama, before leaving Rome, he flung his *Metamorphoses* in the fire, declaring it as yet unfit for publication. No doubt he had Virgil in mind, who died before his epic was completed; but, without being uncharitable, we may feel sure that this gesture was not intended to be final, that Ovid knew there were other copies of his work in circulation, and that he had not any real intention of destroying the poem.

From his exile he continued to write, pouring out polished verse, appealing for pardon, describing the horrors of the land to which he had been exiled, its barbarity and icy chill, deploring the constant threats of war, and again appealing for a reprieve. But the years went on, and the pardon he sought was never granted. There are signs that he became more reconciled to his lot, and varied the laments of the *Tristia* and the *Epistulae ex Ponto* by writing a poem on the fishes of the Black Sea, and even attempting a poem in the Getic language. But he never ceased to speak longingly of Rome, even when his hopes of return gradually faded and disappeared. In A.D. 17 Ovid died, still an exile in Tomis. His fame, however, was securely founded: his own proud boast in the closing lines of the *Metamorphoses* has been supremely justified.

2. THE 'METAMORPHOSES'

When the general plan of the *Metamorphoses* had suggested itself to Ovid, there was no lack of material for him to use. All the best-known myths could be found in the works of Homer, or of the Greek dramatists, with which he would naturally be familiar from his schooldays. Moreover, the idea of collecting such tales into omnibus volumes was one that had already appealed to poets of the Hellenistic age. We know of such a compilation, the *Ornithogonia*, assigned to one Boios, which dealt with the transformation of men into birds, and Nicander of Colophon had been responsible for another collection, which Ovid probably used. In Rome itself, Ovid's friend and contemporary, Aemilius Macer, had translated the *Ornithogonia*, and the Greek Parthenius, tutor to Virgil and Tiberius, had produced a work entitled *Metamorphoses*. It is impossible to say how much Ovid may have derived from these earlier writings, but there is no doubt that, both in its scope, embracing some two hundred and fifty stories, and in the elegance of style and treatment, Ovid's *Metamorphoses* is unique. The narrative skill which the poet possessed was employed to weave his tales into one vast and elaborate tapestry – an appropriate metaphor, for the pictorial effect of Ovid's writing is sometimes almost overwhelming.

After the usual epic invocation of heaven's aid, Ovid launches straightway into an account of the origin of the world from a chaotic mass of elements, and describes their transformation into an ordered whole. We are then told of the four ages of the world, transmuted from gold to silver, then to bronze, and finally to iron. In this last age, all manner of wickedness appeared: there is therefore full scope for the story-teller. An age that is too peaceful and law-abiding makes dull reading, after a while. Jupiter himself reports to the gods the first transformation of man to beast, the punishment inflicted on Lycaon for his wickedness. The father of gods and men then announces his intention to destroy the entire human race. Afraid of fire, he sends the flood, strangely similar to that described in the Old Testament, but saves Deucalion and Pyrrha to repeople the earth. From that point the poem sweeps steadily on with never a break or hesitation. Apollo appears and slays the Python, then falls in love with Daphne, and the amorous adventures of the gods have begun. They continue throughout the next five books, and the first half of the sixth. Then it is the turn of the heroes of ancient Greece, Jason and Theseus and their like, till we come at length to the Trojan war and so, through Aeneas, to the ancient tales of Italy and of the Roman kings. The last and most glorious metamorphosis of all, in a Roman's eyes, is that of Julius Caesar into a star, in order that the father of Augustus may be no mere mortal. And so, with a panegyric on the emperor, the poet ends: having, as he set out to do, spun a thread of continuous narrative from the beginning of the world down to his own times.

Apart, however, from this continuous narrative, Ovid has a host of ingenious devices for introducing his stories. Sometimes one character recounts an anecdote for the benefit of the company, the daughters of Minyas while away the time as they spin by telling each other stories, broken-hearted Orpheus fills a whole book with his repertoire of songs, the Muses have a contest with the daughters of Pierus, which ends in the transformation of those presumptuous sisters. This contest enables Ovid to include the touching tale of Ceres and Proserpine, which he puts into the mouth of Calliope. Without some such excuse, it has no place in a record of transformations, even if the poet seeks to justify himself by recording changes that befell some of the minor characters.

The skill with which he links his tales is no less admirable than the variety of their presentation. There is no obvious connexion, in many cases, but Ovid is never at a loss. A character in one legend suggests another incident in which he was concerned, the name of a tree or flower, some chance remark, will serve to recall another story. No connexion is too slight, and yet there are few that seem forced. Nowadays the *Metamorphoses* is commonly read only in selections, and of course it lends itself admirably to such selective treatment. But it is only when the poem is read as a whole that one can fully appreciate Ovid's achievement. The work gives at least an illusion of unity, and he has managed to produce a semblance of cohesion between incidents where there is no necessary dramatic link.

The same gods are, of course, introduced over and over again, and have no sooner finished with one adventure than they become involved in the next. Jupiter is the chief menace to nymphs and mortal maidens, but Apollo and Mercury are not far behind. These are not by any means gods to be reverenced: but even Homer had at times failed to take the Olympians seriously, and we can hardly blame an Augustan poet for his attitude. If the deities show themselves distressingly susceptible to human faults and frailties, it is just because of these failings that Ovid makes them seem so alive, and gives such verisimilitude to his world of fancy. Jove can, on occasion, be majestic, but for the most part gods and men are treated in the same way, as actors in a universal drama, where Destiny is the only overriding force.

In his previous works Ovid, speaking in his own person, had had a reputation to maintain as a witty and cynical man of the world; in the *Metamorphoses*, a purely narrative poem, he can abandon this standpoint and reveal, not only insight, but a sympathetic insight into human emotions. As he had done in the *Heroides*, he portrays again pity and fear, tenderness and love, the first stirrings of passion, the turbulent jealousy of scorned love, with a faithfulness which no modern psychologist could surpass. His knowledge of human nature, so devastatingly employed in the *Art of Love*, is here used with kindlier intent. In the same way, the satirical wit of the earlier poem is replaced by a gentler kind of humour, such as is seen in the whimsical description of Jupiter changed into a bull for the carrying off of Europa, in the account of Polyphemus decking himself out to attract Galatea, or again in the delightful picture of Baucis and Philemon. He can even be whimsical at his own expense when, in describing Perseus' first glimpse of Andromeda, he almost makes his hero stand still in astonishment, but remembers in time that this would be fatal for one winging his way through the air.

The danger of monotony is avoided, partly by a variation of pace, and partly by changes in the tone of the poem. By lingering over some stories, passing over others briefly, or merely alluding to them in passing, Ovid prevents the feeling that this is a mere mythological handbook. Thus, when he makes the daughters of Minyas consider and reject so many tales, he is able to give us a brief acquaintance with a whole series of metamorphoses which he does not propose to treat at length. Again, when one particular myth has already received full treatment in some other Latin poem, he tends to pass over it rapidly. So we have only a short account of the desertion of Ariadne, which Ovid himself, in the *Art of Love*, and Catullus before him, had already described. The story of Iphigenia, told with such pathos by Lucretius, is given quite a different emphasis: the actual sacrifice is dismissed in one or two lines. The wanderings of Aeneas, familiar from the *Aeneid*, are only touched upon, and that same hero is hurried through the underworld with almost unseemly haste. This is not, of course, universally true: where a story appealed to him particularly, he was not deterred from telling it again. An instance that springs to mind is the tale of Orpheus and Eurydice, which is given in detail, though Virgil had already recounted it in the *Georgics*. The story of Procris and Cephalus, and that of Daedalus and Icarus, both of which had been introduced into the *Art of Love*, are related again at considerable length in the *Metamorphoses*. Lengthy too, and less pleasant reading, are the orgies of horrors in Ovid's descriptions of battle scenes. Like Lucan after him, he leaves nothing to the imagination. On the whole, however, there is a skilful blending of detailed and less detailed narrative, and of stories of different lengths.

Nor is there any lack of variety in tone and style. It has been said that Ovid felt a sustained effort in the grand manner to be beyond him: hence his rejection of the heroic epic in favour of a more intimate variety. None the less he can, when occasion demands, rise to a really noble tone. The first book, in the description of the world's creation, is solemn and dignified, and can bear comparison with any epic verse. The same is true of much of the philosophy in the fifteenth book. There is grandeur in his description of the North wind, lyric ecstasy in the invocation of Bacchus: while passages calling for gentler and more subdued treatment find him ready with an easy flow of musical verse.

It must be admitted, however, that at times his rhetorical training becomes rather obtrusive. We see it in his love of catalogues, admittedly a feature of epic, but carried to quite incredible lengths by Ovid. One has only to think of the list of hounds which tore Actaeon apart, the trees that crowd into a shade round Orpheus, the mountain peaks set alight by Phaethon, the lovesong of Polyphemus, to realize how far he carried this trick, which strikes a modern reader as somewhat tedious. He also shows a fondness for stock themes, where he seems to invite comparison with earlier poets. An instance of this is to be found in his description of the Golden Age, a favourite subject of Augustan authors: another is his account of the plague which carried off the subjects of King Aeacus, and calls to mind the passages in Virgil and Lucretius, dealing with the same topic. The long speech of Pythagoras in the fifteenth book may be taken to be Ovid's answer to philosophical poetry, challenging the Epicurean philosophy of Lucretius, but it has a rather subtle application to the theme of the

Metamorphoses itself. The main doctrine of the Pythagoreans, metempsychosis, taught that the soul migrated from one body to another, even from humans into animals, and this might seem to lend a kind of justification to the transformations that Ovid has been describing in the previous books. This idea is never made explicit: stress is laid not so much on the transmigration of souls, as on the vegetarianism that it entails. None the less the constant state of flux and the changing forms that Pythagoras describes may well have seemed to Ovid to lend colour to the changes he himself recorded. His education in rhetoric makes itself felt most forcibly, however, in the set speeches which he puts into the mouths of his characters, whenever opportunity offers. In times of stress his heroines, debating with themselves possible courses of action, do so with all the accomplished tricks of style which an experienced orator might use. Medea and Byblis, Myrrha and Scylla and the rest, show every sign of having studied profitably in the schools of Rome; so carefully do they weigh up balanced arguments on both sides, presenting the alternatives as persuasively as possible, indulging in rhetorical questions and antitheses, before committing themselves to the course of action which they have obviously been intending to pursue from the start. The most elaborate example of a debate is, however, a more legitimate one, the contest between Ajax and Ulysses, to determine the fate of Achilles' arms: a theme which we learn from Juvenal was a stock subject of debate in the rhetorical schools.

Before leaving our consideration of the *Metamorphoses*, it is worth while to notice how much is contributed to the poem by Ovid's appreciation of the beauties of nature. Ovid as a nature poet is somewhat unexpected, but in the setting of the stories, no less than in their personages, he delights to exercise his vivid imagination and, by his words, conjure up a clear and detailed picture of the scenes of the various adventures. There is no suggestion that he, any more than most classical poets, was concerned to describe the actual landscape with which he was himself familiar, in Italy, Sicily, or Greece. The settings for these conventional tales are themselves conventional: a cave in some secluded glade, a bay of the sea, a mountain overhanging the waters – in each case his artist's eye sees the whole picture, and gives it reality by stressing just the kind of detail that would naturally be noticed. The stream so clear that its pebbles can be counted, the still pool hidden among shady trees, the beach where the sand is of just the right texture for walking, these are places we all know, and yet there is a magic about them too, so that his woodlands and his limpid pools are eminently fit to be peopled by nymphs and rustic deities. This shows yet another side of Ovid's talent, and pastoral poetry could and did derive much from the pages of the *Metamorphoses*. No less effective are the more specialized descriptions of places which, though we are never likely to see them, are made real to us by the poet's words. We have only to think of the house of Envy, where all is slime and rottenness, the hungry haunts of Famine, the whispering home from which Rumour sees and hears and exaggerates news from all the world, the drowsy cave of Sleep, to realize the liveliness of the poet's fancy, and his outstanding descriptive talent.

3. THE 'METAMORPHOSES' IN LATER LITERATURE

Though Ovid ended his life under a cloud, though his *Art of Love* had been banned and his *Metamorphoses* consigned to the flames by his own hand, there is no doubt that these, as well as his other works, circulated freely in Rome in the days of the early empire. Poets of the first century, Manilius, Martial, Statius, and Juvenal, show themselves well acquainted with his poems, and at the end of the century Quintilian, in his literary criticism, considers him as an epic, lyric, and dramatic poet. He accords him rather grudging praise, however, censures him for levity and lack of self-discipline, and calls the *Metamorphoses* 'deserving of praise in parts'. The temper of the times was changing, and Ovid's popularity declined. Nor was he regarded with approval in the centuries that followed, when the influence of the early Christian teachers and preachers was in the ascendant. They disapproved of the pagan writers, especially the poets, as likely to be harmful to the morals of the reader. From their point of view, Ovid's writings, with their worldly attitude, their frank tales of the Olympians' none too respectable behaviour, and their open enjoyment of this world's pleasures, would be calculated to do much harm, however charming they might seem. In fact, their charm made them all the more dangerous. Yet, however much he was frowned upon, he must still have been copied and read. Indeed, if pagan authors were banned, there was little left for men to read, and one could always try to have the best of both worlds by showing that the ancient writers were not wholly unenlightened. So the early Christian father, Lactantius, quotes Ovid's *Metamorphoses* to show that even a pagan poet believed in a single god by whom the world was created. Further evidence that Ovid was not ignored in those early centuries is to be found in the prose summaries of the tales, included in the earliest extant manuscripts. These are generally assigned to a sixth century grammarian, Lactantius Placidus, and it has been suggested that they were most probably intended for use in schools. Whether he had a place in the curriculum at this early date is doubtful, but at any rate he had not been forgotten. In the time of Charlemagne, he is mentioned with approval by Theodolphus, Bishop of Orleans, one of the most distinguished men at the royal court, and a patron of education. Theodolphus includes Ovid among the Latin authors whom he is in the habit of reading, and foreshadows the treatment that was to allow even the devout to read him with impunity, by explaining that, though much of his writing is frivolous, many a truth is to be found hidden beneath the covering of fiction.

On the whole, however, Virgil is the classical poet to whom these early centuries were devoted: it was in medieval times that Ovid's fame spread throughout Europe to such an extent that no other Latin poet was as popular as he. This was natural enough in an age which delighted in romance and adventure, and revelled in stories combining both. It was probably his love poetry which first endeared him to a wider audience, for the Goliards, the wandering scholars of medieval Europe, claimed him as their patron, while the troubadours and Minnesänger found in his works a fertile source of inspiration for their own verse. Others were not slow to recognize his charm, and he rapidly became more widely known both as a model for Latin verse and for his subject matter too. His name appears in the school lists in Germany in the eleventh century, and in the twelfth century in France. Alexander Neckam, who taught in Paris towards the end of the twelfth century, and later in England, includes Ovid's *Metamorphoses* in the books prescribed for a course in Arts. The twelfth and thirteenth centuries of our era have, indeed, been called an 'aetas Ovidiana', and with good reason. A German translation of the *Metamorphoses* was produced in the early years of the thirteenth century, though it is now extant only in a later sixteenth century

version. In Spain there are signs of early Ovidian influence, and that
of the *Metamorphoses* can be recognized in the thirteenth century
Libro de Alexandre. In France, as early as the twelfth century, the first
great French poet Chrétien de Troyes translated portions of the
Metamorphoses: to him is assigned a translation and expansion of
Philomela's story, under the title *Philomena*, and there are versions in
old French, dating from about the same time, which may also be his,
of the tales of Narcissus and of Pyramus and Thisbe. For this last
story, which proved one of the most popular of all, Ovid is our
earliest authority. The influence of the *Metamorphoses* has also been
traced in the *Roman de la Rose*, one of the masterpieces of early French
literature: though this poem again owes more to Ovid's love poetry.
In a Provençal poem of the thirteenth century there is a list of tales
that minstrels ought to know, which includes a number from the
Metamorphoses.

About this time the *Metamorphoses* itself underwent a curious
transformation. In order that its tales might be read without ill-effect
and indeed with profit by the ordinary reader, versions were produced
which contained long allegorical explanations of the myths, and
linked up the stories of Ovid, where possible, with those of the
scriptures. In the matter of the Creation and the Flood, for instance,
there was an obvious resemblance which could be turned to good
account. Morals too were drawn from the myths, which would
assuredly have surprised the poet. So in an old French version, prob-
ably belonging to the early fourteenth century, known as the *Ovide
Moralisé*, the story of the flood is first equated with the Biblical one,
and then given an allegorical interpretation as the flood of sin, in
which all men drown. The Python is the devil, and Apollo who slays
him is Christ. The Daphne and Apollo myth has no less than five
different allegorical interpretations. Another treatise, attributed to a
fourteenth century Italian, offers some rather more prosaic explana-
tions. Actaeon, for instance, was a huntsman who had his eyes
opened to the folly of his sport. He therefore gave it up but, being a
kind-hearted man, kept his pack of hounds, who retaliated by ruining
him with their appetites. This kind of interpretation retained its
popularity, and many of the old translations contained such exposi-
tions, whether as a sop to conscience, or because the authors really
enjoyed such ingenious interpretations.

To return to the thirteenth century, the old Greek legends then suffered another Metamorphoses, back into their original tongue, when Ovid's poem was translated into Greek by the Byzantine monk, Planudes. This translation is still extant, and is of some importance for the verification of geographical names.

Meanwhile, in Ovid's own land of Italy, one of the greatest poets of all time was paying tribute to his genius. If Dante chose Virgil to be his guide through the underworld, he set Ovid in the highest place of honour that was possible for a pagan poet, and placed him in the company of such writers as Homer, Horace, and Lucan. There are constant references in Dante's great poem which reveal the extent of his knowledge of Ovid's work, and his admiration for it. The *Metamorphoses* was his chief source for classical mythology, and at one point he even issues a challenge to its author as he prepares to outdo him in his own field, by effecting a double transformation of man to snake and snake to man. Boccaccio too, himself an inimitable story-teller, was naturally attracted to Ovid. In the *Amorosa Visione* he retells several of Ovid's tales, including the favourite Pyramus and Thisbe. The *Decameron*, though less obviously indebted to Ovid, does recall in its framework, in the decision to relieve the tedium of a country existence by telling stories, until the plague in the city should subside, the occasion when the daughters of Minyas resolved to while away the time in a similar way, while others were engaged in Bacchus' festival.

Ovid came early to England too, and could be happily quoted by such men as Walter Map, before the end of the twelfth century. But it was Chaucer, who had probably gained his love for Ovid in France, who first showed how much the Latin poet could mean to an English one. In the *House of Fame* he dedicates one of the pillars to *Venus clerk Ovyde*, and much else in the poem is derived from the *Metamorphoses*. Indeed, the influence both of Ovid's love poetry and of his narrative verse is clearly to be seen throughout Chaucer's writings. In the *Legend of Good Women*, the story of Pyramus and Thisbe is told again, in a reasonably close version of the original. Other tales in the same collection are partially, if not wholly, indebted to the *Metamorphoses*. The whole idea of the *Canterbury Tales*, too, a number of stories strung together by a very slender thread of connexion, is in the Ovidian tradition, and many allusions in the tales themselves indicate that Ovid's poems were constantly in Chaucer's mind. About the same time the poet Gower, possibly encouraged by Chaucer's success with the ancient stories, recounted many of Ovid's myths from the *Metamorphoses* in his *Confessio Amantis*.

Ovid's popularity probably reached its height in the twelfth to the fourteenth centuries, but once established he continued to be one of the best known and most widely read of classical authors. Translations of the *Metamorphoses* into more or less allegorized versions were produced in great numbers and in various languages – there are sixteenth century versions in English, German, Italian, Spanish, and French. Writers who knew Ovid either through these translations or in the original continued to enrich their works with fables, illustrations, and allusions, which they owed to him. Apart from the poets, painters and sculptors of the renaissance too found an inexhaustible source of inspiration in his works. The famous group of Daphne and Apollo by Bernini, and Benvenuto Cellini's Perseus, still holding up the Gorgon's head in the main square of Florence, are but two of many examples that could be cited of the way in which Ovid's pictorial images have been transmuted into metal or stone, and few of the myths have not, at one time or another, been transferred to some painter's canvas. In the world of literature, too, all Western Europe continued to acknowledge his appeal. Ariosto admired and imitated Ovid, Montaigne devoured the *Metamorphoses* with delight as a story book, before ever he went to school, Cervantes shows himself well acquainted with the spirit and substance of the poem, whether from the original or from translations, the Spanish dramatists of the seventeenth century made extensive use of the *Metamorphoses* in their mythological plays, La Fontaine translated some of its stories in his *Contes*, and used two of the legends in his poem on the death of Adonis. Camoens, too, shows Ovid's influence in his Portuguese epic, the *Lusiads*, and has at least one transformation worthy of Ovid himself. The first European opera, staged at Florence in 1594, was entitled *Dafne*, and presented the favourite story in yet another medium.

In England the *Metamorphoses* was translated and probably published by Caxton, in 1480. But the first important translation of the whole was that of Golding, published in 1567, which gained a deservedly high place in the affections of his readers. Long before this, however, Ovid was being read as a prescribed author in the schools, at least in selections, so that his works were well known to men of letters. No other poet was ever again so completely in sympathy with Ovid as Chaucer had been, but the value of his tales for the embroidery of other themes continued to be recognized. Spenser, himself a sound classical scholar, shows by numerous references and reminiscences in the *Faerie Queene* that he knew the *Metamorphoses* well. Shakespeare, whatever the extent of his knowledge of Latin, seems to have read at least some Ovid in the original. He also knew Golding's translation, and made use of it for his own ends. The remark of the contemporary critic Meres, that 'the sweet witty soul of Ovid lives in mellifluous honey-tongued Shakespeare', might suggest that it was the Ovidian spirit, rather than his matter, that was to be recognized in Shakespeare's pages: but the direct influence of Ovid can be discerned too. Perhaps the best known example is Shakespeare's burlesque of the Pyramus and Thisbe episode, in *A Midsummer-Night's Dream*. Ovid himself would have enjoyed this. Another instance is to be found in *The Tempest*, where Prospero's invocation to the spirits of magic is closely modelled on Medea's incantations in the seventh book of the *Metamorphoses*. Nor is it only in the plays that Ovidian influence is manifest. As Meres points out, Shakespeare's first poem, *Venus and Adonis*, retells one of Ovid's tales, and much of the philosophy of the sonnets, and even their language, is reminiscent of the words which Ovid put into the mouth of Pythagoras.

The lesser Elizabethans, too, were devoted admirers of Ovid, translated portions of his verse, and made use of it in their own works.

Milton's poetry is perhaps more akin to that of Virgil than to Ovid's verse, but he too knew and loved the *Metamorphoses*. Some interesting early stanzas have survived, which he wrote to accompany a set of engravings, illustrating scenes from the poem. These stanzas are in Latin and recount briefly the myth in question: the work is of no great poetic value, but gives an interesting glimpse of the exercises of the young poet. In his later years, his daughter, whose task it was to read aloud to her blind father, noted that the *Metamorphoses* was one of his favourite compositions, second in his affections only to those of Homer.

Another well-known translation was produced in 1626, that of Sandy's, with the impressive title of *Ovid's Metamorphoses Englished, Mythologized, and Represented in Figures*. Ovid was still being interpreted, as well as translated. Towards the end of the century, Dryden too translated large portions of the poem – he regarded the fifteenth book as far the best – and published these translations, along with tales from Homer, Chaucer, and Boccaccio, under the title *Fables Ancient and Modern*.

In the eighteenth century, Ovid was still part of the equipment of every educated man, served as a model for Latin verse, and provided a rich fund of classical allusions. Writers of the time enjoyed turning him into polished English verse, and there were several composite translations as, for example, that published by Samuel Garth, which is described as 'Ovid's *Metamorphoses* translated by Dryden, Addison, Garth, Mainwaring, Rowe, Pope, Gay, Eusden, Croxall, and other eminent hands'. Pope declared that he had himself translated more than a quarter of the *Metamorphoses* as a literary exercise, but only two fragments were ever polished and published, the story of Dryope, and of Pomona and Vertumnus. But in spite of his appeal to these new Augustan poets, Ovid's influence was now waning. He had, in fact, made his contribution to our literature: the essence of what he had to give had been so completely absorbed that it was now part of our own tradition, and poets were looking away from the classics, trying to develop a new kind of verse. They had less sympathy with purely narrative poetry, and reacted against sophistication and too polished urbanity of style. The nineteenth century still knew its classical authors, and there was much that they could use in Ovid's myths and in the freshness of his countryside. His influence can be traced in Keats and Shelley, Byron and Browning, but their main interests lay elsewhere and it is a task only for specialists to seek out the extent of their debt to Ovid. Time would be better spent in returning to the *Metamorphoses*, and familiarizing ourselves with the tales in their original form, as they have appealed to the greatest poets of our own and other languages, both for their own sake and for the heightened appreciation of such poets which comes from the sharing of a common background.

INTRODUCTION

4. THE TRANSLATION

The purpose of this translation has been to produce a version which, while remaining faithful to the text, offers pleasant and easy reading, even to the non-classicist. To achieve this end, it has been necessary to do two things which may require some explanation.

In the first place, it is a common device of Latin epic verse to make frequent use of apostrophe, addressing things animate and inanimate in the second person, partly because the vocative case is often more convenient metrically than the nominative. Such a usage is not a feature of English prose, and has therefore been dropped, except where there seemed to be some definite reason, other than metrical convenience, for the use of the vocative. Thus, when Ovid begins the story of the slaying of the Python with the words: 'It was then, O earth, that you produced the serpent,' he does not have any special reason for addressing the earth in person, and that apostrophe has accordingly been removed: but his lyrical apostrophe of the god Bacchus at the beginning of the fourth book does express the rapture of the Bacchic worshippers, and so the direct mode of address has been retained.

Again, Ovid could count on a reading public more or less familiar with many of the personages in his tales, and he sometimes introduced a character abruptly, knowing that his readers would recognize the connexion for themselves. The result can be confusing for those without specialized classical knowledge. One solution is to append a glossary of names, but constant reference to glossary or footnotes detracts considerably from the pleasure of reading any book. The difficulty can usually be resolved by the insertion of some brief descriptive phrase, and this is the method I have adopted. Only a few words have been added, and that only on a few occasions: they can easily be ignored by those who know their Latin, but should help to clarify the narrative for the non-specialist.

M. M. I.

January 1955

The Metamorphoses

BOOK I

❀

M Y purpose is to tell of bodies which have been transformed into shapes of a different kind. You heavenly powers, since you were responsible for those changes, as for all else, look favourably on my attempts, and spin an unbroken thread of verse, from the earliest beginnings of the world, down to my own times.

Before there was any earth or sea, before the canopy of heaven stretched overhead, Nature presented the same aspect the world over, that to which men have given the name of Chaos. This was a shapeless uncoordinated mass, nothing but a weight of lifeless matter, whose ill-assorted elements were indiscriminately heaped together in one place. There was no sun, in those days, to provide the world with light, no crescent moon ever filling out her horns: the earth was not poised in the enveloping air, balanced there by its own weight, nor did the sea stretch out its arms along the margins of the shores. Although the elements of land and air and sea were there, the earth had no firmness, the water no fluidity, there was no brightness in the sky. Nothing had any lasting shape, but everything got in the way of everything else; for, within that one body, cold warred with hot, moist with dry, soft with hard, and light with heavy.

This strife was finally resolved by a god, a natural force of a higher kind, who separated the earth from heaven, and the waters from the earth, and set the clear air apart from the cloudy atmosphere. When he had freed these elements, sorting them out from the heap where they had lain, indistinguishable from one another, he bound them fast, each in its separate place, forming a harmonious union. The fiery aether, which has no weight, formed the vault of heaven, flashing upwards to take its place in the highest sphere. The air, next to it in lightness, occupied the neighbouring regions. Earth, heavier than

29

these, attracted to itself the grosser elements, and sank down under its own weight, while the encircling sea took possession of the last place of all, and held the solid earth in its embrace. In this way the god, whichever of the gods it was, set the chaotic mass in order, and, after dividing it up, arranged it in its constituent parts.

When this was done, his first care was to shape the earth into a great ball, so that it might be the same in all directions. After that, he commanded the seas to spread out this way and that, to swell into waves under the influence of the rushing winds, and to pour themselves around earth's shores. Springs, too, he created, and great pools and lakes, and confined between sloping banks the rivers which flow down from the hills and continue, each in its own channel, until they are either swallowed up by the earth itself, or reach the sea and enter its expanse of wider waters, there to wash against shores instead of banks. Then the god further ordained that earth's plains should unroll, its valleys sink down, the woods be clothed with leaves, and rocky mountain peaks rise up.

As the sky is divided into two zones on the right hand, and two on the left, with a fifth in between, hotter than any of the rest, so the world which the sky encloses was marked off in the same way, thanks to the providence of the god: he imposed the same number of zones on earth as there are in the heavens. The central zone is so hot as to be uninhabitable, while two others are covered in deep snow: but between these extremes he set two zones to which he gave a temperate climate, compounded of heat and cold.

Over all these regions hangs the air, as much heavier than the fiery aether as it is lighter than earth or water. To the air the god assigned mists and clouds, and thunder that was destined to cause human hearts to tremble: here too he placed the thunderbolts, and winds that strike out lightnings from the clouds. Nor did the builder of the world allow the winds, any more than the rest, to roam at will throughout the air – they can scarcely be prevented from tearing the world apart, even as it is, although each blows in a different direction: so violent is the strife between brothers. The East wind withdrew to the lands of the dawn, to the kingdoms of Arabia and Persia, and to the mountain ridges that lie close to the sun's morning rays. The West, and the shores which are warmed by the setting sun, are subject to Zephyr. Boreas, who makes men shudder with his chill breath, invaded Scythia and the North, while the lands opposite to those are continually drenched with rain and clouds, brought by the South wind.

Above all these, the god set the clear aether that has no weight, and is untainted by any earthly particles.

No sooner were all things separated in this way, and confined within definite limits, than the stars which had long been buried in darkness and obscurity began to blaze forth all through the sky. So that every region should have its appropriate inhabitants, stars and divine forms occupied the heavens, the waters afforded a home to gleaming fishes, earth harboured wild beasts, and the yielding air welcomed the birds.

There was as yet no animal which was more akin to the gods than these, none more capable of intelligence, none that could be master over all the rest. It was at this point that man was born: either the Creator, who was responsible for this better world, made him from divine seed, or else Prometheus, son of Iapetus, took the new-made earth which, only recently separated from the lofty aether, still retained some elements related to those of heaven and, mixing it with rainwater, fashioned it into the image of the all-governing gods. Whereas other animals hang their heads and look at the ground, he made man stand erect, bidding him look up to heaven, and lift his head to the stars. So the earth, which had been rough and formless, was moulded into the shape of man, a creature till then unknown.

In the beginning was the Golden Age, when men of their own accord, without threat of punishment, without laws, maintained good faith and did what was right. There were no penalties to be afraid of, no bronze tablets were erected, carrying threats of legal action, no crowd of wrong-doers, anxious for mercy, trembled before the face of their judge: indeed, there were no judges, men lived securely without them. Never yet had any pine tree, cut down from its home on the mountains, been launched on ocean's waves, to visit foreign lands: men knew only their own shores. Their cities were not yet surrounded by sheer moats, they had no straight brass trumpets, no coiling brass horns, no helmets and no swords. The peoples of the world, untroubled by any fears, enjoyed a leisurely and peaceful existence, and had no use for soldiers. The earth itself, without compulsion, untouched by the hoe, unfurrowed by any share, produced all things spontaneously, and men were content with foods that grew without cultivation. They gathered arbute berries and mountain strawberries, wild cherries and blackberries that cling to thorny bramble bushes: or acorns, fallen from Jupiter's spreading oak. It was a season of everlasting spring, when peaceful zephyrs, with their warm breath, caressed the flowers that sprang up without having been planted. In time the earth, though untilled, produced corn too, and fields that never lay fallow whitened with heavy ears of grain. Then there flowed rivers of milk and rivers of nectar, and golden honey dripped from the green holm-oak.

When Saturn was consigned to the darkness of Tartarus, and the world passed under the rule of Jove, the age of silver replaced that of gold, inferior to it, but superior to the age of tawny bronze. Jupiter shortened the springtime which had prevailed of old, and instituted a cycle of four seasons in the year, winter, summer, changeable autumn, and a brief spring. Then, for the first time, the air became parched and arid, and glowed with white heat, then hanging icicles formed under the chilling blasts of the wind. It was in those days that men first sought covered dwelling places: they made their homes in caves and thick shrubberies, or bound branches together with bark. Then corn, the gift of Ceres, first began to be sown in long furrows, and straining bullocks groaned beneath the yoke.

After that came the third age, the age of bronze, when men were of a fiercer character, more ready to turn to cruel warfare, but still free from any taint of wickedness.

Last of all arose the age of hard iron: immediately, in this period which took its name from a baser ore, all manner of crime broke out; modesty, truth, and loyalty fled. Treachery and trickery took their place, deceit and violence and criminal greed. Now sailors spread their canvas to the winds, though they had as yet but little knowledge of these, and trees which had once clothed the high mountains were fashioned into ships, and tossed upon the ocean waves, far removed from their own element. The land, which had previously been common to all, like the sunlight and the breezes, was now divided up far and wide by boundaries, set by cautious surveyors. Nor was it only corn and their due nourishment that men demanded of the rich earth: they explored its very bowels, and dug out the wealth which it had hidden away, close to the Stygian shades; and this wealth was a further incitement to wickedness. By this time iron had been discovered, to the hurt of mankind, and gold, more hurtful still than iron. War made its appearance, using both those metals in its conflict, and shaking clashing weapons in bloodstained hands. Men lived on what they could plunder: friend was not safe from friend, nor father-in-law from son-in-law, and even between brothers affection was rare. Husbands waited eagerly for the death of their wives, and wives for that of their husbands. Ruthless stepmothers mixed brews of deadly aconite, and sons pried into their fathers' horoscopes, impatient for them to die. All proper affection lay vanquished and, last of the immortals, the maiden Justice left the blood-soaked earth.

The heights of heaven were no safer than the earth; for the giants, so runs the story, assailed the kingdom of the gods and, piling mountains together, built them up to the stars above. Then the almighty father hurled his thunderbolt, smashed through Olympus, and flung down Pelion from where it had been piled on top of Ossa. The terrible bodies of the giants lay crushed beneath their own massive structures, and the earth was drenched and soaked with torrents of blood from her sons. Then, they say, she breathed life into this warm blood and, so that her offspring might not be completely forgotten, changed it into the shape of men. But the men thus born, no less than the giants, were contemptuous of the gods, violent and cruel, with a lust to kill: it was obvious that they were the children of blood.

When the father of the gods, the son of Saturn, looked down from his high citadel, and saw what was going on, he groaned aloud. He recalled the horrid banquet of Lycaon which had not yet become common knowledge, so recent was the deed, and his heart swelled with dreadful wrath, worthy of Jupiter. He called together his council, and they did not delay when they heard his summons.

There is a track across the heavens, plain to see in the clear sky. It is called the Milky Way, and is famous for its brightness. It is by this road that the gods come to the palace of the mighty Thunderer, and to his royal home. On the right hand and on the left stand the houses of distinguished gods, filled with crowds that throng their open doors. The ordinary inhabitants of heaven live elsewhere, in different places. Here the powerful and noble divinities have made their homes. This is the spot which, were I allowed to speak boldly, I would not hesitate to call the Palatine district of high heaven.

So the gods took their seats in the marble council chamber, and their lord sat, throned high above them, leaning on his ivory sceptre. Three times, four times, he shook those awe-inspiring locks and with them moved the earth, the sea, the stars. Then he opened his lips, and spoke these indignant words: 'Never was I more anxious concerning the sovereignty of the universe, no, not even at that time when each of the snaky-footed giants was preparing to throw his hundred arms round the sky and take it captive. For then the attack was made by one small group of enemies and, although they were fierce ones, still the trouble originated from one source. Now the entire human race must be destroyed, throughout all the lands which Nereus surrounds with his roaring waters. I swear by the rivers of the underworld that flow through the Stygian grove beneath the earth: all other remedies have already been tried. This cancer is incurable, and must be cut out by the knife, in case the healthy part become infected. We have the demigods to care for, the spirits of the countryside, nymphs and fauns, satyrs and silvani, who roam the hills. Since we have not, as yet, considered them worthy of the honour of a place in heaven, let us at least ensure that they can live on the earth which we have given them. For can you believe, you gods, that they will go unmolested when Lycaon, a man notorious for his savagery, has laid plots against me, the lord and master of the thunderbolt, aye, and your king and master too?'

All the gods muttered uneasily, and eagerly demanded the punishment of the man who had dared to do such a deed. Their dismay was such as was felt by the human race, when a wicked band of fanatics tried to extinguish the Roman name by shedding Caesar's blood: all men were seized by panic fear of instant destruction, and the whole world shuddered. Just as the loyal devotion of your subjects pleases you, Augustus, so did that of the gods please Jupiter. He checked their murmurs with a word, and as he raised his hand, all fell silent. When the uproar had subsided, hushed by the authority of the king of heaven, Jupiter again broke the silence with these words: 'As far as he is concerned, he has paid the penalty. Have no fear on that score. But I shall tell you what his crime was, and what his punishment.

'Scandalous rumours concerning the state of the times had reached my ears. Hoping to find them false, I descended from the heights of Olympus, and walked the earth, a god in human form. It would take long to tell what wickedness I found on every side. Even the scandalous rumours were less than the truth. I had crossed over the ridge of Maenalus, a place bristling with the lairs of wild beasts, over Cyllene, and through the pinewoods of chill Lycaeus. From there, when the last shades of twilight were heralding the night, I entered the inhospitable home of the Arcadian tyrant. I revealed myself as a god, and the people began to do me homage. Lycaon, however, first laughed at their pious prayers, and then exclaimed: "I shall find out, by an infallible test, whether he be god or mortal: there will be no doubt about the truth." His plan was to take me unawares, as I lay sound asleep at night, and kill me. This was the test of truth on which he was resolved. Not content with that, he took a hostage sent him by the Molossian people, slit the man's throat with his sharp blade, and cooked his limbs, still warm with life, boiling some and roasting others over the fire. Then he set this banquet on the table. No sooner had he done so, than I with my avenging flames brought the house crashing down upon its household gods, gods worthy of such a master. Lycaon fled, terrified, until he reached the safety of the silent countryside. There he uttered howling noises, and his attempts to speak were all in vain. His clothes changed into bristling hairs, his arms to legs, and he became a wolf. His own savage nature showed in his rabid jaws, and he now directed against the flocks his innate lust for killing. He had a mania, even yet, for shedding blood. But, though he was a wolf, he retained some traces of his original shape. The greyness of his hair was the same, his face showed the same violence, his eyes gleamed as before, and he presented the same picture of ferocity.

'One house has fallen, but far more than one have deserved to perish. To the ends of the earth, the dread Fury holds sway. You would think men had sworn allegiance to crime! They shall all be punished, forthwith, as they deserve. Such is my resolve.'

Some of the gods shouted their approval of Jove's words, and sought to increase his indignation: others played the part of silent supporters. Yet all were grieved at the thought of the destruction of the human race, and wondered what the earth would be like, in future, when it had been cleared of mortal inhabitants. They inquired who would bring offerings of incense to their altars, whether Jove meant to abandon the world to the plundering of wild beasts. In answer to their questions, the king of the gods assured them that they need not be anxious, for he himself would attend to everything. He promised them a new stock of men, unlike the former ones, a race of miraculous origin.

Now he was on the point of launching his thunderbolts against every part of the earth, when he felt a sudden dread lest he should set light to the pure upper air by so many fiery bolts, and send the whole vault of heaven up in flames. He remembered, too, one of fate's decrees, that a time would come when sea and earth and the dome of the sky would blaze up, and the massive structure of the universe collapse in ruins. So he laid aside the weapons forged by the hands of the Cyclopes, and resolved on a different punishment, namely to send rain pouring down from every quarter of the sky, and so destroy mankind beneath the waters.

He wasted no time, but imprisoned the North wind in Aeolus' caves, together with all the gusts which dispel the gathering clouds; and he let loose the South wind. On dripping wings the South wind flew, his terrible features shrouded in pitchy darkness. His beard was heavy with rain, water streamed from his hoary locks, mists wreathed his brow, his robes and feathers dripped with moisture. When he crushed the hanging clouds in his broad hand, there was a crash; thereafter sheets of rain poured down from heaven. Juno's messenger Iris, clad in rainbow hues, drew up water and supplied nourishment to the clouds. The corn was laid low, and the crops the farmer had prayed for now lay flattened and sadly mourned, the long year's toil was wasted and gone for nothing.

Nor was Jupiter's anger satisfied with the resources of his own realm of heaven: his brother Neptune, the god of the sea, lent him the assistance of his waves. He sent forth a summons to the rivers, and when they entered their king's home: 'No time now for long exhortations!' he cried. 'Exert your strength to the utmost: that is what we need. Fling wide your homes, withdraw all barriers, and give free course to your waters.' These were his orders. The rivers returned to their homes and, opening up the mouths of their springs, went rushing to the sea in frenzied torrents.

Neptune himself struck the earth with his trident; it trembled, and by its movement threw open channels for the waters. Across the wide plains the rivers raced, overflowing their banks, sweeping away in one torrential flood crops and orchards, cattle and men, houses and

temples, sacred images and all. Any building which did manage to sur-
vive this terrible disaster unshaken and remain standing, was in the end
submerged when some wave yet higher than the rest covered its roof,
and its gables lay drowned beneath the waters. Now sea and earth could
no longer be distinguished: all was sea, and a sea that had no shores.

Some tried to escape by climbing to the hilltops, others, sitting
in their curved boats, plied the oars where lately they had been
ploughing; some sailed over cornlands, over the submerged roofs of
their homes, while some found fish in the topmost branches of the
elms. At times it happened that they dropped anchor in green
meadows, sometimes the curved keels grazed vineyards that lay
beneath them. Where lately sinewy goats cropped the grass, now
ugly seals disported themselves. The Nereids wondered to see groves
and towns and houses under the water; dolphins took possession of
the woods, and dashed against high branches, shaking the oak trees
as they knocked against them. Wolves swam among the flocks, and
the waves supported tawny lions, and tigers too. The lightning stroke
of his strong tusk was of no use, then, to the wild boar, nor his swift
legs to the stag – both alike were swept away. Wandering birds
searched long for some land where they might rest, till their wings
grew weary and they fell into the sea. The ocean, all restraints
removed, overwhelmed the hills, and waves were washing the
mountain peaks, a sight never seen before. The greater part of the
human race was swallowed up by the waters: those whom the sea
spared died from lack of food, overcome by long-continued famine.

There is a land, Phocis, which separates the fields of Boeotia from
those of Oeta. It was a fertile spot while it was land, but now it had
become part of the sea, a broad stretch of waters, suddenly formed. In
that region a high mountain, called Parnassus, raises twin summits to
the stars, and its ridges pierce the clouds. When the waters had
covered all the rest of the earth, the little boat which carried Deucalion
and his wife ran aground here. Of all the men who ever lived,
Deucalion was the best and the most upright, no woman ever showed
more reverence for the gods than Pyrrha, his wife. Their first action
was to offer prayers to the Corycian nymphs, to the deities of the
mountain, and to Themis, the goddess who foretold the future from
its oracular shrine.

Now Jupiter saw the earth all covered with standing waters. He perceived that one alone survived of so many thousand men, one only of so many thousand women, and he knew that both were guiltless, both true worshippers of god. So, with the help of the North wind he drove away the storm clouds and, scattering the veils of mist, displayed heaven to earth and earth to heaven. The sea was no longer angry, for the ruler of ocean soothed the waves, laying aside his trident. Then he called to the sea-god Triton, who rose from the deep, his shoulders covered with clustering shellfish. Neptune bade him blow on his echoing conch shell, and recall waves and rivers by his signal. He lifted his hollow trumpet, a coiling instrument which broadens out in circling spirals from its base. When he blows upon it in mid-ocean, its notes fill the furthest shores of east and west. So now, too, the god put it to his lips, which were all damp from his dripping beard, and blew it, sending forth the signal for retreat as he had been bidden. The sound was heard by all the waters that covered earth and sea, and all the waves which heard it were checked in their course. The sea had shores once more, the swollen rivers were contained within their own channels, the floods sank down, and hills were seen to emerge. Earth rose up, its lands advancing as the waves retreated, and after a long interval the woods displayed their treetops uncovered, the mud left behind still clinging to their leaves.

The world was restored: but when Deucalion saw its emptiness, the desolate lands all deeply silent, tears started to his eyes, and he said to Pyrrha: 'My cousin, my wife, the only woman left alive, related to me first by birth and blood, then joined to me in marriage – now, Pyrrha, our very dangers unite us. We two are the sole inhabitants of all the lands which east and west behold. The sea has taken the rest. Indeed, even yet, I feel no certainty that we shall survive; even now the clouds strike terror to my heart. What would your feelings be now, my poor wife, had fate snatched you to safety, without saving me? How could you have endured your fears, had you been left all alone? Who would have comforted you in your grief? For believe me, if the sea had taken you with the rest, I should follow you, my dear one, and the sea would have me too. If only I could create the nations anew, by my father's skill! If only I could mould the earth and give it breath: now the human race depends upon us two. It is god's will: we have been left as samples of mankind.' So he spoke, and they wept together.

Then they decided to pray to the god in heaven, and to seek help from the holy oracle. Without delay, they went side by side to the waters of Cephisus which, though not yet clear, were already flowing in their accustomed channel. When they had sprinkled their heads and garments with water drawn from the river they turned their steps to the shrine of the holy goddess. The gables of the temple were discoloured with foul moss, and its altars stood unlit. At the temple steps they both fell forward, prone upon the ground, and timidly kissed the chill rock, saying: 'If the gods may be touched and softened by the prayers of the righteous, if divine anger may be thus turned aside, tell us, O Themis, how we may repair the destruction that has overtaken our race. Most gentle goddess, assist us in our distress.'

The goddess pitied them, and uttered this oracle. 'Depart from my temple, veil your heads, loosen the girdles of your garments and throw behind you the bones of your great mother.' For long they stood in speechless wonder at this reply. Pyrrha was the first to break the silence, by declaring that she would not obey the commands of the goddess. With trembling lips she prayed to be excused: for she was afraid to injure her mother's ghost by disturbing her bones. But meanwhile they considered again the words of the oracle, so puzzling and obscure, and pondered them deeply: till after a time the son of Prometheus soothed the fears of Epimetheus' daughter with these comforting words: 'Oracles are righteous, and never advise guilty action; so, unless my intuition deceives me, our great mother is the earth, and by her bones I think the oracle means the stones in the body of the earth. It is those we are instructed to throw behind our backs.' The Titan's daughter was impressed by her husband's surmise; but she did not trust her hopes, for neither of them had any confidence in heaven's counsels. Still, there could be no harm in putting the matter to the test.

They went down the hillside, veiled their heads, loosened their tunics, and threw the stones behind them, as they had been bidden. Who would believe what followed, did not ancient tradition bear witness to it? The stones began to lose their hardness and rigidity, and after a little, grew soft. Then, once softened, they acquired a definite shape. When they had grown in size, and developed a tenderer nature, a certain likeness to a human form could be seen, though it

was still not clear: they were like marble images, begun but not yet
properly chiselled out, or like unfinished statues. The damp earthy
parts, containing some moisture, were adapted to make the body: that
which was solid and inflexible became bone. What was lately a vein
in the rock kept the same name, and in a brief space of time, thanks to
the divine will of the gods, the stones thrown from male hands took
on the appearance of men, while from those the woman threw,
women were recreated. So it comes about that we are a hardy race,
well accustomed to toil, giving evidence of the origin from which we
sprang.

Other animals of different kinds were produced by the earth, of
its own accord, when the long-lingering moisture was warmed
through by the rays of the sun. Then the mud and soggy marshes
swelled under the heat, and fertile seeds, nourished in the life-giving
earth as in a mother's womb, grew and in the fullness of time acquired
a definite shape. This is what happens when the Nile, the river with
seven mouths, recedes from the flooded fields and returns its streams
to their original bed. The new mud becomes burning hot under the
sun's rays, and the farmers, as they turn over the sods of earth, come
upon many animals. Among these creatures they see some just begun,
but already on the point of coming alive, others unfinished, lacking
their full complement of limbs; and often in one and the same body
one part is alive, while another is still only raw earth. Indeed, when
heat and moisture have reached the proper balance, they bring forth
life, and all things are born from these two elements. Although fire
and water are always opposites, none the less moist heat is the source
of everything, and this discordant harmony is suited to creation.

So when the earth, all muddied by the recent flood, grew warm
again, under the kindly radiance of the sun in heaven, she brought
forth countless forms of life. In some cases she reproduced shapes
which had been previously known, others were new and strange. It
was at that time that she gave birth to the huge Python, among the
rest, though indeed she had no wish to do so; and this snake, whose
body covered so great a stretch of the hillside, struck terror into the
new-born race of men, for they had never known its like. The archer
god, Apollo, who had never before used such weapons against any-
thing but fleeing deer or timid wild goats, almost emptied his quiver
to destroy the serpent, overwhelming it with a thousand arrows, till

the venom flowed out from all its dark wounds. Then, in case the passage of time should blot out the memory of his glorious deed, the god established sacred games, which he called Pythian, after the serpent he had vanquished. Contests of many kinds were held at these games, and when the young athletes had been successful there in wrestling, running, or chariot-racing, they received a wreath of oak-leaves as a prize. There was no laurel in those days, and any tree served to provide the garland which Phoebus wore around his temples, to crown his handsome flowing locks.

Daphne, the daughter of Peneus, was Phoebus' first love, and it was not blind chance which brought this about, but Cupid's savage spite. Not long before, the Delian god, still exultant over his slaying of the serpent, had seen Cupid bending his taut bow, and had said: 'You naughty boy, what have you to do with a warrior's arms? Weapons such as these are suited to my shoulders: for I can aim my shafts unerringly, to wound wild beast or human foe, as I lately slew the bloated Python with my countless arrows, though it covered so many acres with its pestilential coils. You be content with your torch to excite love, whatever that may be, and do not aspire to praises that are my prerogative.' But Venus' son replied: 'Your bow may pierce everything else, Phoebus, but mine will pierce *you*: and as all animals are inferior to the gods, your glory is to that extent less than mine.'

With these words he swiftly winged his way through the air, till he alighted on the shady summit of Parnassus. From his quiver, full of arrows, he drew two darts, with different properties. The one puts love to flight, the other kindles it. That which kindles love is golden, and shining, sharp-tipped; but that which puts it to flight is blunt, its shaft tipped with lead. With this arrow the god pierced the nymph, Peneus' daughter, but Apollo he wounded with the other, shooting it into the marrow of his bones. Immediately the one fell in love; the other, fleeing the very word 'lover', took her delight in woodland haunts and in the spoils of captured beasts, emulating Diana, the maiden goddess, with her hair carelessly caught back by a single ribbon.

Many a suitor wooed her but, turning away from their entreaties, she roamed the pathless woods, knowing nothing of men, and caring nothing for them, heedless of what marriage or love or wedded life might be. Again and again her father said: 'It is your duty to marry and give me a son-in-law, my child.' Often he repeated: 'My child, it is your duty to give me grandchildren.' But she blushed, hating the thought of marriage as if it were some crime. The modest colour crimsoned her fair face and, throwing her arms round her father's neck, she cried imploringly: 'My dear, dear father, let me enjoy this state of maiden bliss for ever! Diana's father granted her such a boon in days gone by!' Her father did, indeed, yield to her request, but her very loveliness prevented her from being what she desired, and her beauty defeated her own wishes.

As soon as Phoebus saw Daphne, he fell in love with her, and wanted to marry her. His own prophetic powers deceived him and he hoped to achieve his desire. As the light stubble blazes up in a harvested field, or as the hedge is set alight, if a traveller chance to kindle a fire too close, or leaves one smouldering when he goes off at daybreak, so the god was all on fire, his whole heart was aflame, and he nourished his fruitless love on hope. He eyed her hair as it hung carelessly about her neck, and sighed: 'What if it were properly arranged!' He looked at her eyes, sparkling bright as stars, he looked at her lips, and wanted to do more than look at them. He praised her fingers, her hands and arms, bare almost to the shoulder. Her hidden charms he imagined lovelier still.

But Daphne ran off, swifter than the wind's breath, and did not stop to hear his words, though he called her back: 'I implore you, nymph, daughter of Peneus, do not run away! Though I pursue you, I am no enemy. Stay, sweet nymph! You flee as the lamb flees the wolf, or the deer the lion, as doves on fluttering wings fly from an eagle, as all creatures flee their natural foes! But it is love that drives me to follow you. Alas, how I fear lest you trip and fall, lest briars scratch your innocent legs, and I be the cause of your hurting yourself. These are rough places through which you are running – go less swiftly, I beg of you, slow your flight, and I in turn shall pursue less swiftly!

'Yet stay to inquire whose heart you have charmed. I am no peasant, living in a mountain hut, nor am I a shepherd or boorish herdsman who tends his flocks and cattle in these regions. Silly girl, you do not know from whom you are fleeing: indeed, you do not, or else you would not flee. I am lord of Delphi, Claros, and Tenedos, and of the realms of Patara too. I am the son of Jupiter. By my skill, the past, the

42

present, and the future are revealed; thanks to me, the lyre strings thrill with music. My arrow is sure, though there is one surer still, which has wounded my carefree heart. The art of medicine is my invention, and men the world over give me the name of healer. All the properties of herbs are known to me: but alas, there are no herbs to cure love, and the skill which helps others cannot help its master.'

He would have said more, but the frightened maiden fled from him, leaving him with his words unfinished; even then, she was graceful to see, as the wind bared her limbs and its gusts stirred her garments, blowing them out behind her. Her hair streamed in the light breeze, and her beauty was enhanced by her flight. But the youthful god could not endure to waste his time on further blandishments and, as love itself prompted, sped swiftly after her. Even so, when a Gallic hound spies a hare in some open meadow he tries by his swiftness to secure his prey, while the hare, by her swiftness, seeks safety: the dog, seeming just about to fasten on his quarry, hopes at every moment that he has her, and grazes her hind quarters with outstretched muzzle, but the hare, uncertain whether she has not already been caught, snatches herself out of his very jaws, and escapes the teeth which almost touch her.

Thus the god and the nymph sped on, one made swift by hope and one by fear; but he who pursued was swifter, for he was assisted by love's wings. He gave the fleeing maiden no respite, but followed close on her heels, and his breath touched the locks that lay scattered on her neck, till Daphne's strength was spent, and she grew pale and weary with the effort of her swift flight. Then she saw the waters of the Peneus: 'O father,' she cried, 'help me! If you rivers really have divine powers, work some transformation, and destroy this beauty which makes me please all too well!' Her prayer was scarcely ended when a deep languor took hold on her limbs, her soft breast was enclosed in thin bark, her hair grew into leaves, her arms into branches, and her feet that were lately so swift were held fast by sluggish roots, while her face became the treetop. Nothing of her was left, except her shining loveliness.

Even as a tree, Phoebus loved her. He placed his hand against the trunk, and felt her heart still beating under the new bark. Embracing the branches as if they were limbs he kissed the wood: but, even as a tree, she shrank from his kisses. Then the god said: 'Since you cannot be my bride, surely you will at least be my tree. My hair, my lyre, my quivers will always display the laurel. You will accompany the generals of Rome, when the Capitol beholds their long triumphal processions, when joyful voices raise the song of victory. You will stand by Augustus' gateposts too, faithfully guarding his doors, and keeping watch from either side over the wreath of oak leaves that will hang there. Further, as my head is ever young, my tresses never shorn, so do you also, at all times, wear the crowning glory of never-fading foliage.' Paean, the healer, had done: the laurel tree inclined her newmade branches, and seemed to nod her leafy top, as if it were a head, in consent.

There is a grove in Haemonia, shut in on every side by steep wooded slopes. Men call it Tempe. Through this grove flow the foaming waters of Peneus, gushing out from the bottom of Pindus' range. As the river roars downwards, it gathers mists of light spray, and scatters its drops on the treetops. The noise of its waters wearies the ear, far beyond its own neighbourhood. This was the home, the dwelling, the most secret haunt of the great river. Sitting here, in a cave hewn out of the cliffs, he was dispensing justice to the waves and to the nymphs who inhabited his stream.

To this spot there came first the rivers of his own country – Spercheus, poplar-fringed, the never-resting Enipeus, old Apidanus, gentle Amphrysus, and Aeas: none of them knowing whether to congratulate or to condole with Daphne's father. Then all the other rivers came, all the streams which, wherever their course has carried them, at last bring down their waters, weary with wandering, to the sea.

Only Inachus was not present, but remained hidden away in the depths of his cave, swelling his stream with tears, and in utter misery lamenting the loss of his daughter Io. He did not know whether she was alive or among the shades of the dead: but since he could not find her anywhere he assumed that she was nowhere to be found, and his heart feared worse than he knew.

Jupiter had caught sight of her as she was returning from her father's stream, and had said: 'Maiden, you are fit for Jupiter himself to love, and will make someone divinely happy when you share his couch. Now, while the sun is at its zenith, seek shelter from its heat in the depths of the greenwood,' – and he indicated the shady grove –

44

'and do not be afraid to go alone into the haunts of wild beasts: you will be safe, though you make your way into the very heart of the forest, for you will be under the protection of a god; no common god at that, but the one who holds heaven's great sceptre, and launches the roving thunderbolt. Do not run away from me!' – for the girl was already fleeing. She had left the pasture lands of Lerna behind her, and the Lyrcean fields, thickly planted with trees, when the god spread darkness over the wide earth, concealing it from view. Then he halted the maiden's flight, and robbed her of her maidenhood.

Meanwhile Juno looked down over the heart of Argos, and wondered that floating clouds should give the appearance of night during the bright daytime. She realized that these were no river mists, nor were they exhaled from the damp earth. She looked round to see where her husband was: for by now she knew well the deceptions practised by that husband, who had so often been caught behaving as he ought not. When she could not find him in the sky, 'Unless I am mistaken,' she said, 'he is doing me some wrong.' Then, gliding down from high heaven, she stood on earth and bade the clouds disperse.

Jupiter had sensed his wife's arrival before she appeared, and had changed Inachus' daughter into a sleek heifer. Even as a cow she was lovely. Juno, though against her will, admired the look of the animal, and inquired whose it was, where it came from, and from what herd – as if she did not know the truth! Jupiter lied to her, and to stop her asking further questions about its parentage, said that it had been born of the earth. Then Saturn's daughter asked to have it as a present. What was he to do? It would be cruel to hand over his darling to another, but not to give her looked suspicious. On the one hand shame persuaded him to yield, but on the other love made him reluctant. His love would have triumphed over his sense of shame: but if a gift as trivial as a cow were refused to one who was his sister and his wife, it might seem to be more than a cow.

Her rival was handed over, but yet the goddess did not immediately lay aside all her fears. She was suspicious of Jove, and afraid of trickery, until she had given the heifer into the keeping of Argus, son of Arestor. Argus had a head set round with a hundred eyes, of which two in turn were always resting, while the others kept watch and remained on guard. In whatever position he stood he was watching Io; though he had his back to her, Io was still before his eyes. By day he allowed her to graze, but when the sun sank far below the earth he shut her up, and chained her innocent neck. Leaves of trees were her food, and bitter-tasting grass. Instead of a bed she lay on ground not always even grassy, and for drink, poor thing, she had the muddy rivers. Even when she wished to stretch out her arms in appeal to Argus, she had no arms to stretch. When she tried to complain, a lowing sound issued from her lips, and she was afraid, terrified by her own voice. Moreover, when she came to the banks of Inachus' river, where she often used to play, she saw her gaping jaws and her strange horns, reflected in the water. Frightened and dismayed, she fled from herself.

The nymphs of the stream, and even Inachus himself did not know who she was: but she followed her father and her sisters about, allowing them to stroke her, and offering herself to their attentions. The aged Inachus plucked some grasses, and held them out to her. She licked his hand, kissing her father's palms, and could not restrain her tears. If only the words would come, she would have asked for help, and told him her name and her misfortune. Instead of words, she traced letters in the dust with her foot, and thus conveyed the sad news of her changed shape. 'Alas,' cried her father, clinging to the horns of the mourning heifer, and to her snowy neck. 'Alas,' he cried again, 'are you the daughter I have sought the world over? My sorrow was less keen when you were lost than it is now that you have been found. You do not speak, do not answer my words, but only heave sighs from deep down in your heart, and make lowing sounds in reply – all indeed that you can do. And I knew nothing of this, I was preparing a home and arranging a marriage for you, hoping for a son-in-law, first of all, and then for grandchildren. Now you must have a bull from the herd for husband, and your children will be cattle. I cannot even put an end to such grief by death: it is a hateful thing to be a god, for my sorrow is prolonged to eternity, since the gate of death is closed to me.'

So they mourned together, till starry-eyed Argus moved her on; driving the daughter away from her father, he herded her into distant pastures. Then he himself sat down on a lofty mountain top, near at hand: for, from that seat, he was able to keep watch in every direction.

The ruler of the gods could not any longer bear that Io should suffer so. He called his son Mercury, whom the shining Pleiad bore, and ordered him to slay Argus. Mercury delayed only long enough to put on his winged sandals, to take in his potent hand the rod which induces slumber, and to set his cap upon his head. Thus arrayed, the son of Jupiter left his father's citadel, and swooped down to earth. There he removed his cap and laid aside his wings, retaining only his staff. With this in his hand, he made his way along winding country paths, in the guise of a herdsman, driving a flock of goats he had collected on the way, and playing on reed-pipes as he went.

Juno's watchman, charmed by the novel sound and by this new accomplishment, hailed him. 'You there, whoever you are, you could sit here beside me on this rock. There is no richer grass anywhere for your flock, and the shade, as you see, is convenient for herdsmen.' The son of Atlas' daughter sat down; with many a tale he whiled away the day in talking and playing on his pipe, as he tried to overcome the watchful eyes. But Argus fought to keep the charms of sleep at bay, and although some of his eyes slumbered, yet some remained awake. He also inquired how the pipe had been discovered: for it was a new invention.

Then Mercury told this story: 'In the chill mountains of Arcadia there lived a nymph, the most famous of all the wood nymphs of Nonacris. The other nymphs called her Syrinx. Many a time she had eluded the pursuit of satyrs and of other spirits who haunt the shady woodlands or the fertile fields. She was a follower of the Ortygian goddess, imitating her in her pastimes, and in her virtue too. When she had her garments caught up out of the way, for hunting, as Diana wears hers, she could easily have been mistaken for Leto's daughter, save that her bow was of horn, Diana's of gold; even in spite of this, she used to be taken for the goddess.

'As she was returning from Mount Lycaeus Pan caught sight of her, Pan who wears on his head a wreath of sharp-leaved pine, and he spoke these words. . . .' Mercury still had to tell what Pan said to the nymph and how she, scorning his prayers, ran off through the pathless forest till she came to the still waters of sandy Ladon. When the river halted her flight, she prayed her sisters of the stream to transform her; and when Pan thought that he had at last caught hold of Syrinx, he found that instead of the nymph's body he held a handful of marsh reeds. As he stood, sighing, the wind blew through the reeds, and produced a thin plaintive sound. The god was enchanted by this new device and by the sweetness of the music. 'You and I shall always talk together so!' he cried; then he took reeds of unequal length, and fastened them together with wax. These preserved the girl's name.

This was the tale Mercury was about to tell, when he saw that Argus' eyelids were closed, and all his eyes fast asleep. At once he stopped speaking, and deepened Argus' slumbers, gently touching those drowsy eyes with his magic wand. Without delay, as the watchman sat nodding, he struck him with his crescent-shaped sword, just where his head joined his neck; then he flung the body down the cliff, all dripping with blood, and spattering the precipitous rocks as it fell. Argus lay dead – the light of his many eyes was quenched, the whole hundred shrouded in a single darkness.

Saturn's daughter took those eyes and placed them on the feathers of her own bird, covering its tail with jewelled stars. Her anger blazed up instantly, and she did not hesitate to show it. She conjured up a dreadful Fury, to torment the eyes and the mind of her Greek rival and, implanting goads of madness in her heart, drove her all over the world, a terrified fugitive.

Finally the Nile put an end to Io's interminable wanderings. When she reached it, she fell forward on her knees on the edge of the bank, and bending back her neck raised her face, all she could raise, to the sky. Her groans and tears and mournful lowings seemed to be reproaching Jove, and begging for an end to her troubles. He threw his arms round his wife's neck, and pleaded with her to put a stop to the punishment. 'Have no fear for the future,' he said, 'she will never give you any cause for indignation' – and he called the Stygian waters to witness his words.

When the goddess was appeased Io resumed her former appearance, and became what she had been before. The hairs fell from her body, her horns disappeared, her eyes grew smaller, and her gaping mouth was reduced to human size. Her shoulders and hands were restored, her hooves vanished, each dividing into five nails. Nothing remained of her cowlike shape, except her snowy whiteness. Then the nymph stood upright, happy to be walking on two feet again. She was afraid to speak, in case she should low like a heifer, and timidly attempted the words which she had not used for so long.

Now she is a goddess of high renown, and linen-clad worshippers throng her shrines. She had a son Epaphus, so men believe, born long afterwards, from the seed of mighty Jupiter, and in the cities he has temples beside those of his mother.

Phaethon, the child of the sungod, was of the same age as Epaphus, and like him in temper. One day, when he was boasting and bragging about his father Phoebus, refusing to give way to Epaphus, Io's son could bear it no longer. 'You are a fool to believe all your mother says,' he exclaimed; 'you are giving yourself airs on the score of a father who is not your real father at all.' Phaethon blushed, but suppressed his anger, from very shame. He carried the tale of Epaphus' insults to his mother Clymene, 'and to make it worse, mother,' he said, 'I, outspoken and spirited as I am, was silenced. I am ashamed that such insults can be uttered, and I be unable to refute them. Come now, if my father really is a god, give me proof of my noble birth, and allow me my place in heaven.' As he spoke, he wound his arms round his mother's neck, and begged her by his own head, by the head of Merops, and by his sisters' hopes of marriage, to give him evidence of his real parent.

Clymene was roused, though it would be hard to say whether it was more because of Phaethon's prayers or because of the implied insult to herself. She stretched out both arms to heaven and looking up at the bright sun she said: 'By this shining orb with radiant beams which sees and hears me as I speak, I swear to you that you are the child of the sun which you behold, the sun which guides the world. If my words are false, may he deny himself to my sight, may the light of this day be the last I ever see.

'But it would not be difficult, nor would it take long for you to become acquainted with your father's dwelling-place: the home from which he rises lies on the borders of our own land. If you wish to do so, go and question the sun himself.'

When he heard his mother's words, Phaethon rushed out at once, highly elated, his mind filled with thoughts of heaven. He passed through the land of his own people, the Ethiopians, and through the country where the Indians live, close to the fiery sun: then he eagerly approached the place from which his father rises.

BOOK II

❁

THE sun's palace was a lofty building with towering columns, bright with glittering gold, and bronze that shone like fire. The roof was covered with polished ivory, and the double doors reflected the light from their silver surface. Their workmanship was even more wonderful than their material: for on them Mulciber had engraved the seas that hold the earth in their embrace, the earth itself, and the heavens above the earth. The waves contained the gods of the sea, tuneful Triton, Proteus, who has no settled shape, and Aegeon, supporting himself on two huge whales, his arms thrown across their backs. Doris and her daughters were there also, some of them swimming, some riding fishes, some perched on rocks, drying their sea-green hair. They were not all exactly alike, but there was a resemblance, such as sisters should have. On the earth, men and cities were to be seen, woods and wild beasts, rivers and nymphs and other spirits of the countryside; above these was a picture of the shining sky, with six signs of the zodiac on the right-hand door, and the same number on the left.

Clymene's son climbed up the steep approach, and entered the palace of his parent, whose relationship to him Epaphus had questioned. He went at once into his father's presence, but stood some way off: for he could not bear his light too close. The sun, dressed in a purple robe, was sitting on a throne bright with shining emeralds. On his right hand and on his left stood Day, Month, Year, the Generations and the Hours, all ranged at equal intervals. Young Spring was there, his head encircled with a flowery garland, and Summer, lightly clad, crowned with a wreath of corn ears; Autumn too, stained purple with treading out the vintage, and icy Winter, with white and shaggy locks.

The boy stood, trembling and marvelling at the strangeness of it all, till the sun himself, seated amid his retinue, turned upon him those eyes which see all things, and addressing him, inquired: 'Why have you come? What do you want in this citadel, Phaethon, my son? Son I call you, for indeed you are one whom no parent would fail to acknowledge.' Phaethon answered: 'O god, in whose light all the wide universe shares, father Phoebus, if you grant me the right to call you by that name, if Clymene is not lying to conceal some guilty secret, give me evidence, to prove that I am indeed your son, and remove this doubt from my mind.'

So he spoke, and his father laid aside the rays that gleamed all round his head, and bade Phaethon come closer. Then he embraced the lad, and said: 'You deserve that I should claim you as my son; Clymene told you the truth about your birth. To clear away your doubts, ask any boon you wish, and you shall have it from me. Let the lake by which the gods take their oaths, that lake which my eyes have never seen, be witness to my promise.'

Scarcely had these words left the sun's lips, than Phaethon asked for his father's chariot: to be allowed for one day to control and drive the wing-footed steeds.

Then his father repented of his oath. Shaking his bright head, three times and again, he said: 'Your words show me how rashly I spoke. If only promises could be broken! For I confess, my boy, that this is the one thing I would deny you. But I can try to dissuade you. What you want to do is dangerous. It is a major privilege that you are asking for, Phaethon, and one unsuited to your strength or to your boyish years. You are but a mortal, whereas the thing you desire is not one that a mortal can attempt. In your ignorance, you aim at more than can be granted even to the gods. However pleased with his own powers each one of those gods may be, yet none other than myself can stand in that fiery chariot. Even the ruler of mighty Olympus, who hurls fierce thunderbolts from his dreadful hand, will not drive this car: and what is mightier than Jove?

'The first part of the way is steep, and the horses can scarcely force their way up it, fresh though they are, in the morning. Then it rises to its zenith in high heaven, and to look down from there on earth and sea often gives me myself a sense of panic. My heart beats faster, and throbs with palpitating fear. Finally, as the path slopes down, a firm guiding hand is necessary: then even Tethys, who receives me in her waters below, is often afraid, lest I fall headlong. Consider, too, that the sky is spinning in ceaseless revolutions, carrying with it the stars on high, and whirling them in swift circles. I force my way against it, and its impetus does not carry me away, as it does all else – I alone ride in the opposite direction to the revolving sphere. Suppose I give you the chariot: what will you do? Will you be able to confront the whirling poles, and prevent the reeling vault of heaven from sweeping you away?

'Perhaps you think that, in the sky, there are sacred groves and cities of the gods, and shrines, richly endowed? On the contrary, you must make your way through dangerous ambushes and among monstrous wild beasts: even though you keep to the path, and do not wander from it, still you will have to go past the horns of the hostile Bull, past the Thracian Archer and the jaws of the raging Lion, past the Scorpion's cruel pincers, whose sweeping embrace threatens you from one quarter, while the clutching claws of the Crab attack you from another.

'Further, it would not be easy for you to control the horses when their spirits are fired by those flames which they house in their breasts and breathe forth from mouth and nostrils. They scarcely suffer me to curb them, when their keenness is aroused: their necks chafe against the rein. Take care, my son, that I do not bestow upon you a gift that brings about your ruin; while it is possible, ask for something better. If you reply that you want some definite sign, in order to be sure that you are indeed my son, I give you that definite sign by being afraid for you: the fact that I show a father's fears proves that I am your father. Come now, look at my face – I only wish your eyes could see into my heart, and perceive the fatherly anxiety within it.

'Look round, then, at all the rich world contains, and ask for anything from among all the good things in earth or air or sea. You will not be refused. This one thing only am I reluctant to grant you, and in fact it would be a punishment, not an honour. It is a punishment, Phaethon, not a boon, which you are seeking.

'Why throw your arms persuasively round my neck, not knowing what you ask? Never fear, you will obtain your request, for I have sworn by the Styx; only show more wisdom in the request you make.'

So he ended his warnings; but his son, rebelling against his advice pressed for what he had first proposed, and was on fire with eagerness to drive the sun's car. His father had held him back as far as he could: now he led the youth out to the lofty chariot, which Vulcan had made. The axles were of gold, golden the chariot pole, of gold the rims of the wheels, their spokes of silver. Along the yoke chrysolites and jewels in orderly array reflected a brilliant light when Phoebus shone upon them.

As Phaethon, full of confidence in himself, was examining and admiring the chariot, far in the crimsoning east wakeful Dawn threw wide the shining doors of her rosefilled chambers. The stars fled away, the Morning Star shepherding their long columns, and leaving his post in heaven last of all. When the sungod saw this star setting, when he saw the sky reddening, and the horns of the vanishing moon fading from sight, he told the swift Hours to yoke his team. Quickly the goddesses carried out his orders: from the lofty stables they led out his horses, breathing fire and replete with essence of ambrosia, and fastened on the jingling harness.

Then the father rubbed his son's face with a divine ointment, to enable him to endure the searing flames. On his head he placed his own rays, and, sighing deeply from his troubled heart – for he foresaw the grief that was in store for him – he said: 'At least obey your father's instructions, my son, if you can. Use the goad sparingly, and hold in the reins with all your strength. The horses set a fast pace of their own accord: the difficulty is to check their keenness. And do not try to drive straight across the five zones of heaven – there is a track that slants in a broad curve, confined within the boundaries of three zones, which avoids the Southern Pole, and also the North with its chilling winds. Travel by this road, where you will see clear marks of wheels. To allow earth and heaven to share equally in your warmth, do not go too low, nor yet force your way into the upper air: if you drive too high, you will set the dome of heaven on fire, and if you are too low you will scorch the earth. The middle way is safest. Nor must you swerve to the right, towards the coiling Serpent, nor to the left, where the low-lying Altar shines. Hold your course between them both.

'I leave the rest to Fortune, and pray that she may help you, and look after you better than you can look after yourself. While I have been talking, dewy night has reached its goal, far off on the western shore. We can delay no longer: we must appear. Dawn shines forth, putting darkness to flight. Grasp the reins tightly; or, if I can yet change your mind, take my advice rather than my chariot. While you can, while you still stand firm on solid ground, while you have not yet, in your inexperience, mounted the skies, which you long for to your cost, let me give light to the earth, a light which you may look upon in safety.'

But Phaethon, in the pride of his youth and strength, leaped into the light chariot, delighted to hold the reins his father gave him. He took his stand in the car, and cried his thanks to his unhappy parent.

Meanwhile Pyrois and Eous and Aethon, the winged horses of the sun, together with Phlegon, the fourth member of the team, were filling the air with their fiery whinnyings, and pawing at the barriers. Tethys, knowing nothing of her grandson's fortunes, pulled these aside, and the wide sky lay open before the horses. They hurled themselves forward, and, galloping into the air, tore through the clouds that hampered their way. Soaring on winged feet, they sped past the East winds, which rise in the same region.

But the sun's horses felt that their burden was too light. They did not recognize the chariot which they drew, for their yoke was not pulling its usual weight. Just as curved ships toss about, if they are not carrying their full cargo, and ride the waves unsteadily, because they are not heavy enough, so this chariot, lacking its normal load, leaped into the air, and was thrown about on high, as if it were empty.

As soon as the horses felt this happen, they raced away out of the well-beaten track, and galloped off, no longer following their usual course. Their driver was panic-stricken, and had not the skill to handle the reins that had been entrusted to him: he did not know where the path lay, and could not control the horses, even had he known. Then for the first time the chill stars of the Northern Plough grew hot, and vainly tried to bathe themselves in the forbidden ocean. The Serpent which lay close to the icy pole, and had till then been sluggish with the cold, no danger to anyone, now sweltered in the heat, and was roused to unprecedented fury. They say that even Bootes was disturbed, and fled, slow-moving though he was, and hampered by his plough. Finally, when the luckless Phaethon glimpsed the earth from the heights of heaven, and saw it lying outspread far, far below, he grew pale, his knees trembled in sudden terror, and his eyes were dazzled by excess of light. He wished now that he had never touched his father's horses; he regretted that he had learned his parentage, and that his request had been granted. He was eager enough, now, to pass as Merops' son, as he was carried along like some pinewood ship driven before a Northern gale when her helmsman, finding the rudder useless, looses his hold on the ropes, and abandons his ship to the mercy of the gods, putting his trust in prayer. What was he to do? Much of the sky lay behind him, still more stretched before his eyes. Mentally he measured them both, now looking onwards to the west, which he was not fated to reach, now back to the east. He stood, dazed with indecision, neither letting go the reins, nor having the strength to hold them. He did not even know the names of the horses.

To add to his fear, he now perceived the monstrous beasts of huge size, which lay scattered over the spangled face of heaven. There is a certain place where the Scorpion stretches out his pincers in two hollow arcs, and with his tail and curving claws outspread on either side sprawls over two signs of the zodiac. When the boy saw him, exuding his baneful poison, and menacing him with his curved sting, he was so completely unnerved and numb with fear that he dropped the reins. They fell from his hands, and lay loose on the horses' backs. At once, the team galloped away, out of their course. With none to restrain them, they sped through regions of air unknown, and rushed wherever their headlong career carried them, quite beyond control. They dashed against the stars set in highest heaven, and hurled the car along where there was no pathway, now soaring up to the heights of the sky, now hurtling down its steep incline, to be borne along close to the earth. The moon was amazed to see her brother's horses lower than her own, and smoke rose from the scorched clouds.

The earth caught fire, starting with the highest parts. With all its moisture dried up, it split and cracked in gaping fissures. The meadows turned ashy grey; trees, leaves and all, were consumed in a general blaze, and the withered crops provided fuel for their own destruction. But these are trifles to complain of, compared with the rest. Great cities perished, their walls burned to the ground, and whole nations with all their different communities were reduced to ashes. The woods on the mountains were blazing, Athos was on fire, Cilician Taurus and Timolus, Oeta and Ida, a mountain once famous for its springs, but now quite dry. Helicon, the Muses' haunt, was burning, and Haemus, later to be linked with Orpheus' name. Etna's flames were redoubled, and shot up to immense heights, the twin peaks of Parnassus and Eryx and Cynthus were alight, Othrys and Rhodope, destined at last to lose its snows, Mimas and Dindyma and Mycale and Cithaeron, the natural abode of sacred rites. Scythia did not escape, in spite of its chilly clime, Caucasus was in flames and Ossa too, and Pindus; Olympus, a greater mountain than either of these, was ablaze, as were the airy Alps and cloud-capped Apennines.

Then, indeed, Phaethon saw every part of the world on fire, and found the scorching heat more than he could endure. He breathed in blasts of burning air, like those from some deep furnace, and felt his chariot glowing white hot. No longer could he bear the cinders and sparks which were flying through the air; enveloped in hot smoke and pitchy darkness, he did not know where he was, or whither he was going, but was swept along, according to the whim of his swift-footed team.

It was then, so men believe, that the Ethiopians acquired their dark skins; for the blood rose to the surface of their bodies. It was then that Libya became a desert, when the heat dried up her waters, then the nymphs tore their hair, and lamented their vanished springs and lakes. Boeotia looked in vain for Dirce's fountain, Argos for Amymone, Ephyre for Pyrene's waters. The rivers, though they ran in more open channels, were no safer than the springs. Tanais steamed in the depths of his waters, and so did aged Peneus, Mysian Caicus and swift Ismenus. Arcadian Erymanthus suffered, and Xanthus, who was later to be consumed by fire a second time: yellow Lycormas too, and Maeander who flows in looping curves, Thracian Melas and Spartan Eurotas. Euphrates, the river of Babylon, was kindled also, Orontes and swift-running Thermodon, Ganges and Phasis and Hister; Alpheus boiled, Spercheus' banks were all aflame, the gold that Tagus carries in his stream was made molten by the fires, and the river birds, for whose singing Maeonia's banks are famous, found no coolness in Cayster's pools. The Nile was terrified and, fleeing to the ends of the earth, hid his head, which still is hidden. His seven mouths were left dusty and empty, seven channels without a river. The same fate dried up the waters of Ismarus, the Hebrus and the Strymon, as

well as the rivers of Hesperia, the Rhine and the Rhône, the Po, and
even the Tiber, which had been promised sovereign power.

Everywhere the ground gaped open, and the light descended
through the cracks into Tartarus, frightening the king of the under-
world, and his queen beside him. The seas contracted, and an expanse
of barren sand appeared where there had lately been ocean. Moun-
tains which had been submerged beneath deep waters rose above the
surface, and increased the number of the scattered Cyclades. Fish
swam down into the depths of their pools, and the dolphins did not
dare to leap out into the air, arching their backs over the sea, as was
their usual habit. Lifeless bodies of seals floated upturned on the top of
the waves. They say that Nereus himself, and Doris and her daugh-
ters, as they lurked in their caves, found them warm.

Three times Neptune tried to raise his arms and his grim counten-
ance above the waters: three times the fiery air was too much for him.
But when the goodly earth goddess found herself entirely girdled by
waters, between those of the sea and the springs which, shrinking in
from every side, had buried themselves in her dark bowels, then,
parched though she was, she lifted up her head and neck from the
smothering ashes. Sheltering her face behind her hand, she made
everything tremble with her convulsive shudderings. Then she sank
down a little lower than she used to be, and spoke in majestic tones.
'If this be fate's resolve, if I have deserved this doom, why, most
mighty god, why are your thunderbolts slow to come? If I must
perish by fire, let it be by yours: disaster is easier to bear when you
are its author. I can scarcely open my lips to speak these words!' –
for the heat had gripped her throat – 'Look, see my scorched hair,
and the ashes in my eyes, covering my face. Are these my rewards, is
this the honour you bestow in return for my fertility and my services?
Is it for this that I endure the wounds inflicted by the mattock and
the crooked plough, for this that I am given no rest throughout the
whole year? Is this what I get for supplying the cattle with leaves and
tender grazing, for providing grain for the human race, aye and
incense for you gods?

'Even if I have deserved destruction, what have the waves done, or
what your brother? Why should the seas, which have fallen by lot to
him, contract their waters and shrink away further from the sky? But
if neither your brother's influence nor mine has any power to touch

you, at least show pity for your own realm of heaven. Look around on either side: both poles are smoking hot; if the fire should undermine them, it is your own palace which will crash. See, Atlas himself is in difficulties, and can scarcely hold up the glowing sky on his shoulders. If earth and sea and the citadel of heaven perish, we shall be thrown into primeval chaos. Save anything that still survives from the flames, and take thought for the safety of the universe.'

When she had made this plea, unable to bear the heat any longer, or to say more, the earth goddess withdrew her head into herself, into the caves that lie close to the shades of the dead.

The omnipotent father called upon the gods and even upon the sun himself, who had bestowed his car upon Phaethon, to be his witnesses that, if he did not bring help, the whole world would come to a grievous end. Then he mounted up to the highest point of heaven, that height from which he is wont to spread clouds over the broad lands of earth, whence he sends forth his thunderings and hurls his flashing bolts: he had no clouds then to draw over the world, no rain to shower down from the skies. He sent forth a thunderclap and, poising his bolt close by his right ear, launched it against the charioteer. With one and the same blow he dashed him from his car, and from the realms of life: with his own cruel flames, he quenched the other's fire.

The horses, dismayed, leaped apart, broke free from the yoke, and escaped from among the broken reins. Here lay the harness, there the axle, torn from its pole, and there the spokes of the shattered wheels. The fragments of the wrecked car were scattered far and wide. But Phaethon, with flames searing his glowing locks, was flung headlong, and went hurtling down through the air, leaving a long trail behind: just as sometimes a star, though it does not really fall, could yet be thought to fall from the clear sky. Far from his native land, in a distant part of the world, the great river Eridanus received him, and bathed his charred features. The Italian nymphs buried his body, which was still smouldering from the three-forked flame, and on the rock they set this inscription:

> *Here Phaethon lies: his father's car he tried –*
> *Though proved too weak, he greatly daring died.*

The nymphs attended to this, for his unhappy father, sick with sorrow, had veiled his face, and hidden it from sight. If we can believe it, they say that one day passed without the appearance of the sun: the burning fires gave light, so that the disaster served some useful purpose. Clymene, Phaethon's mother, first made such lament as was in keeping with the tragedy. Then, out of her mind with grief, tearing at her breast in anguish, she roved the whole world, seeking the lifeless limbs, and later the bones, of her son. She found his bones, buried on the foreign river bank. Brooding over the spot, she bathed with tears the name she read upon the marble, and pressed it to her naked breast.

The daughters of the sun, no less than she, offered their vain tribute of tears and lamentations to their dead brother; beating their breasts with their palms, they flung themselves on Phaethon's tomb and called upon him, day and night, though he would never hear their piteous cries. Four times had the moon rounded her crescent horns into a full circle: the sisters, as was their habit – for constant practice had made it a habit – were mourning by the tomb: when Phaethusa, the eldest of them, as she tried to fling herself upon the ground, complained that she could not move her feet. Fair Lampetie would have gone to her assistance, but she was held fast by roots which had suddenly formed. A third made to tear her hair, and plucked out leaves. One cried out that her legs were caught in the grip of a tree trunk, another was indignant to find her arms had become long branches. While they were marvelling at this, bark surrounded their thighs, and gradually spread over womb and breast, shoulders and hands, till only their lips remained, vainly calling for their mother.

What could that mother do, but rush this way and that, wherever her impulse bore her, and snatch kisses while she could? Not content with that, she tried to tear their bodies out of the tree trunks and broke off the tender branches in her hands: but drops like blood trickled from the gash, as if from a wound. 'Oh mother, please, don't hurt me!' was the cry of whichever girl she touched. 'Do not hurt me, please! It is my body you are injuring, though it has been transformed into a tree. And now, farewell!' The bark closed over the last words, and from that bark there flowed tears which, hardened into amber by the sun, dropped from the new-made branches and were received by the shining river. It bore them off in its waters, to be an ornament one day for Roman brides.

Cygnus, the son of Sthenele, was present at the scene of this marvel. He was related to Phaethon on his mother's side, but the bond of affection between them was closer than that of blood. He had held sway over the peoples of Liguria and their great cities, but now he left his kingdom and made the stream and the grassy banks of Eridanus echo with his lamentations. The woods which had been increased by the addition of Phaethon's sisters were filled with his sorrowful cries. As he mourned, his voice became thin and shrill, and white feathers hid his hair. His neck grew long, stretching out from his breast, his fingers reddened and a membrane joined them together. Wings clothed his sides, and a blunt beak fastened on his mouth. Cygnus became a new kind of bird: but he put no trust in the skies, or in Jupiter, for he remembered how that god had unjustly hurled his flaming bolt. Instead, Cygnus made for marshes and broad lakes, and in his hatred of flames chose to inhabit the rivers, which are the very antithesis of fire.

Meanwhile Phaethon's father, clad in sordid mourning, his usual brightness gone, looked as he does when he suffers an eclipse. He loathed the light, hated himself and the bright day, and gave himself up to grief. He was angry too, and refused to perform his duty to the world. 'I have had enough of my fated task, which has allowed me no rest from the beginning of time: I am tired of my endless work, my efforts which bring me no honour. Anyone else who cares to do so, may drive the chariot of light. If there is no volunteer, if all the gods declare themselves unfit, let Jupiter drive it himself. Then, at least, while he tries to control my team, he will have to lay aside for a time those thunderbolts which rob fathers of their sons. When he has some experience of the strength of the fiery-footed horses, he will realize that nobody deserves to die for being unable to guide them.'

Such were the sun's words: but all the gods stood around and earnestly begged him not to persist in shrouding the world in darkness. Even Jupiter apologized for hurling his bolts, and, as kings do, mingled threats with his entreaties.

Phoebus rounded up his frenzied horses, which were still quivering with fear. In his bitter grief, he lashed them with his whip, and pricked them with the goad: for he was indeed in a savage temper, blaming them for the death of his son, and laying the disaster to their account.

Meanwhile the omnipotent father of the gods made a tour of the great walls of heaven, inspecting them to see whether any damage had been done by the violence of the fire. When he saw that all was in good repair, and that their original strength was unshaken, he looked abroad over the earth and man's handiworks. Most of all was he anxious about his dear Arcadia. He restored its springs and the rivers which had not yet dared to flow; he clothed the earth with grass, the trees with leaves, and commanded the blasted forests to grow green again.

As he was hurrying busily to and fro, he stopped short at the sight of an Arcadian maiden. The fire of passion kindled the very marrow of his bones. This girl was not one who spent her time in spinning soft fibres of wool, or in arranging her hair in different styles. She was one of Diana's warriors, wearing her tunic pinned together with a brooch, her tresses carelessly caught back by a white ribbon, and carrying in her hand a light javelin or her bow. None of the nymphs who haunt Maenalus was dearer than she to the goddess of the Cross-ways: but a favourite is never a favourite for long.

The sun on high had passed its zenith, when she entered a grove whose trees had never felt the axe. Here she took her quiver from her shoulders, unstrung her pliant bow, and lay down on the turf, resting her head on her painted quiver. When Jupiter saw her thus, tired and unprotected, he said: 'Here is a secret of which my wife will know nothing; or if she does get to know of it, it will be worth her reproaches!'

Without wasting time he assumed the appearance and the dress of Diana, and spoke to the girl. 'Dearest of all my companions,' he said, 'where have you been hunting? On what mountain ridges?' She raised herself from the grass: 'Greetings, divine mistress,' she cried, 'greater in my sight than Jove himself – I care not if he hears me!' Jove laughed to hear her words. Delighted to be preferred to himself, he kissed her – not with the restraint becoming to a maiden's kisses: and as she began to tell of her hunting exploits in the forest, he prevented her by his embrace, and betrayed his real self by a shameful action. So far from complying, she resisted him as far as a woman could – had Juno seen her she would have been less cruel – but how could a girl overcome a man, and who could defeat Jupiter? He had his way, and returned to the upper air.

The nymph was filled with loathing for the groves and woods that had witnessed her fall. As she left, she almost forgot to pick up the quiver that held her darts, and the bow she had hung up.

Now, as Diana with her attendant company was making her way along the lofty ridge of Maenalus, in high fettle after successful hunting, she caught sight of the nymph, and called to her. At the sound of her name the girl fled, afraid at first lest this was Jupiter in disguise: but when she saw the nymphs accompanying Diana she realized that there was no trickery here, and she joined them. Alas, how difficult it is not to betray guilt by one's looks! She scarcely raised her eyes from the ground, and did not stay close by the goddess as she usually did, nor did she take her place in the forefront of them all. Instead she remained silent, and by her blushes gave clear indication of the wrong she had suffered. If Diana herself had not been a virgin goddess, she could have perceived her guilt by a thousand signs; the nymphs perceived it, so men say.

Now the moon's horns were filling out to complete their ninth circle, when the goddess wearied with hunting in the fierce heat of the sun, came to a cool grove, from which there flowed a murmuring stream that rippled over its smooth sandy bed. Diana exclaimed with pleasure at the sight, and dipped her foot in the water: delighted with this too, she called to her companions: 'There is no one here to see us – let us undress, and bathe in the brook.' The Arcadian maiden blushed. All the rest took off their garments, while she alone sought excuses to delay. As she hesitated, the others pulled off her tunic, and at one and the same time revealed her body and her crime. She stood dismayed, and with her hands vainly tried to cover up the evidence of her guilt. But Diana cried: 'Off with you! Do not defile this sacred spring!' and ordered her to withdraw from her company.

The wife of the mighty Lord of Thunder had long since realized what had happened, and was resolved to inflict stern punishment, but had postponed doing so until a suitable opportunity should arise. There was now no reason for delay: already a child, Arcas, had been born to her rival, and that in itself enraged Juno. She regarded the boy, with anger in her heart and in her eyes. 'This is the one insult that was lacking, you shameless woman,' she cried, 'that you should bear a son. Now the wrong done to me has been made public by the birth of your child, and there is proof of my husband's misdemeanour. But you will not escape unpunished! For I shall rob you of that beauty, in which both you and my husband take such delight, you minx!'

With these words she seized the hair above her rival's brow, and tugged till the girl fell forward on the ground. As she lay there, stretching out her arms to beg for mercy, these arms began to bristle with coarse black hairs, and her hands curved round, turning into crooked claws, which then served her as feet. Her face, which Jupiter had once praised, was disfigured by wide gaping jaws. Then, lest her prayers and imploring words should wake sympathy, the goddess deprived her of the power of speech. A harsh growling issued from her throat, angry and quarrelsome, frightening to hear; she had become a bear, but even so her mind remained unchanged, and she declared her grief with continual lamentations, raising to the stars in heaven such hands as she had, and feeling Jove's ingratitude, though she could not speak of it. Many a time, not daring to rest in the lonely wood, she wandered before the home and in the fields that once were hers. Many a time, barking hounds drove her through rocky places, and the huntress fled, terrified of the hunters. Often she forgot what she was, and hid when she saw wild beasts; though a bear herself, she shuddered at the sight of bears in their mountain haunts, and feared wolves too, though her father was one of them.

Meanwhile her son Arcas had reached the age of fifteen. He was quite unaware of what had happened to his mother, Lycaon's daughter. But one day, when he was engaged in tracking wild creatures in the woods, choosing suitable hunting grounds and encircling the copses of Erymanthus with his nets, he came face to face with her. She stopped when she saw Arcas, and seemed to recognize him: but he, not knowing the reason for such behaviour, shrank back, terrified of this beast, which gazed at him so fixedly, never taking her eyes off him. As she tried, in her eagerness, to approach him, he would have pierced her heart with his deadly spear: but almighty Jupiter stayed his hand, and prevented a crime being committed, by removing both mother and son. A whirlwind carried them up, together, through the void of heaven, and then he set them in the sky, as neighbouring constellations.

When her rival was shining among the stars, Juno's wrath knew no bounds. She went down to the wide waters to visit hoary-headed Tethys and the aged Oceanus, for whom the gods have often shown reverence. When they inquired the reason for her coming, she replied: 'You ask me why I, the queen of the gods, have left my heavenly abode to come here? It is because another, in my place, holds sway in the sky! Unless I am mistaken, when night darkens the world, you will see two constellations newly raised to the honour of a place in highest heaven, expressly to insult me! Look for them where the last and narrowest circle surrounds the tip of the pole. And do you suppose that anyone will hesitate to wrong Juno, or fear to offend her, when I alone actually do good to those I try to harm? Great indeed are my achievements, and mighty my strength; I denied her the rights of a human being, and she has become a goddess! So much for the punishment I inflict on the guilty! So much for my tremendous power! Let Jupiter now restore her former shape, and rid her of her bestial appearance, as he did before in the case of the Argive Io. Why does he not go so far as to divorce Juno, and marry this new love – set her in my wedding chamber, and take Lycaon as a father-in-law?

'I implore you, if this contemptuous treatment of one who was your nursling distresses you, prevent the Bear from entering your dark blue waters: repulse those stars which have been received into heaven as a reward for shameless conduct, and do not let my rival bathe in your pure tide.'

The gods of the sea nodded in consent. Then Saturn's daughter drove off through the clear air in her light chariot, drawn by gaily-coloured peacocks. They had only recently acquired their bright plumage, at the time of Argus' death: and just as recently the shining white wings of the chattering raven had been suddenly changed to dusky black.

This bird was once of a silvery hue, with such snowy feathers that it could rival any spotless dove. It was no less white than the geese who were one day to save the Capitol with their wakeful voices, as white as the swan that haunts rivers. But its tongue brought about the raven's downfall. Thanks to its chattering tongue, its plumage, once white, is now the very opposite.

In all Thessaly there was no one lovelier than Coronis of Larissa. At any rate, she won the heart of the god of Delphi, while she remained true to him, or at least while her faults passed unobserved. But the bird of Phoebus detected her in wrongdoing, and, a pitiless informer, hurried to its master, determined to reveal her guilt. The crow, another garrulous bird, pursued the raven on swiftly beating wings, anxious to learn the whole story. When it heard the object of the raven's flight, it said: 'No good will come of your journey. Pay heed to my warning. Look at what I was, and what I now am. If you inquire into the cause of this change, you will find it was my faithfulness that ruined me.

'Once upon a time, Pallas took Erichthonius, a baby born without a mother, and shut him in a chest woven from Actaean osiers. This chest she entrusted to the three unmarried daughters of Cecrops, that king whose nature was part human and part snake, imposing the condition that they should not pry into her secret. I was hidden in the light foliage of a leafy elm, and I watched to see what they would do. Two of them, Pandrosos and Herse, honourably guarded the trust they had been given: but the third, Aglauros, taunted her sisters with cowardice, and undid the knots. Inside they saw the infant, with a serpent stretched out beside him.

'I told the goddess what had happened, and my reward for that service was that I was ousted from my place as Minerva's attendant, and ranked lower than the bird of night. The punishment I suffered may serve as a warning to other birds, not to court danger by telling tales. It was not as if I had ever asked for any mark of favour from her – she, of her own accord sought me out. Ask Pallas herself – angry though she is, her anger will not make her deny the truth.

'It is a well-known story. Phocis was my country, and the famous Coroneus my father. Do not think me a person of no importance: I was a king's daughter, and wooed by rich suitors. But beauty was my undoing: for, as I was strolling on the smooth sand, as I used to do, the god of the sea saw me, and fell in love. When he found that he was wasting his time uselessly in prayers and entreaties, he prepared to resort to force, and pursued me. I fled, leaving the firm shingle, and tiring myself to no purpose in the soft sand. Then I called on gods and men to help me. No mortal ear heard my cry, but the maiden goddess pitied one of her own kind, and brought me her aid. As I stretched my arms towards the sky, they began to grow dark with downy plumage: I tried to throw my robe back from my shoulders, but it too had turned to feathers, with roots deep in my skin. I made to beat my bared breast with my hands, but neither breast nor hands were bare any more. When I ran, the sand did not clog my footsteps as before: instead I skimmed along the surface of the ground. Then I soared up into the air, and was appointed Minerva's blameless attendant.

'But of what use was that to me, if Nyctimene, who became a bird as a result of a foul crime, has replaced me in the post of honour? Or have you not heard the tale, so widely known through all Lesbos, of how Nyctimene violated her father's bed? She is a bird now, it is true, but her guilty conscience makes her flee the sight of men and the light of day. She hides her shame in darkness, and is driven off by all the birds, from every quarter of the sky.'

But the raven answered the crow in these words: 'I hope your attempts to hold me back may recoil on your own head! I have no time for your futile predictions!' – and it did not abandon the journey it had begun, but went and told its master, Phoebus, that it had seen Coronis lying with a young Thessalian.

When her lover heard this charge against Coronis, the wreath of laurel slipped from his head, his face changed, his colour ebbed away, and the plectrum fell from his fingers. His heart was in a fever of swelling rage. Seizing his customary weapons, he strung his bow, bending it from its horns, and, with the arrow that none can avoid, pierced the breast he had so often clasped to his own. As the shaft struck home, Coronis groaned; when she drew it out, scarlet blood welled over her fair white limbs. 'O Phoebus,' she cried, 'you could have let me bear your child, and then have punished me. Now, in my one person, two will perish.' That was all she said, before her spirit ebbed out with her blood. A deathly chill crept over her lifeless body.

Too late, the lover repented of the cruel punishment he had exacted, and hated himself for listening to the tale, for allowing his anger to blaze up in such a way. He hated the bird, whose officiousness had forced him to learn of Coronis' guilt, forced him to know that he had cause for indignation; and no less did he hate his bow, his hands, his arrows too, shafts he had so rashly launched. Fondling her lifeless frame, he tried to thwart the fates, but he employed his healing art without avail: his aid came too late.

When he saw that his attempts were vain, that the pyre was being got ready, and that her limbs were about to be consumed by the funeral fires, then indeed Apollo groaned from the very depths of his heart – tears are forbidden to the gods. Even so does a heifer mourn when, before her eyes, the mallet is poised close to the slaughterer's right ear, and then brought crashing down with a resounding blow upon the hollow forehead of her unweaned calf. Then he poured upon Coronis' breast perfumes which she could never enjoy, clasped her to him for the last time, and performed all too soon the rites that death demands.

That his own seed should perish in those same ashes was more than he could bear. He snatched his son from his mother's womb, saved him from the flames, and carried him to the cave of Chiron, the centaur.

As for the raven, which was hoping for a reward for revealing the truth, Phoebus decreed that never again should it be numbered among white birds.

The centaur, meanwhile, was delighted at having the son of a god as his ward, and was rejoicing in the honour and responsibility it brought him: when suddenly his daughter appeared, her red-gold hair streaming over her shoulders. This daughter was his child by the nymph Chariclo, who had called her Ocyrhoe, after the racing stream on whose banks she had been born. She had not been content merely to learn her father's arts, but could reveal in prophecy the secrets of the fates.

So now the prophetic frenzy gripped her mind, and the god's presence set her breast aglow. She looked upon the babe, and said: 'Grow and prosper, my child, you who are destined to bring health to all the world. Often mortal men will owe their lives to you, and you will be granted the right to restore those who are already dead; till, in one case, you will incur the gods' displeasure by daring to do so, and will be prevented by your grandfather's bolt from ever again bestowing such a boon. From an immortal god you will be reduced to a lifeless corpse, but later, from being a corpse, you will be raised up to be a god again, and will twice renew your destiny.

'You too, my dear father, who are now an immortal, fated by the conditions of your birth to live to all eternity, you too will long for death, when through your poisoned wounds the awful venom of the serpent creeps into your body, and tortures you: till in the end the gods will take away your immortality, and enable you to die, and the three goddesses will unloose the threads of your destiny.'

Some secrets of fate still remained to be revealed: but she sighed

deeply, tears started to her eyes, and flowed down her cheeks, as she
sobbed: 'The fates forestall me, and forbid me to say more. My
words are checked; too dearly bought were these powers which have
drawn down heaven's wrath upon me. Would that I did not know
the future! Now I seem to see my human form stolen away; now
meadow grass is my food, to gallop over the broad plains is my
delight. I am changed into a mare, a creature to which I am already
akin. Yet why should I be wholly such? Surely my father is half
human?' Even as she spoke, the last part of her lament was barely
intelligible, for her words became blurred. Then the sound seemed to
be neither human speech, nor yet the neighing of a horse, but it was
like someone trying to imitate a horse. In a little while, she gave vent
to shrill whinnyings, and drooped her arms towards the grass. Her
fingers grew together and a thin hoof of smooth continuous horn
bound her five finger nails. Her head grew larger, her neck lengthened
out, the greater part of her trailing robe became a tail, and her
loosened hair, as it streamed down her neck, fell as a mane on her
right shoulder. Her voice and her shape altered together: and from
the miracle she acquired a new name too.

Vainly did the half-divine son of Phylira weep, and beg for Apollo's
aid. Apollo could not undo the commands of mighty Jupiter nor,
even if he could have done so, was he at hand to help, for he was
sojourning in Elis and in the fields of Messenia. That was the time
when he clothed himself in a shepherd's cloak and carried a crook in
his left hand, in his right the panpipes, seven reeds of unequal length.

While he was thinking only of his love, and comforting himself
with his reedpipes, his cattle, unguarded, so the story goes, strayed into
the fields of Pylos. There Maia's son, Mercury, espied them, and by his
cunning drove them off and hid them in the woods. No one had
noticed the theft, except one old man, well known in the neighbour-
hood, whom everyone called Battus. His duty was to patrol the
glades and grassy meadows of wealthy Neleus, keeping watch over
his herds of pedigree mares. Mercury was afraid of Battus, and so he
led him aside and said coaxingly: 'Whoever you are, my friend, if
anyone should happen to ask for these herds, say that you haven't
seen them. Here is a sleek cow, as a reward for doing me this favour.'
The other took the cow he gave him, and replied: 'Go on your way,
you are quite safe.' – and pointing to a stone, he added: 'Sooner will

that stone tell of your theft than I.' Jove's son pretended to depart; but later he returned in a different guise, and spoke in a different voice. 'Herdsman,' he said, 'if you have seen any cattle passing this way, help me, and do not be party to a theft by keeping silent. In return you will have a bull and its mate for yourself.' Now when the reward was doubled, the old man was tempted. 'You will find them at the bottom of those hills' – and in fact, that was where they were. Mercury laughed. 'You rogue,' he said. 'You would betray me to my face? Actually betray me to myself?' and he turned the faithless heart to hard flint, the stone which even today is called 'touchstone'. The innocent rock still bears the stigma of that shameful deed of long ago.

Then the god who carries the magic rod flew off, soaring upwards on level wings. As he flew, he looked down on the fields of Munychia, the land dear to Minerva, and the cultivated groves of the Lyceum.

It so happened that it was the festival of Pallas, and on that day in accordance with religious custom, a procession of pure young girls used to carry the sacred symbols to her temple, bearing them on their heads in flower-wreathed baskets. As they were on their home-ward way, the winged god saw them, and instead of continuing on a straight course, he wheeled round in his tracks: just like a hawk, the swiftest of birds, when it sees the entrails of a sacrifice. As long as the attendants are crowding closely round, it circles above them, afraid, yet not daring to go further off, but eagerly hovering with beating wings over its hoped-for prey. Even so did nimble Mercury fly round the Actaean citadel, and circle there in the same breezes.

As Lucifer shines brighter than all the other stars, as golden Phoebe is brighter than Lucifer, so Herse outshone every other maiden, and was the loveliest sight of the whole procession, surpassing all her companions. Jupiter's son was astonished at her beauty, and as he hovered in the air, a fire of love was kindled in his heart as hot as when the leaden bullet from a Balearic sling catches fire as it travels through the air, finding in the clouds the heat it did not have before. He changed his course and, leaving the sky, flew down to earth; nor did he conceal his true shape, so confident was he in his beauty. He had good reason for his confidence, but yet he took pains to enhance his looks, smoothed his hair, and arranged his cloak to hang grace-fully, so that its embroidered edge and all its gold array were well dis-played. He looked to his polished rod, which he carries in his right hand to induce or ward off slumber, and took care that his winged sandals were gleaming on his smooth feet.

Far within the house were three rooms, decorated with ivory and tortoiseshell. The one on the right belonged to Pandrosos, that on the left to Aglauros, while Herse occupied the middle one. The girl who had the room on the left was the first to see Mercury when he came, and she ventured to ask him his name, and why he had come. This was his reply. 'I am he who carries his father's commands through the sky, the son of Jupiter himself. I shall not invent any reasons – it is because of Herse that I am here. Only show yourself a true friend to your sister, and consent to become aunt to my son. I ask you to lend your favour and help to a lover.' Aglauros looked at him with those same hard eyes with which she had lately pried into the secrets of fair-haired Minerva, and demanded a heavy weight of gold, in return for her services. For the present she forced him to leave her home.

The warrior goddess turned her angry eyes upon this girl, and sighed so deeply that her breast heaved, and with it the aegis which covered her brave heart. She recalled how, with profane hands, Aglauros had laid bare her secrets at the time when, breaking the conditions imposed on her, she had looked upon the son of the Lemnian god, the baby born without a mother. Now this girl would be dear to Mercury and to her sister, and rich as well, if she acquired the gold she greedily demanded.

Immediately the goddess made her way to the house of Envy, a house filthy with dark and noisome slime. It is hidden away in the depths of the valleys, where the sun never penetrates, where no wind blows through; a gloomy dwelling, permeated by numbing chill, ever fireless, ever shrouded in thick darkness. When the dread warrior maiden reached this spot she stopped in front of the house, for it was not permitted for her to enter: she struck the doors with the tip of her spear, and at the blow they flew open and revealed Envy within, busy at a meal of snake's flesh, the food on which she nourished her wickedness. At the sight, Minerva turned her eyes away. But the other rose heavily from the ground, leaving the half-eaten corpses, and came out, with dragging steps. When she saw the goddess in all the brilliance of her beauty, in her flashing armour, she groaned, and frowned when she heard the goddess' sighs.

Envy's face was sickly pale, her whole body lean and wasted, and she squinted horribly; her teeth were discoloured and decayed, her poisonous breast of a greenish hue, and her tongue dripped venom. Only the sight of suffering could bring a smile to her lips. She never knew the comfort of sleep, but was kept constantly awake by care and anxiety, looked with dismay on men's good fortune, and grew thin at the sight. Gnawing at others, and being gnawed, she was herself her own torment.

The Tritonian maid, in spite of her loathing, yet addressed her briefly: 'Instil your poison into one of Cecrops' daughters – her name is Aglauros. This is what I require of you.' Without another word she pushed against the ground with her spear, left the earth, and soared upwards.

From the corner of her eye the other watched the goddess out of sight, muttering and angry that Minerva's plan should be successful. Then she took her staff, all encircled with thorny briars, wrapped herself in dark clouds, and set forth. Wherever she went she trampled down the flowery fields, withered up the grass, seared the treetops, and with her breath tainted the peoples, their cities and their homes, until at length she came to the Athenian citadel, the home of wit and wealth, peaceful and prosperous. She could scarcely refrain from weeping when she saw no cause for tears.

Then entering the chamber of Cecrops' daughter, she carried out Minerva's orders. She touched the girl's breast with a hand dipped in malice, filled her heart with spiky thorns, and breathing in a black and evil poison dispersed it through her very bones, instilling the venom deep in her heart. That the reason for her distress might not be far to seek, she set before Aglauros' eyes a vision of her sister, of that sister's fortunate marriage, and of the god in all his handsomeness; and she exaggerated the glory of it all.

So Cecrops' daughter was tormented by such thoughts, and the jealous anger she concealed ate into her heart. Day and night she sighed, unceasingly wretched, and in her utter misery wasted away in a slow decline, as when ice is melted by the fitful sun. The fire that was kindled within her at the thought of Herse's luck and good fortune was like the burning of weeds which do not burst into flames, but are none the less consumed by smouldering fire. Often she prayed for death, that she might not have to see such a sight, often she planned to tell her stern father of the affair, as if it were some crime.

Finally, she sat down on her sister's threshold, with the idea of preventing the god's entrance when he came. He addressed her with flattery and prayers and tender words. 'Enough!' she cried, 'I shall not move from this spot until I have driven you away!' Swift-footed Mercury accepted her ultimatum. 'Let us keep to that agreement!' he said, and opened up the door with a touch of his magic wand.

Then, as Aglauros tried to rise, she found her limbs so sluggish and heavy that they could not be moved from a sitting position. She struggled to stand upright, but her knee joints had become rigid, a coldness pervaded her body to her very fingernails, and the blood drained from her pallid veins. As some evil growth that cannot be cured spreads rapidly, infecting sound flesh as well as the parts already diseased, so a deadly chill gradually crept over her breast, sealing the passages through which the breath of life must come. She did not try to speak nor, had she tried, could her voice have found a way. Already stone held her neck in its grip, her lips had hardened, and she sat, a lifeless statue. The stone was not even white, for her dark thoughts had lent it their own hue.

When Atlas' grandson had thus punished her for her wicked words and schemes, he left the land which takes its name from Pallas, and soared through the air on beating wings. His father called him aside and, without confessing his love as the reason, gave him his orders. 'My son, you who faithfully carry out my commands, hurry, glide swiftly down on your accustomed path, and make your way to the land which looks up to your mother's star from the left. The inhabitants call it Sidon. You will see a herd of cattle belonging to the king, grazing some distance off on the mountain slopes: drive them towards the shore.'

No sooner had he spoken than the bullocks, driven from their mountain pastures, were on their way to the beach, as Jove had directed; they were making for the sands where the daughter of the great king used to play with the young girls of Tyre, who were her companions.

Majesty and love go ill together, nor can they long share one abode. Abandoning the dignity of his sceptre, the father and ruler of the gods, whose hand wields the flaming three-forked bolt, whose nod shakes the universe, adopted the guise of a bull; and, mingling with the other bullocks, joined in their lowing and ambled in the tender grass, a fair sight to see. His hide was white as untrodden snow, snow not yet melted by the rainy South wind. The muscles stood out on his neck, and deep folds of skin hung along his flanks. His horns were small, it is true, but so beautifully made that you would swear they were the work of an artist, more polished and shining than any jewel. There was no menace in the set of his head or in his eyes; he looked completely placid.

Agenor's daughter was filled with admiration for one so handsome and so friendly. But, gentle though he seemed, she was afraid at first to touch him; then she went closer, and held out flowers to his shining lips. The lover was delighted and, until he could achieve his hoped-for pleasure, kissed her hands. He could scarcely wait for the rest, only with great difficulty did he restrain himself.

Now he frolicked and played on the green turf, now lay down, all snowy white on the yellow sand. Gradually the princess lost her fear, and with her innocent hands she stroked his breast when he offered it for her caress, and hung fresh garlands on his horns: till finally she even ventured to mount the bull, little knowing on whose back she was resting. Then the god drew away from the shore by easy stages, first planting the hooves that were part of his disguise in the surf at the water's edge, and then proceeding farther out to sea, till he bore his booty away over the wide stretches of mid ocean. The girl was sorely frightened, and looked back at the sands behind her, from which she had been carried away. Her right hand grasped the bull's horn, the other rested on his back, and her fluttering garments floated in the breeze.

BOOK III

❀

JUPITER was now resting in the fields of Crete. He had laid aside the disguise of a bull, under which he had deceived the princess, and revealed himself for what he was.

Meanwhile King Agenor, her father, did not know what had happened; he told his son Cadmus to search for his lost sister, and threatened him with exile if he did not find her. Thus by the same act the king showed himself at once an affectionate and a villainous father.

Cadmus wandered over the whole world: for who can lay hands on what Jove has stolen away? Driven to avoid his native country and his father's wrath, he made a pilgrimage to Apollo's oracle, and begged him to say what land he should dwell in. This was Phoebus' reply: 'In solitary pastures you will come upon a heifer, which has never felt the yoke, nor drawn the crooked plough. Go on your way with her to guide you, and when she lies down in the grass, there build your city walls, and call the place Boeotia.'

Cadmus went down from the Castalian grotto: almost at once he saw a heifer walking slowly along with none to guard her. There was no trace of harness upon her neck. He followed her, keeping close behind, and offered a silent prayer of thanksgiving to Phoebus, who had directed his way.

They passed by the shallow pools of Cephisus and through the lands of Panope. When they had gone so far, the heifer stopped, lifted up her head, graced with lofty horns, and raising it towards the sky filled the air with her lowings. She looked back at the friends who were following her; then, sinking to her knees, lay down on her side in the tender grass. Cadmus gave thanks, kissed the foreign soil, and greeted fields and mountains to which he was as yet a stranger. Then, intending to offer sacrifice to Jove, he ordered his attendants to go in search of fresh spring water, for a libation.

There was an ancient forest which no axe had ever touched, and in the heart of it a cave, overgrown with branches and osiers, forming a low arch with its rocky walls, rich in bubbling springs. Hidden in this cave dwelt the serpent of Mars, a creature with a wonderful golden crest; fire flashed from its eyes, its body was all puffed up with poison, and from its mouth, set with a triple row of teeth, flickered a three-forked tongue. The Phoenician travellers entered the grove on their ill-omened errand, and dipped their pitchers in the waters. At the sound, the dark gleaming serpent put forth its head from the depths of the cave, hissing horribly. The blood drained from the men's limbs, the jugs fell from their grasp and they shuddered with sudden dread. As for the snake, it coiled its scaly loops in writhing circles, then with a spring shot up in a huge arc, raising more than half its length into the insubstantial air, till it looked down upon the whole expanse of the forest. It was as huge as the Serpent that twines between the two Bears in the sky, if its full length were seen uncoiled. Without a moment's pause the monster seized upon the Phoenicians, while some of them were getting their weapons ready, and some were preparing to flee. Others were too terrified to do either. With its fangs, its constricting coils, and tainted poisonous breath, it slew them all.

The noonday sun had reduced the shadows to their shortest. Agenor's son, wondering what was detaining his friends, went out to look for them. His shield was a lion's skin, his weapon a lance with shining point. He had a javelin too, and courage that was of more avail than any weapon. When he entered the grove he saw the dead bodies, and their monstrous foe, towering triumphant above them, the blood dripping from its tongue as it licked their cruel wounds. 'My faithful friends,' cried Cadmus, 'I shall avenge your death, or share it!' As he spoke he lifted a great boulder in his right hand, and hurled this huge missile with tremendous force. Towering walls with lofty battlements would have been shaken by the impact: but the serpent was unharmed. Protected by its scales as by a breastplate, and by the toughness of its black skin, it repelled the stoutest blows. But that same toughness was not proof against the javelin, which struck home in a coil in the middle of the creature's sinuous back: the whole iron tip sank deep into its belly. Maddened with pain, the serpent twisted its head round to look at its back, and seeing the wound, bit at the shaft of the spear that was lodged there. By violent efforts it loosened the shaft all round, and just managed to drag it out: but the iron remained fixed in its bones. Then indeed, when this fresh irritation increased its normal savagery, the veins of the snake's throat filled and swelled with poison and white foam flecked its venomous jaws. Its scales rasped along the ground and its breath, rank as that from Stygian caves, spread foulness through the air. Now it coiled itself into huge spirals, now shot up straighter than a tree, or again, like a river swollen by the rains, swept violently along, its breast brushing aside the woods which barred the way. Cadmus drew back a little, received the onslaught on his lion's shield and, using his spear point as a barrier, blocked the threatening jaws. The serpent, in a frenzy, bit uselessly at the hard iron, and fastened its teeth on the point of the spear. Now the blood began to flow from its poison-laden throat, spattering the green grass. But the wound was a slight one, for the snake retreated from the blow, drawing back its injured neck; by yielding ground, it prevented the weapon from striking home, or entering more deeply. Meanwhile the son of Agenor kept pressing close, driving in the iron he had fixed in its throat; until an oak tree blocked its backward movement, and its neck was pinned to the trunk. The tree bent beneath the serpent's weight, and groaned as the end of the creature's tail thrashed against its bark.

While the victorious Cadmus stood, eyeing the huge bulk of his defeated foe, suddenly a voice was heard. It was not easy to tell where it came from, but heard it was. 'Son of Agenor, why stare at the snake you have slain? You, too, will become a serpent, for men to gaze upon.' The colour drained from Cadmus' cheeks, and for a long time he stood panic-stricken, frozen with fear, his hair on end, his senses reeling.

Then Pallas, the hero's patroness, suddenly appeared, gliding down through the upper air. She told him to plough up the earth, and to sow the serpent's teeth, as seeds from which his people would spring. He obeyed, and after opening up furrows with his deep-cutting plough, scattered the teeth on the ground as he had been bidden, seeds to produce men. What followed was beyond belief: the sods began to stir; then, first of all a crop of spearheads pushed up from the furrows, and after them came helmets with plumes nodding on their painted crests. Then shoulders and breasts and arms appeared, weighed down with weapons, and the crop of armoured heroes rose into the air. Even so, when the curtains are pulled up at the end of a show in the theatre, the figures embroidered on them rise into view, drawn smoothly upwards to reveal first their faces, and then the rest of their bodies, bit by bit, till finally they are seen complete, and stand with their feet resting on the bottom hem.

Cadmus was terrified at the sight of this new enemy, and was about to seize his weapons: but one of the warriors whom the earth had produced cried out to him: 'Don't take to arms! Keep clear of this family conflict!' With these words he drove his unyielding sword into one of his earthborn brothers, who was standing close at hand; then fell himself, pierced by a javelin thrown from a distance. The man who had killed him lived no longer than he did himself; he, too, gasped out the breath he had so lately received. The whole host fought madly in the same way, dealing each other wounds in turn. In the struggle which they had themselves begun, these short-lived brothers perished; until, of all the young warriors granted so brief a span of life, only five remained – the rest lay writhing on the bosom of their mother earth, which was all warm with their blood. One of the five survivors, Echion, flung down his arms, at the bidding of Pallas, promising to fight no more, and asking for the same promise from his brothers. These were the companions with whom the foreigner from Phoenicia undertook the task of founding his city, as instructed by Phoebus' oracles.

Now the city of Thebes was built, and it might have seemed that exile had been a blessing for Cadmus. He was married to the daughter of Mars and Venus, and his noble wife had borne him a family of many sons and many daughters. He had grandchildren too, dearly loved descendants, who kept close the bonds of family affection. He even saw these grandchildren grown to manhood. But indeed, one must ever wait for the last day of a man's life, and call no one happy until he is dead and buried.

Amid so much prosperity, it was one of his grandsons, Actaeon, who first brought distress to Cadmus, when antlers, foreign to his human shape, sprouted from the youth's forehead, and his hounds gorged themselves on their master's blood. But calm reflection will show that destiny was to blame for Actaeon's misfortunes, not any guilt on his own part; for there is nothing sinful in losing one's way.

The scene of this event was a mountain where the ground was stained with the bloodshed of wild beasts of many kinds. The heat of mid-day had shortened the shadows, and the sun was midway between his eastern and his western goal, when the young Actaeon called to his comrades, as they roamed the lonely thickets, saying in a gentle tone: 'My friends, our nets and swords are dripping with blood from the beasts we have taken – we have had enough success for one day. When tomorrow's dawn, riding in her saffron car, brings us another day, we shall return to our chosen task. But now the sun is at its highest, halfway on its course, cracking open the fields with its heat. For the present, then, put an end to your hunting, and gather in your knotted nets.' The men did as he suggested and stopped, for a time, their strenuous activities.

There was a valley, thickly overgrown with pitchpine, and with sharp-needled cypress trees. It was called Gargaphie, and was sacred to Diana, the goddess of the hunt. Far in its depths lay a woodland cave, which no hand of man had wrought: but nature by her own devices had imitated art. She had carved a natural arch from the living stone and the soft tufa rocks. On the right hand was a murmuring spring of clear water, spreading out into a wide pool with grassy banks. Here the goddess, when she was tired with hunting in the woods, used to bathe her fastidious limbs in the pure water. When she entered the grotto she handed her javelin to one of the nymphs, who acted as her armour-bearer, along with her quiver and her bow, un-strung. Another nymph received her cloak and hung it across her arm, while two more took off her sandals. Yet another attendant, more skilled than the rest, Crocale, the daughter of Ismenus, gathered up the tresses which lay scattered on the goddess' shoulders, and bound them into a knot, though her own hair hung loose. Nephele, Hyale, Rhanis, Psecas, and Phiale drew up the water in capacious jars, and poured it over their mistress.

Now while Diana was bathing there in her stream, as usual, the grandson of Cadmus, who had for the present abandoned his hunting, came wandering with hesitant steps through this wood which he had never seen before. He reached the grove – so were the fates directing him – and entered the cave, which was moist with spray. The nymphs, discovered in their nakedness, beat their breasts at the sight of a man, and filled all the grove with their sudden outcry. Crowding round Diana, they sheltered her with their own bodies, but the goddess was taller than they, head and shoulders above them all. When she was caught unclad, a blush mantled her cheeks, as bright as when clouds reflect the sun's rays, as bright as rosy dawn. Though hidden by her comrades, who gathered closely round her, she stood turned aside, looking back over her shoulder. She wished she had her arrows ready to hand: instead, she caught up a handful of the water which she did have, and threw it in the young man's face. As she sprinkled his hair with the vengeful drops she also spoke these words, ominous of coming disaster. 'Now, if you can, you may tell how you saw me when I was undressed.' She uttered no more threats, but made the horns of a long-lived stag sprout where she had scattered water on his brow. She lengthened his neck, brought the tips of his ears to a point, changed his hands to feet, his arms to long legs, and covered his body with a dappled skin. Then she put panic fear in his heart as well. The hero fled, and even as he ran, marvelled to find himself so swift. When he glimpsed his face and his horns, reflected in the water, he tried to say 'Alas!' but no words came. He groaned – that was all the voice he had – and tears ran down his changed cheeks. Only his mind remained the same as before. What was he to do? Return home to the royal palace, or hide in the woods? He was ashamed to do the first, afraid to do the second.

As he hesitated, his hounds caught sight of him. Melampus and the wise Ichnobates were the first to give tongue, Ichnobates of the Cretan breed, and Melampus of the Spartan. Then the others rushed to the chase, swifter than the wind, Pamphagus and Dorceus and Oribasus, all Arcadians, and strong Nebrophonus, fierce Theron and Laelaps too. Pterelas, the swift runner, was there, and keen-scented Agre, Hylaeus who had lately been gored by a wild boar, Nape, offspring of a wolf, Poemenis, the shepherd dog, Harpyia with her two pups, Ladon from Sicyon, slender-flanked, and Dromas and Canace, Sticte and Tigris, Alce, white-coated Leucon, and black-haired Asbolus; with them was Lacon, a dog of outstanding strength, Aello the stout runner, Thous and swift Lycisce with her brother Cyprius, Harpalus, who had a white spot in the middle of his black forehead, and Melaneus and shaggy Lachne, Lebros and Agriodus, both cross-bred of a Cretan mother and a Spartan father, shrill-barking Hylactor, and others whom it would take long to name. The pack, eager for its prey, swept over the rocks and crags, over un-approachable cliffs, through places where the going was difficult, and where there was no way at all. Actaeon fled, where he had himself so often pursued his quarry, fled, alas, before his own faithful hounds. He longed to cry out: 'I am Actaeon! Don't you know your own master?' but the words he wanted to utter would not come – the air echoed with barking. First Melanchaetes fastened his teeth in his master's back, then Theridamas and Oresitrophus clung to his shoul-der. They had been slow to begin the chase, but had outstripped the others by taking a short cut over the mountains. While they held their master down, the rest of the pack gathered, and sank their teeth in his body, till there was no place left for tearing. Actaeon groaned, utter-ing a sound which, though not human, was yet such as no stag could produce. The ridges he knew so well were filled with his mournful cries. Falling to his knees, like a suppliant in prayer, he silently swayed his head this way and that, as if stretching out beseeching arms. But his friends, not knowing what they did, urged on the ravening mob with their usual encouragements and looked round for Actaeon, shouted for Actaeon, as if he were not there, each trying to call louder than the other. They lamented that their leader was absent, and that his slowness prevented him from seeing the booty chance had offered. Actaeon turned his head at the sound of his name. Well might he wish to be absent, but he was all too surely present. Well might he wish to see and not to feel the cruel deeds of his hounds. They surrounded him on every side, fastening their jaws on his body, and tore to pieces the seeming stag, which was in fact their master. Only when he had been dispatched by wounds innumerable, so men say, was the anger of Diana, the quiver-bearing goddess, appeased.

When the story was told, opinions were divided: some thought that the goddess had been too cruel, others praised her, and declared her act in keeping with her strict chastity. Both sides could justify their views.

Only the wife of Jupiter spoke no word of praise or blame, but rejoiced in the disaster that had come upon the house descended from Agenor, transferring to Europa's kinsmen the hatred she had con-ceived against her Phoenician rival. Then fresh fuel was added to the fire of her former wrath, and she was indignant to find that Semele was heavy with child by Jove. She checked the words of abuse that sprang to her lips: 'What good have my oft-repeated reproaches ever done?' she said. 'It is the girl I must deal with. As I am rightly called Juno most mighty, as it is fitting that I should bear the jewelled sceptre in my hand, I will destroy her: as surely as I am queen of heaven, and sister and wife of Jupiter – his sister I certainly am. I suppose some may excuse her on the grounds that she asks no more than this furtive love, and that the wrong done to my marriage is of brief duration. My answer is that she is with child, and that is all that was needed. She carries in her womb clear proof of her guilt, and hopes to become a mother by Jove, and by him alone – something I myself have scarcely achieved. So confident is she in her beauty! But I shall see to it that her confidence is misplaced. Call me not Saturn's daughter, if she does not descend to the waters of the Styx, plunged there by that Jupiter of hers!' With these words she rose from her throne and, wrapped in a golden cloud, approached Semele's threshold; nor did she remove the cloud until she had adopted the guise of an old woman, streaking her temples with white hairs, and furrowing her skin with wrinkles. She walked with bowed back and shaking steps, and made her voice to quaver with age. She was the very double of Beroe, Semele's nurse from Epidaurus.

The two began to talk and, in the course of their lengthy gossiping, finally mentioned Jupiter. Then Juno sighed, and said: 'I pray that it may be Jupiter! But the whole business disturbs me: many a man has made his way into an honest girl's bedroom by calling himself a god. Anyhow, even if it is Jupiter, that is not enough – he should give proof of his love. If he is Jupiter indeed, ask him to appear in all the greatness and glory in which he shows himself to Juno on high. Let him first deck himself in his grandeur, and then embrace you.'

With such words Juno worked on the mind of Cadmus' daughter. She, quite unsuspicious, asked Jupiter to grant her a boon she would not name, and the god said: 'Choose what you want, you will not be refused. To show that you can trust me, I call the god of the Stygian torrent to be my witness: for the gods themselves stand in awe of his divinity.' Semele, all too persuasive, and fated to perish by her lover's compliance, rejoiced in obtaining the promise that was to be her ruin. 'Show yourself to me,' she said, 'as you appear to Juno, when you share love's embrace with her!' The god tried to stop her lips as she spoke, but already her hasty utterance had escaped into the air. He groaned; for neither her request nor his oath could now be altered. So, deeply grieving, he mounted high into the upper air. By his nod he drew together obedient mists, and coupled them with stormclouds and lightnings, with winds and thunderclaps, and with that bolt which none can escape. Yet he tried to diminish his strength as far as possible, rejecting as too fierce the fire with which he had struck down the hundred-handed Typhoeus. There is another lighter thunderbolt which the Cyclopes' hands have forged with a flame less cruel, a less wrathful weapon. The gods call such bolts his secondary armament. With these in hand, he entered the house of Agenor's descendants. But Semele's mortal frame could not endure the exaltation caused by the heavenly visitant, and she was burned to ashes by her wedding gift. Her child, still not fully formed, was snatched from his mother's womb and, if the tale may be believed, the feeble baby was sewn into his father's thigh till the months for which his mother should have carried him were fulfilled. Then his aunt, Ino, brought him up secretly, in his early infancy. Later he was given to the nymphs of Nysa who hid him in their caves, and fed him with milk.

While these things were being done on earth by fate's decree, while the cradle of twice-born Bacchus was safely guarded, it happened, so the story goes, that Jupiter put aside his weighty cares; mellowed by deep draughts of nectar, he indulged in idle banter with Juno, who shared his leisure, and teased her, saying: 'Of course, you women get far more pleasure out of love than men do.' Juno denied that this was true. They decided to ask the opinion of the wise Tiresias, for he had experienced love both as a man and as a woman.

Once, when two huge serpents were intertwining themselves in the depths of the green wood, he had struck them with his staff; from being a man he was miraculously changed into a woman, and had lived as such for seven years. In the eighth year he saw the same serpents again and said: 'If there is such potent magic in the act of striking you that it changes the striker to the opposite sex, I shall now strike you again.' So, by striking the same snakes, he was restored to his former shape, and the nature with which he was born returned.

He, then, was chosen to give his verdict in this playful argument, and he confirmed what Jupiter had said. Then, they say, Juno was more indignant than she had any right to be, more so than the case demanded, and she condemned the judge to eternal blindness. It is not possible for any god to undo the actions of another god, but in return for his loss of sight, the omnipotent father granted Tiresias the power to know the future and softened his punishment by conferring this honour upon him.

His fame spread throughout the Aonian cities, and when the people consulted him he gave replies with which none could find fault.

The dark river nymph, Liriope, was the first to test his reliability and truthfulness. She was the nymph whom Cephisus once embraced with his curving stream, imprisoned in his waves, and forcefully ravished. When her time was come, that nymph most fair brought forth a child with whom one could have fallen in love even in his cradle, and she called him Narcissus. When the prophetic seer was asked whether this boy would live to a ripe old age, he replied: 'Yes, if he does not come to know himself.' For a long time this pronouncement seemed to be nothing but empty words: however it was justified by the outcome of events: the strange madness which afflicted the boy and the nature of his death proved its truth.

Cephisus' child had reached his sixteenth year, and could be counted as at once boy and man. Many lads and many girls fell in love with him, but his soft young body housed a pride so unyielding that none of those boys or girls dared to touch him. One day, as he was driving timid deer into his nets, he was seen by that talkative nymph who cannot stay silent when another speaks, but yet has not learned to speak first herself. Her name is Echo, and she always answers back.

Echo still had a body then, she was not just a voice: but although she was always chattering, her power of speech was no different from what it is now. All she could do was to repeat the last words of the many phrases that she heard. Juno had brought this about because often, when she could have caught the nymphs lying with her Jupiter on the mountainside, Echo, knowing well what she did, used to detain the goddess with an endless flow of talk, until the nymphs could flee. When Juno realized what was happening, she said: 'I shall curtail the powers of that tongue which has tricked me: you will have only the briefest possible use of your voice.' And in fact she carried out her threats. Echo still repeats the last words spoken, and gives back the sounds she has heard.

So, when she saw Narcissus wandering through the lonely countryside, Echo fell in love with him, and followed secretly in his steps. The more closely she followed, the nearer was the fire which scorched her: just as sulphur, smeared round the tops of torches, is quickly kindled when a flame is brought near it. How often she wished to make flattering overtures to him, to approach him with tender pleas! But her handicap prevented this, and would not allow her to speak first; she was ready to do what it would allow, to wait for sounds which she might re-echo with her own voice.

The boy, by chance, had wandered away from his faithful band of comrades, and he called out: 'Is there anybody here?' Echo answered: 'Here!' Narcissus stood still in astonishment, looking round in every direction, and cried at the pitch of his voice: 'Come!' As he called, she called in reply. He looked behind him, and when no one appeared, cried again: 'Why are you avoiding me?' But all he heard were his own words echoed back. Still he persisted, deceived by what he took to be another's voice, and said, 'Come here, and let us meet!' Echo answered: 'Let us meet!' Never again would she reply more willingly to any sound. To make good her words she came out of the wood and made to throw her arms round the neck she loved: but he fled from her, crying as he did so, 'Away with these embraces! I would die before I would have you touch me!' Her only answer was: 'I would have you touch me!' Thus scorned, she concealed herself in the woods, hiding her shamed face in the shelter of the leaves, and ever since that day, she dwells in lonely caves. Yet still her love remained firmly rooted in her heart, and was increased by the pain of having been rejected. Her anxious thoughts kept her awake, and made her pitifully thin. She became wrinkled and wasted; all the freshness of her beauty withered into the air. Only her voice and her bones were left, till finally her voice alone remained; for her bones, they say, were turned to stone. Since then, she hides in the woods, and, though never seen on the mountains, is heard there by all: for her voice is the only part of her that still lives.

Narcissus had played with her affections, treating her as he had previously treated other spirits of the waters and the woods, and his male admirers too. Then one of those he had scorned raised up his hands to heaven and prayed: 'May he himself fall in love with another, as we have done with him! May he too be unable to gain his loved one!' Nemesis heard and granted his righteous prayer.

There was a clear pool, with shining silvery waters, where shepherds had never made their way; no goats that pasture on the mountains, no cattle had ever come there. Its peace was undisturbed by bird or beast or falling branches. Around it was a grassy sward, kept ever green by the nearby waters; encircling woods sheltered the spot from the fierce sun, and made it always cool.

Narcissus, wearied with hunting in the heat of the day, lay down here: for he was attracted by the beauty of the place, and by the spring. While he sought to quench his thirst, another thirst grew in him, and as he drank, he was enchanted by the beautiful reflection that he saw. He fell in love with an insubstantial hope, mistaking a mere shadow for a real body. Spellbound by his own self, he remained there motionless, with fixed gaze, like a statue carved from Parian marble. As he lay on the bank, he gazed at the twin stars that were his eyes, at his flowing locks, worthy of Bacchus or Apollo, his smooth cheeks, his ivory neck, his lovely face where a rosy flush stained the snowy whiteness of his complexion, admiring all the features for which he was himself admired. Unwittingly, he desired himself, and was himself the object of his own approval, at once seeking and sought, himself kindling the flame with which he burned. How often did he vainly kiss the treacherous pool, how often plunge his arms deep in the waters, as he tried to clasp the neck he saw! But he could not lay hold upon himself. He did not know what he was looking at, but was fired by the sight, and excited by the very illusion that deceived his eyes. Poor foolish boy, why vainly grasp at the fleeting image that eludes you? The thing you are seeing does not exist: only turn aside and you will lose what you love. What you see is but the shadow cast by your reflection; in itself it is nothing. It comes with you, and lasts while you are there; it will go when you go, if go you can.

No thought of food or sleep could draw him from the spot. Stretched on the shady grass, he gazed at the shape that was no true shape with eyes that could never have their fill, and by his own eyes he was undone. Finally he raised himself a little. Holding out his arms to the surrounding woods: 'Oh you woods,' he cried, 'has anyone ever felt a love more cruel? You surely know, for many lovers have found you an ideal haunt for secret meetings. You who have lived so many centuries, do you remember anyone, in all your long years, who has pined away as I do? I am in love, and see my loved one, but that form which I see and love, I cannot reach: so far am I deluded by my love. My distress is all the greater because it is not a mighty ocean that separates us, nor yet highways or mountains, or city walls with close-barred gates. Only a little water keeps us apart. My love himself desires to be embraced: for whenever I lean forward to kiss the clear waters he lifts up his face to mine and strives to reach me. You would think he could be reached – it is such a small thing that hinders our love. Whoever you are, come out to me! Oh boy beyond compare, why do you elude me? Where do you go, when I try to reach you? Certainly it is not my looks or my years which you shun, for I am one of those the nymphs have loved. With friendly looks you proffer me some hope. When I stretch out my arms to you, you stretch yours towards me in return: you laugh when I do, and often I have marked your tears when I was weeping. You answer my signs with nods, and, as far as I can guess from the movement of your lovely lips, reply to me in words that never reach my ears. Alas! I am myself the boy I see. I know it: my own reflection does not deceive me. I am on fire with love for my own self. It is I who kindle the flames which I must endure. What should I do? Woo or be wooed? But what then shall I seek by my wooing? What I desire, I have. My very plenty makes me poor. How I wish I could separate myself from my body! A new prayer this, for a lover, to wish the thing he loves away! Now grief is sapping my strength; little of life remains for me – I am cut off in the flower of my youth. I have no quarrel with death, for in death I shall forget my pain: but I could wish that the object of my love might outlive me: as it is, both of us will perish together, when this one life is destroyed.'

When he had finished speaking, he returned to gazing distractedly at that same face. His tears disturbed the water, so that the pool rippled, and the image grew dim. He saw it disappearing, and cried aloud: 'Where are you fleeing? Cruel creature, stay, do not desert one who loves you! Let me look upon you, if I cannot touch you. Let me, by looking, feed my ill-starred love.' In his grief, he tore away the upper portion of his tunic, and beat his bared breast with hands as white as marble. His breast flushed rosily where he struck it, just as apples often shine red in part, while part gleams whitely, or as grapes, ripening in variegated clusters, are tinged with purple. When Narcissus saw this reflected in the water – for the pool had returned to its former calm – he could bear it no longer. As golden wax melts with gentle heat, as morning frosts are thawed by the warmth of the sun, so he was worn and wasted away with love, and slowly consumed by its hidden fire. His fair complexion with its rosy flush faded away, gone was his youthful strength, and all the beauties which lately charmed his eyes. Nothing remained of that body which Echo once had loved.

The nymph saw what had happened, and although she remembered her own treatment, and was angry at it, still she grieved for him. As often as the unhappy boy sighed 'Alas,' she took up his sigh, and repeated 'Alas!' When he beat his hands against his shoulders she too gave back the same sound of mourning. His last words as he gazed into the familiar waters were: 'Woe is me for the boy I loved in vain!' and the spot re-echoed the same words. When he said his last farewell, 'Farewell!' said Echo too. He laid down his weary head on the green grass, and death closed the eyes which so admired their owner's beauty. Even then, when he was received into the abode of the dead, he kept looking at himself in the waters of the Styx. His sisters, the nymphs of the spring, mourned for him, and cut off their hair in tribute to their brother. The wood nymphs mourned him too, and Echo sang her refrain to their lament.

The pyre, the tossing torches, and the bier, were now being prepared, but his body was nowhere to be found. Instead of his corpse, they discovered a flower with a circle of white petals round a yellow centre.

When this story became known, it brought well-deserved fame to the seer Tiresias. It was told throughout all the cities of Greece, and his reputation was boundless.

Now Pentheus, son of Echion, was a man who despised the gods. He alone among mortals scorned their prophet, and laughed at the old man's words of warning, taunting him with his loss of sight, and with the calamity of his blindness. But the seer, shaking his white head, spoke these words to him: 'How lucky it would be for you, if you too were to be deprived of sight, so that you could not behold Bacchus' sacred rites! For a day will come, and I warrant it is not far off, when the new god Liber, son of Semele, will come hither; and unless you accord him the honour of worship in holy shrines, you will be torn limb from limb, and scattered in a thousand places, bespattering the woods with your blood, and your mother and her sisters too. This thing will come to pass! You will deny the god his honour, and lament that in my darkness I saw all too clearly.' Even as he was uttering these warnings, the son of Echion thrust him aside – but his words were proved true, his prophecies fulfilled.

Bacchus was now at hand, and the fields were ringing with the wild shrieks of his worshippers. The whole populace streamed out of the city, men and women, old and young, the humbly born and those of high estate, all rushing to celebrate the new rites. But Pentheus objected: 'Descendants of the serpent's race,' he cried, 'children of Mars, what madness has robbed you of your senses? Can brazen cymbals clashing, pipes with curving horns, trickery and magic have an effect so great that men who faced the swords of battle and heard its trumpets, undismayed, who were undaunted by the ranks of war with weapons drawn, should quail before wailing women and tinkling tambourines, drunken madmen and disgusting fanatics? I do not know which of you surprise me more, you older men who, after sailing far across the sea and building a new Tyre in this land, a refuge for your exiled gods, now allow it to be captured without a struggle – or the younger men, those of a more spirited age, nearer to my own, who should be wearing helmets, not garlands, and be carrying martial arms, not Bacchic wands. Remember your parentage, I implore you, and show the spirit of that serpent who, one against many, destroyed them all. He gave his life for the sake of a pool and a spring of water: do you, by defeating the foe, defend the honour of your name. He slew men of valour: you, then, must rout this feeble enemy, and so maintain the glory of your fathers. If Thebes is fated to fall so soon, how I wish that gallant foemen were bringing down her walls with their engines of war, that the roar of flames and the din of battle were sounding in our ears. Then, though wretched, we should be free from blame; though our lot would be lamentable, there would be no need for concealment, our tears would bring us no shame. But now, Thebes will be taken by an unarmed boy, one who takes no pleasure in war, its weapons and its cavalry, but delights in tresses dripping with myrrh, in fresh garlands and garments embroidered with purple and gold. Only stand aside, and I shall compel him forthwith to confess that he has himself invented this tale of a divine father, that his sacred rites are empty mockeries. Acrisius had courage enough to despise his empty boast of divine power, and to shut the gates of Argos in his face: and will this new arrival frighten Pentheus and all Thebes? Go quickly' – this order was given to his slaves – 'Go and drag that leader here in chains. Waste no time in carrying out my commands.'

His grandfather and Athamas, and indeed his whole family reproached and warned Pentheus: vainly they tried to stop him. Their warnings only roused him the more, and his mad rage was excited and increased by their attempts to restrain it. Their very efforts to control him did harm. So have I seen a mountain stream, flowing smoothly downhill, with gentle murmuring, as long as nothing blocked its course; but wherever trees or rocks obstructed it, it foamed and boiled, made fiercer by the obstacles.

Now the band of slaves returned, all stained with blood. When their master inquired where Bacchus was, they declared they had not seen him. 'But here is one of his companions we have captured,' they said, 'a priest who celebrates his sacred mysteries.' And they handed over a prisoner, whose hands were bound behind his back. He was a man of Lydian parentage, and a follower of the god. Pentheus looked at him, terrible anger in his eyes. He could scarcely bear to delay punishment for an instant: however, he questioned the prisoner, and said: 'You are on the point of death, and by your death you will serve as a warning to others. Speak, then, reveal your name and the names of your parents, tell me where you were born, and why you celebrate the rites of this new cult.' The other was quite unperturbed. He replied: 'My name is Acoetes, I was born in Lydia, and my parents were of humble stock. My father did not leave me any fields for sturdy bullocks to till, or any woolly flocks, or herds. He was a poor man, as I am, and used to catch fish with hook and line: with his rod he drew them, leaping, from the stream. His fisherman's skill was all his wealth. This he passed on to me, saying: "Take such riches as I have, be my successor and heir to my craft." So he died, leaving me nothing but the waters. These alone can I call my inheritance. But I did not wish to spend the rest of my life on those selfsame rocks, so I soon learned to put my hand to a ship's rudder, and I

marked well the rainy constellation of the Olenian goat, Taygete and
the Hyades, and the Bears, and made myself familiar with the homes
of the winds, and harbours fit for ships. It happened that as I was mak-
ing for Delos, I put in to the shores of Chios. The oarsmen rowed
easily to the beach; I leaped lightly from the boat, and landed on the
moist sand. There we spent the night.

'When the first flush of dawn appeared I rose, and showed my
comrades the way that led to a spring, telling them to fetch fresh
water. I myself climbed a high hill to see what the breeze promised:
then I called my men, and made my way back to the ship. Opheltes
was the first of my friends to return. "Here we are!" he cried, and
came along the shore, bringing with him a boy, as pretty as a girl.
He had found him alone in a field, and had taken possession of this
prize, as he thought. The boy, drowsy with sleep and wine, seemed to
stumble, and was scarcely able to follow. I looked at his clothes, at
his features, and his bearing, and saw that everything indicated him to
be more than mortal. When I realized this, I said to my companions:
"What god is within that body, I cannot tell, but a god there is. I
pray you, whoever you are, be gracious and assist our labours. Grant
pardon, too, to these your captors." "No need to pray on our behalf!"
cried Dictys, the quickest man who ever climbed to the topmost
halyard and slid down again by the rope. Libys and blond Melanthus,
who was our look-out, and Alcemidon said the same; so did Epopeus,
whose task it was to apportion spells of rest, and to set the time for the
rowers, spurring them on with his voice. All the others agreed with
them – so blind was their lust for plunder. But I retorted: "I have the
chief say in this matter. I will not allow a ship of mine to become
accursed by carrying off holy cargo," – and I barred the gangway of
the ship. This enraged Lycabas, who was the boldest of them all. He
had been banished from his city in Lydia for a horrible murder, and
was enduring exile as a punishment. When I tried to resist him, he
tore at my throat with his strong young fists, and would have dashed
me overboard into the sea, if I had not, half-stunned as I was, clung to
a rope which held me back. The scoundrelly crew applauded his
deed; and then at last Bacchus, for it was Bacchus, intervened, as if
his slumbers had been dispelled by the shouting and his senses restored
again, after his drinking bout. "What goes on here? What means all
the shouting?" he asked. "Tell me, sailors, how came I to this place?

Where do you intend to take me?" "Do not be afraid," Proreus soothed him. "Tell us what harbour you want to reach, and you will be set down in the land of your choice." "Direct your course towards Naxos," Liber told them. "My home is there, and that land will give you hospitality." By the sea and by all the gods they treacherously swore that so it would be, and they told me to hoist sail in the painted ship. Naxos was on the right hand: but as I set my sail towards the right, Opheltes shouted: "You fool, what are you doing? What madness has possessed you?" And every man joined in, crying: "Make for the left!" Most of them indicated their purpose by a nod, but some whispered in my ear what they meant to do. I was horrified. "Someone else can take the rudder!" I cried, and refused to have any share in their wickedness, or in the sailing of the ship. They all cursed me, my whole crew muttered angrily. Then one of them, Aethalion by name, exclaimed: "I suppose you think the safety of us all depends on you alone!" and he himself took my place, and performed my duties. Leaving Naxos behind, he sailed off in a different direction.

'Then the god made sport of them. As if he had only just perceived their treachery, he stood on the curved stern, looking out over the sea, and pretended to weep. "These are not the shores you promised me, sailors, this is not the land I asked for. What have I done to deserve such treatment? What credit is it for a large band of grown men to cheat a solitary boy?" I had long been weeping; but my wicked crew laughed at my tears, and sped on, striking the sea with their oarblades.

'Now I swear to you by that god himself – for there is no god greater than he – that what I tell you is as surely true as it seems past belief. The ship stood still in the water, as if held in a dry dock. The sailors, in surprise, kept on plying their oars and spread their sails, trying to run on with the help of both; but their oars were hampered with ivy, which twined up the blades in curling tendrils, and adorned the sails with heavy clusters. The god himself wreathed his head with bunches of grapes, while in his hand he flourished a wand draped with vine-leaves. Around him lay phantom shapes of wild beasts, tigers and lynxes and panthers with dappled skins. The sailors leaped overboard, whether in madness or in fear I cannot tell. Medon's body was the first to darken in colour, and his spine arched into a well-marked curve. Lycabas began to say to him: "What kind of monster are you turning into?" But even as he spoke, his own mouth widened, his nostrils became hooked, and his skin hardened into scales. Libys, as he strove to pull the sluggish oars, saw his hands shrinking into small compass, saw that they were no longer hands, but might rather be called fins. Yet another, as he tried to lift his arms to handle the twisted ropes, found that he had no arms and, arching his limbless body, sprang backwards into the waves. The end of his tail was sickle-shaped, bent round like the horns of a half-moon. On all sides these creatures leaped-about, dashing up clouds of spray: they sprang out of the water, and dived under again, throwing their bodies about in wanton play, like some troupe of dancers, and blowing out the sea-water that washed into their broad nostrils. Where there had lately been twenty men – for that was the ship's crew – I alone remained. I was trembling with cold and fear, scarcely in my right mind; but the god comforted me, saying: "Be not afraid, make for Dia's isle." Brought safely to that island, I was initiated into the sacred mysteries and, since then, I have been one of Bacchus' worshippers.'

Then spoke Pentheus: 'We have listened to a long and rambling tale, in order that delay might serve to calm our anger. Slaves, remove this man now, with all speed, rack his frame with your worst torments, and consign him to the shades of the Styx.'

Immediately the Lydian Acoetes was dragged away and shut up in a stout prison chamber: but the story goes that while the cruel instruments, the fire, and the sword were being got ready to kill him, as the king had ordered, the doors flew open of their own accord and, of their own accord, though no one loosed them, the fetters fell from his arms. Still the son of Echion persisted in his folly. He no longer commanded others to go, but went himself to Cithaeron, the mountain chosen for the sacred rites, where the songs and shrill cries of the worshippers filled the air. As a spirited horse on the battle-field whinnies, eager for the fray, when the trumpeter sounds the charge on his brazen instrument, so Pentheus was roused by the long-drawn howlings, which set the very air a-quiver, and, when he heard the shouting, his anger blazed up hotly once more.

Halfway up the mountain is a stretch of level ground hemmed in by forests but itself bare of trees so that it can be clearly seen from every side. Here Pentheus looked upon the mysteries with uninitiated eyes. The first to see him, the first to make a frenzied rush, the first to hurl her thyrsus and wound him, was his own mother. As she did so, she cried: 'Sisters, come, both of you, come and help! That huge boar, roaming in our preserves, that boar, I say, must be the victim of my spear.' The whole frenzied throng rushed madly upon him, all gathering to pursue the panic-stricken king. For now he was indeed panic-stricken, now he spoke less violently; he cursed himself, and confessed himself at fault. Wounded as he was, still he called out: 'Help me, aunt Autonoe, let the ghost of your Actaeon move you to pity me!' But the name of Actaeon meant nothing to her; even as he prayed for mercy, she tore off his right arm, while Ino seized the other and wrenched it away. With no arms left to stretch towards his mother, the hapless man showed her instead the gaping wounds where his limbs had been torn out, and cried: 'Look, Mother!' At the sight Agave uttered a wild shriek, tossed her head till her hair streamed through the air, then tore his head from his shoulders. Clutching it in blood-stained fingers, she called: 'See, my friends, this victory, my own achievement!' Swiftly as the wind strips a tall tree of its autumn leaves, when a touch of frost has left them only just clinging to the branches, so swiftly did those terrible hands tear the king's limbs apart.

Taught by such a warning, the Theban women thronged to celebrate the new rites, and made offerings of incense, worshipping at the holy altars.

BOOK IV

❋

BUT Alcithoe, the daughter of Minyas, was not among them: for she did not believe that the god's wild worship should be permitted in their land. In her rashness she still denied that Bacchus was the son of Jupiter, and she had her sisters, too, as partners in her wickedness.

The priest had announced that Bacchus' festival was to be celebrated, and that servant girls should be released from their tasks. Then they and their mistresses were to drape animal skins across their breasts, untie the ribbons that bound their hair, set garlands on their heads, and take in their hands the leaf-decked thyrsus. Further, he had prophesied that, if the god were slighted, his wrath would be terrible. The women, old and young, obeyed the priest's commands. They put aside their looms, their baskets of wool, and their unfinished tasks. Then they made offerings of incense, and called upon Bacchus, hailing him by different titles, as Bromius and Lyaeus, as the son of the thunderbolt, the twice-born, the only child ever to have two mothers. He was invoked as Nisaeus, as Thyoneus of the flowing tresses, as Lenaeus, and as planter of the genial vine, as Nyctelius and father Eleleus, as Iacchus and Euhan, and by all the other names besides that Bacchus bears among the Greeks. For he is one whose youth never fades: he remains always a boy, the loveliest god in the heights of heaven. When he appears before us, without his horns, his head is like that of a young girl. He has conquered the East, as far as the land where swarthy India is watered by remote Ganges' stream.

O god most worshipful, for their sacrilege you slew Pentheus, and Lycurgus, who carried the two-headed axe, you cast the Lydian sailors into the sea, you set that harness bright with broidered reins upon the necks of the twin lynxes which draw your car. Bacchants and satyrs follow in your train, and with them that tipsy old man who supports his staggering steps with a staff, or clings unsteadily to his crook-backed ass. Wherever you go, young men's voices are raised in cheering, and women's voices join in the chorus, palms beat upon tambourines, hollow cymbals clash, to the sound of the boxwood flute's shrill piping.

The Theban women offered up their prayer to Bacchus, saying: 'May your gracious and gentle presence be with us now!' Then they celebrated the rites which had been ordained. Only the daughters of Minyas remained indoors, desecrating the festival by their untimely spinning. They drew out strands of wool, twirled the threads with their thumbs, and applied themselves to their looms, keeping their servant maids busy about their tasks.

By-and-by, one of them, as she drew the thread smoothly over her thumb, said to her sisters: 'All the other girls are on holiday, crowding to take part in this unwarranted festival. Let us amuse ourselves too. While our hands are usefully engaged in the service of Pallas, a greater divinity than Bacchus, let us take turns in telling stories and each contribute something to while away the time. The rest will listen.' Her sisters were pleased with the idea, and said that she should begin.

She knew a great many stories, so she considered which of them she ought to tell. She hesitated as to whether it should be the tale of Dercetis of Babylon who, so the people of Palestine believe, was changed into a fish and swam in their pools, her limbs all covered with scales; or the story of how Dercetis' daughter grew wings, and spent her last years in a white-washed dove-cote; or how the naiad, by means of spells and all too potent herbs, changed young men into dumb fishes, until she herself suffered the same fate; or how the tree which used to have white berries now bears fruit dyed deep purple by the stain of blood. Finally she chose this last, for it was a little-known tale. Spinning her wool the while, she began as follows:

'Pyramus and Thisbe lived next door to each other, in the lofty city whose walls of brick are said to have been built by Semiramis. Pyramus was the most handsome of young men, and Thisbe the fairest beauty of the East. Living so near, they came to know one another, and a friendship was begun; in time, love grew up between them, and they would have been married, but their parents forbade it. None the less – for this their parents could not forbid – both their hearts were caught in love's snare, and both burned with equal passion. No one shared their secret: they communicated by nods and signs, and the more it was concealed, the more their hidden love blazed up.

'There was a crack, a slender chink, that had developed in the party wall between their two houses, when it was being built. This fault had gone unnoticed for long years, and the lovers were the first to find it: nothing can escape a lover's eyes! They used it as a channel for their voices, and by this means their endearments were safely conveyed to one another, in the gentlest of whispers. Often when Pyramus stood on this side, Thisbe on that, when in turn they felt each other's breath, they used to exclaim: "Jealous wall, why do you stand in the way of lovers? How little it would be to ask that you should let us embrace or, if that is too much, that you should at least open wide enough for us to exchange kisses! Not that we are ungrateful – we admit that it is thanks to you that we have any way at all by which our words can reach our true love's ears." So they talked, in vain, on their opposite sides. At nightfall, they said good-bye, and though they could not reach each other with their kisses, they kissed their own side of the wall.

'Next day, when Aurora had put out night's starry fires and the sun's rays had dried the frosty grass, they came to their usual meeting place. At first, softly sighing, they lamented their sad lot. Then they determined that, at dead of night, they would try to slip past the watchmen and steal out of doors; once outside their homes, they would make their way out of the city too; and in case they should miss each other, wandering aimlessly in the open country, they agreed to meet at Ninus' tomb, and to hide in the shade of its tree. For a tree grew there, a tall mulberry, hung thick with snowy fruits; it stood close by a cool spring. They were enraptured with their plan. The daylight seemed slow to depart, but at last the sun plunged into the waters, and from those waters came forth the night. Stealthily Thisbe turned the door on its hinges, and slipped out into the darkness, unseen by any. Her face hidden by her veil, she came to the tomb, and sat down under the appointed tree. Love made her bold. But suddenly a lioness, fresh from the kill, her slavering jaws dripping with the blood of her victims, came to slake her thirst at the neighbouring spring. While the animal was still some distance off, Thisbe saw her in the moonlight. Frightened, she fled into the darkness of a cave, and as she ran her veil slipped from her shoulders, and was left behind.

'When the savage lioness had drunk her fill, and was returning to the woods, she found the garment, though not the girl, and tore its fine fabric to shreds, ripping it with bloodstained jaws.

'Pyramus came out of the city a little later. He saw the prints of the wild beast, clearly outlined in the deep dust, and the colour drained from his face. Worse still, he found the veil, all stained with blood. Then he cried out: "This night will bring about the death of two fond lovers, and of the two she deserved to live far more than I. 'Tis I who am to blame: poor girl, it was I who killed you! I told you to come, by night, to a place that was full of danger, and did not arrive first myself. Come, all you lions who live beneath this cliff, come and tear me limb from limb! With your fierce jaws, devour my guilty person. But it is a coward's trick, only to pray for death!" He picked up Thisbe's veil, and carried it into the shade of the tree where they should have met. Weeping and kissing the garment he knew so well, he said: "Drink deep, now, of my blood too." And as he spoke he took the sword which hung at his waist, and thrust it into his side: then, with a dying effort, pulled it out of the warm wound. As he lay, fallen back upon the ground, his blood spouted forth, just as when a water pipe bursts, if there is some flaw in the lead, and through the narrow hissing crack a long stream of water shoots out, and beats on the air. The fruits of the tree were sprinkled with his blood, and changed to a dark purple hue. The roots, soaked in his gore, tinged the hanging berries with the same rich colour.

'Now, though Thisbe had not yet quite recovered from her fear, she came back; for she was anxious not to disappoint her lover. She looked about for the youth with eager eyes and heart, impatient to tell him of the perils she had escaped. But although she recognized the spot, and the shape of the tree, yet the colour of its fruit made her uncertain; she was unable to decide whether this was the place or not. As she stood in doubt, she saw the quivering limbs writhing on the bloodstained ground, and started back. Her cheeks grew paler than boxwood, and she trembled as the sea shivers when a soft breeze ripples its surface. After a moment's pause, she recognized her love. Wailing aloud, she beat her innocent arms, tore her hair, and embracing his beloved form, bathed his wound with her tears, mingling the salt drops with his blood, and passionately kissing his cold cheeks. "Pyramus," she cried. "What mischance has taken you from me?

Pyramus, speak to me! It is your own dear Thisbe who is calling you!
Hear me, and raise your drooping head!'' At Thisbe's name, Pyramus
opened his eyes, which were already heavy with death's stupor; then,
with one last look, closed them for ever. Thisbe, when she recognized
her veil, and saw the ivory scabbard empty of its sword, exclaimed:
"Alas, your own hand and your love have destroyed you. I, too, have
a hand resolute for this one deed; my love, as great as yours, will give
me strength to deal the wound. I shall follow you in death, and men
will speak of me as at once the unhappy cause and the companion of
your fate. Only death could have separated you from me, but not
even death will part us. Most wretched parents, mine and his, I beg
this one boon for us both: since our steadfast love and the hour of
our death have united us, do not grudge that we be laid together in a
single tomb. And you, O tree, already sheltering one hapless body,
soon to shelter two, bear for ever the marks of our death: always
have fruit of a dark and mournful hue, to make men remember the
blood we two have shed!'' As she spoke, she placed the sword blade
beneath her breast, and fell forward on the steel, which was still
warm from Pyramus' death. Her prayers touched the gods, and they
touched the parents also: for the berry of the tree, when ripe, is a
dark purple colour, and the remains of the two lovers, gathered from
the funeral fires, rest together in a single urn.'

She had finished her story. There was a brief pause, and then
Leuconoe began to speak, while her sisters listened in attentive
silence. 'Even the sun there, who rules the whole world with his
flashing rays, even the sun became Love's captive! I shall tell you how
he fell in love. This god was the first, so it is thought, to see the
shameful behaviour of Venus and Mars: for he sees everything before
anyone else. Indignant at their actions, he showed Vulcan, who was
Juno's son and Venus' husband, how and where they were mis-
behaving. Vulcan's senses reeled, and the iron he was forging fell
from his hand. At once, he began to fashion slender bronze chains,
nets and snares which the eye could not see. The thinnest threads
spun on the loom, or cobwebs hanging from the rafters are no finer
than was that workmanship. Moreover, he made them so that they
would yield to the lightest touch, and to the smallest movement.
These he set skilfully around his bed.

'When his wife and her lover lay down together upon that couch, they were caught by the chains, ingeniously fastened there by her husband's skill, and were held fast in the very act of embracing. Immediately, the Lemnian Vulcan flung open the ivory doors, and admitted the gods. There lay Mars and Venus, close bound together, a shameful sight. The gods were highly amused; one of them prayed that he too might be so shamed. They laughed aloud, and for long this was the best-known story in the whole of heaven.

'The lady of Cythera did not forget. In her turn, she punished the informer, wounding with like passion the god who had ruined her secret love affair. Of what use then was his beauty to the son of Hyperion, his brightness, or his radiant light? He who makes all lands glow with his fires was himself most surely aglow with a new kind of flame. Those eyes which should see all, and range over the universe, caught sight of Leucothoe, and were riveted on a single girl. Sometimes he rose too early in the eastern sky, sometimes he was later than he should have been in plunging into the waves. Lingering to gaze at her, he lengthened the hours of the winter days. Sometimes his light failed, and the sickness of his mind affected his rays, so that he grew dim, striking terror into mortal hearts. It was not the moon's orb, journeying between him and the earth, which made him wan, by cutting off his light: love was the cause of his pallor. All his affection was centred on this girl alone. He had no thought for Clymene, or for Rhodos, for the lovely mother of Aeaean Circe, or for Clytie, who sought his company, in spite of his scorning her, and at that very time was bitterly hurt. Leucothoe caused him to forget his many former loves.

'She was the daughter of Eurynome, who had been the fairest beauty in the land of perfumed spices: but when Leucothoe grew up, she surpassed her mother in loveliness, just as her mother surpassed all others. Her father was Orchamus, who ruled over Persia's cities, seventh in descent from Belus, the ancient founder of the kingdom.

'Beneath the western sky lie the meadows where the sun's horses pasture, feeding not on grass but on ambrosia. When they are exhausted by their daily duties, this nourishment builds up their limbs, and refreshes them for their tasks. While his steeds were there cropping their divine food, while night was taking its turn in the sky, the sungod entered the home of his loved one, disguised as her mother, Eurynome. Leucothoe was sitting in the lamplight, with her twelve servant maids about her, drawing out smooth threads with her whirling spindle. When he saw her, he kissed her, just as if he were a mother kissing her dear daughter; then he said: "I have a secret to tell you. Leave us, servants. Do not deprive a mother of the right to speak to her daughter in private." The servants did as they were told, and when there was no one else in the room to see, the sun revealed himself to Leucothoe. "I am that god," he said, "who measures out the path of the long year, who sees everything, and by whose light the earth sees all. I am the eye of the universe and, believe me, I am in love with you!" The girl was afraid. In her fear, spindle and distaff dropped from her nerveless fingers, but her very panic enhanced her loveliness. The sun waited no longer, but returned to his true shape, and to his wonted brilliance. Leucothoe, though frightened by the unexpected sight, was overcome by his magnificence, and accepted the god's embraces without a murmur.

'Clytie was jealous, for her love for the sun had been beyond all measure. Spurred on by anger against her rival, she spread the story of Leucothoe's guilt and, by publishing it abroad, brought it to the notice of the girl's father. Orchamus was furious. Though Leucothoe entreated him, though she stretched out her hands to the sun and cried: "It was he who forced me to it! I did not wish it!" still, her father would not be appeased, but cruelly buried her in a living grave, and piled a heavy heap of sand on top. Hyperion's son scattered this with his rays, and made a passageway for his loved one to lift up her buried head. But to raise her head was now more than the nymph could do, crushed as it was by the weight of earth. She lay, lifeless. They say that never, since the thunderbolt slew Phaethon, had the god who drives the winged steeds seen anything which caused him more bitter grief. He tried whether the strength of his rays could restore living warmth to her chilled limbs, but fate made all his efforts useless. Then he sprinkled her body, and the spot where it lay, with perfumed nectar. Many were the laments he uttered, and finally he cried: "You will reach heaven, none the less!" Straightway her body, which he had anointed with divine nectar, dissolved away, soaking the earth with sweet-scented essence. Gradually a shrub of incense spread its roots down through the earth, and itself rose into the air, its shoots breaking through the mound.

'As for Clytie, she could have been forgiven for her indignation, since it was due to love, and indignation might have excused her tale-bearing. However, the lord of light did not go near her any more – his affection for her was at an end. From that day she wasted away, for she had been quite mad with love. She had no use for the company of the nymphs, but sat upon the bare ground, night and day, under the open sky, her head uncovered, and her hair all disarrayed. For nine days she tasted neither food nor drink, but fed her hunger only on dew and tears. She never stirred from the ground: all she did was to gaze on the face of the sungod, as he journeyed on, and turn her own face to follow him. Her limbs, they say, became rooted to the earth, and a wan pallor spread over part of her complexion, as she changed into a bloodless plant: but in part her rosy flush remained, and a flower like a violet grew over her face. Though held fast by its roots, this flower still turns to the sun, and although Clytie's form is altered, her love remains.'

This was the end of the story. The miracle described by Leuconoe had held them all enthralled. Some declared it could not have happened: others said that real gods could do anything. But Bacchus was not one of those. When the sisters were quiet again, Alcithoe was asked for the next tale. She stood, running her shuttle through the threads of the vertical loom, and said:

'I won't tell you about the love affair of Daphnis, the shepherd of Ida, for everyone knows the story – how the nymph, angry at the thought of a rival, turned him into stone. So fierce is the indignation felt by lovers! Nor shall I tell how once the laws of nature were altered, and Sithon hovered between both sexes, now male, now female. There is the story of Celmis, once the faithful guardian of the infant Jove, but now a block of adamant, and that of the Curetes, who were created from showers of rain: or again there is the tale of Crocos and Smilax, both of whom were changed into tiny flowers. But I shall pass over these, and delight you with a new and charming story. Listen, and I will tell you how the fountain Salmacis acquired its ill repute and why its enervating waters weaken and soften the limbs they touch. This property of the fountain is well known, but the reason for it has remained obscure.

'Once a son was born to Mercury and the goddess Venus, and he was brought up by the naiads in Ida's caves. In his features, it was easy to trace a resemblance to his father and to his mother. He was called after them, too, for his name was Hermaphroditus. As soon as he was fifteen, he left his native hills, and Ida where he had been brought up, and for the sheer joy of travelling visited remote places, and saw strange rivers. His enthusiasm made him count the hardships as nothing. He even went as far as the cities of Lycia, and on to the Carians, who dwell nearby. In this region he spied a pool of water, so clear that he could see right to the bottom. There were no marshy reeds around it, no barren sedge or sharp-spiked rushes. The water was like crystal, and the edges of the pool were ringed with fresh turf, and grass that was always green. A nymph dwelt there: not one skilled in hunting or practised in the art of drawing her bow, nor yet a swift runner. She was the only naiad unknown to the fleet-footed Diana. Often, so runs the story, her sisters would say to her: "Salmacis, get yourself a javelin, or a gaily painted quiver, and join in the chase. It is good exercise, in contrast to hours of leisure." But she did not get herself a javelin, nor any gaily painted quiver, nor did she take part in the chase, as good exercise to vary her hours of leisure: all she would do was bathe her lovely limbs in her own pool, frequently combing out her hair with a boxwood comb, and looking into the water, to see what hair style was becoming to her. Then she would drape herself in her transparent robes, and lie down among the soft leaves, or on the grass.

'Often she would gather flowers, and it so happened that she was engaged in this pastime when she caught sight of the boy, Herma-phroditus. As soon as she had seen him, she longed to possess him. But, eager as she was to approach him, she did not do so until she had composed herself, taken pains with her attire, assumed a charming expression, and seen to it that she was at her loveliest. Then she addressed him: "Fair boy, you surely deserve to be thought a god. If you are, perhaps you may be Cupid? Or if you are mortal, blessed are your parents, happy your brother, most fortunate your sister, if you have a sister, and happy too the nurse who reared you. But far and away more blessed than any of these is the maiden, if such there be, who is engaged to you, whom you will deign to make your wife. If there is such a girl, let me enjoy your love in secret: but if there is not, then I pray that I may be your bride, and that we may enter upon marriage together." The naiad said no more; but a blush stained the boy's cheeks, for he did not know what love was. Even blushing became him: his cheeks were the colour of ripe apples, hanging in a sunny orchard, like painted ivory or like the moon when, in eclipse, she shows a reddish hue beneath her brightness, and bronze instruments clash vainly in attempts to aid her. Incessantly the nymph demanded at least sisterly kisses, and tried to put her arms round his ivory neck. "Will you stop!" he cried, "or I shall run away and leave this place and you!" Salmacis was afraid: "I yield the spot to you, stranger, I shall not intrude," she said; and, turning from him, pretended to go away. Even then she kept glancing back till, slipping into a thick clump of bushes, she hid there, kneeling on the ground. The boy, meanwhile, thinking himself unobserved and alone, strolled this way and that on the grassy sward, and dipped his toes in the lapping water – then his feet, up to the ankles. Then, tempted by the enticing coolness of the waters, he quickly stripped his young body of its soft garments. At the sight, Salmacis was spell-bound. She was on fire with passion to possess his naked beauty, and her very eyes flamed with a brilliance like that of the dazzling sun, when his bright disc is reflected in a mirror. She could scarcely bear to wait, or to defer the joys which she anticipated. She longed to embrace him then, and with difficulty restrained her frenzy. Hermaphroditus, clapping his hollow palms against his body, dived quickly into the stream. As he raised first one arm and then the other, his body gleamed in the clear water, as if someone had encased an ivory statue or white lilies in transparent glass. "I have won! He is mine!" cried the nymph, and flinging aside her garments, plunged into the heart of the pool. The boy fought against her, but she held him, and snatched kisses as he struggled, placing her hands beneath him, stroking his unwilling breast, and clinging to him, now on this side, and now on that.

'Finally, in spite of all his efforts to slip from her grasp, she twined around him, like a serpent when it is being carried off into the air by the king of birds: for, as it hangs from the eagle's beak, the snake coils round his head and talons and with its tail hampers his beating wings. She was like the ivy encircling tall tree trunks, or the squid which holds fast the prey it has caught in the depths of the sea, by wrapping its tentacles round on every side. Atlas' descendant resisted stubbornly, and refused the nymph the pleasure she hoped for; but she persisted, clinging to him, her whole body pressed against his. "You may fight, you rogue, but you will not escape. May the gods grant me this, may no time to come ever separate him from me, or me from him!" Her prayers found favour with the gods: for, as they lay together, their bodies were united and from being two persons they became one. As when a gardener grafts a branch on to a tree, and sees the two unite as they grow, and come to maturity together, so when their limbs met in that clinging embrace the nymph and the boy were no longer two, but a single form, possessed of a dual nature, which could not be called male or female, but seemed to be at once both and neither.

'When he saw that the clear water into which he had descended as a man had made him but half a man, and that his limbs had become enfeebled by its touch, Hermaphroditus stretched out his hands and prayed – even his voice was no longer masculine – "O my father, and my mother, grant this prayer to your son, who owes his name to you both: if any man enter this pool, may he depart hence no more than half a man, may he suddenly grow weak and effeminate at the touch of these waters." Both his parents were moved with compassion, and granted this request of their child, who was now but half male, and half female. They infected the pool with this horrible magic power.'

That was the end of the story. Still the daughters of Minyas were busy about their tasks, scorning the god, and dishonouring his festival, when suddenly there came a harsh throbbing of unseen drums, and the sound of the curved flute was heard, accompanied by the clashing of cymbals. The scent of myrrh and saffron filled the air. Then the looms began to grow green, and, though it sounds past belief, the fabric which the sisters were weaving put forth leaves like ivy. Part was changed into vines, and what had been threads became vine tendrils. Vine leaves grew out from the warp, and bunches of coloured grapes borrowed their bright hue from the purple tapestry.

Now the day was ended, and the hour was approaching which can be called neither daylight nor darkness, when the light still lingers, but the night is almost come. Suddenly a tremor shook the house, the oil in the lamps seemed to burn brighter, the rooms were agleam with ruddy fires, and ghostly effigies of wild beasts howled around. Long before this, the sisters had concealed themselves in different parts of their smoke-filled home, shrinking from the fires and lights. As they crept into dark corners, a skinny covering stretched over their slender limbs and enclosed their arms, forming thin wings. The darkness prevented them from knowing how they lost their former shape. They had no feathery plumage with which to fly, but they did raise themselves into the air on transparent wings. When they tried to talk, they uttered a thin sound, in keeping with their changed bodies, and continued their complaints in faint squeaks. They haunt houses, rather than woods; shunning the light, they fly by night, and derive their name from late evening.

Then throughout all Thebes the divinity of Bacchus was on everyone's lips, and his aunt Ino went about everywhere telling of the mighty powers of the new god: for of all those sisters, she alone had no cause to mourn, except such cause as her sisters' fate gave her. Juno looked at this woman, and saw how proud she was of her sons, of her marriage to Athamas, and of having been nurse to a god. It was more than the queen of heaven could bear, and she said to herself: 'The son my rival bore has been able to change the Lydian sailors into fishes and cast them into the sea, he has induced a mother to tear her son in pieces, and has enshrouded three of the daughters of Minyas in wings of a strange new kind. And can Juno do nothing but weep for her wrongs, unavenged? Is that enough for me? Is that the limit of my power? Why, Bacchus himself teaches me what to do, and it is right to learn even from one's enemies. He has shown all too clearly, by Pentheus' murder, what madness can achieve. Why should not Ino be driven mad, and perish by her own frenzy, as her sisters have done?'

There is a road that slopes downhill, all gloomy with funereal yew. It leads to the underworld, through regions mute and silent. There the sluggish Styx breathes forth its mists, and by that path descend the ghosts of those newly dead, the shades of mortals duly laid to rest in their tombs. Far and wide the desolate spot is wrapped in gloomy chill. The ghosts, but lately come, do not know where the road lies, that leads to the Stygian city, nor where to go to find the grim palace of dusky Dis. His populous city has a thousand approaches, and gates on every side, all standing open. As the sea absorbs rivers from all over the earth, so does that place receive every soul: it is never too small, however great the throng. New crowds arriving make no difference. Lifeless shadows without body or bones wander about, some jostling in the market-place, some round the palace of the underworld's king, while others busy themselves with the trades which they practised in the old days, when they were alive. Others again, are subjected to punishment, each according to his crime.

Saturnian Juno left her home in heaven, and braced herself to visit this place: so much was she willing to do to satisfy her anger and hatred. As soon as she entered, making the threshold groan under the pressure of her divine form, Cerberus lifted his three heads, and uttered three barks, all at the same time. Then Juno summoned those dread and awful sister goddesses, the children of Night. They were sitting before the adamantine gates of hell's prison, combing out their dark snaky locks. When they recognized her, amid the gloomy shadows, they rose up in her honour. This place is known as the Abode of the Accursed. Here Tityus, lying stretched out over nine acres, exposes his entrails for the vulture to tear. Here Tantalus reaches for the water he can never catch, and the overhanging tree for ever eludes his grasp. Sisyphus now pursues, now pushes the stone that always comes rolling back. Ixion whirls round, following and fleeing from himself, and the grand-daughters of Belus, who dared to plan the deaths of their cousin-husbands, continually seek again the waters which they always lose.

Juno glared fiercely at them all, especially at Ixion. Then her eyes passed on from him to Sisyphus, and she said: 'Why does this man here suffer perpetual punishment, while his arrogant brother Athamas, in spite of the contempt that he and his wife have always shown for me, lives in a luxurious palace?' She went on to explain the reasons for her anger, and told the goddesses why she had come, and what she wanted. Her aim was that the royal house of Cadmus should be destroyed, and that the sister Furies should drive Athamas to crime. Pouring out promises, commands, entreaties indiscriminately, she besought the goddesses to help her. When Juno had spoken in this way, Tisiphone tossed her white head, already all disordered, and flinging back from her face the snakes that covered it, she said: 'No need for long and involved explanations! Count as done whatever you command. Leave this unpleasant domain, and return to the healthier air of heaven.' Juno went back home rejoicing. As she was about to enter the sky Iris, daughter of Thaumas, cleansed her, sprinkling her with drops of spray.

Without delay, pitiless Tisiphone took up her torch, all soaked in gore, donned her cloak that streaming blood had dyed crimson, fastened a twining snake around her waist, and went forth from the house. Along with her went Grief and Fear and Terror, and Madness too, with palsied features. She stopped upon the threshold of the house of Aeolus, where Athamas, his son, now lived; the door posts trembled, so men say, the beechwood doors turned pale, and the sun fled from his usual place in the sky. Athamas' wife was terrified by these portents, and he was no less frightened than she. They tried to escape from their home, but the dire Fury planted herself in the entrance, and blocked their way. Then, stretching out her arms, round which the serpents were knotted and coiled, she gave her head a toss. The snakes of her hair hissed as they were disturbed: some lay upon her shoulders, some slipped down around her breast, uttering sibilant sounds, vomiting gore and flickering their tongues. Next, she tore two snakes from amongst her tresses, and hurled them with deadly aim. They slid over Ino's bosom, and round Athamas' breast, breathing their poisonous breath into their victims. The limbs of the royal pair received no wound: it was their minds which felt those ominous fangs. Tisiphone had also brought a noisome witch's brew, compounded of foam from Cerberus' jaws, and the venom of the Lernaean hydra, mixed with vague hallucinations, blind forgetfulness, tears, crime and madness, and lust for murder. These she had ground up together, moistened them with fresh blood and cooked the mixture in a bronze cauldron, stirring it with a green hemlock stalk. While the king and queen stood trembling, she poured this maddening poison over their breasts, disturbing the very depths of their souls. Then she made a ring of fire, brandishing her torch round and round, in the same circle, over and over again. When Juno's orders had been successfully carried out, the Fury returned to the yawning kingdoms of great Dis, and unloosed the snake which she had used as a girdle.

Athamas, son of Aeolus, was smitten with instant madness. Though he was within the walls of his own palace, he cried out: 'Ho there, my friends, spread out your nets in these woods! Just now I saw a lioness here, with her two cubs!' Quite demented, he tracked down his wife, following her footprints as if she were some wild beast. Then, from her arms he snatched the baby Learchus, who lay smiling and stretching out his little hands towards his father. But

Athamas whirled him round in the air like a sling, twice, three times, and then let go, madly smashing the child's head against a hard rock. At this the mother was roused to utter frenzy, either by her grief, or because of the poison which had been sprinkled upon her. Howling like an animal, she fled, completely distraught, tearing her hair. In her bare arms she carried the infant Melicerta, and as she ran, she cried on Bacchus' name. Juno heard her, and laughed: 'May the babe you reared ever bring you such blessing!' she exulted.

There is a cliff which overhangs the sea; its lower part has been eaten away by the waves, and shelters the waters beneath it from the rain. The top is a rocky pinnacle, whose brow stretches far out over the open sea. Ino climbed up here – her madness lent her strength – and undeterred by any fear, flung herself and the child she carried far out into the waters. The waves foamed whitely where she fell. But Venus pitied the distress of her innocent grand-daughter, and coaxed her uncle Neptune, saying: 'Great god of the sea, whose dominion is second only to that of heaven, it is a great boon I ask: but take pity on my dear ones, whom you see being tossed about in the Ionian waves. Add them to your company of seagods. I, too, have some influence with the sea, for I was once fashioned from foam, in its divine depths, and my Greek name still recalls that origin.' Neptune granted her prayer, stripped Ino and her son of their mortal parts, clothed them in serene majesty, and gave them new names to go with their new shapes. The new god he called Palaemon, and his mother Leucothoe.

Her Phoenician attendants followed the track of Ino's footsteps as far as they could, and saw her last prints on the edge of the rock. Never doubting that she was dead, they bewailed the fate of the house of Cadmus. They beat their breasts, tore their hair, and rent their garments, reviling Juno as unjust, and too cruel to her rival. The goddess was indignant at their reproaches: 'You yourselves,' she cried, 'will afford the most striking reminder of my cruelty!' And at once her threat was made good: for, as Ino's most devoted attendant was about to fling herself from the cliff, crying, 'I shall follow my queen into the sea!' she found that she could not move at all, but was held fast, rooted to the rock. Another, who had been beating her breast in lamentation, felt her arms grow rigid, as she tried to raise them. One, by chance, had stretched out her hand, pointing to the sea-waves – turned to stone, she remained, still stretching out her hand towards those same waters. There was another, whose fingers, as she clutched and tore at her hair, could have been seen suddenly hardening amongst her tresses. Each of them remained fixed in the act in which she had been caught. Others, again, were changed into birds, which even now still fly over that pool, skimming its surface with their wings, birds which were once Theban women.

Cadmus, son of Agenor, did not know that his daughter and his little grandson had been transformed into gods of the sea. Overwhelmed with grief at his series of misfortunes, and daunted by the many portents he had seen, the founder departed from his city, as if it were the fortune of the place and not his own which was oppressing him. After long wanderings he and his wife, who had accompanied him in his flight, came to the land of Illyria. Both bowed down now with age and sorrow, they were recalling the early fortunes of their house, and as they talked they reviewed their sufferings. 'Surely,' said Cadmus, 'that must have been a holy snake I slew, the one whose teeth I scattered over the soil as a new kind of seed, long ago in the days when I first left Sidon. If it is his death which the gods are avenging with such unerring anger, I pray that I myself may become a serpent, that my body may be stretched out into that of a long-bellied snake.' As he was speaking, his body did indeed begin to stretch into the long belly of a snake; his skin hardened, and turned black in colour, and he felt scales forming on it, while blue-green spots appeared, to brighten its sombre hue. Then he fell forward on his chest, and his legs, united into one, were gradually thinned away into a smooth pointed tail. His arms yet remained: so, holding out these remaining arms, with tears streaming down his still human cheeks: 'Come, my wife, my most unhappy wife,' he said. 'Come, and while something of me yet remains, touch me: take my hand, while it is a hand, before I am entirely changed into a snake.' He tried to say more, but suddenly his tongue divided into two parts – though he wished to speak, words failed him: whenever he made an attempt to lament his fate, he hissed. That was all the voice that Nature left him.

His wife beat her hands against her naked breast. 'Cadmus,' she cried, 'stay, my unhappy Cadmus, rid yourself of this monstrous shape! Cadmus, what is happening? Where are your feet, your hands and shoulders, your fair complexion, your features? – All that is you is vanishing as I speak. You heavenly powers, will you not

turn me also into the same kind of snake?' Such were her words.
Her husband licked her cheeks, and slipped into his wife's bosom,
as if into a familiar resting place, embracing and twining himself
about the neck he knew so well. All who were there – for their friends
were with them – were terrified: but his wife stroked the glistening
neck of the crested snake, and suddenly there were two of them,
gliding along with coils intertwined, till they disappeared into the
shelter of a neighbouring grove. Even now they are friendly snakes,
and do not shun mankind, or do them harm, for they remember their
former state.

Both Cadmus and his wife, however, found great consolation for
their loss of human shape in their grandson, who had conquered
India, and was there worshipped as a god. The Achaeans, too,
flocked in adoring throngs to the temples they had built in his honour.
Only Acrisius of Argos, who was the son of Abas, and of the same
lineage as Bacchus himself, still persisted in shutting the god out of his
city and kept him from its walls by armed force, refusing to believe
that he was of divine birth: just as he refused to believe that Perseus,
the child whom Danae conceived in a shower of golden rain, was the
son of Jupiter. But soon, such is the present force of truth, Acrisius
repented equally of having wronged a god, and of having failed to
acknowledge his own grandson.

Of these two the one, Bacchus, had now been received into heaven:
the other, Perseus, was returning home, beating his way through the
thin air on whirring wings. He was bringing back the Gorgon's
head, the memorable trophy he had won in his contest with that
snaky-haired monster. As the victorious hero hovered over Libya's
desert sands, drops of blood fell from the head. The earth caught
them as they fell, and changed them into snakes of different kinds. So
it comes about that that land is full of deadly serpents. Thereafter,
Perseus was driven by warring winds all over the vast expanse of sky:
like a raincloud, he was blown this way and that. He flew over the
whole earth, looking down from the heights of heaven to the land
which lay far below. Three times he saw the frozen north, three
times, borne southwards, he beheld the claws of the Crab; often he
was swept away towards the east, and often towards the west.

Now day was declining. Afraid to trust himself to the darkness,
he came to a halt in the regions of the west, the kingdom of Atlas.

This Atlas, the son of Iapetus, surpassed all mortal men in size. He was the lord of earth's furthest shores, and of the sea which spreads its waters to receive the panting horses of the sun, and welcomes his weary wheels. No neighbouring kingdoms encroached upon Atlas' realm. In his meadows strayed a thousand flocks, all his, and as many herds of cattle; and he had a tree on which shining leaves of glittering gold covered golden boughs and golden fruit. Here Perseus begged for a brief respite, till the morning star should summon dawn's fires, and Aurora yoke the chariot of day. 'My friend,' he said to Atlas, 'if you are impressed by noble birth, Jupiter is my father: or, if you admire heroic deeds, you will surely admire mine. I ask you to give me hospitality, and a chance to rest.' Atlas, however, remembered the ancient decree of fate, which Themis had uttered once, on Parnassus' height. 'The time will come, Atlas, when your tree will be robbed of its gold, and a son of Jupiter will have the glory of gaining such spoil.' Afraid lest this should come to pass, he had surrounded his orchards with stout walls, put them under the protection of a great serpent, and made a practice of excluding all strangers from his land. So now to Perseus, as to the rest, he said: 'Be off with you, in case that heroism of which you falsely boast be found wanting here, and Jupiter himself should fail you.' When Perseus hesitated, Atlas passed from threats to violence, and tried to thrust him forcibly away, while the other made a brave attempt to resist, at the same time endeavouring to soothe the giant by his words. However, when he found himself the weaker – for indeed who could equal the strength of Atlas? – he cried: 'Very well! Since you think my gratitude of so little importance, here is a gift for you!' and, turning his own face away, he produced in his left hand the horrid head of Medusa. Atlas was changed into a mountain as huge as the giant he had been. His beard and hair were turned into trees, his hands and shoulders were mountain ridges, and what had been his head was now the mountain top. His bones became rock. Then, expanding in all directions, he increased to a tremendous size – such was the will of the gods – and the whole sky with its many stars rested upon him.

Now Aeolus had shut up the winds in their everlasting prison; the daystar Lucifer had risen and was shining brightly, high in the heavens, warning mortals to be about their daily tasks. The hero took up his wings again, and bound them on either foot. He fastened on his curved sword, and with the motion of his winged sandals cut his way through the clear air. He flew over countless peoples, whose lands stretched out in all directions below him, till he caught sight by-and-by of the Ethiopian tribes and the domain of Cepheus. There Jupiter Ammon had unjustly ordered that the innocent Andromeda should pay the penalty for the boastful utterances of her mother the queen.

When Perseus saw the princess, her arms chained to the hard rock, he would have taken her for a marble statue, had not the light breeze stirred her hair, and warm tears streamed from her eyes. Without realizing it, he fell in love. Amazed at the sight of such rare beauty, he stood still in wonder, and almost forgot to keep his wings moving in the air. As he came to a halt, he called out: 'You should not be wearing such chains as these – the proper bonds for you are those which bind the hearts of fond lovers! Tell me your name, I pray, and the name of your country, and why you are in chains.'

At first she was silent; for, being a girl, she did not dare to speak to a man. She would have concealed her face modestly behind her hands, had they not been bound fast. What she could do, she did, filling her eyes with starting tears. When Perseus persisted, questioning her again and again, she became afraid lest her unwillingness to speak might seem due to guilt; so she told him the name of her country, and her own name, and she also told him how her mother, a beautiful woman, had been too confident in her beauty.

Before she had finished, the waters roared and from the ocean wastes there came a menacing monster, its breast covering the waves far and wide. The girl screamed. Her sorrowing father was close at hand, and her mother too. They were both in deep distress, though her mother had more cause to be so. No help could they offer, but only tears and lamentations, suited to such a time. They clung to her, as she hung in her chains, till the newcomer, Perseus, addressed these words to them: 'There will be plenty of time hereafter for tears, but now the time for helping her is short. My name is Perseus, son of Jupiter and of Danae, whom Jupiter made pregnant with his fertile gold, and that though she was imprisoned in a tower. I am that same Perseus who conquered the snaky-tressed Gorgon, the man who dared to travel through the airy breezes on beating wings. If I were to ask for this girl's hand, I ought surely to be preferred to all other suitors as a son-in-law: but I shall try to add a further service to my present claims, if only the gods are on my side. I make this contract with you, that she shall be mine, if my valour can save her.' Her parents agreed to his conditions – who, indeed, would have hesitated? They begged his help, promising that, in addition to their daughter, they would give him their kingdom as a wedding gift.

Then, just as a swift ship cleaves the waves with her sharp prow, when she is driven forward by the stout arms of her lusty crew, so the monster came on, parting the waves with the impact of its breast. It was as far from the cliffs as a Balearic sling can send a bullet whirling through the air: when suddenly the hero, springing from the earth, shot up high into the clouds. His shadow was cast on the surface of the sea, and the monster attacked that shadow in a fury. Then Perseus flew downwards. As Jove's eagle swoops on the serpent he has seen, sunning its mottled coils in some deserted field, as he seizes it from behind, and sinks his greedy talons in the reptile's scaly neck, in case it should twist its cruel fangs backwards, so swooping swiftly through the sky, Perseus attacked the monster's back and, to the sound of its bellowing, buried his sword up to its crooked hilt in the beast's right shoulder. Tormented by this deep wound, the creature now reared itself upright, high in the air, now plunged beneath the waters, now turned itself about like some fierce wild boar, encircled and, terrified by a pack of baying hounds. The hero, on his swift wings, avoided the greedily snapping jaws, and dealt blows with his curved sword, wherever an opportunity offered; at one time striking at its back, which bristled all over with hollow shells, at another piercing its ribs, or again the point where its tail dwindled away into that of a fish. From its mouth the monster spat out waves dyed red with blood, and Perseus' wings grew wet and heavy with spray. Not daring to trust his drenched feathers any longer, he espied a rock whose summit emerged above the surface when the waters were still, but was covered over by the breaking waves. He braced himself against this and, holding on to the sharp pinnacles of the rock with his left hand, three times, four times, he drove his sword through the beast's flanks, striking it again and again. The shores of the sea, and homes of the gods in heaven re-echoed with shouting and applause.

Cassiope and Cepheus were filled with joy: they greeted Perseus as their son-in-law, calling him the saviour and preserver of their house.

The girl stepped down, freed from her bonds, she who was at once the cause and the reward of his heroic deed. The victor himself washed his hands in water drawn from the sea, and in case Medusa's head, with its growth of snakes, should be injured by the harsh sand, he made a soft bed of leaves on the ground, covered it with seaweed, and there laid down the head of Phorcys' daughter. The freshly gathered weed, still living and absorbent, drew into itself the power of the monster; hardening at the touch of the head, it acquired a strange new rigidity in its leaves and branches. The sea nymphs tested this miracle, trying it on several twigs, and were delighted to find the same thing happening again. By scattering seeds from these plants over the waves, they produced more of the substance. Even today coral retains this same nature, hardening at the touch of air: that which was a plant when under water becomes rock when brought above the surface.

Then Perseus set up three turf-built altars in honour of three gods: one on the left to Mercury, one on the right to the warrior maiden, and an altar to Jupiter between them. To Minerva he made offering of a cow, to the wing-footed god he gave a calf, and a bull to Jupiter, the mightiest of the gods. Then, without delay, he claimed Andromeda as his reward for so great an exploit, and took her without a dowry. Cupid and Hymen flourished the tossing marriage torches before them. Incense in abundance fed the flames, garlands hung from the roof, and everywhere was heard the sound of lyres and pipes, and singing that gives happy proof of joyful hearts. The folding doors were thrown open, the whole of the golden palace revealed, and the noble leaders of the Ethiopians went in to the luxurious banquet that had been prepared.

When the feast was over, and they had indulged freely in wines, the gift of generous Bacchus, then Perseus, offspring of Lynceus, asked about the country and its ways, and about the customs and character of its inhabitants. One of the diners told him what he asked, and went on: 'Now, bravest Perseus, tell us, pray, how you cut off that head which has snakes instead of hair; a deed requiring the maximum of courage and skill.' The descendant of Agenor's house then told them of his adventures.

There is a place beneath the chill slopes of Atlas, that is securely shut away behind a mass of solid rock. At the entrance to this spot dwelt two sisters, the daughters of Phorcys, who shared the use of a single eye. Perseus had managed by his skill and cunning to get hold of that eye, by interposing his hand when it was being transferred from one sister to the other. Then, by remote and pathless ways, through rocky country thickly overgrown with rough woods, he reached the Gorgon's home. Everywhere, all through the fields and along the roadways he saw statues of men and beasts, whom the sight of the Gorgon had changed from their true selves into stone. But he himself looked at dread Medusa's form as it was reflected in the bronze of the shield which he carried on his left arm. While she and her snakes were wrapped in deep slumber, he severed her head from her shoulders. The fleet-winged steed Pegasus and his brother were born then, children of the Gorgon's blood.

He told, too, of the other dangers, all too real, which he had encountered on his long journeyings, spoke of the seas and the lands which he had locked down on, from on high, and the stars to which he had soared on beating wings. Yet, when he stopped, they were still eager to hear more. One of the princes further asked why, of all the sisters, only Medusa had snakes twining themselves amongst her hair. Perseus replied: 'Since the story you ask for is one worth telling, listen and I shall explain. Medusa was once renowned for her loveliness, and roused jealous hopes in the hearts of many suitors. Of all the beauties she possessed, none was more striking than her lovely hair. I have met someone who claimed to have seen her in those days. But, so they say, the lord of the sea robbed her of her virginity in the temple of Minerva. Jove's daughter turned her back, hiding her modest face behind her aegis: and to punish the Gorgon for her deed, she changed her hair into revolting snakes. To this day, in order to terrify her enemies and numb them with fear, the goddess wears as a breastplate the snakes that were her own creation.'

BOOK V

❁

MEANWHILE, as Danae's heroic son was relating his adventures to the assembled company of the Ethiopians, a riotous mob crowded into the royal palace, their raised voices singing no festive wedding hymn, but issuing a fierce challenge to fight. The banquet, suddenly thrown into confusion, could be compared with the sea, when its still waters are lashed to fury by the wild wind. Foremost among the intruders, rashly inciting the rest to war, was Phineus. Brandishing his ashen spear, with its bronze-tipped point, 'Behold, here am I!' he cried, 'come to avenge the theft of my promised bride. Neither your wings nor Jupiter, who changed himself to spurious gold, will save you from me.' As he made to throw his weapon, Cepheus intervened. 'What are you doing, brother?' he exclaimed. 'What mad impulse drives you to this criminal behaviour? Is this your gratitude for so great a service? Is this the dowry with which you reward one who has saved my daughter's life? If you want the truth, it was not Perseus who took her away from you, but rather the stern god of the Nereids, and the horned Ammon, and the monster who came forth from the sea to glut himself on my flesh and blood. It was then she was lost to you, then when she almost perished. You have no complaint now, unless it is, in fact, her death that you are cruelly demanding, to comfort your own grief by the sight of mine. It is not enough, I suppose, that you stood by and watched, while she was put in chains, and did nothing to aid her, you who were at once her uncle and her betrothed? You further dare to be indignant that anyone else should save her, and you would snatch his prize away? If that prize seems to you so valuable, you should have tried to carry it off from the cliffs where it was fastened. As things stand, let the man who did rescue her, and saved me from a childless old age, have the reward which he was promised in return for his services. Understand that he has been chosen, not in preference to you, but in preference to certain death.'

Phineus made no reply, but looked from the king to Perseus, not knowing at which of the two to aim his weapon. After a brief moment of hesitation, he hurled his spear at the latter, with all the force which anger lent him: but his throw was vain. The spear stuck fast in Perseus' couch. Then, at last, the hero leaped from the cushions. In his fury, he hurled back the weapon, and would have pierced his enemy's breast, but Phineus took refuge behind the altar, which afforded the guilty wretch a protection he did not deserve. Still, the spear was not thrown in vain, for it pierced Rhoetus' forehead. He fell to the ground. When the iron was dragged out of his skull, his heels drummed on the floor, and his blood spattered the well-spread tables. At that, the anger of the mob blazed up, quite beyond control. Weapons were hurled, and there were some who said that Cepheus should die, as well as his son-in-law. But Cepheus had taken his departure from the palace, calling upon Justice and Good Faith and the gods of hospitality to bear him witness that this disturbance was contrary to his express command. Then the warrior Pallas arrived, offering her brother Perseus the protection of her aegis, and filling him with courage.

There was one Athis, an Indian, who was supposed to have been born under the glassy waters of the Ganges, his mother Limnaee being one of the nymphs of the river. He was a wonderfully handsome boy, whose beauty was enhanced by his rich clothing. Just sixteen years old, and in the flower of his strength, he wore a cloak of Tyrian purple, bordered with gold; chains of gold adorned his neck, and a golden headband encircled his perfumed locks. He threw his javelin with such skill that he could hit any mark, however distant, and was even more adept with his bow. But on this occasion, as he was forcibly bending its pliant horns, Perseus snatched up a brand which lay smoking on the altar, and struck him down. The bones of his skull were smashed, his face crushed into them.

Lycabas, an Assyrian, was Athis' closest comrade, and had never concealed his true affection for him. When he saw Athis breathing out his life, sorely wounded, the features he had praised so highly twitching in a welter of blood, Lycabas first wept for his friend. Then, snatching up the bow which Athis had strung, he cried: 'Now you have me to contend with; not for long will you rejoice in the death of a mere lad, which brings you more disgrace than glory.' Before he had finished speaking, the keen arrow flashed from his string. Perseus managed to avoid it, but it stuck in the folds of his garment. Then the son of Acrisius turned against his enemy his curved sword, proved true by Medusa's slaying, and drove it into the other's breast. Lycabas, though dying, looked round with swimming eyes, as the darkness closed in on him: he looked for Athis, fell beside him, and bore to the shades the comfort that they were together in their death.

After that Phorbas, the son of Metion from Syene, and the Libyan Amphimedon, who were both eager to join battle, slipped and fell in the blood with which the ground was warm and sodden all around. As they tried to rise, Perseus' sword prevented them; for he drove it through the ribs of Amphimedon, and through Phorbas' throat. Erytus, son of Actor, whose weapon was a broad-bladed axe, met a different fate. It was not with his hooked sword that Perseus struck him, but instead, he lifted in his two hands a huge drinking-cup, weighty and massive, with decorations in high relief, and brought this crashing down on his opponent. Erytus vomited up a stream of scarlet blood and, falling backwards, beat his head upon the ground in his dying agony. Then Polydaemon, a descendant of Semiramis, and Abaris from Caucasus, and Lycetus, who lived by the Spercheus, Helices with his flowing locks, Phlegyas and Clytus, all were slain, and Perseus trampled over heaps of dying men.

Phineus did not dare to meet his enemy at close quarters. He flung his javelin at him, but his aim was faulty, and the weapon lodged in Idas' body. Idas had held aloof from the fight and refused to identify himself with either side: all in vain. Now, glaring furiously at cruel Phineus, he cried: 'Since I have been forced to take sides, Phineus, accept the enemy you have made for yourself, and pay with a wound for the wound you have dealt.' He dragged the weapon from his body, and was on the point of hurling it back, when he collapsed and fell, his limbs drained of their life blood. Then Hodites, who was the most important man in Ethiopia next to the king, was killed by Clymenus' sword, Hypseus struck down Prothoenor, and Perseus slew Hypseus. Among the rest, a certain Emathion was present there, a man advanced in years, just and god-fearing. His age prevented him from fighting, but he did battle with his tongue and, stepping forward, called down curses on the attackers' guilty weapons. As he was clinging to the altar with trembling hands, Chromis attacked him, sword in hand, and struck off his head. It fell right on to the altar, and there the dying tongue uttered imprecations, as the head breathed out its life amid the flames.

Then the twin brothers, Broteas and Ammon, invincible boxers, if only swords could be defeated by boxing-gloves, fell beneath the hand of Phineus, as did Ampycus, Ceres' priest, who wore a white fillet on his brow. Lampetides, too, was struck down, a man who should never have been invited to such scenes as these, a musician, whose singing and harp-playing were essentially for times of peace. He had been summoned to provide songs and musical entertainment during the banquet and the festivities; but when Pettalus saw him, standing on the edge of the company, fingering his plectrum, no fit instrument for war, he cried mockingly: 'Sing the rest of your song to the Stygian shades.' As he spoke he drove his sword into Lampetides' left temple. The poet fell, his dying fingers plucking the strings of his lyre, and as he fell, sounded a mournful strain. Fierce Lycormas did not allow him to die unavenged. Seizing the stout bar from the gate-post on the right, he brought it crashing down on the bones of Pettalus' neck, and his victim fell to the ground, like a calf slain for sacrifice. Pelates, who came from the banks of the Cinyps, tried to tear out the bar from the gatepost on the left also, but his right hand was pinned in the very act by the spear of Corythus, from Marmarica, and held fast to the wood. He stood, fastened there, and when Abas thrust him through the side, he did not fall to the ground, but died, still hanging to the gatepost by his hand. Melanus was killed too, one of Perseus' followers, and Dorylas, the richest landowner in Nasamonia, lord of wide acres. No one else possessed estates as large as his, no one else could pile up so many heaps of spices. Now Halcyoneus of Bactria hurled a javelin at him, and it entered his thigh obliquely, wounding him in a vital spot. When his assailant saw him panting out his life and rolling his eyes, he said: 'Of all your broad lands, keep but this patch of earth on which you lie!' and he left him there, dead. But Perseus avenged Dorylas, snatching up the spear which was still warm with his blood, and hurling it back at his foe. The weapon pierced Halcyoneus' nose and forced its way out through his neck, projecting both in front and behind. With fortune still guiding his hand, Perseus next killed the two brothers, Clytius and Clanis, who were born of one mother, but died by different wounds. For Clytius lost his life when an ashen spear, hurled by Perseus' mighty arm, passed through both his thighs, while Clanis fell with his teeth clenched on the javelin which had pierced his throat. Mendesian Celadon was killed too, and Astreus, whose mother came from Palestine: who his father was is uncertain. Aethion, once skilled in foretelling the future, was on this occasion deceived by a false omen, and met his end. The king's armour-bearer Thoactes perished also, and Agyrtes, a man notorious for having killed his own father.

But there still remained more to do than had been accomplished: for all the attackers were determined to overwhelm one man. Banded together, their companies assailed Perseus from every side, as they championed a cause which refused to recognize his services, or the king's promise. Vainly did the hero's father-in-law show him loyal support and, along with the new bride and her mother, range himself on Perseus' side, filling the palace with lamentation. The clash of arms, the groans of the falling drowned their cries, while at the same time Bellona, goddess of war, was busy, drenching and defiling the household gods with blood, and stirring up fresh strife.

Phineus and his thousand followers surrounded the solitary Perseus. Thicker than winter's hail weapons flew on either side, past his eyes and past his ears. He set his shoulders against a great stone column and, with this to protect his rear, faced the opposing host and withstood their attack. Molpeus from Chaonia threatened him from the left, Ethemon of Nabataea on the right. Just like a tiger when, maddened by hunger, it hears the lowing of two herds in different valleys, and does not know in which direction to rush, but would like to charge both ways at once, so Perseus hesitated whether to attack to the right or to the left. He cleared Molpeus out of his way first, dealing him a blow that pierced his leg. Then he was content to let him go, for Ethemon, allowing him no respite, came at the hero in a frenzy of rage, aiming high, eager to wound Perseus in the neck. However, as he drove his sword forward with heedless violence, he struck it on the edge of the column, and broke it. The blade flew off, and lodged in its owner's throat. The wound was not enough in itself to cause death, but as he stood trembling and vainly stretching out his defenceless hands, Perseus ran him through with Mercury's curved sword.

Finally, however, the hero realized that his valour was no match for the numbers against him. Then he exclaimed: 'Since you yourselves force me to it, I shall seek the aid of my enemy. If I have any friends here, let them hide their faces!' and he brought out the Gorgon's head. 'Find someone else to frighten with your miracles!' retorted Thescelus, and was preparing to launch his deadly javelin, when he became fixed in that attitude for ever, a statue of stone. Ampyx was the next to aim his sword-thrust at Perseus' courageous breast, but in the act his hand grew rigid: it moved no more, neither forward nor back. At this point Nileus, who falsely claimed descent from the Nile with its seven mouths, displayed his shield on which the river's seven streams were engraved, partly in gold, partly in silver, and cried: 'Look, Perseus, see here the ancestor of my race! It will be a great comfort to you to carry with you to the silent shades the knowledge that you died at the hands of so noble a hero!' His last words were choked in the midst of what he was saying. His parted lips looked as if they were speaking, and yet no words came through them. Eryx upbraided these warriors, and shouted: 'It is your own cowardice, not the power of the Gorgon, which has numbed you. Forward with me, and overthrow this youth with his magic weapon!' But as he was about to rush forward, he was rooted to the spot and stood there, a rigid stone image of an armed man.

All these deserved the punishment they suffered, but there was one soldier on Perseus' side, Aconteus, who, while fighting on the hero's behalf, caught sight of the Gorgon and froze into stone. Astyages, thinking him still alive, struck him with his long sword, and the echoing steel rang out shrilly. The attacker stopped short in amazement and, as he did so, he himself was similarly changed; his features, turned to marble, retained their expression of surprise.

It would take long to tell the names of all the common folk who perished. Two hundred men survived the fight, two hundred were turned to stone by the sight of the Gorgon's head. Then at last Phineus regretted the conflict he had unjustly begun, but what could he do? He saw the statues in their various attitudes, recognized his men, and called each one by name, begging for help. Unable to believe his eyes, he touched the nearest bodies – they were marble. He turned away and, in confession of failure, held out his hands like a suppliant. With arms outstretched, not facing Perseus, but turned to one side, he cried: 'You are the victor, Perseus! Put your horrible weapon out of sight: hide away the head of your Medusa, whoever she may be, that head which turns men to stone. Hide it away, I beg of you. It was not hatred nor yet lust for power that drove me to war; it was for my promised bride I took up arms. You had done more to deserve her, but I had known her longer. I am not ashamed to yield to you. Grant me but one thing, most mighty hero, only my life, and let the rest be yours!' As Phineus spoke, he did not dare to look at the man of whom he made this request. 'Most cowardly Phineus,' Perseus replied, 'what I can give, I will: and a great boon it is, for one of so poor a spirit. Do not be afraid, no sword will injure you. Why, I shall even make you a lasting memorial; you will always be seen, standing in my father-in-law's palace, so that my wife may comfort herself with the sight of the man to whom she was once engaged!' With these words, he swung round the head of Phorcys' daughter, in the direction in which Phineus had timidly averted his face. Even now, the coward tried to turn his eyes away, but his neck grew rigid, the moisture in his eyes hardened into stone and still, though turned to marble, he retained his frightened look and his suppliant expression. His hands admitted defeat, and his face showed submission.

Then the victorious Perseus entered his native city, accompanied by his bride. There, though his grandfather had done nothing to deserve his aid, he nevertheless showed himself Acrisius' champion and avenger. For he attacked Proetus, Acrisius' brother, who had routed the king by force and taken possession of his citadel. Neither the armed strength of the usurper nor the stronghold he had wickedly seized could defend him from the glaring eyes of the snaky monster.

But Polydectes, the ruler of the tiny island of Seriphos, was quite unmoved by the young man's courage, to which so many exploits bore testimony, or by his sufferings. He nursed a harsh and inexorable hatred, and there was no limit to the groundless anger which he felt against Perseus. He even belittled his glorious deed, asserting that his claim to have slain Medusa was false. 'I shall prove its truth to you – all others, hide your eyes!' cried Perseus: and he turned the king's face to bloodless stone, by showing him the Gorgon's head.

All this time, Minerva had accompanied her hero brother, who had been conceived in a shower of gold. Now, concealed in a hollow cloud, she departed from Seriphos and, leaving Cythnus and Gyarus behind her on the right, took the shortest way over the sea to Thebes and Helicon, the home of the Muses. When she reached the mountain the goddess alighted, and addressed the learned sisters. 'A rumour has come to my ears,' she said, 'of a new fountain that gushed out of the earth at a blow from the hard hoof of the winged horse Pegasus, Medusa's offspring. That is why I have come; I wanted to see this miraculous spring, for I saw the horse himself being born, from his mother's blood.' Urania answered her: 'Whatever your reason for visiting our home, goddess, you are most welcome. All the same, the story is true: Pegasus it was, who produced this spring' – and she led Pallas to the sacred stream. The goddess stood for a long time, gazing in wonder at the waters produced by a kick from the horse's hoof. Then she looked round at the ancient groves of the forest, the caves and grassy slopes, starred with countless flowers, and congratulated the daughters of Mnemosyne on their good fortune in having a home and an occupation which were both alike so pleasant. One of the sisters answered her in these words: 'Tritonian Pallas, you who would have been one of our company, had not your courage directed you to greater tasks, what you say is true, and you are right to praise our pursuits and our home. Ours is indeed a happy lot, if only we may enjoy it safely. But there is no limit to what wicked men may do, and so unprotected women have all manner of cause for fear. Constantly before my eyes, I seem to see grim Pyreneus; even yet, I have not completely recovered myself, after that adventure.

'He was a fierce warrior who, with his Thracian soldiers, had seized the lands of Daulis and Phocis, and was ruling as king the territory he had unjustly acquired. We Muses were on our way to our temple on Parnassus. He saw us passing and, feigning respect for our divine persons, invited us in, out of the rain. "Daughters of Mnemosyne," he said – for he had recognized us – "pray stop a while, and do not hesitate to seek shelter under my roof from the storm and rain: the gods have often entered humbler homes." We were persuaded by his words, and by the bad weather, to accept his invitation, and went into the hall of the palace. By and by, the rains stopped, the North wind drove off the wind from the south, the dark clouds dispersed, and the sky cleared. We wished to go on our way, but Pyreneus barred his home, and prepared to lay violent hands upon us. By taking to our wings, we escaped his assault: whereupon the king perched himself on the battlements, as if he would follow us: "Where you go, there I will go also!" he cried, and in his madness flung himself from the top of a high tower. He fell headlong, shattering the bones of his skull, and in his death-throes drummed upon the ground he had dyed red with his guilty blood.'

While the Muse was still speaking, there was a sound of wings in the air, and from the high branches of the trees came words of greeting. Jove's daughter looked up to see where the sound of those tongues was coming from. The words were so clear, she thought it was a man who had spoken: but it was a bird. Nine magpies, birds who can imitate any kind of sound, had settled on the boughs, and were lamenting their fate. As Minerva showed her surprise, the Muse explained: 'These, too, have but recently joined the ranks of the birds, as a result of being defeated in a competition. Their father was Pierus, a rich landowner of Pella, and Euippe of Paeonia was their mother. Nine times she called upon powerful Lucina to come to her assistance, for nine times she found herself with child. Then the foolish band of sisters, swollen with pride in their number, journeyed through the many cities of Haemonia and Achaea, till they came to Helicon, where they issued this challenge to us: "Stop imposing upon uneducated people, pretending to be sweet singers: if you have confidence in your powers, divine daughters of Thespis, enter into competition with us. We are not inferior to you in voice or skill, we are your equals in number. If you are defeated, you will leave the spring that Medusa's offspring produced, and Boeotian Aganippe: or else we, in our turn, shall withdraw beyond the plains of Macedon, as far as snowy Paeonia. Let the nymphs judge our performance."

'Truly, it shamed us to compete with them, but it seemed even more shameful to yield without a struggle. Nymphs were chosen, and sworn in by their rivers. Then they took their seats on blocks of living rock. We dispensed with drawing lots: the one who had declared that she would begin the contest sang of the wars of the heaven-dwellers, falsely assigning honour to the giants, and belittling the deeds of the mighty gods. She told how Typhoeus issued forth from the very depths of the earth, and filled the inhabitants of heaven with terror; how the gods all fled, till the land of Egypt and the Nile with its seven separate mouths gave them refuge in their weariness.

Even here, the earthborn giant Typhoeus pursued them, and they concealed themselves under false shapes. Jupiter, she said, became a ram, the leader of the flock, and that is why even now Libyan Ammon is represented with curling horns. Apollo hid himself in the guise of a crow, Semele's child became a goat, Phoebus' sister changed into a cat, Juno into a snowy cow, Venus into a fish, while Mercury donned the wings of an ibis. So much did she sing, to the accompaniment of the harp. This was her challenge to the Muses.

'But perhaps you may not have time to spare? You may not be free to listen to the Muses' song?' 'Don't be afraid of that,' said Pallas. 'Tell me what you sang, with everything in its proper order' – and she sat down in the gentle shade of the trees. The Muse went on with her story.

'We chose one of our number, Calliope, to represent us all. She rose to her feet, an ivy wreath binding her flowing locks, and ran her thumb over the plaintive strings: then she sang this song, accompanying herself with sweeping chords. "Ceres was the first to break up the sods of earth with the crooked plough, she first planted corn and cultivated crops, she imposed the first laws on the world. All we have, we owe to Ceres. Of her must I sing: I pray that my songs may be worthy of the goddess, for surely the goddess is worthy of my song.

'"The vast island of Sicily had been piled on top of Typhoeus' limbs, and the giant who had dared to hope for a home in heaven was crushed and held under by its mighty mass. He struggled, it is true, and often tried to rise again: but his right hand was pinned under Ausonian Pelorus, his left under Pachynus, while his legs were fastened down by Lilybaeum. Etna weighed heavily upon his head; as he lay stretched on his back beneath it, he spat forth ashes and flame from his cruel jaws. Often he strove to throw aside the weight of earth, and roll off the towns and massive hills that secured him. At such times the earth trembled and even the king of the silent shades was afraid lest the ground should split and gape wide open, and the daylight thus admitted to his kingdom frighten the trembling ghosts.

'"Dreading such a disaster, the tyrant had come up from his dark dwelling and, in his chariot drawn by black horses, was cautiously driving round the foundations of the Sicilian land. He had made sufficiently sure that there were no weak places, and his fears had been set at rest: but meanwhile the lady of Eryx, who was seated on her mountainside, saw him on his travels. Embracing her winged son, she said: 'My son, you who are arms and hands to me, and all my power, take those all-conquering darts, my Cupid, and shoot your swift arrows into the heart of the god to whose lot fell the last of the three kingdoms. You have conquered the divinities of the upper air, including Jupiter himself, and hold them in subjection; yes, and the gods of the sea, also, not excepting their overlord. Why is Tartarus left alone? Why not extend your mother's domain, and your own? A third part of the world is at stake, while we display such tolerance that we are being scorned in heaven. The powers of the god of love are dwindling, no less than my own. Don't you see how Pallas and the huntress Diana have been lost to me? Ceres' daughter, too, will remain a virgin, if we allow it, for she has that same ambition. But do you, if you have any feeling for the kingdom which we share, bring about a union between the goddess and her uncle.' Such were Venus' words. Cupid opened his quiver and, at his mother's wish, selected one of his thousand arrows, the sharpest and surest, and most obedient to the bow. Then, bending his pliant bow against his knee, he struck Pluto to the heart with the barbed shaft.

"Not far from Henna's walls, there is a deep lake, called Pergus. The music of its swans rivals the songs that Cayster hears on its gliding waters. A ring of trees encircles the pool, clothing the lakeside all around, and the leaves of the trees shelter the spot from Phoebus' rays, like a screen. Their boughs afford cool shade, and the lush meadow is bright with flowers. There it is always spring. In this glade Proserpine was playing, picking violets or shining lilies. With childlike eagerness she gathered the flowers into baskets and into the folds of her gown, trying to pick more than any of her companions. Almost at one and the same time, Pluto saw her, and loved her, and bore her off – so swift is love. With wailing cries the terrified goddess called to her mother, and to her comrades, but more often to her mother. She rent and tore the upper edge of her garment, till the flowers she had gathered fell from its loosened folds: and she was so young and innocent that even this loss caused her fresh distress. Her captor urged on his chariot, called each of his horses by name, encouraging them to greater efforts, and shook his reins, dyed a dark and sombre hue, above their necks and manes. On they raced, across deep lakes and over the sulphurous pools of the Palici, that boil up, bubbling, through the earth, past the place where the Bacchiadae, a people who came originally from Corinth on its isthmus, had built their city walls between two harbours, a larger and a smaller one.

'"Half-way between Cyane and Pisaean Arethusa there is a narrowing stretch of sea, shut in by jutting headlands. Cyane herself lived there: she was the most famous of the Sicilian nymphs, and from her the pool itself took its name. She rose from the midst of her waters as far as her waist, and recognized the goddess. 'You will go no further, Pluto!' she cried. 'You cannot be the son-in-law of Ceres, if she does not wish it. You should have asked for the girl, instead of snatching her away. If I may make a humble comparison, I too have been loved, by Anapis. But it was after he had won me by his prayers that I became his bride, I was not frightened into marriage like this child.' As she spoke, she stretched out her arms on either side, to block their path. Pluto, Saturn's son, contained his wrath no longer, but urged on his grim steeds, and with his strong arm hurled his royal sceptre into the depths of the pool. Where it struck the bottom, the ground opened up to afford a road into Tartarus, and the yawning crater received his chariot as it hurtled down. As for Cyane, she lamented the rape of the goddess, and the contempt shown for her fountain's rights, nursing silently in her heart a wound that none could heal; until, entirely wasted away with weeping, she dissolved into those waters of which she had lately been the powerful spirit. Her limbs could be seen melting away, her bones growing flexible her nails losing their firmness. The slenderest parts of her body dissolved first of all, her dark hair, her fingers, her legs and feet. It needed but a little change to transform her slight limbs into chill waters; after that her shoulders, her back, her sides, her breast disappeared, fading away into insubstantial streams, till at last, instead of living blood, water flowed through her softened veins, and nothing remained for anyone to grasp.

'"Meanwhile Proserpine's mother Ceres, with panic in her heart, vainly sought her daughter over all lands and over all the sea. When Aurora came forth, with dewy tresses, she never found the goddess resting, nor did Hesperus, the evening star. Holding in either hand a blazing pine torch kindled at Etna's fires, she bore them through the darkness of the frosty nights, never relaxing her search. When kindly day had dimmed the stars, still she sought her daughter from the rising to the setting sun. She grew weary with her efforts, and thirsty too, but before she found a spring of water to moisten her lips, she chanced to see a thatched cottage. She knocked at the humble door, and an old woman came out. When she saw the goddess and heard that she wanted some water, she gave her a sweet drink, into which she had sprinkled roasted barley. While Ceres was drinking this, a cheeky bold-faced boy stopped in front of her, taunting her, and calling her greedy. While he was still speaking, the offended goddess threw in his face the mixture of liquid and barley grains which she had not yet finished. As it soaked into his skin his complexion became spotted; he developed legs where previously he had had arms, and in his changed shape he acquired a tail as well. To prevent him from doing much mischief, he shrivelled up until he was like a tiny lizard, but even smaller. The old woman wondered and wept; she put out her hand to touch the strange creature, but it fled away, seeking a hiding-place; and now it bears a name appropriate to its disgrace, derived from the multi-coloured spots which star its body.

'"It would take a long time to name the lands and seas over which the goddess wandered. She searched the whole world – in vain: and when there was no place left for her to search, she came back to Sicily. As she journeyed over the length and breadth of the island, she visited Cyane amongst other places. Had the nymph not been changed to water, she could have told Ceres everything: but though she wished to speak, she had no mouth, no tongue, nothing with which to talk. However, she did give the mother an obvious clue, by displaying on the surface of the water Proserpine's girdle, which happened to have fallen in her sacred pool. Ceres knew it well, and as soon as she recognized it, tore her dishevelled hair, as if she had only then learned of her loss: again and again she beat her breast. She still did not know where her daughter was, but she reproached all the lands of the earth, calling them ungrateful, undeserving of the gift of corn. More than all the rest, she blamed Sicily, where she had found traces of her lost one. So, in that island, she broke with cruel hands the ploughs which turned up the earth, and in her anger condemned the farmers and the oxen which worked their fields to perish alike by plague. She ordered the fields to betray their trust, and caused seeds to be diseased. The land whose fertility had been vaunted throughout the whole world lay barren, treacherously disappointing men's hopes. Crops perished as soon as their first shoots appeared. They were destroyed, now by too much sun, now by torrential rain: winds and stormy seasons harmed them, and greedy birds pecked up the seeds as they were sown. Tares and thistles and grass, which could not be kept down, ruined the corn harvest.

"'Then the nymph whom Alpheus loved, Arethusa of Elis, raised her head from her pool and, shaking back the dripping locks from her brow, said to Ceres: 'Great mother of the corn crops, you who have sought your daughter throughout the whole world, enough of unending toil, enough of violent rage against the faithful earth! No blame attaches to the earth: if it gaped open to receive that robber, it did so reluctantly. It is not for my own land that I plead; I was born in Elis, Pisa was my birthplace. I came here as a stranger, but though I am not a native of Sicily, I love this land beyond all others. This is now Arethusa's home, and this her dwelling. Do you, most gentle goddess, keep it safe. As to why I left my country and travelled across such a stretch of sea to Ortygian Sicily, it will be time enough to tell of that later, when you are relieved of your anxieties, and can look more cheerful: suffice it now, that the earth opened up a way for me and, after passing deep down through its lowest caverns, I lifted up my head again in these regions, and saw the stars which had grown strange to me. So it happened that, while I was gliding through the Stygian pool beneath the earth, there I saw your Proserpine, with my own eyes. She was sad, certainly, and her face still showed signs of fear: none the less, she was a queen, the greatest in that world of shadows, the powerful consort of the tyrant of the underworld.'

"'When she heard these words, the mother stood, as if turned to stone, and for a long time seemed to be dazed; till her crushing distress was replaced by bitter indignation, and she went soaring up in her chariot, into the realms of aether. There she stood before Jupiter, with clouded brow, her hair all disarrayed, and said accusingly: 'I have come, Jupiter, to intercede for one who is your child as well as mine. If her mother has no influence with you, at least let your daughter move her father's heart to pity. Do not regard her with any less affection because she is my child. For behold, the daughter I have sought so long has now at last been found — if you call it "finding" to be more certain that I have lost her, or if knowing where she is is finding her. But I shall overlook the theft, provided she be returned. A pirate is no fit husband for your daughter, even if she is no longer mine.' Jupiter answered her: 'Our child is as dear to me as she is to you, and I feel my responsibility no less. But if you will only call things by their proper names, this deed was no crime, but an act of love. Only give your consent, and this son-in-law will not disgrace us. Though he had no other qualities to recommend him, it is a great thing to be the brother of Jove. What then, when he does possess other qualities, and yields place to me only because of the luck of the draw? However, if you are so eager to separate them, Proserpine may return to heaven, but on one definite condition, that no food has passed her lips in that other world. Such is the provision made by the decree of the fates.' Jupiter had finished. Ceres was still resolved to rescue her daughter, but the fates would not allow it to be so, for the girl had broken her fast. While wandering in the well-tended gardens, she had innocently picked a pomegranate from a drooping branch, and had placed in her mouth seven seeds taken from its pale husk. The only person who saw her was Ascalaphus, the son whom Orphne bore, so men say, to her own Acheron long ago in the dusky woods of Avernus, where she herself was not the least famous of the nymphs of the grove. He saw Proserpine and, by telling what he had seen, cruelly prevented her return. Then the queen of Erebus moaned in distress, and changed the informer into a bird of evil omen. Sprinkling his head with water from Phlegethon she gave him a beak and feathers and huge eyes. He lost his human shape, and found himself clad in tawny wings; his head increased in size in proportion to his body, he developed long hooked talons, and could scarcely raise the feathers which had sprouted along his languid arms. He became a sluggish screech owl, a loathsome bird, which heralds impending disaster, a harbinger of woe for mortals.

'"Now Ascalaphus may be thought to have earned his punishment, by revealing what he knew about Proserpines. But how did the daughters of Achelous come to have feathers and claws like birds, while retaining their human faces? Was it because these skilful singers were among Proserpine's companions, when she was gathering the spring flowers? And after seeking her in vain the world over, they prayed that they might fly across the waves on beating wings, so that the seas, too, might know of their anxiety. The gods consented, and suddenly they saw their limbs covered with golden plumage. But in case those melodies that fell so sweetly on the ear should be silenced, if the maidens lost their tongues, and their rich gift of song be denied expression, they retained the features of young girls, and kept their human voices.

"'Jupiter, however, intervening between his brother and his sorrowing sister, divided the circling year in equal parts, and now the goddess whose divinity is shared by two kingdoms spends the same number of months with her husband and with her mother. Her expression and her temperament change instantly: at one moment she is so melancholy as to seem sad to Dis himself; the next, she appears with radiant face, as when the sun breaks through and disperses the watery clouds that have previously concealed him. Then kindly Ceres, restored to cheerfulness by the return of her daughter, inquired the reason for Arethusa's flight, and why she was now a holy spring. The waters were stilled as their goddess raised her head from the pool and, wringing the moisture from her green tresses, told the story, now an old one, of the love of the Elean river.

"'I was one of the nymphs who dwelt in Achaea,' she said, 'and none took more delight than I in roaming the forests, and spreading my hunting nets. Though I was a maid of action, and never sought a reputation for beauty, still, I was famous for my loveliness. But my appearance, all too highly praised, gave me no pleasure; in my simplicity, I blushed for those attractive looks on which other girls pride themselves, and thought it wicked to please men's eyes.

"'I was returning from the Stymphalian wood, I remember, quite tired out. It was very hot, and my exertions had made the heat seem twice as fierce. I came to a stream that flowed silently and smoothly, so clear that I could see right to the bottom, and count every pebble in its depths. You would scarcely have thought that it was moving at all. Silvery willows and poplars, drawing nourishment from the water, spread natural shade over its sloping banks. I went up and dipped my feet in the stream, and then my legs, up to the knees. Not content with that, I unfastened my girdle, hung my soft garments on a drooping willow, and plunged naked into the waters. As I swam with a thousand twists and turns, striking the water and drawing it towards me, threshing my arms about, I felt a kind of murmuring in the midst of the pool and, growing frightened, leaped on to the nearer bank. "Whither away so fast, Arethusa?" cried Alpheus, from his waters; and then again, in harsh tones, "Whither away so fast?" I fled, just as I was, naked, for my garments were on the other bank: all the more passionately did he pursue me, and because I was undressed I seemed more ready for his assault. I ran on, and he pressed fiercely after, just as doves flee from the hawk on fluttering wings, and the hawk closely pursues the trembling doves. Right on past Orchomenus and Psophis, past Cyllene and the ridges of Maenalus, past chill Erymanthus and Elis, I kept on running, and he was no swifter than I. But my strength was no match for his, and I could not keep up my pace for long, whereas he could make a sustained effort. Still over the open plains and the tree-clad mountain slopes, over rocks and crags, and where there was no path, on I sped. The sun was behind me. I saw a long shadow stretching before my feet – unless fear made me imagine it – but certainly the sound of his footsteps terrified me, and as he panted heavily behind me his breath stirred my hair. Weary with my efforts to escape, I cried out to Dictynna: "Help me, or I am lost! Help your armour-bearer, to whom you have so often given the task of carrying your bow, and your quiver full of arrows!" The goddess was moved by my cry, and sent a thick cloud which she cast over and around me. The river god circled about me as I stood shrouded in darkness, and, not knowing what had happened, searched all round the hollow cloud. Twice, unwittingly, he walked round the place where the goddess had hidden me, and twice he called: "Ho there, Arethusa! Hallo, Arethusa!" Alas, what feelings did I have then! Assuredly I was like a lamb when it hears the wolves howling round the high sheepfold, or like a hare, hiding in the brambles, watching the jaws of hostile hounds, and not daring to move. Still Achelous did not depart; for he did not see any footprints leading further on. He kept watch on the spot where the mist was. A cold sweat broke out on my limbs, when I was thus trapped, and dark drops fell from my whole body. Wherever I moved my foot, a pool flowed out, moisture dripped from my hair. More quickly than I can tell of it, I was changed into a stream. Then, indeed, the river recognized the waters that he loved, divested himself of the human shape he had adopted, and resumed his proper form, to join his waves with mine. But the Delian maiden split open the earth, and I plunged into its gloomy caverns. By that route I reached Ortygia: this land, dear to me because it bears the name of my own goddess, first restored me to the upper air.'

'"That was the end of Arethusa's tale. The goddess of fertile fields then yoked her two dragons to her car, fastening the bits in their mouths, and rode off through the air, midway between heaven and earth. She guided her light chariot to the city of Pallas, where she handed it over to Triptolemus, bidding him scatter the seeds she gave him, partly in virgin soil, partly in fields that had long lain fallow.

'"The boy drove high above Europe and the land of Asia, and then turned his course towards the realm of Scythia where Lyncus was king. He entered the royal palace and, when asked to tell his name and country, how he had come, and why, he answered thus: 'My name is Triptolemus, and famous Athens is my native city. I did not come by sea, nor yet by land, neither on board ship, nor on foot: the skies were my highway. I bring the gifts of Ceres which, if they are scattered widely over the fields, will produce fruitful harvests and cultivated crops.' The barbarian king was jealous. Hoping that he himself might have the honour of bestowing so great a blessing on mankind, he welcomed Triptolemus into his house and then, when his guest lay fast asleep, attacked him with a sword. But, as he tried to pierce the boy's breast, Ceres turned the villain into a lynx. Then she told the young Athenian to continue his journey through the air, borne by her sacred team."

'With these words Calliope, the oldest of our sisterhood, ended her song, the song I have just recited. The nymphs agreed unanimously that the goddesses of Helicon were the victors. Our defeated opponents replied by hurling abuse at us, until I exclaimed: "So, it is not enough that you have deserved punishment by forcing this contest, but you add insult to injury? Our patience is not unlimited: we shall follow where our anger prompts, and proceed to punish you." The Macedonian women laughed and scorned my threats, but as they tried to speak, menacing us with loud cries and wanton gestures, they saw feathers sprouting from their nails and plumage covering their arms. They looked at each other, watching their faces narrow into horny beaks, as a new addition was made to the birds of the forest. When they tried to beat their breasts, the movement of their arms raised them, to hover in the air. They had become magpies, the scandalmongers of the woods. Even now, as birds, they still retain their original power of speech. They still chatter harshly and have an insatiable desire to talk.'

BOOK VI

❀

WHEN Minerva had listened to such stories, she expressed her approval of the Muses' song, and of their righteous indignation. Then she said to herself: 'It is not enough to praise other people: what I want is to be praised myself, and not to have others scorn my divine powers with impunity.' As she spoke, her thoughts turned to the fortunes of Arachne, a young woman of Maeonia, whose skill in spinning, so the goddess had heard, was earning no less admiration than that of Minerva herself. Arachne was not of high rank, or noble family, but her talent had made her famous. Her father was a native of Colophon, called Idmon, who earned his living by dying absorbent wool with Phocaean purple. Her mother was dead, but she also had been of humble origin, no better than her husband. Their daughter, however, although she had been born in a cottage and still lived in the small village of Hypaepae, had gained a reputation throughout all Lydia by reason of her skill. Often the nymphs used to leave the vine-clad slopes of their beloved Tmolus to admire her work, and the river nymphs came from the waters of Pactolus. They enjoyed seeing the cloths, not only when they were completed, but even while they were still being woven. There was such grace in Arachne's skilful movements, whether she was winding the coarse yarn into balls in the first stages of her task, or working the stuff with her fingers, drawing out the fleecy cloud of wool, with constant handling, into one long soft thread, or whether she was twirling the slender spindle with deft thumb, or embroidering the finished material.

It was easy to see that she had been taught by Pallas: but the girl herself denied this. Offended at the suggestion that she had had any teacher, no matter how distinguished, 'Let Pallas come and compete with me!' she cried. 'If I am defeated, she can do what she likes with me!' Pallas made herself up as an old woman, put false streaks of grey in the hair at her temples, and took a stick to support her tottering steps. Then she began to speak to Arachne, saying: 'Not all the things that old age brings in its train are to be shunned: with advancing years, we gain experience. Pay heed, then, to my advice; seek recognition as the best of all mortal spinners, but admit the supremacy of the goddess, and humbly ask her pardon for your hotheaded words. She will forgive you, if you ask her.' Arachne left the piece of weaving which she had begun. She eyed the old woman sullenly, and could scarcely keep herself from striking her. Anger showed plainly on her face, as she answered Pallas, whom, of course, she did not recognize. 'You have lived too long,' she said, 'that is what is wrong with you. You are worn out with old age, and your mind is feeble too. If you have any daughters or daughters-in-law, let them listen to what you have to say. I can look after myself. Don't imagine that your warnings have had any effect on me; I am still of the same opinion. Why does Pallas not come in person? Why does she avoid my challenge?' 'She has come!' cried the goddess and, throwing off the disguise of an old woman, she revealed that she was indeed Pallas.

The nymphs and the women of Mygdonia reverently humbled themselves before the goddess. They were all terrified, except Arachne, and even she leaped to her feet, and a sudden flush swept over her unwilling cheeks, and receded again, just as the sky crimsons when Aurora first stirs, but in a little while shines white with the light of sunrise. She persisted in going on with her plan and, in her eagerness for a victory which she foolishly thought she could win, rushed upon her fate. Jove's daughter uttered no more warnings; she accepted the challenge, and postponed the competition no further. Without wasting any time, she and Arachne took their stance in different parts of the room, and each stretched the slender threads on her loom. Then they bound their frames to the crossbeams, separated the threads of the warp with the heddle and, with flying fingers wove the crossthreads in between, by means of the sharp-tipped shuttles. As these threads were drawn through the warp, a blow from the comb with its notched teeth beat them into place. With their garments tucked up beneath their breasts, out of the way, the goddess and the girl

worked with all speed, their hands moving skifullly over the looms.
In their eagerness, they were not conscious of the labour involved.
Into the cloth they wove threads dyed purple in Tyrian coppers,
shades of colour differing so slightly that they could scarcely be
distinguished: so, after a shower, when the sunlit rainbow paints
heaven's vault with its long arc, though a thousand different colours
shine there, the transition from one to another is so gradual that the
eye of the beholder cannot perceive it. Where they meet, the colours
look the same, yet their outer bands are completely different. Pliant
gold thread, too, was interwoven, as old stories were pictured on the
looms.

Pallas' tapestry showed the rock of Mars, on the acropolis of
Cecrops' city, and the ancient contest that took place there, to deter-
mine what name the land should have. Twelve gods, in all their
glorious majesty, were seated on lofty thrones, with Jupiter in their
midst. Each of the gods was recognized by his own particular features:
the figure of Jove was one of royal dignity, while Neptune was stand-
ing up, striking the rugged rocks with his long trident. From the
cleft, the sea gushed out, and by this token he claimed the city. To
herself, Pallas gave a shield and a sharp-tipped spear. On her head she
wore her helmet, and her breast was protected by the aegis. Then she
showed the earth putting forth a hoary olive tree, complete with
berries, where she had struck the ground with her spear. The gods
were gazing in awe at this miracle, and the figure of Victory com-
pleted the picture.

Then, to give her rival illustrations of the reward she might expect
for her insane audacity, the goddess added four scenes, depicting
contests, one in each corner, all brilliantly coloured, though shown in
miniature. One corner held Haemon and Thracian Rhodope, now icy
mountains but once human beings, who dared to give themselves
the names of the greatest of the gods. A second corner showed the un-
happy fate of the queen of the Pygmies. Juno, after defeating her in a
contest, had ordained that she become a crane, and declare war on her
own people. The goddess portrayed Antigone too, who once dared
to compete with the consort of almighty Jupiter: royal Juno changed
her into a bird. Neither the city of Troy nor her father, Laomedon,
could save her then. She grew wings and, as a shining white stork,
still applauds herself with clattering beak. The remaining corner

showed Cinyras after his bereavement, embracing the temple steps which had once been his daughters' limbs, and weeping as he lay on the stone. Then Pallas embroidered the edges with olives, the symbol of peace. This was the end of her task: she finished her weaving with her own tree.

Arachne wove a picture of Europa, deceived by Jupiter when he presented himself in the shape of a bull. You would have thought that the bull was a live one, and that the waves were real waves. Europa herself was seen, looking back at the shore she had left behind, crying to her companions, and timidly drawing up her feet, shrinking from the touch of the surging waters. The tapestry showed Asterie too, held fast by the struggling eagle, and Leda reclining under the swan's wings. Then the girl added further pictures of Jupiter in disguise, showing how he turned himself into a satyr to bestow twins on fair Antiope, and assumed the likeness of Amphitryon when he embraced the lady of Tiryns: how he tricked Danae by changing into a shower of gold, deceived Asopus' daughter as a flame, Mnemosyne as a shepherd, and Demeter's daughter, Proserpine, as a spotted snake.

She showed Neptune, too, changed into a fierce bull for his affair with Aeolus' daughter. Disguised as the river god Enipeus, he was making love to Aloeus' wife, who later bore him twin sons, and he was deceiving Bisaltis as a ram. The golden-haired mother of the corn crops, gentlest of goddesses, knew him in the shape of a horse, Melantho as a dolphin, and to the snaky-haired princess, who was the mother of the winged steed, he appeared as a bird. All these incidents were correctly depicted, people and places had their authentic features.

Phoebus was there, in peasant garb, and other scenes showed how he dressed himself, at one time in a hawk's plumage, at another in a lion's skin, and how he disguised himself as a shepherd to deceive Macareus' daughter, Isse. There was also a picture of Bacchus, tricking Erigone with the semblance of a bunch of grapes, and one of Saturn, in the shape of a horse, creating the centaur Chiron, half horse, half man. The outer edge of the cloth, bordered by a fine hem, was gay with flowers, intertwined with clustering ivy.

Neither Pallas nor even Jealousy personified could find any flaw in the work. The golden-haired goddess, wild with indignation at her rival's success, tore to pieces the tapestry which displayed the crimes committed by the gods. Then, with the shuttle of Cytorian boxwood which she held in her hand, three times, four times, she struck Idmon's daughter on the forehead. Arachne found her plight beyond endurance: with a fine show of spirit, she fastened a noose round her neck, to hang herself. But Pallas pitied her, as she hung there; lifting her up, the goddess said: 'You may go on living, you wicked girl, but you must be suspended in the air like this, all the time. Do not hope for any respite in the future – this same condition is imposed on your race, to your remote descendants.' Then, as she departed, she sprinkled Arachne with the juice of Hecate's herb. Immediately, at the touch of this baneful potion, the girl's hair dropped out, her nostrils and her ears went too, and her head shrank almost to nothing. Her whole body, likewise, became tiny. Her slender fingers were fastened to her sides, to serve as legs, and all the rest of her was belly; from that belly, she yet spins her thread, and as a spider is busy with her web as of old.

All Lydia was in an uproar at the news. The rumour of what had happened spread through the cities of Phrygia, and set the whole world talking. Niobe who, before her marriage, had lived in Maeonia, at Sipylus, had known Arachne in the old days. But not even the fate of her fellow-countrywoman warned her to speak more humbly, and give precedence to the gods. Many things contributed to her pride: her husband's talents, the noble birth they shared, the pomp and power of their kingdom. But none of those things, pleasing though they were, gave her such satisfaction as did her children. Niobe would have been called the happiest of mothers, had she not considered herself to be so.

It happened that Tiresias' daughter, Manto, who could foretell the future, had been filled with divine frenzy, and had gone rushing through the streets, crying the will of the gods. 'Women of Thebes,' she called, 'come, crown your heads with laurel wreaths, and crowd to the altars with offerings of incense and humble prayers to Leto, and Leto's children. The goddess herself commands you through my lips.' The Theban women obeyed: decking their brows with the foliage they were told to wear, they made offerings of incense on the holy altars, praying the while. Then Niobe appeared, surrounded by a throng of attendants. She was a handsome sight, in her Phrygian robes of gold tissue; as she tossed her lovely head, and with it the hair that streamed loose over her shoulders, she was as beautiful as an

angry woman can be. She halted and, drawing herself up to her full
height, swept her proud gaze over the scene. 'What madness is this,'
she cried, 'to honour the gods in heaven, of whom you have only
heard, more highly than those whom you can actually see? Why is
Leto worshipped at altars built in her honour, while my divinity as
yet receives no tribute of incense? I am the daughter of Tantalus,
who was the only mortal ever allowed to participate in the banquets
of the gods: my mother is a sister of the Pleiads, and Atlas, the
mighty god who carries the vault of heaven on his shoulders, is my
grandfather. On the other side, Jupiter is my grandparent, and I can
proudly boast that he is my father-in-law as well. The peoples of
Phrygia stand in awe of me, with my husband Amphion I rule over
the city whose walls were built to the strains of his lyre, and I am the
mistress of Cadmus' royal palace. Wherever I turn my eyes, every-
where throughout my home, I see unlimited wealth. Moreover, I am
as beautiful as any goddess. Add to all this my seven sons and seven
daughters, and the fact that soon I shall have sons- and daughters-in-
law as well. Can you still ask what cause I have for pride? Can you
still ignore me in favour of Leto, the daughter of the Titan Coeus,
whoever he may be, a goddess to whom the great earth once refused
even the tiniest resting-place, when she was about to give birth to her
children? She was rejected by heaven, by earth, by sea, cast out from
the whole world, this divinity of yours, until Delos took pity on her
wanderings, and said: "You roam the earth as I the sea, a wanderer
with no fixed abode." And then the island granted her a resting-place,
which was itself never at rest. Leto became the mother of twins, only
a seventh part of my family. I am blessed – who can deny it? And who
can doubt that I shall remain so? The very abundance of my blessings
is my safeguard. I am beyond the reach of Fortune's blows, for
though she may take much away from me, still she will leave me
much more than she takes. I have so many good things, there is no
room for fear. Suppose some of my many children could be taken
from me: though bereaved, still I should not be reduced to a mere
two, such as Leto's family consists of – one might as well have no
children at all! Have done! Enough of this sacrifice. Remove the
wreaths of laurel from your heads!' The women took off their
garlands, and left their rites unfinished: but Niobe could not stop
them from offering unspoken prayers to their goddess.

Leto was highly indignant. Standing on the summit of Mount Cynthus, she spoke to her children, Apollo and Diana. 'Here am I, your mother,' she said, 'so proud of having borne you, I would not take second place to any of the goddesses, save only Juno herself! Yet now my divinity is being questioned, and I am excluded from the altars where I have been worshipped all through the ages, unless you, my children, lend me your assistance. Nor is this the only thing that annoys me: that daughter of Tantalus has added insult to injury, by daring to say that her family is superior to mine, and by calling me childless. May her insults recoil on her own head! She has shown herself her father's daughter in the matter of blasphemy.' She would have gone on to add entreaties to this tale of woe, but Phoebus broke in: 'Enough,' he cried, 'the longer you complain, the longer we are kept from punishing her!' His sister agreed with him, and together they glided swiftly through the air, concealed in clouds, till they reached the citadel of Cadmus.

There was an extensive stretch of level ground near the city walls, the scene of constant horse-riding, where the passage of many wheels and the hard hooves of the horses had worn down the sods. There, some of Amphion's seven sons had mounted their strong horses and, firmly seated on the riding cloths, gay with Tyrian purple, which covered the backs of their steeds, were handling the gold-studded reins. One of the princes, Ismenus, Niobe's eldest son, was wheeling his horse round in a circle, guiding it surely, and pulling hard on the foaming bit, when he suddenly uttered a wild cry, as an arrow pierced his breast. The reins dropped from his dying hands, and he gradually slipped down the side of his mount, falling over its right shoulder. Sipylus was the next to hear the rattle of a quiver in the empty air, and he gave his horse free rein: just as the helmsman, when he sees a stormcloud, speeds on his way, anticipating squalls, and crowds on all canvas, not to let the slightest breath of wind escape. Yet, although Sipylus slackened the reins, none the less the inescapable dart overtook him; the arrow stuck quivering in the nape of his neck, and its iron tip protruded from his throat. Leaning forward as he was, he fell down over his horse's mane, rolled in among its galloping hooves, and stained the earth with his warm blood.

Phaedimus, poor boy, and Tantalus, who had inherited his grandfather's name, had finished their usual exercise, and passed on to the sport which young men most enjoy, wrestling with one another, their bodies slippery with oil. Now they were tightly clinched, their breasts locked together, when, joined as they were, one arrow sped from the taut bowstring pierced them both. They groaned in unison and, as one man, fell to the ground, their limbs contorted with pain. Together, as they lay there, they looked round for the last time, together breathed their last. Alphenor saw them fall: beating his breast, rending it with his own hands in his grief, he rushed up to them, to clasp and raise their cold limbs in his arms. But, even as he was performing this service for his loved ones, he was himself brought down. The Delian god pierced his diaphragm with deadly steel and, as the shaft was drawn out, part of his lung, caught on the barb, was drawn out too. Blood and life poured from his body together.

In contrast to the others, long-haired Damasichthon was injured by more than just a single wound. He had been struck at the top of the leg, where the sinews behind the knee offer a soft vulnerable spot. While he was trying with all his might to drag the fatal weapon out, another arrow sank into his throat, as far as its feathers. A rush of blood drove out this arrow, and the crimson stream, gushing forth, spouted upwards, piercing the air with its leaping column. Last of all, Ilioneus raised his arms in supplication, though it was to be of no avail. 'O gods,' he cried, 'I pray you, one and all, spare me!' So he prayed, not knowing that there was no need to address them all. The archer Apollo was moved to sympathy, but already his shaft had gone beyond recall: still, the wound that killed the boy was only a slight one, and the arrow was not driven deep into his heart.

Rumours of the disaster, the sight of the people's grief, and the tears of her own family advised Niobe of the calamity which had so suddenly befallen her. She was amazed to think that the gods had been able to do such a thing, furious that they should have so much power, and that they had dared to use it. For, to crown all, the boys' father, Amphion, had driven a sword into his heart, thus ending at once his life and his heartache. Ah, how different was that Niobe, from the one who had lately scattered the people from Leto's altars; who, with head held high, had walked proudly through the centre of the city, stirring envious hatred in the hearts of her own citizens. Now she was an object of pity, even to her enemies. She bent over her sons' bodies, cold in death, and distractedly kissed them all a last farewell. Then, turning from them, she stretched her bruised arms to the sky, and moaned: 'Feast your heart, cruel Leto, on my misery; have your fill of gloating over my grief. Yes, feast your barbarous heart to the full: for I have died seven deaths in the death of my sons. Exult and enjoy the triumph of a victor over her enemy. But why should I call you victor? Wretched though I am, I have still more children left alive than you have, for all your happy fortune. Even after losing so many, I still surpass you.' As she finished speaking a bowstring twanged, terrifying all, save Niobe alone: misery had made her bold.

The sisters of the dead boys were standing before the biers on which their brothers lay. They were in mourning garb, and their hair streamed loosely over their shoulders. The arrow struck one of them, piercing her to the heart, and as she drew it out of her body, she fell forward, fainting and dying, her cheek against her brother's. Another sister, as she was trying to comfort her mother's wretchedness, suddenly checked herself, doubled up by a wound from an unseen hand. She pressed her lips tightly together, but it was too late; the breath of life had already escaped. One girl vainly tried to flee, and fell in her tracks: yet another collapsed and died, on top of the first. One hid herself away, and one stood trembling, in full view of everyone. When six had been dispatched by wounds of various kinds, one last child remained. With garments outspread and with her own body, Niobe shielded her, crying as she did so: 'Leave me this one, the youngest of them all! Of all my many children, I ask only for the littlest, only for one!' But even as she made this prayer, the child for whom she prayed fell dead. Utterly bereft now, she sank down surrounded by the bodies of her sons, her daughters, her husband, and grief turned her to stone. The breeze could not stir her hair, the blood drained from her colourless face, her eyes stared in an expression of fixed sorrow. There was nothing to show that this image was alive. She could not turn her head, nor move her arms or legs: even inside her, her tongue clove to her palate and froze into silence, there was no pulsing in her veins, and her internal organs too were turned to stone: yet still she wept. A violent whirlwind caught her up, and carried her away to her own country, where she was set down on a mountain top. There she wastes away, and even now, tears trickle from her marble face.

Then all the people, men and women alike, frightened by this open manifestation of divine wrath, worshipped the great goddess, the mother of the twins, more zealously than ever before. As so often happens, they told stories of earlier incidents, recalled by the recent events, and one of them said: 'Long ago, in the fertile land of Lycia, there were peasants who, like Niobe, showed contempt for this goddess, and were punished for it. The story is not well-known, for the men it concerns were of humble birth, but it is a strange tale all the same. I myself have been to the pool, and seen the place that is famous for this miracle; for my father, when he was growing old and unfit for travel, ordered me to go to that land, and bring home some special cattle. He himself found me a guide, a native of the country. While I was travelling across the pastures with this man, I caught sight of an ancient altar, standing in the middle of a lake, surrounded by quivering reeds, and black with the ashes of past sacrifices. My guide stopped and, in a superstitious whisper, muttered: "Oh, be gracious unto me!" I echoed his murmur, "Be gracious!" Then I asked whether this altar was in honour of the Naiads or of Faunus, or of some native god, and he replied: "It is no mountain spirit who dwells by that altar, my boy. The goddess who claims it as her own is the one whom the queen of heaven once debarred from settling anywhere in the world: till at last wandering Delos, still a floating island then, heard her prayer, and barely consented to receive her. There, leaning against a palm, and with the help of Pallas' olive tree, Leto gave birth to her twins, in spite of their stepmother. But as soon as the babes were born, Juno's wrath forced her to flee from this refuge too, carrying her two divine children clasped to her breast.

'"At last, she found herself wandering in the land of Lycia, the home of the Chimaera, while the relentless sun blazed down, scorching the fields. Tired with her long journeying, and parched with the heat of the sun, the goddess grew thirsty: and her children, too, had greedily sucked all the milk from her breasts. Then it so happened that she saw a medium-sized lake, far down in the valley. Beside the lake, peasants were gathering bushy osiers and reeds and sedge, that grew abundantly in the marshy soil. The Titan's daughter drew near, and knelt down to drink the cool water, but the country folk tried to prevent her. Then the goddess appealed to them: 'Why do you keep me away from the water?' she said. 'Water is there for the use of all.

143

Nature has made rippling streams, as she made air and sunlight, not for individuals, but for the benefit of all alike. I come in search of something to which all men have a right. Still, I ask you on bended knee to give it me. I had no intention of bathing my body or my weary limbs in this lake: all I want is to quench my thirst. My mouth is too dry to talk, and my voice can scarcely come out, my throat is so parched. A drink of water will be nectar to me and, if you give it, I shall freely confess that you have saved my life. You will bestow on me, not merely water, but life itself. Have pity on these children too, who are holding out their tiny arms to you, from my breast!' – and indeed the children were, as it happened, holding out their arms. Who could have resisted the persuasive words of the goddess? But in spite of her entreaties, those peasants stubbornly continued to prevent her from drinking, threatening what they would do, if she did not take herself off, and heaping insults on her as well. Not content with that, they stirred up the waters of the lake itself with their hands and feet, and leaped about, this way and that, in pure malice, churning up the soft mud at the bottom of the pool. Coeus' daughter forgot her thirst, in her anger; no longer did she waste time asking favours of people who did not deserve such consideration, or addressing them in tones too humble for a goddess. Instead she raised her hands to the stars, and cried: 'Live then for ever in that lake of yours!' Her prayer was granted. The peasants were seized with a desire to plunge beneath the water; now they submerged themselves entirely in the depths of the pool, now popped their heads up, and swam on the surface. Often they rested on the banks of the lake, often sprang back again, into its cool waters. But even then, their foul tongues still kept up their bickering, and with no sense of shame at all, even under the water, they still tried to be abusive. Their voices became harsher, their throats puffed and swollen, and their ill-natured croakings stretched their gaping mouths still wider. Their heads sank down on to their shoulders, for their necks seemed to have disappeared; their backs turned green and their bellies, the largest part of their bodies, were white. So they were changed into frogs, and, in their new shape, leaped about in the muddy pool.'"

When the story-teller, whoever he was, had related the disaster which befell the Lycians, another man remembered the tale of the satyr whom Apollo punished, after having defeated him in a competition on the reed-pipes, the instrument Minerva invented. 'Help!' Marsyas clamoured. 'Why are you stripping me from myself? Never again, I promise! Playing a pipe is not worth this!' But in spite of his cries the skin was torn off the whole surface of his body: it was all one raw wound. Blood flowed everywhere, his nerves were exposed, unprotected, his veins pulsed with no skin to cover them. It was possible to count his throbbing organs, and the chambers of the lungs, clearly visible within his breast. Then the woodland gods, the fauns who haunt the countryside, mourned for him; his brother satyrs too, and Olympus, dear to him even then, and the nymphs, and all who pasture woolly sheep or horned cattle in these mountains. The fertile earth grew wet with tears, and when it was sodden, received the falling drops into itself, and drank them into its deepest veins. Then from these tears, it created a spring which it sent gushing forth into the open air. From its source the water goes rushing down to the sea, hemmed in by sloping banks. It is the clearest river in Phrygia, and bears the name of Marsyas.

As soon as these tales were told, the people's thoughts returned to the present, and they mourned the death of Amphion and his whole house. Everyone blamed the mother: yet even for her, they say, one man spared a tear. Her brother Pelops wept for her, and tore the garments from his breast, displaying the piece of ivory on his left shoulder. When he was born, this shoulder was no different from his right one, in colour or in substance. But soon afterwards his limbs were cut in pieces by his own father. The gods joined them together again, but though they found all the rest, one bit was missing from between his neck and upper arm. A piece of ivory was substituted for the part which could not be found, and Pelops was thus made whole again.

All the neighbouring princes came to Thebes, and the near-by cities begged their rulers to go and convey their sympathy. Argos and Sparta, Mycenae, the home of Pelops' line, Calydon, which was later to incur the hatred of cruel Diana, fertile Orchomenus, Corinth famous for its bronze, and fierce Messene, Patrae and humble Cleonae, and Pylos, the city of Neleus, Troezen, not yet under the sway of Pittheus, and all the other cities shut off by the Isthmus with its two seas, as well as those outside, but visible from it. Athens alone failed to appear, incredible as it may seem. War prevented her from fulfilling this solemn duty, for barbarian hordes from across the sea were warring round her walls, filling the citizens with terror. Then Tereus came to their aid, from Thrace, and routed the foe with his troops, winning great renown by his victory.

Pandion, king of Athens, seeing that Tereus was rich and powerful, and a descendant of mighty Mars himself, gave him his daughter's hand in marriage. But neither the Graces nor Hymen nor Juno, who bestows her blessing upon brides, was present at that ceremony. Furies lit the bridal pair upon their way, with torches stolen from funeral processions, Furies prepared the marriage couch, and the cursed screech-owl brooded over their house, perched on the roof above their marriage chamber. Such were the omens when Procne and Tereus were married, such the omens when they became parents. Thrace, little knowing what impended, rejoiced with their king and queen, as the royal pair themselves gave thanks to the gods; proclamation was made that the day on which Pandion's daughter had married the noble king of Thrace, and the birthday of their son Itys, too, should be celebrated as public holidays. So blind are men, regarding what is truly to their advantage.

Now five autumns had passed away, as the sun rolled on his yearly course, when Procne spoke coaxingly to her husband: 'If you love me at all, send me to see my sister, or else have my sister come here. You can promise my father that she will not be long away from home. A chance to see Philomela will be a magnificent gift for me.' Tereus gave orders for ships to be launched and, with the help of sail and oars, came to the harbours of Cecrops' land, where he disembarked on the shore of Piraeus. As soon as he was admitted to the presence of his father-in-law, the king, they shook each other by the hand, and exchanged the usual greetings. Then Tereus began to explain the reason for his coming, and to deliver his wife's message, promising that if her sister were allowed to visit her, she would not be kept away too long, when suddenly Philomela appeared, richly attired in gorgeous robes, but richer still in her own beauty. She was like the descriptions that one often hears of the naiads and dryads who haunt the depths of the woodlands, if only they wore ornaments and garments such as hers. A flame of desire was kindled in Tereus' heart when he saw her, flaring up as quickly as the fire that burns withered corn, or dry leaves, or stores of hay. Her beauty, indeed, was excuse enough, but he was further excited by his own passionate nature, for the people of his country are an emotional race. So, thanks to the fault of the national temperament and of his own, he burned with ardent passion. His impulse was to bribe the attendants who guarded her, to undermine her nurse's loyalty, to tempt the girl herself with magnificent gifts, lavishing his whole kingdom on her: or else to seize her and carry her off, and then to defend his prize by savage fighting. There was nothing that his unbridled passion would not dare. His heart could not contain the fires that burned within. He was impatient, now, of delay, and eagerly turned back to deliver Procne's message, and to put forward his own plea under cover of hers. Love made him eloquent, and whenever his request seemed too pressing, he declared that Procne would have it so. He enforced his arguments with tears, as if his wife had entrusted him with those as well.

O gods above, how blind we mortals are! The very acts which furthered his wicked scheme made people believe that he was a devoted husband, and he was praised for his criminal behaviour. Moreover, Philomela shared his eagerness. Throwing her arms round her father's neck, she coaxed him to let her go to visit her sister, and begged him, as he hoped for her welfare, to agree to a plan which was, in fact, entirely contrary to it. Tereus gazed at the princess and already, in anticipation, held her in his arms. As he watched her kissing Pandion, throwing her arms about his neck, the sight of all this goaded him to greater frenzy, and added food and fuel to his desire. When he saw her embrace the king, how he wished that *he* were her father! Yet even had he been so, his desires would still have been equally wicked. The king yielded to the wishes of his two daughters: Philomela, overjoyed, thanked her father and supposed, poor girl, that his decision was a victory for herself and her sister, when in fact it was to be the ruin of them both.

Now the sun had but a little way to go, and his horses were galloping down the slope of the evening sky: a kingly banquet was spread upon the tables, and the golden goblets were filled with wine. After the feast, the guests retired to peaceful slumbers. But the Thracian king, though he had gone to bed, was in a fever of love for the princess and lay, recalling her face, her movements, her hands, and imagining the parts he had not seen to be just as he would have them. So he fostered his love, too restless to sleep.

When the dawn came, and Tereus was on the point of departure,

Pandion clasped his hand and, with tears in his eyes, begged him to look after his companion. 'My dear son,' he said, 'since your affection-ate pleading leaves me no choice, I entrust this child of mine to you, in accordance with your own wishes, Tereus, and those of my two daughters. I beg you, by your honour, by the gods above, and by the relationship that binds us, to watch over her like a father, and to send back to me, as soon as may be, this dear girl who is the comfort of my old age. The time will drag for me, all the while she is away. And you, Philomela, if you love me at all, come back to me as soon as you can. It is enough that your sister is so far from home.' With these injunc-tions, he kissed his daughter good-bye, crying quietly as he did so. He asked them both to give him their hands as a pledge that they would keep their promise and then, joining their hands together, begged them to remember to convey his greetings to his absent daughter and to his grandson. Sobs choked him, so that he could scarcely manage to utter a last farewell: his mind was filled with anxious foreboding.

Once Philomela was on board the painted ship, when the sea was churned up under the oar-blades, and the land left behind, then the barbarous prince cried out: 'I have won! I have on board with me the girl I prayed for!' In his triumph he could scarcely wait for the joys which he anticipated, could not tear his eyes away from his prize: as when an eagle, seizing a hare in its crooked talons, deposits the prize in its lofty eyrie – then the captor gazes gloatingly on the prisoner, for whom there is no escape.

They had accomplished their journey and, on reaching their own shores, disembarked from the travel-worn ship. The king dragged Pandion's daughter to a high-walled steading, hidden in the dark depths of an ancient forest, and there he shut her up. She, for her part, pale and trembling, frightened of everything, begged him with tears to tell her where her sister was. Instead, he told her of his guilty passion and, by sheer force, overcame the struggles of the lonely and defenceless girl, while she vainly called aloud to her father, to her sister, and above all to the gods, for help. She was quivering with fear, like some timid lamb which has been mauled and cast aside by a grey wolf, and cannot yet believe in its safety: or like a dove, its feathers matted with its own blood, still trembling and afraid of the greedy talons which held it fast.

Soon, when she came to herself again, she tore her disordered hair, clawed at her arms and beat them against her breast, as if she were in mourning. Then, stretching out her hands, she cried: 'You horrible barbarian, you cruel scoundrel! Are you quite unmoved by the charges my father laid upon you, by the affectionate tears he shed as he let me go? Do you care nothing for my sister's anxiety, for my innocent youth, or for your own marriage? You have confounded all natural feelings: I am my sister's rival, you a husband twice over, and Procne ought, by rights, to be my enemy. You traitor, why not take my life from me as well, to complete your crime? How I wish that you had done so, before I was forced into that unspeakable union! Then my ghost would have been guiltless. Yet if the gods above take notice of these things, if the power of heaven is more than an empty name, if all has not been lost, though I am lost, then one day no matter when, you will pay the penalty for this. I myself will throw aside all modesty, and proclaim your deeds. If I have the chance, I shall come forward before your people, and tell my story. If I am to be kept shut up in the woods, I shall fill the forests with my voice, and win sympathy from the very rocks that witnessed my degradation. Heaven will hear my cries, and any god that dwells there!'

Her words roused the fierce tyrant to anger, and to fear no less. Goaded on by both these passions, he snatched his sword out of its scabbard where it hung at his waist, and seizing his victim by the hair, twisted her arms behind her back, and bound them fast. Philomela, filled with hopes of death when she saw the sword, offered him her throat. But even as she poured out her scorn, still calling upon her father, and struggling to speak, he grasped her tongue with a pair of forceps, and cut it out with his cruel sword. The remaining stump still quivered in her throat, while the tongue itself lay pulsing and murmuring incoherently to the dark earth. It writhed convulsively, like a snake's tail when it has newly been cut off and, dying, tried to reach its mistress' feet. Even after this atrocity, they say, though I can hardly bring myself to believe it, that the king in his guilty passion often took his pleasure with the body he had so mutilated.

After such behaviour, he had the audacity to go back to Procne. When the queen saw her husband, she inquired for her sister, and he then told her a tale of his own invention: he declared that Philomela was dead, groaning in pretended grief, and convincing the listeners by his tears. Procne tore from her shoulders her bright robes, with their broad golden hems, clothed herself in black, and set up an empty tomb, at which she made offerings to a ghost that was no ghost, and lamented the sad fate of her sister, whose sufferings were far other than she thought.

The sungod had driven his car through the twelve signs of heaven, and a full year had passed. What could Philomela do? She was closely guarded to prevent her escape, the walls of the steading were stout, built of solid stone, her dumb lips could not reveal what had happened. But grief and pain breed great ingenuity, and distress teaches us to be inventive. Cunningly she set up her threads on a barbarian loom, and wove a scarlet design on a white ground, which pictured the wrong she had suffered. When it was finished, she gave it to one of her servants and, by her gestures, conveyed to the girl that she wished her to take it to the queen. The servant did as she was asked, and carried the tapestry to Procne, without knowing what she was giving her.

When the cruel tyrant's wife unfolded the woven cloth, she read there the unhappy story of her own misfortunes. She uttered not a word: it was incredible how she restrained herself, but her grief was too great for speech and, when she sought for words, she could find none bitter enough. There was no time for tears. Instead, she concentrated on schemes for revenge, and rushed ahead with a plan that was to confound completely the issues of right and wrong.

It was the time of the solemn festival which the young women of Thrace celebrate every three years in honour of Bacchus. Their sacred rites are carried on by night, by night Rhodope rings with the clashing of shrill cymbals. By night, therefore, the queen left her home, all ready for the worship of the god, and carrying the ritual weapons of his frenzied followers. Her head was wreathed with vine leaves, a deerskin was slung over her left side, and she carried a light spear resting on her shoulder. Then she went whirling through the woods, accompanied by her attendants, a figure that struck terror to the heart. She pretended that she was being driven by Bacchus' frenzy, but it was the fury of grief that drove her on. At length she came to the hidden steading. Amid howls and Bacchic cries the gates were broken down; then Procne seized her sister, dressed her in the costume of one of Bacchus' worshippers, concealing her face with ivy leaves, and led the bewildered girl back to the palace.

When Philomela realized that she had come to that accursed house, she shuddered in distress, and grew deathly pale: but Procne, having gained her home, removed the emblems of Bacchus' festival from her unhappy sister's brow, and uncovered her downcast face. She flung her arms around her, but Philomela did not dare to lift her head or meet her sister's eyes, considering herself the cause of the other's sorrow. She gazed steadfastly at the ground, and her gestures conveyed what her voice could not: for she was eager to swear by the gods that she had been forcefully assaulted and disgraced. Procne, blazing with uncontrollable anger, cut short her sister's sobs, saying: 'This is no time for tears, but rather for the sword, or anything more effective than the sword, if such you have. I am prepared to go to any lengths of crime, my sister – either to set the palace alight, and trap that scheming Tereus in the flames, or to cut out his tongue and his eyes, to hew off the limbs which wronged you, and drive his guilty soul from his body, through a thousand gaping wounds. The revenge prepared must be something tremendous: but I am still in doubt as to what it should be.'

While Procne was speaking, Itys came up to his mother. The sight of her son suggested what she could do and, looking at him with ruthless eyes, she murmured: 'How like his father he is!' Without another word, seething with silent rage, she prepared for her terrible deed. Even so, when her son came close and greeted her, drawing down her head with his little arms, kissing her and prattling childish endearments, the mother was shaken. Her anger was checked and, against her will, tears gathered in her eyes. But as soon as she felt her excessive love for the child weakening her resolution, she turned away from him again, to look at her sister's face. As her eyes went from one to the other, she upbraided herself, saying: 'Why does one of them speak to me lovingly, while the other has no tongue to speak at all? Why does he call me mother, when she cannot call me sister? See the kind of man you have married, you, Pandion's daughter! You are not worthy of your father! It is criminal to feel affection for a husband such as Tereus!'

She hesitated no longer, but dragged Itys away to a distant part of the lofty palace, like some tigress on the Ganges' banks, dragging an unweaned fawn through the thick forest. He realized what was in store for him and, stretching out his hands, cried 'Mother, Mother!' and tried to throw his arms round her neck. But Procne drove a sword into his side, close to his breast, and did not even turn her face away. That wound alone was enough to kill him, but Philomela took the sword, and cut his throat as well. While his limbs were still warm, still retained some vestiges of life, the two sisters tore them apart: the room was dripping with blood. Then they cooked his flesh, boiling some in bronze pots, and roasting some on spits.

Next, Procne invited her husband, who knew nothing of what she had done, to partake of this feast. She pretended that it was a sacred ritual, practised in her own country, and that only her husband might be present at the meal. On this pretext, she got rid of their attendants, and the servants. So Tereus, all by himself, sat in state on his ancestral throne, and ate what was before him, swallowing down mouthfuls of flesh that was his own. He was so utterly blind to what was going on, that he called out: 'Bring Itys here!' Procne could not conceal her cruel exultation. Eager to be the first to announce the catastrophe she had brought about, she told her husband: 'The boy you are asking for is here, inside, with you.' Tereus looked round, asking where his son was. As he inquired for him and called his name once more, Philomela leaped forward in all her disarray, her hair spattered with the blood of the boy she had madly murdered. She thrust Itys' head, dripping with gore, before his father's face. Never would she have been more glad to have been able to speak, to express her glee in fitting words. With a roar of fury the Thracian king pushed away the tables, invoking the snaky-haired sisters from the Stygian depths. Could he have done so, he would willingly have burst open his breast and disgorged from it the frightful banquet of human flesh which he had eaten. Then again he wept, calling himself the wretched tomb of his own son. Drawing his sword, he was rushing in pursuit of Pandion's daughters, when it almost seemed that the girls' bodies were hovering in the air, raised up on wings: in fact, they were hovering on wings. One of them flew off to the woods, the other flew under the eaves of the roof: traces of the murder were still visible on her breast, her feathers were still crimson with blood. The king, made swift by grief and longing for revenge, was also turned into a bird. He had a crest of feathers on his head and, in place of his long sword, wore a huge jutting beak. This bird is called the hoopoe, and it looks as if it were accoutred for battle.

When Pandion heard the story, his grief brought him down to the shades of Tartarus before his time, before he had completed the full span of a long life. Erechtheus succeeded to the kingship, and took over the government of the state, a man as upright as he was powerful in arms. He had four young sons, and as many daughters, and of his daughters there were two who rivalled each other in beauty. One of these, Procris, made Aeolus' grandson Cephalus, happy, by becoming his wife. Boreas fell in love with the other, who was called Orithyia, but he long wooed her in vain. He pleaded for her favour, preferring to use persuasion rather than force, but the memory of the Thracians, his countrymen, and of Tereus, their king, hampered his suit. When his endearments were of no avail, the wind bristled with rage, his normal temper which he all too commonly displays. 'And rightly so,' he cried. 'Why did I abandon my own weapons, violent savagery, anger and threats, and make humble prayers, quite unsuited to my character? Violence is natural to me: by violence I drive away the grim clouds, by violence stir up the sea, bring gnarled oaks crashing down, freeze the snow, and lash the earth with hail. Yes, and when I come upon my brothers in the open sky, the scene of our combats, I wrestle with them so stoutly that the intervening air rings with our clashes, and lightning darts from the hollow clouds; again, when I enter the hollow caverns beneath the earth, and fiercely thrust my back against its lowest vaults, my gusts make the whole world shake, and trouble even the ghosts. This is how I should have asked for the princess' hand in marriage, not begging but forcing Erechtheus to be my father-in-law.'

With these words and more in the same haughty strain, Boreas shook out the wings which, as he beats his way through the air, cause gusts of wind to blow over all the earth, and ruffle the surface of the sea. Trailing his dusty cloak over the mountain tops, the lover swept along the ground and, shrouded in darkness, engulfed the panic-stricken Orithyia in his dusky wings. As he flew, he fanned the flames of his passion, and it burned more strongly; nor did he check his onrush through the air, till he had borne his prize to the walls of the city where the Cicones dwell. There the Actaean maiden became the icy despot's wife, and she was made a mother too, for she bore him twin sons, who resembled their mother in all respects, except that they had wings like their father. However, they were not born with these; while their golden hair hung over cheeks still smooth and beardless, young Calais and Zetes showed no trace of plumage: but then, as the yellow down covered their chins, feathers began to grow on either shoulder too, just as if they were birds.

So, when they had grown to manhood, they joined the Minyans in sailing over the unknown sea, in the first ship ever built, in search of the shining golden fleece.

BOOK VII

❋

NOW the Minyans were cutting their way through the waters, on board the ship built at Pagasae. They had seen Phineus, old and helpless, dragging on his life in the eternal darkness of the blind, and the young sons of the North wind had scared away from his lips the harpies that tormented the wretched old man. At last, when they had come through many dangers and difficulties under the leadership of the famous Jason, they reached the swift-flowing waters of the muddy river Phasis.

While they were entering the presence of King Aeetes, and were asking for the fleece of the ram which had carried Phrixus, while Aeetes was imposing his monstrous conditions, requiring them to perform prodigious tasks, the king's daughter, Medea, was seized by an overwhelming passion of love and, though she long fought against it, her reason could not subdue her mad desire. 'Medea, your struggles are useless,' she said to herself, 'for some god, though I know not which, is opposing you. Surely this, or something like it, is what men call love. Why else do my father's commands seem to me too harsh? And indeed they are too harsh! Why am I afraid lest Jason perish, when I have only just seen him? What is the reason for such fear? Unhappy girl, rid your inexperienced heart, if you can, of the flames that have been kindled there. Oh, if I could, I should be more like myself! But against my own wishes, some strange influence weighs heavily upon me, and desire sways me one way, reason another. I see which is the better course, and I approve it; but still I follow the worse. Why do you, a princess, burn with love for a stranger? Why dream of marriage with a foreigner? This land, as much as any other, can provide you with one to love. Whether Jason lives or dies, is in the lap of the gods. Yet I hope that he may live! I can pray for that, even without loving him: for what wrong

has he done? Who but a monster of cruelty could fail to be stirred by
his youth, his noble birth, his valour? Though he had none of these
virtues, who would not be moved by his words? He has certainly
touched my heart. But, unless I help him, he will be blasted by the
breath of the bulls, or come into conflict with the crop of earth-born
foemen, raised from the seeds which he himself must sow; or else,
like some creature of the wilds, he will become the prey of the greedy
dragon. To allow this to happen is to confess myself the child of a
tigress, to admit that I have a heart of stone or iron. Why should I not
go further, and incriminate my eyes by watching him die? Why
should I not encourage the bulls against him, urge on the earth-born
warriors and the sleepless dragon? Heaven grant him a happier fate!
But I must work for that, not pray for it!

'Shall I then betray my father's kingdom, and by my help rescue
an unknown stranger so that, thanks to my efforts, he may set sail
without me, and become another woman's husband, while I, Medea,
am left to my punishment? If he could do such a thing, if he could
prefer some other women to me, then let him perish, the ungrateful
wretch! But his face, his noble character, his handsome person are
such, that I need have no fear of his deceiving me, or forgetting my
services. Besides, he will give me his promise before I act, and I shall
call the gods to witness our compact. Why be afraid, when there is
nothing to fear? Prepare yourself for action: away with all delay!
Jason will always owe his life to you. He will wed you with solemn
ceremony, and throughout all the cities of Greece women will flock
to honour you as their saviour.

'Shall I then leave my sister and my brother, my father and my
gods, even my native land, and sail away across the seas? And why
not? My father is cruel, my land a barbarous one, my brother still a
child. My sister's prayers are on my side, and the greatest god of all is
within my breast. The things I leave behind are of little worth, but
precious are the objects I pursue – the glory of having saved the
Greek heroes, a knowledge of a better land than this, and cities whose
fame has spread even to these shores. I shall become acquainted with
all the art and culture of such cities, and I shall have Jason, for whom
I would barter all the wealth the world holds. With him as my
husband, men will call me the fortunate favourite of heaven, and
my head will touch the stars!

'But what of the tales of mountains that clash together in mid-ocean, of Charybdis, the dread of sailors, sucking down the sea, and then vomiting it out once more, of greedy Scylla, girdled with savage dogs, barking in the depths of the Sicilian waves? Ah, but my long sea voyage will be made in the arms of him I love; I shall be clinging to Jason's breast. In his embrace, I shall fear nothing; or, if I do fear at all, it will be for my husband and for him alone. But do you call this marriage, Medea? Do you gloss over your sin, by giving it a fine-sounding name? Far better consider what an unspeakable thing you are about to do, and while you may, shun such wickedness.' As she spoke, she had before her eyes a vision of what was right, of what filial affection and modesty required. Cupid, defeated, was already on the point of flying off.

The princess was on her way to the ancient altars of Hecate, Perseus' daughter, which were hidden away in a shady grove in the depths of the wood. She was strong in her resolution now, and love had been routed and driven from her heart, when she caught sight of the son of Aeson. Her cheeks blushed scarlet, and then the colour drained from her face entirely. The passion that had been quenched was rekindled, and just as a tiny spark that lurks beneath a covering of ash is nourished by the wind's breath and, increasing as it is fanned, regains its original strength, so Medea's cooling love, which had seemed to be dying, blazed up anew at the sight of the young man, there before her in person. And, so it chanced, Jason was more than usually handsome that day: there was every excuse for her to love him. She gazed at the hero, her eyes fixed on his face, as if she were seeing it for the first time, and was so carried away that she did not believe that she was looking at an ordinary human face: she could not take her eyes from him. When the stranger began to speak to her, taking her hand, and humbly begging her help, promising to marry her, she burst into tears, and cried: 'I see clearly what I am doing: love, not ignorance of the truth, will lead me astray. I shall make you a present of your safety and do you, when you have been saved, give me what you have promised.' By the mysteries of the threefold goddess he swore, by the divine presence that was in the grove, by the father of his future father-in-law, the sun who sees all things, by his own fortunes and by the mighty dangers to which he was exposed. He persuaded Medea to believe him, and received from her forthwith the herbs over which she had woven her spells. He learned how to use them, and returned home rejoicing.

When next day's dawn had put the shining stars to flight, the people assembled in the sacred field of Mars, and took their stand on the upper slopes. The king himself sat in the midst of the company, clad in purple, a conspicuous figure with his ivory sceptre. Suddenly the brazen-footed bulls were seen, blowing fire from adamantine nostrils. The grass flared up at the touch of their hot breath and, as furnaces roar when they are stoked, as limestones baked in the kiln hiss and grow hot when sprinkled with drops of water, so from the breasts of the bulls and from their parched throats came the roar of the flames enclosed within. Yet Aeson's son went forward to face them. Fiercely they swung round their awful heads, with iron-tipped horns, in the direction of the new arrival, pawing the dusty ground with their cloven hooves, and filling the place with bellowings that issued from their mouths amid clouds of smoke. The Argonauts were rigid with fear. But Jason went up to the bulls, and never felt their fiery breath: so potent were his magic drugs. Boldly he stroked their hanging dewlaps and, harnessing the animals to the yoke, made them draw the heavy plough behind them and, with its iron share, break up the virgin soil. The Colchians were amazed, while the Minyans heartened and encouraged Jason by their cheers.

Then he took the serpent's teeth from the brazen helmet and scattered them over the land he had ploughed. These seeds, which had been steeped beforehand in a virulent poison, softened when planted in the ground: as they grew, the teeth that had been sown took on new forms. Just as a baby acquires human shape in its mother's womb, and has all its parts perfectly formed inside her body, only emerging into the light of day when it is complete, so there rose up from the soil, in teeming abundance, a crop of human bodies which had been perfected in the womb of the pregnant earth. More surprising still, they emerged brandishing weapons, produced at the same time as themselves. When the Pelasgi saw them preparing to hurl their sharp-pointed spears at the head of the Thessalian hero, their faces fell, and their spirits too, and they were afraid for Jason. Even Medea herself, though she had rendered him safe, felt a surge of panic: as she sat there and saw so many foes attacking one solitary youth, she grew pale, the blood drained from her limbs, and she felt a sudden chill. Then, in case the herbs she had given Jason were not strong enough, she chanted a spell to help him, and called her secret art to her aid. Jason, however, tossed a heavy stone into the midst of the enemy and turned their attack away from himself, on to their own ranks. Then these brothers, whom the earth had produced, took to wounding one another and, struck down by the bands of their own kin, perished in civil war. The Achaeans cheered, and grasped the victor's hand, hugging him with eager embraces. The barbarian princess would have liked to embrace him too, but the thought of what people would say kept her from doing so. What she could do, she did, rejoicing secretly, and giving thanks to her magic spells, and to the gods who were responsible for them.

It remained to lull to sleep with magic drugs the watchful dragon which grimly guarded the golden tree. It was a striking sight, this creature, with its crest and three-forked tongue and curving fangs; but when Jason had sprinkled it with a herb whose juices bring ob-livion, and had three times recited spells that produce tranquil slumbers, spells which soothe the tossing sea and raging rivers, then sleep fell upon those eyes which had never known it before, and the heroic son of Aeson gained possession of the gold. Exultant in his spoil, and carrying with him as a further prize the one who had enabled him to win it, he sailed homewards in triumph and, with his wife Medea, came in time to Iolcos' harbour.

The mothers of Thessaly brought thank-offerings for their sons' safe return. The aged fathers of the heroes did likewise, and burned great heaps of incense on the altars. A victim with gilded horns was sacrificed, as they had vowed. Only Aeson was not present at this festive scene, for he was now worn out with age and near to death. So Jason turned to his wife, and said: 'My own wife, to whom, I con-fess, I owe my present safety, though you have already given me everything, and the sum of your services to me passes belief, yet if it is possible – and nothing is impossible for your magic – take some years from my span of life, and add them to my parent's.' His tears flowed freely. Medea was touched by her husband's affection for his father, and into her mind, so different from his, came the thought of Aeetes, and of how she had deserted him. She did not, however, confess her true feelings, but said: 'What a wicked suggestion this is, that you have made! Do you think that I can transfer part of your life to anyone else? Hecate would not allow such a thing, and you have no right to ask it. But, Jason, I shall try to give you a boon even greater than that for which you ask. With the help, not of your years, but of my skill, we shall try to renew your aged father's life, if only the threefold goddess be pleased to help, and lend me her present aid in my daring attempt'!

It wanted three nights to the time when the horns of the moon would be rounded into its full circle. When it was shining at its fullest, looking down on earth with its disc complete, Medea stole out of her home, dressed in flowing robes, with her feet bare, her head uncovered, and her hair streaming over her shoulders. Through the still silence of midnight she directed her uncertain steps, alone. Birds and beasts and men lay relaxed in deep slumbers. There was no murmuring from the hedgerows, the leaves hung motionless and quiet, and the misty air was still. Only the stars, unresting, sparkled in the sky. Stretching up her arms towards these stars, Medea turned herself about three times, three times sprinkled her head with water drawn from the river, and three times uttered a wailing cry. Then, sinking to her knees on the hard earth, 'O night,' she prayed, 'most faithful guardian of my secrets, and golden stars, who, with the moon, succeed the brightness of the day, goddess Hecate, triple-formed, you who ever know my undertakings, and come to aid my spells and magic arts and you, O earth, the source of the magician's powerful herbs: you too, breezes and winds, mountains, rivers and lakes, all spirits of the groves and of the night, be present! By your help I can at will turn rivers to run backwards to their source, between their astonished banks, I can soothe the stormy seas, or rouse their placid surface with my songs, dispel or bring up the clouds, summon or dismiss the winds, burst open serpents with my spells and incantations: I can move living rocks and trees, making oaks uproot themselves from the soil, even whole forests; I bid the mountains tremble, the earth produce dull rumblings, and the ghosts rise from their tombs. The moon, too, I draw down from the sky, though the bronze cymbals of Temesa do their best to aid her struggles. Even my grandfather's chariot grows pale at my song, and Dawn loses her colour as a result of my potions. It was you who dulled for me the fiery breath of the bulls, and harnessed to the crooked plough those necks which had never drawn a load before. You stirred up fierce strife in the ranks of the warriors who sprang up from the serpent's teeth, you lulled to sleep the ever-wakeful dragon, and when you had tricked the guardian, sent the golden fleece to Greece. Now I have need of essences by which an old man may be restored to the flower of his youth, and regain the prime of life. And you will give me them: it is not for nothing that the stars have flashed in answer to my call, not for nothing that a chariot stands near, drawn by a team of winged dragons!'

A chariot had indeed descended from heaven, and was standing close beside her. Climbing into it, Medea stroked the necks of the dragons which were harnessed to the car, and shook the light reins. High in the air she soared, and saw Thessalian Tempe lying far below her. Then she directed her dragons towards certain definite regions. She examined the herbs which grew on Ossa, on lofty Pelion, and on Othrys, on Pindus, and on Olympus, a greater mountain still, and gathered the ones she wanted, plucking some out by the roots, severing others with the curved blade of a bronze knife. She also chose many grasses from the banks of the Apidanus, many from Amphrysus, and Enipeus too contributed his share. Peneus and the waters of Spercheus likewise added to her store, as did the reedy shores of Boebe. At Anthedon, opposite Euboea, she picked a plant which bestows long life, later to become famous for the change it wrought in Glaucus' body.

Nine days and nine nights had seen her visiting all countries, in the chariot which the winged dragons drew: then she returned home. The dragons had done no more than inhale the perfume of her drugs, yet they sloughed off the skins that showed their weight of years. When she reached the door of her home, Medea stopped at the threshold, and remained outside the house. Avoiding all male contact, she set up two turf-built altars, under the open sky, one on the right to Hecate, and one on the left to Youth, and wreathed them with branches from the wild wood. She dug two trenches close at hand, and offered sacrifice, plunging her knife into the throat of a black-fleeced sheep. Then she filled the wide trenches with its blood and, as she poured on top cups of wine, and again cups of warm milk, she chanted her spells, calling up the spirits of the earth, and praying the king of the shades and his stolen queen not to be too eager to rob the old man's body of its spirit. When by her prayers, recited at great length, she had gained their favour, she bade Jason bring out

Aeson's worn and withered frame into the open air. By her spells she
relaxed the old man's limbs in profound slumber, stretching him,
like one dead, on a carpet of strewn herbs. Then she ordered his son
and the attendants to retire from the spot, warning them that their
uninitiated eyes must not look upon her mystic rites. They scattered
quickly at her bidding, while Medea herself, with streaming hair,
circled the flaming altars, like some bacchant. She dipped her well-
cleft torches in the trench, full of black blood, and when they were
impregnated with this, set fire to them, on the two altars: thrice she
cleansed the old man with fire, thrice with water, and thrice with sul-
phur. Meanwhile a potent liquid of mysterious power was boiling in
the cauldron she had set on the flames, bubbling and foaming, froth-
ing whitely. In this she brewed the roots she had cut in Haemonian
valleys, the seeds and flowers and sharp-tasting juices. To these she
added stones sought from the furthest East, and sands once washed by
the everflowing tide of Oceanus. Hoar frosts, too, gathered at night
by the light of the moon, the flesh and wings of a horrid screech-owl,
the entrails of a werewolf, that monster which can change its bestial
features for those of man – all these went in: nor did she forget the
scaly skin of a scraggy Cinyphian water-snake, and a stag's liver (for
stags survive to a great age) and the head and beak of a crow more
than nine generations old. With these and a thousand other nameless
ingredients the barbarian princess prepared to accomplish a deed
beyond mortal power.

She mixed the whole concoction thoroughly, stirring it with a
long-withered branch from a fruitful olive when suddenly, as she
moved the old stick round and round in the bowl of hot liquid, it
first grew green, then after no long space clothed itself in leaves, and
an instant later was laden with heavy clusters of olives. Whenever
the heat of the fire caused the froth to boil over out of the bronze caul-
dron, so that warm drops fell on the earth, the ground at that point
grew green, and flowers and soft grass sprang up. When Medea saw
this, she drew her sword and, slitting the old man's throat, let his
aged blood drain out and refilled his veins with her potion. Aeson
absorbed it, both by mouth and through the wound she had made.
Quickly his beard and his hair lost their whiteness, and turned dark
once more. The shrivelled, neglected look of old age was dispelled
and vanished, his pallor disappeared. New flesh filled out his sagging

wrinkles, and his limbs grew young and strong. The old king marvelled at the change in himself, recalling that this was the Aeson of forty years ago.

Bacchus saw the miracle, from the heights of heaven; realizing that his nurses, too, could have their youth restored, he obtained this boon from the Colchian princess.

But there was to be no end to her witchcraft. Pretending that she had quarrelled with her husband, she went to the house of Pelias, Aeson's brother, who had usurped his throne, and begged for shelter. The king's daughters received her, for he himself was bowed down with age. In a short time, the cunning Colchian insinuated herself into their affections, with a false pretence of friendship. While she was telling them what she had done for Jason, lingering over the tale of how, as one of her greatest services, she had restored Aeson's youth, she inspired the daughters of Pelias with the hope that their father could be rejuvenated in a similar fashion. They begged her to do this, and told her to name her own price. Medea remained silent for a space, and seemed to be hesitating: by pretending to weigh the matter deeply, she kept her petitioners in suspense.

Eventually she promised her aid, and said: 'To give you greater confidence in this gift of mine, I shall turn the oldest of the rams who lead your flocks into a lamb again, by my magic potion.' Immediately a woolly ram, with curling horns at its hollow temples, was dragged before her, an animal quite worn out with the weight of years beyond number. Medea cut its scraggy throat with her Thessalian knife, staining the iron blade with only a thin stream of blood. Then the enchantress plunged the limbs of the ram into a hollow pot, and flung in her potent magic herbs as well. These caused its limbs to shrink, burned away its horns, and with them its years, until a thin bleating was heard, issuing from the midst of the brazen vessel. While the onlookers were marvelling at the sound, all at once a lamb leaped out, and ran friskily off, in search of some udder to give him milk. Pelias' daughters watched in amazement; now that she had given them reason to believe her promises, they pressed her the more urgently.

Three times had Phoebus unyoked his horses after their descent into the Spanish main: on the fourth night, when the stars were shining in the sky, the deceitful daughter of Aeetes set a cauldron of clear water on the blazing fire, containing herbs that had no virtue in them. The king lay relaxed in a deathlike sleep, and his attendants too were in a deep slumber, caused by Medea's spells and by the powerful magic words she had pronounced. The king's daughters, at Medea's bidding, had accompanied her into his room, and were standing around his bed. Then she encouraged them: 'Why do you stand hesitating, doing nothing? Draw your swords,' she cried, 'drain out the old blood, so that I can fill his emptied veins with that of youth. Your father's life, the renewal of his years, is in your own hands. If you have any affection for him, if there is anything in the hopes you cherish, do your duty by your father: drive out his old age with your weapons, and by a stroke of the knife let the thin blood flow from his body.' With such exhortations in their ears, Pelias' daughters performed the wicked deed, thinking they would be wicked not to do it: the more each loved her father, the quicker she was to hurt him. Yet not one of them could bear to look at the blows she struck: they averted their eyes and turned their heads away, while their hands fiercely inflicted wounds they could not see. The king raised himself on his elbow, all covered in blood and, mutilated as he was, tried to get out of bed. Finding himself encircled by so many swords he stretched out his bloodless arms, and cried: 'My daughters, what are you doing? What has made you take up arms to destroy your father?' At his words, their courage and strength collapsed: but as he was about to say more, Medea cut short his words by drawing her knife across his throat. Then she flung his mangled body into the boiling water.

Had she not soared away into the breezes, borne by her winged dragons, she would surely have been punished. She escaped on high, over wooded Pelion, the home of the centaur Chiron, above Othrys, and the regions made famous by the fate of Cerambus in days of old. At the time when the flooding waters of the sea inundated the solid earth, he was helped by the nymphs, and flew up into the air on wings: so he escaped drowning in the flood that is linked with Deucalion's name.

As she journeyed on, she passed by Aeolian Pitane on her left hand, with its huge stone image of a serpent, over the grove of Ida, where Bacchus concealed the calf his son had stolen, changing it into a stag, and over the place where Corythus' father lies buried under a tiny heap of sand. She continued past the fields where Maera filled men with terror by her strange barking, and past the city of Eurypylus, where the Coan women displayed horns on their brows, in the days when Hercules and his company were leaving their country. Past Rhodes she flew, the island which Phoebus loved, and over the Telchines, inhabitants of Ialysus, whose eyes defiled everything they looked upon, till Jupiter in his loathing drowned them in the waters of his brother Neptune. Then came the walls of Carthaea, an ancient Cean city, where Alcidamas was one day to marvel that a peaceful dove could be born from his daughter's body.

After that, she saw lake Hyrie and Tempe, the home of Cygnus, which was made famous by his transformation into a swan. For there Phyllius, to satisfy the demands of Cygnus, had tamed birds, and after the birds a savage lion, and given them as presents to the boy. Then he was ordered to subdue a wild bull, and he did that too: but he was angry that his affection should have been scorned so often, and when Cygnus asked for the bull, Phyllius refused him this last gift. The boy was wildly indignant. 'You will be sorry you did not give me it!' he cried, and flung himself over a high cliff. Everyone thought that he had fallen, but he was changed into a swan, and hovered in the air on snowy wings. His mother, Hyrie, not knowing that he had been saved, wasted away with weeping, and turned into the pool that bears her name.

Next to this land lies Pleuron, where Ophis' daughter, Combe, escaped on fluttering wings from her own sons who would have injured her. Then Medea looked down on the fields of Calaurea, Leto's island, which saw its king, and his wife with him, transformed into birds. On her right was Cyllene, where Menephron was one day to behave like some fierce wild beast, sharing his mother's bed. Some distance off, she saw Cephisus, lamenting the fate of his grandson who had been changed by Apollo into a lumbering seal, and she glimpsed the house of Eumelus too, who was mourning his son, now one of the birds of the air.

At length her winged dragons brought her to Corinth, and Pirene's sacred spring. An ancient legend tells that here, in the beginning of time, mortals were created from fungi, nourished by the rain. The new bride whom Jason had married was consumed by fire, kindled by the Colchian's poisons, and the seas on either side of the isthmus saw the king's home in flames. Medea's guilty sword dripped with the blood of her sons, and after such wicked vengeance their mother fled from Jason's armed wrath. Borne off by her dragons, steeds sprung from the Titans, she entered the city of Athens, Pallas' citadel, which once saw Phene, who had been the most honourable of women, and aged Periphas flying side by side, and Alcyone too, Polypemon's grand-daughter, soaring aloft on strange new wings. The king Aegeus welcomed Medea, the only thing he ever did that deserved censure and, not content with giving her hospitality, made her his wife.

Presently Theseus, who by his valiant deeds had been establishing peace and order throughout the Isthmus with its two seas, arrived in Athens. He was Aegeus' son, but the king did not know this. In order to destroy him, Medea mixed a draught of aconite, which she had brought with her long ago, from the shores of Scythia. This herb is said to have come from the teeth of Cerberus, the Echidnean dog; for there is a cave in Scythia, with a shadowy entrance, through which the road slopes down to the underworld. It was by this route that Hercules, the hero of Tiryns, dragged Cerberus up, after he had bound him fast with chains of adamant. The dog struggled, twisting its head away from the daylight and the shining sun. Mad with rage, it filled the air with its triple barking, and sprinkled the green fields with flecks of white foam. These flecks are thought to have taken root and, finding nourishment in the rich and fertile soil, acquired harmful properties. Since they flourish on hard rock, the country folk call them aconites, rock-flowers. Aegeus himself, thanks to Medea's wiles, offered this poison to his own son, imagining him to be an enemy. Theseus, suspecting nothing, had already taken the cup in his hand, when his father recognized his family crest on the ivory hilt of the hero's sword, and dashed the guilty goblet from his lips. But Medea escaped death by shrouding herself in clouds which she summoned by her spells.

Aegeus, though rejoicing in his son's safety, was none the less dismayed that a crime so dreadful had been so narrowly averted. He lit fires on the altars, and plied the gods with gifts. Oxen were led up, wreathed with garlands, and the sacrificial axe struck down upon their sturdy necks. That day is famous as the most glorious that ever dawned for the Athenians. The leaders of the state and the common people united in feasting and merriment, and as wine made them eloquent, they said: 'O mighty Theseus, you are the wonder of Marathon, for having slain the Cretan bull, thanks to you and your valour, the farmers till Cromyon's fields without fear of the wild boar, Epidaurus saw Vulcan's son brought down by your hands, in spite of the club he carried, the banks of Cephisus saw cruel Procrustes slain, and Ceres' town, Eleusis, beheld Cercyon dead. Sinis, notorious for the evil use he made of his mighty strength, could bend trees with his hands, and used to draw down pines till their tops touched the ground so that, when released, they tore his victims limb from limb, and scattered them far and wide: yet he perished at your hands. The road to Alcathoe, the city of Megara, now lies open and safe for all, since you dealt with the robber Sciron, to whose scattered bones both earth and sea refused a tomb. For long they were tossed from place to place, till finally, men say, they hardened into rocky crags, that still bear Sciron's name. If we were to reckon up your years and your achievements, the tale of your exploits would far outweigh your count of years. On your behalf, bravest of heroes, we, as a people, offer up our prayers, and drink our toasts to you.' The palace rang with the applause of the nation, and with the prayers of his admirers – nowhere in the city was there any room for sadness.

But it is all too true that no pleasure is unalloyed: some trouble ever intrudes upon our happiness. So the joy Aegeus felt at his son's return was tempered with anxiety, for Minos of Crete was making preparations for war. This king had a strong army, a strong fleet, but stronger than either was his rage at the fate of his son Androgeus. It was his death that Minos was seeking to avenge by a war that was fully justified. First of all, however, he scoured the seas with his swift ships, wherein lay his chief strength, gathering troops to be his allies in the conflict. He gained the support of Anaphe and of Astypalaea, winning the former by promises and the latter by force. The low-lying island of Myconus joined him, and Cimolus with its chalky soil, Syros where the wild thyme grows, and the level plains of Seriphos, Paros with its marble quarries, and the land which Thracian Arne wickedly betrayed. After this girl had received the gold she greedily demanded, she was changed into a bird, the black-footed, black-winged jackdaw, and even as a bird she still loves gold. On the other

hand Oliaros and Didymae, Tenos and Andros, Gyarus and Pepar-
ethos, where the shining olive grows in abundance, refused to help
the Cretan ships.

From there, Minos made for Oenopia, which lay on his left. This
was Aeacus' kingdom. It had been called Oenopia in the old days, but
Aeacus himself called it Aegina, after his mother. A crowd rushed
down to meet Minos, eager to welcome so famous a hero. Telamon
ran to greet him, accompanied by his younger brother Peleus, and by
Phocus, the youngest of the three princes. Even Aeacus himself came
out, though he moved slowly under the burden of his years. He in-
quired of Minos what brought him to the land. Then the ruler of a
hundred cities, reminded thus of his grief for his son, sighed and
answered in these words: 'I seek your assistance in a war which I am
undertaking for the sake of my son. I would have your men form part
of my army, to fight in a just cause: I ask you to help give repose to
one who is in his tomb.' But Aeacus, grandson of Asopius, replied:
'Your requests are made in vain. My city cannot do as you ask. For
no land is more closely allied to that of Cecrops than this land of
mine: so binding are the treaties that unite us.' Gloomily Minos took
his departure. 'Your treaties will cost you dear,' he said. But he deemed
it better to threaten war than to fight, and thereby diminish his own
strength too soon.

The Cretan fleet was still visible from Oenopia's walls, when a
ship from Athens came speeding in under full sail. It entered the
friendly harbour, bringing Cephalus and with him messages from his
native land. Though it was long since the young sons of Aeacus had
seen Cephalus, they recognized him, grasped his right hand, and led
him to their father's house. The hero still retained some traces of his
former handsomeness, and drew all men's eyes to him, as he came
forward, carrying a branch of the olive that is native to his country.
On his right hand and his left, walked two ambassadors younger than
himself, Clytus and Butes, the sons of Pallas.

When the conventional words of greeting had been exchanged,
Cephalus delivered the message of the Athenian people, asking for
assistance, and reminding his hosts of the treaty rights which their
ancestors had established. He added that Minos was aiming at the
sovereignty of the whole of Greece. When the ambassador had put
forward the plea with which he had been entrusted, giving it greater

weight by the eloquence of his appeal, Aeacus replied, his left hand resting on the hilt of his sceptre: 'Men of Athens, do not ask my help, but take it. There is no question but that you may count all the forces of this island yours, as well as everything which the present state of my fortunes can provide. There is no lack of military strength here: I have soldiers in plenty, both for my own defence, and to meet the enemy. Thanks be to the gods, my affairs are in a prosperous state, and give me no reason to refuse you.' 'So may it ever be!' cried Cephalus. 'May your city increase in numbers as time goes on. Indeed, it gave me great pleasure, on my arrival, to see so many young people, all of an age and all so handsome, coming out to meet me. Yet I miss many of those whom I saw before, when I was welcomed into your city on a previous occasion.'

Aeacus groaned, and there was sadness in his voice, as he answered: 'Though better fortune followed, we had a wretched time of it at the start; I only wish that I could give you an account of the one without the other. But as it is, I shall tell you the whole story in the order in which it happened. Not to waste your time with unnecessary details, those men whom you remember and look for in vain, are now in their graves, mere bones and ashes: and how great a part of my kingdom perished with them! Cruel Juno visited her wrath upon our land, hating it because it had been named after her rival, and a dreadful plague fell upon my people. At first we believed this to be an ordinary epidemic, and while we were ignorant of the baleful origin of our disaster fought it by means of medical skill. But the pestilence was too much for us: our science was defeated and collapsed.

'At first the sky, dark and heavy, pressed down upon the earth, shutting in beneath its clouds a sultry heat which sapped all energy. Four times the moon had brought together the points of her horns, to form her disc's full circle, four times she waned, her orb dwindling away, and all this time the South wind blew with hot and deadly blasts. It is common knowledge that even the lakes and springs became infected: thousands of serpents crawled over our neglected fields, and polluted the rivers with their poisons. The violence of the disease and the suddenness with which it struck were first realized when dogs and birds, sheep and oxen, and wild creatures began to die. The wretched farmers watched in dismay as their sturdy oxen collapsed at their work, and sank to the ground in the midst of ploughing. The fleecy sheep gave vent to sickly bleatings. Their wool fell out of its own accord, and their bodies wasted away. Horses, once full of spirit, famous for their performance on the dusty race-course, disgraced their previous victories. Past triumphs forgotten, they stood groaning in their stables, waiting for an ignominious death. The wild boar forgot his fury, and the hind no longer fled away, relying on her swiftness for safety; bears ceased to attack the herds which were no weaker than themselves. Lassitude laid hold upon them all. Through the woods, in the fields and along the roads, lay decaying corpses. A foul stench filled the air. Strange to relate, the dogs did not touch these bodies, nor did grey wolves or greedy vultures. They were left to rot and fall apart, polluting the atmosphere with their smells, and spreading infection far and wide.

'The disaster became worse still when the plague spread to the unhappy farmers themselves, and gained the upper hand within the walls of our great city. First of all the inner organs of the victim became burning hot: a flushed skin and panting breath were symptoms of internal fever. The tongue was rough and swollen, dry lips gaped open to catch breaths of the warm air, as men gaspingly tried to gulp in an atmosphere heavy with pollution. The sick could not endure their beds, or any kind of covering, but lay face downwards on the hard ground, and even so their bodies found no coolness from the earth, but rather the earth became fevered from their bodies. No one could check the disease: it broke out fiercely among the doctors themselves, and medical skill only served to harm its own practitioners. The more closely and faithfully a man attended the sick, the sooner he met his death. Moreover, as the hope of being cured left them, and men saw that the sickness must end in death, they abandoned themselves to their desires, and paid no attention to what was good for them: since nothing was, in fact, for their good. Everywhere, with no regard for decency, they attached themselves to springs or rivers or deep wells, suffering from a thirst that was quenched only when life was gone. Many of them were too weak to rise again, and died in the very waters. Even so, men still drank from those streams! Other poor wretches grew so tired of lying on their hated sickbeds that they leaped out of them or, lacking the strength to stand, rolled themselves on to the floor and one and all fled from their homes. Each thought his own house fatal to him and, because the real source

of the trouble was unknown, blamed his cramped quarters for his ill-
ness. Men who were only half conscious could be seen wandering
about the streets, as long as they had strength to stand. Others lay on
the ground, weeping, rolling their weary eyes upwards in one last
effort. They stretched their arms towards the stars in the lowering
sky, and breathed out their lives here, there, wherever death had over-
taken them.

'Need you ask what my feelings were then? Surely the natural
reaction was a hatred of life, and a desire to share my people's fate!
Wherever I turned my eyes, bodies lay strewn on the ground, like
overripe apples, that fall from the trees when the boughs are shaken,
or like acorns beneath a storm-tossed oak. You see that temple
opposite, built on the hill, with a long flight of steps leading up to it?
Jupiter is the god who dwells there. Was there anyone who did not
make offerings of incense on those altars? But it was all to no purpose.
How often did husbands, praying for their wives, or fathers for their
sons, fall dead at the very altar, their petitions unheard, while part of
their offering of incense was found clutched in their hands, still in-
tact! Time and again, the bulls which had been brought into the
temple collapsed and died without waiting for the stroke of the knife,
while the priest was still reciting his prayers, and pouring neat wine
between their horns. When I myself was offering sacrifice to Jupiter
on behalf of my country, my three sons, and myself, the victim sud-
denly gave vent to dreadful moanings and, before ever it had been
struck, fell to the ground, staining the knives beneath its throat with
only a few drops of blood. Furthermore, the entrails of the sick
animals showed none of the signs which used to reveal the truth to
mortals, and convey the warnings of the gods; for the awful sickness
penetrated to their vital organs.

'I have seen corpses thrown down before the temple doors or, to
make their deaths still more of a reproach to the gods, before the very
altars. Some of my people hanged themselves, and by dying escaped
the fear of death, anticipating of their own accord the fate that was
approaching. The bodies of the dead received none of the usual funeral
rites, nor were they even carried out of the city: its gates could not
have found room for all those funerals to pass. Corpses lay on the
ground unburied, or were thrown without further ceremony on to
pyres, heaped with bodies. By now all respect for death had vanished,

and men fought over the funeral fires, and were burned in other people's flames. No one was left to mourn, and the ghosts of mothers and young wives, young men and old, wandered about unwept. There was not enough land for graves, not enough trees for the funeral pyres.

'Utterly distraught by such a storm of disasters, I cried to heaven: "O Jupiter, if it is true, as men say, that you entered the embrace of Aegina, Asopus' daughter, and if you are not ashamed, mighty father, to acknowledge me your son, either restore my people, or lay me too to rest in my tomb." Jupiter gave me a sign that he had heard, a lightning flash, followed by a peal of thunder. "I receive your token," I exclaimed, "and pray that those indications of your purpose may augur well for me. I accept the pledge you give me."

'It so happened that there was an oak tree close by, with spreading branches widely spaced, which was sacred to Jupiter, grown from the seed of Dodona's grove. There we saw a long column of ants, which had been gathering grain, carrying massive burdens in their tiny mouths, as they followed a path along the wrinkled tree trunk. I looked at their numbers admiringly. "O best of fathers," I cried, "grant me so many citizens to fill up my desolate city!" The tall oak trembled, and its branches groaned as they moved, though there was no wind to move them. My limbs quivered with panic fear, and my hair stood on end. Nevertheless, I kissed the earth and the trunk of the tree. Though I did not confess that I indulged any hope, yet in fact I did hope, and fondly cherished my prayers in my own heart.

'Night came on and, weary with anxiety as we were, sleep laid hold on us. Then the same oak tree seemed to appear before me, with just the same number of branches, the same number of insects on them. It seemed to tremble as it had done before, and scattered the column of ants, with the grain they had collected, upon the fields below. Suddenly the creatures began to grow; they became bigger and bigger, raised themselves from the ground, and stood upright. Their superfluous feet and their dark colouring disappeared, their bodies swelled out, and their limbs too took on human shape. Sleep left me then. Once I was awake, I discounted what I had seen, and complained that there was no help in heaven. But there was a loud murmur of voices within the palace, and I thought I heard men talking, a sound that had long ceased to be familiar.

'While I was imagining that this too was a dream, Telamon came hurrying to my room, and burst open the door: "Father," he shouted. "Come out, and you will see something beyond all your hopes, beyond belief!" I went out, and saw men such as I had seemed to see in my dream. I recognized their ranks. They approached, and hailed me as their king. Then I fulfilled the vows I had made to Jupiter, by giving these new people a share in the city, and in the fields which had lost their former cultivators. I called them Myrmidons, giving them a name that did not conceal their origin. You have seen their persons. As to their characters, they still retain the traits they had before: a thrifty people, willing to endure hard labour, holding on to what they have, and storing their gains away. They will follow you to war, an army all alike in age and valour, just as soon as the East wind which gave you a prosperous voyage hither' – for it was the East wind that had brought the Athenians – 'veers round to the South.'

They whiled away the long day with such tales, and spent the last hours of daylight in feasting: the night was given over to sleep. Now the golden sun had risen with his radiant light. The East wind was still blowing, and held the ships in harbour, though they were impatient to return. The sons of Pallas joined their older companion, and then Cephalus and the two young men made their way to the king. Aeacus was still fast asleep, and the princes Telamon and Peleus were enlisting soldiers for the war. However Phocus, the third son of Aeacus, received the Athenians at the entrance to the palace, and led them inside into a handsome inner chamber, where he sat down with them. He noticed that Aeolus' grandson carried in his hand a javelin, made from some unknown wood, and tipped with gold. So, when they had first exchanged a few words of conversation, the prince said:

'I take a keen interest in the forests and in hunting, yet I have been wondering for some time what wood was used to fashion the javelin you are holding. If it were of ash, surely it would be yellow in colour, and if it were cornel there would be knots in the grain. What tree it comes from I do not know, but I have never set eyes on a more beautiful missile than yours.' One of the two brothers from Athens answered him: 'You will admire its performance even more than its

looks,' he said, 'for it never fails to reach its mark. No mere chance
guides it when it is thrown, and no one has to bring it back, for it
returns of its own accord, all bloodstained, to its master.' Then indeed
the young descendant of Nereus was full of questions as to why this
was so, where the javelin had come from, and who had given
Cephalus so valuable a possession. Cephalus told him what he wanted
to know but said nothing of what the weapon had cost him, for he
was ashamed to speak of that. Filled with grief at the thought of his
lost wife, tears started to his eyes as he told his tale.

'This javelin, goddess-born Phocus, brings the tears to my eyes,
incredible as it sounds, and will do so for years to come, if the fates
have apportioned me so long a life. This weapon destroyed me and
my dear wife together – I wish it had never been given to me!
Procris was my wife, but you are more likely to have heard of
Orithyia, the princess who was swept away from Athens. If you have,
Procris was Orithyia's sister; though if you compare the beauty and
the character of the two, it was Procris rather than her sister who
deserved to be carried off. She and I were joined in marriage by her
father Erechtheus, and we were united too by our own love. Men
called me happy, and indeed I was: but the gods wished things other-
wise, else perhaps I should be happy still.

'It was in the second month after our marriage. I was spreading nets
to capture antlered deer when, from the summit of flower-decked
Hymettus, saffron-robed Aurora, dispelling the darkness with her
morning light, caught sight of me, and snatched me away against
my will. I hope I may tell the truth with all respect to the goddess:
she was fair to see, with her rosy lips, she was the queen of the border-
land of night and day, she was nurtured on draughts of nectar, but it
was Procris I loved. Procris was always on my lips and in my heart. I
kept on talking of the ties of matrimony, of my recent marriage, my
new home, the promises so lately made to the bride I had deserted,
till the goddess grew annoyed, and said: "Enough of your complaints,
you thankless man – have your Procris! But, as surely as my mind
foresees the future, you will wish you had never had her." So she
angrily sent me back to my wife.

'As I was returning, and pondering on what the goddess had said,
I began to be afraid lest Procris had not been true to her marriage
vows. Her youth and beauty bade me suspect her loyalty, but her

character precluded such suspicions. Still, I had been away, and I was returning home from a goddess who had been guilty of just such conduct. Besides, we lovers are always afraid. I decided to look for my own torment and to test her virtue by offering her gifts. Aurora encouraged this fear of mine, and altered my appearance: I seemed to feel myself changing. Then I entered Athens, Pallas' city, so disguised that none could recognize me, and made my way to my own home. I found an exemplary household, which gave every evidence of living a blameless life, its only distress the disappearance of its master. By a thousand contrivances I managed to gain an audience with Procris. When I saw her, I stood, quite overcome, and almost abandoned my schemes for testing her loyalty. I could scarcely restrain myself from telling the truth and kissing her, as I should have done. She was sad, grieving for the loss of the husband who had been snatched from her: but no one could have been lovelier than she was, even in her sadness. Imagine, Phocus, how beautiful she was, when grief itself became her so well. Why should I tell you how often her purity rejected my advances, how often she said: "I am keeping myself for one alone; wherever he is, I reserve the joys that I can give for him only." Who in his sound senses would not have found that sufficient proof of loyalty? But I was not content, I fought on, to wound myself; by increasing the gifts I offered, by promising a fortune for a night in her company, I forced her at length to hesitate. Then, having gained my end at the cost of my own happiness, I cried out: "You wicked woman! The man you see here was only pretending when he tried to seduce you – it was your own true husband all the time! Now you have been caught, and I myself have convicted you of unfaithfulness." She said nothing. Overwhelmed as she was by silent shame, she fled from the home where she had been tricked, and from her wicked husband. She loathed all men, because of what I had done, and roamed the mountains, devoting herself to the pursuits of the huntress Diana. Then, when she had left me, my love for her blazed up more fiercely than ever, searing me to the very marrow. I begged her to forgive, confessed that I had been in the wrong, and that I myself might have fallen into the same fault, had I been offered such gifts. When I had made this confession, and she had sufficiently avenged her outraged modesty, she was restored to me, and we spent blissful years together, living in perfect harmony.

'Now when she returned, as if the gift of herself were of little account, she also made me a present of a dog which she had received from the goddess she had served. As she gave the animal to Procris, Diana had said: "He will run faster than any other dog." At the same time, my wife gave me a javelin as well, which, as you see, I am still carrying. You would like to know what became of the other gift? Listen, and you will be astonished at the strange and wonderful thing that happened.

'Oedipus, son of Laius, had solved the riddles that had baffled all before him, and that dark prophetess, the Sphinx, had flung herself from the cliff and now lay dead, her puzzles forgotten. But righteous Themis did not allow even this, it seems, to go unavenged: so a second plague was immediately loosed on Aonian Thebes, in the shape of a wild beast which struck terror into the hearts of many of the countryfolk, making them afraid for themselves and for their cattle. Then all the young men of the neighbourhood gathered together; we laid our snares in a wide circle, encompassing the fields, but the animal charged away with all speed and leaped easily across the nets, clearing the topmost cords of the traps we had set. A pack of hounds was released, a hundred strong, but the beast, as swift as any bird, escaped from their pursuit and made sport of them all. With one consent, the huntsmen shouted to me for Laelaps: that was the name of the dog I had been given. He had long been struggling to free his neck from its chain, straining at the end of the leash that held him back. Scarcely was he well set free, than we lost all knowledge of where he was. The warm dust showed the marks of his paws, but he himself had vanished, moving with the speed of a bullet shot from a whirling sling, as fast as a thrown spear, or a light arrow sped by a Cretan bow.

'There was a hill, whose summit gave a view of the surrounding fields. I climbed up there, and watched the spectacle of this strange race, in which the wild beast seemed at one moment to be caught by the dog, and at the next to snatch itself out of his very mouth. The creature was cunning, and did not run straight ahead, but eluded the jaws of its pursuer by circling round, preventing its enemy from launching his attack. The dog pressed on the heels of his quarry; following closely, neither gaining nor losing ground, he seemed to have his victim, but never quite had it, and snapped uselessly at the air. I turned to my javelin for aid. While I was balancing it in my hand, trying to fit my fingers into the thongs, I took my eyes off the chase: when I looked back again at the same spot, to my amazement I saw two marble statues on the plain below, such that you would think the one was fleeing and the other in the act of seizing its prey. Assuredly, if there was some god watching them, he did not want either to be defeated in that chase.'

When he had reached this point in his story, Cephalus fell silent. But Phocus questioned him: 'Now about the javelin itself,' he said. 'What fault have you to find with it?' Then Cephalus told the story of his weapon's crime, as follows: 'My happiness, Phocus, was the origin of my sorrow, and I must tell you of it first. How gladly I remember that blissful time when, in the first years of my marriage, I was happy with my wife – and rightly so – and she was happy with her husband. We were both equally in love, cared equally for each other, and she would not have exchanged my love for marriage with Jupiter himself, nor could any other woman interest me: no, not if Venus herself had come to me. The same passionate love burned in both our breasts.

'When the first rays of the sun struck the hilltops, I used to go hunting in the woods, as young men do. I took no servants or horses, no keen-scented hounds or knotted nets: my javelin was all I needed. But when my arm grew tired with killing wild creatures, I used to seek cool shade, and the zephyr that blew from the chill depths of the valleys. I looked for this gentle zephyr in the midday heat, and used to wait for it, to refresh me after my exertions. I remember I used to call "Come, zephyr, come to my breast, a most welcome visitor, and soothe me; be pleased to relieve, as you most surely do, the burning heat that scorches me." Perhaps I may have added other endearments: for so my fate led me on. I used to say: "You are my dear delight, you refresh and restore me: you make me love the woods and lonely places, and my lips are ever seeking your breath!" Someone over-heard these words, and mistook their meaning. He thought that the "zephyr" to whom I called so often was the name of a nymph, and imagined that I was in love with her. Hastily this rash informer hur-ried to Procris with the tale of my supposed unfaithfulness, and whispered to her what he had heard. Love makes us ready to believe: Procris was so overcome by her sudden distress that she fainted, so they told me. After a long time she came to herself and, bemoaning her wretchedness and the cruelty of her fate, lamented my disloyalty. Distraught by those groundless accusations, she feared something which had no real existence, a mere name without a body, and mourned unhappily, as if over a real rival. Still, even in her misery, she often doubted the story, and hoped that she was mistaken, declaring that she did not believe it, and would not condemn her husband unless she saw his guilt with her own eyes.

'The next day the light of dawn had put darkness to flight when I left home, and went to the woods. After I had made my kill, I lay down on the grass, and said: "Come, zephyr, soothe my weariness!" and suddenly, as I spoke, I seemed to hear a sound of moaning: but I continued: "Come, best beloved!" A leaf made a slight rustle as it fell, and I, thinking it was some wild creature, hurled my javelin. It was Procris! Clutching the wound in her breast, she cried out: "Ah, woe is me!" I recognized the voice of my faithful wife, and raced madly to the spot from which it came. There I found her, only half-conscious, her garments smeared and stained with blood: as a crowning touch of misery, she was dragging from her wounded breast the missile she herself had given me. Gently I lifted in my arms that form, dearer to me than my own. Tearing the dress from her breast, I bound up her cruel wounds, and tried to staunch the blood, begging her not to leave me, not to make me guilty of her death. Though she was fainting and on the point of death, she forced herself to utter a few words: "By the marriage we two have shared, by the gods above and those who watch over me, by that love that has brought about my death and yet still lives, even now when I am dying, I beg you, if ever I deserved well of you, do not let Zephyr take my place as your wife." Only when she spoke did I at last realize her mistake, and then I told her the truth. But what use was there in the telling? Her senses were slipping away, the little strength she had ebbed with her blood: as long as she could look at anything, she looked at me, and breathed her last breath on my lips. But her expression was happier, and she seemed to die content.' The hero was in tears as he told his story, and those who heard him were weeping too.

But now Aeacus and his other two sons appeared, leading the soldiers they had newly enlisted, and Cephalus took command of these strongly-armed forces.

BOOK VIII

❁

WHEN the morning star had banished the night, unveiling the brightness of the day, the East wind fell, and rainclouds gathered in the sky. Sped on his way by the mild South wind, Cephalus returned home, accompanied by the sons of Aeacus. After a prosperous voyage they reached the harbour they were making for, sooner than they had dared to hope.

Meanwhile Minos was plundering the shores of Megara, and trying out his military strength against the town of Alcathous, where Nisus ruled. This venerable white-haired king had one bright purple tress right in the middle of his head. On its safety depended the safety of his kingdom.

The rising moon was now displaying her horns for the sixth time, and still the outcome of the struggle hung in the balance. Winged victory had long been hovering between the two sides, undecided. There was a tower belonging to the king, built on to those tuneful city walls where Leto's son, they say, laid down his golden lyre, so that its music was imparted to the masonry. Often in the days of peace Nisus' daughter had been in the habit of climbing up there, and flinging pebbles against the stones to make them ring. During the war, too, she used often to watch the grim struggle from that vantage point and, as the conflict dragged on, she had come to know the names of the leaders and to recognize their arms and their horses, their attire and their Cretan quivers. Better than any of the others, she knew their general, Europa's son; indeed she knew him better than she should have done. In her eyes, Minos was perfect. When he wore his helmet with its plumed crest, she thought how handsome he looked in a helmet; if he was carrying his shield of shining bronze, the shield became him well; when, with straining muscles, he hurled his pliant spear, the princess praised his strength and skill: when he

179

fitted an arrow to his bowstring and bent the bow in a wide arc, she swore that Apollo looked just like that when he stood with his arrows in his hand. But when Minos laid aside his helmet and revealed his features, when, decked in purple, he bestrode his white horse with its embroidered trappings and pulled on its foam-flecked bit, Nisus' daughter was almost driven out of her senses, and was all but out of her mind with love. Happy the javelin he touched, she declared, and happy the reins he gathered in his hands. Had it but been possible, her impulse was to rush to him, braving the enemy's lines, though she was only a girl. She wanted to throw herself from the top of some tower, into the Cretan camp, or to open to the enemy the gates that brazen bolts held fast, or to do anything else to please Minos. As she sat gazing at the shining canvas of the Cretan king's tent, 'I do not know,' she mused, 'whether to be glad or sorry that this miserable war is being fought. I am sorry that Minos is my enemy, when I love him so: but if there had been no war, I should never have known him! Now, if he were to take me as a hostage, he could abandon the war, and have me as his companion, as a pledge of peace. O my handsome hero, if your mother was herself as beautiful as you, it is no wonder that a god fell in love with her! Thrice blessed would I be, if I could take wing and, gliding through the air, light down in the camp of the Cretan king, there to confess my feelings and my love, and ask what dowry would make Minos take me for his wife: anything, short of my father's kingdom! For I would rather lose the marriage I dream of, than obtain it by treachery: though indeed many people have found it profit them to be defeated, when their victor has been reasonable and kindly. There is no doubt that Minos is justified in waging war to avenge his murdered son: he is strong in the cause for which he fights, strong in the arms that defend it. We shall be conquered, I feel sure, and if that is the fate that awaits our city, why should not I, in my love, open up these gates to him, instead of waiting for his military strength to breach the walls? It is better that he should be able to win without delay, without slaughter, without the cost of his own blood. At any rate, I should not then have to fear lest someone unwittingly wound your breast, my Minos. Unwittingly, I say, for there is no one so hard-hearted that he would dare to aim his cruel spear against you, if he knew who you were.'

The plan she had begun to make appealed to her, and she resolved to give herself up to Minos, with her father's kingdom as a dowry, and so put an end to the war. But the will to do this was not enough. 'There is a garrison on sentry duty at the entrance to the city,' she said to herself, 'and my father has the keys to the gates. Wretched girl that I am, he is the only one I have to fear: he alone prevents me from accomplishing what I desire. Would to the gods I were rid of my father! But surely every man is his own god: Fortune refuses her aid to those who merely pray, and take no action. Anyone else, fired with a desire as great as mine, would long ago have destroyed anything that stood in the way of her love, and have been glad to do so. Why should I be less brave than another? I would make my way boldly through fire and sword, and in this case there is no need of either, but only of a lock of my father's hair. That lock is more precious to me than gold, for the purple tress will make me happy, and bring me that for which I pray!' As she was musing thus, night, the mighty healer of men's cares, came on, and with the darkness she grew bolder. During those first peaceful hours, when sleep enfolds the hearts of mortals whom day's anxieties have wearied, she silently entered her father's bedroom, and performed her awful deed. His own daughter robbed her father of the hair on which his whole destiny depended. When she had obtained her horrible prize, she made her way through the very midst of the enemy – so confident was she in the service she had done them – till she came to the king. He was startled by her arrival, but she addressed him in these words: 'Love has driven me to crime. I, Scylla, daughter of King Nisus, hand over to you the gods of my country and my home. I ask nothing in return except yourself. Take this pledge of my love, this purple tress of hair, and believe that it is not my father's hair but his head which I deliver up to you!' She held out her gift in her guilty hand, but Minos shrank back from what she offered him. Shaken at the thought of so unnatural a deed, he cried: 'You are a disgrace to our times! I pray that the gods may rid the earth of you, that land and sea may deny you any refuge! Certainly I shall not allow my world, the island of Crete which was the cradle of Jupiter, to come in contact with such a monster!' This was his reply. Then he imposed his own conditions, which were eminently just, upon his captured enemies and, when he had done so, ordered the mooring cables to be unloosed, and told the rowers to take their places in the bronze-beaked ships.

Scylla watched the ships being dragged down to the sea and, when she saw them already afloat upon the waves, realized that the enemy leader was not going to reward her for her crime. She had no more prayers to utter; her mood changed to one of violent rage instead. In a fury, she tore her hair and shook her fists at Minos. 'Where are you going?' she cried. 'You whom I have preferred to my country and to my own father? Where are you going, leaving behind the one who made your recent conquest possible? Where are you off to, hard-hearted man, after gaining a victory for which I deserve all the credit and all the blame? Does the gift I have made you move you not at all? Does my love mean nothing, or the fact that all my hopes are centred on you alone? For, if you leave me, where shall I go? My own country lies vanquished and, even supposing it still survived, it is closed to me since I betrayed it. Shall I go to my father, after delivering him up to you? The citizens hate me, as they have every right to do, and neigh-bouring peoples are afraid of the example I have set. All the world is shut against me, so that Crete is my only refuge. If you prevent me from finding shelter there, if you are so lost to all sense of gratitude as to abandon me, then you are the son, not of Europa, but rather of the inhospitable Syrtis, of an Armenian tigress, or of Charybdis' pool, which the South wind lashes to fury: you are no child of Jove, and the story of your birth is a lie! It was not a god disguised as a bull who lured your mother away, but a real bull, a wild beast that had never known love for any heifer. O Nisus, my father, punish me! You walls that I lately betrayed, rejoice in my misfortunes! For I freely confess that I have earned your hatred, and that I deserve to die. But let it be one of those whom I have treacherously wronged who destroys me; why do you, Minos, punish my crime, when it has brought you vic-tory? What my father and my country regard as guilt should be to you a proof of devotion. In very truth, that unfaithful wife who tricked a fierce bull by means of a wooden model, and bore a child half animal, half human, was a fit mate for you! Tell me, do my words reach your ears, or do those same winds that speed your ships carry away my pleas, you ungrateful wretch, and make them vain? Now, indeed, I am not surprised that Pasiphae preferred her bull to you: of the two, you were the more savage. Alas, he is ordering his crews to make haste: the wave roars under the beat of the oarblades, and I and my country together fade into the distance. But it is no use!

You need not try to forget the service I have done you. I shall follow you, even against your will. I shall seize hold of your vessel's curving stern, and be carried with you far across the seas!'

No sooner had she said this, than she jumped into the water, and swam after the ships; her violent passion lending her strength, she grasped and clung to the Cretan vessel, an unwelcome companion. Her father caught sight of her (for he had been newly changed into a sea eagle, with tawny feathers, and was now hovering in the air) and attacked her, as she clung there, intending to rend her flesh with his hooked beak. In her terror she let go her hold on the boat, but as she fell the light breeze seemed to bear her up, and prevent her from touching the waters. She found herself all feathers: and when downy plumage had changed her into a bird she was called Ciris, or Shearer, a name she owes to the cutting off of her father's hair.

When Minos had returned safely to Crete, he disembarked, and sacrificed a hundred oxen to Jupiter in payment of his vows. The trophies he had won were hung up to adorn the palace. In his absence the monstrous child which the queen had borne, to the disgrace of the king's family, had grown up, and the strange hybrid creature had revealed his wife's disgusting love affair to everyone. Minos determined to rid his home of this shameful sight, by shutting the monster away in an enclosure of elaborate and involved design, where it could not be seen. Daedalus, an architect famous for his skill, constructed the maze, confusing the usual marks of direction, and leading the eye of the beholder astray by devious paths winding in different directions. Just as the playful waters of the Maeander in Phrygia flow this way and that, without any consistency, as the river, turning to meet itself, sees its own advancing waves, flowing now towards its source and now towards the open sea, always changing its direction, so Daedalus constructed countless wandering paths and was himself scarcely able to find his way back to the entrance, so confusing was the maze.

There Minos imprisoned the monster, half-bull, half-man, and twice feasted him on Athenian blood; but when, after a further interval of nine years, a third band of victims was demanded, this brought about the creature's downfall. For, thanks to the help of the princess Ariadne, Theseus rewound the thread he had laid, retraced his steps, and found the elusive gateway as none of his predecessors had managed to do. Immediately he set sail for Dia, carrying with him the daughter of Minos; but on the shore of that island he cruelly abandoned his companion. Ariadne, left all alone, was sadly lamenting her fate, when Bacchus put his arms around her, and brought her his aid. He took the crown from her forehead and set it as a constellation in the sky, to bring her eternal glory. Up through the thin air it soared and, as it flew, its jewels were changed into shining fires. They settled in position, still keeping the appearance of a crown, midway between the kneeling Hercules and Ophiuchus, who grasps the snake.

Meanwhile Daedalus, tired of Crete and of his long absence from home, was filled with longing for his own country, but he was shut in by the sea. Then he said: 'The king may block my way by land or across the ocean, but the sky, surely, is open, and that is how we shall go. Minos may possess all the rest, but he does not possess the air.' With these words, he set his mind to sciences never explored before, and altered the laws of nature. He laid down a row of feathers, beginning with tiny ones, and gradually increasing their length, so that the edge seemed to slope upwards. In the same way, the pipe which shepherds used to play is built up from reeds, each slightly longer than the last. Then he fastened the feathers together in the middle with thread, and at the bottom with wax; when he had arranged them in this way, he bent them round into a gentle curve, to look like real birds' wings. His son Icarus stood beside him and, not knowing that the materials he was handling were to endanger his life, laughingly captured the feathers which blew away in the wind, or softened the yellow wax with his thumb, and by his pranks hindered the marvellous work on which his father was engaged.

When Daedalus had put the finishing touches to his invention, he raised himself into the air, balancing his body on his two wings, and there he hovered, moving his feathers up and down. Then he prepared his son to fly too. 'I warn you, Icarus,' he said, 'you must follow a course midway between earth and heaven, in case the sun should scorch your feathers, if you go too high, or the water make them heavy if you are too low. Fly halfway between the two. And pay no attention to the stars, to Bootes, or Helice or Orion with his drawn sword: take me as your guide, and follow me!'

While he was giving Icarus these instructions on how to fly, Daedalus was at the same time fastening the novel wings on his son's shoulders. As he worked and talked the old man's cheeks were wet with tears, and his fatherly affection made his hands tremble. He kissed his son, whom he was never to kiss again: then, raising himself on his wings, flew in front, showing anxious concern for his companion, just like a bird who has brought her tender fledgelings out of their nest in the treetops, and launched them into the air. He urged Icarus to follow close, and instructed him in the art that was to be his ruin, moving his own wings and keeping a watchful eye on those of his son behind him. Some fisher, perhaps, plying his quivering rod, some shepherd leaning on his staff, or a peasant bent over his plough handle caught sight of them as they flew past and stood stock still in astonishment, believing that these creatures who could fly through the air must be gods.

Now Juno's sacred isle of Samos lay on the left, Delos and Paros were already behind them, and Lebinthus was on their right hand, along with Calymne, rich in honey, when the boy Icarus began to enjoy the thrill of swooping boldly through the air. Drawn on by his eagerness for the open sky, he left his guide and soared upwards, till he came too close to the blazing sun, and it softened the sweet-smelling wax that bound his wings together. The wax melted. Icarus moved his bare arms up and down, but without their feathers they had no purchase on the air. Even as his lips were crying his father's name, they were swallowed up in the deep blue waters which are called after him. The unhappy father, a father no longer, cried out: 'Icarus!' 'Icarus,' he called. 'Where are you? Where am I to look for you?' As he was still calling 'Icarus' he saw the feathers on the water, and cursed his inventive skill. He laid his son to rest in a tomb, and the land took its name from that of the boy who was buried there.

As Daedalus was burying the body of his ill-fated son, a chattering lapwing popped its head out of a muddy ditch, flapped its wings and crowed with joy. At that time it was the only bird of its kind, and none like it had ever been seen before. The transformation had been a recent one, and was a lasting reproach to Daedalus: for his sister, knowing nothing of fate's intention, had sent her son, an intelligent boy of twelve, to learn what Daedalus could teach him. This lad, observing the backbone of a fish, and taking it as a pattern, notched a series of teeth in a sharp iron blade, thus inventing the saw. He was the first, too, to fasten two iron arms together into one joint, so that, while remaining equidistant, one arm might stand still, and the other

describe a circle round it. Daedalus was jealous, and flung his nephew
headlong down from Minerva's sacred citadel. Then he spread a false
report that the boy had fallen over. But Pallas, who looks favourably
upon clever men, caught the lad as he fell and changed him into a
bird, clothing him with feathers in mid-air. The swiftness of intellect
he once displayed was replaced by swiftness of wing and foot. His
name remained the same as before. However, this bird does not soar
high into the air, nor does it build its nest on branches in the tree-tops:
rather it flutters along the ground, and lays its eggs in the hedgerows,
for it is afraid of heights, remembering its fall in the days of long ago.

Daedalus, weary with wandering, had now found refuge in Etna's
land and Cocalus, who had taken up arms in answer to his request for
aid, had won a reputation for clemency. Athens had now ceased to
pay her mournful tribute, thanks to Theseus' victory. The temples
were decked with garlands of flowers, and the people were singing
hymns to the warrior Minerva, to Jove, and to the other gods,
honouring them with gifts, with offerings of incense, and with the
sacrifices which they had promised. Rumour, swiftly travelling, had
spread Theseus' fame through the various cities of Argos, and the
peoples of rich Achaea sought his help in their hour of peril. Among
the rest, Calydon begged and besought him to come to its aid, though
it had its own hero, Meleager. The request was occasioned by a boar,
which was at once the servant and the avenging minister of Diana.
The goddess was angry with the people: for, according to the tale,
King Oeneus, out of the bountiful harvests of a good year, made
offering of the first fruits of corn to Ceres, poured a libation of wine
in honour of Bacchus, and one of olive oil in honour of Minerva.
First the gods of the farmers, and then all the gods in heaven, received
the honours they desired – except Leto's daughter. She alone was
neglected, and her altars were the only ones left without an offering
of incense. Now the gods feel anger, too. 'I shall not submit to this
without protest: men may say that I went unhonoured, but they will
not say I went unavenged!' cried Diana; and she let loose a wild boar
in Oeneus' land, to punish him for having scorned her. This boar was
as big as the bulls found in grassy Epirus, bigger than the Sicilian ones.
There was a fiery gleam in its bloodshot eyes, it held its neck high and
stiff, its hide bristled with hairs that stuck straight out like spears. It
bellowed harshly, the hot foam flecking its broad shoulders, and its

teeth were like elephants' tusks: fire issued from its jaws, the leaves were set alight by its breath.

This monster trampled down the tender shoots of the growing crops, or again, when the harvest had fulfilled the farmers' hopes, it turned their joy to tears by ravaging the fields and breaking down the corn in the ear. The threshing floor and barns waited in vain for the promised harvests. Heavy vine clusters with their trailing leaves were strewn on the ground among berries and branches from the ever-green olive. The boar launched furious attacks on the flocks also: neither shepherds nor dogs could save them, nor could the fierce bulls defend the herds. People fled in all directions, thinking themselves safe only when protected by the walls of the city: till Meleager and a handful of picked men banded themselves together in a desire to win fame and glory.

There were the twin sons of Tyndareus, one renowned as a boxer, and the other as a horseman: Jason who had built the first ship, Theseus and Pirithous, inseparable companions, and the two sons of Thestius. Aphareus' sons were there, Lynceus and swift Idas; Caeneus too, who had once been a woman, the warrior Leucippus, Acastus, noted for his javelin-throwing, Hippothous and Dryas, along with Phoenix, Amyntor's son, the two sons of Actor, and Phyleus who had come from Elis. Telamon joined them, and Peleus, the father of great Achilles, as well as the son of Pheres, and Iolaus from Boeotia. Eury-tion was with them too, a man full of vigour, and Echion, whom none could surpass in running, the Locrian Lelex, and Panopeus and Hyleus, fierce Hippasus and Nestor, then still in the prime of life. There was also the contingent which Hippocoon had sent from ancient Amyclae, and Penelope's father-in-law Laertes came, accompanied by the Arcadian Ancaeus. The wise seer, Ampycus' son, was there, and Amphiaraus, who had not yet fallen a victim to his wife's treachery. The girl warrior from Tegea, the pride of the Lycaean grove, came too; a polished buckle fastened the neck of her garment, and her hair was simply done, gathered into a single knot. An ivory quiver, con-taining her arrows, hung from her left shoulder, and rattled as she moved, while she carried her bow as well, in her left hand. Such was her attire – she had features which in a boy would have been called girlish, but in a girl they were like a boy's.

As soon as the hero of Calydon saw her, he fell in love, though the gods would not sanction it, and was fired with secret desire. 'Happy indeed, the man whom she thinks worthy of her hand!' he sighed. He was too modest, and had no time, to say more; for there was a matter of greater urgency on hand, the mighty battle with the boar.

A dense forest of trees, which had never felt the woodman's axe, rose up from the level plain, affording a wide view over the sloping fields. When the warriors reached this wood, some of them spread out their hunting nets, some unleashed the dogs, while others, looking for danger, followed the trail of the boar's footprints. In the depths of a sunken hollow into which rainwater drained from above, grew pliant willows and thin sedge, marsh grasses and osiers and tall bullrushes, rising from a carpet of short reeds. The boar was driven out from this retreat, and rushed furiously into the midst of its foes, like a lightning flash struck out from the clouds as they are dashed together. Trees were brought down by its charge, and there was a sound of crashing as the animal blundered against their trunks. The young heroes raised a shout, and grasped their weapons in their strong hands, holding them poised for the throw, with broad iron tips thrust forward. The boar rushed on, scattering the dogs as they tried to block its furious onset, tossing the yapping beasts out of the way with sidelong blows from its tusks. Echion hurled the first spear: but it missed its mark, and merely scarred the bark of a maple tree. The next missile looked as if it would lodge in the boar's back, but Jason of Pagasae, who threw it, put too much force behind the blow, and his spear overshot the mark. Then Mopsus, son of Ampycus, cried out: 'O Apollo, as I have worshipped you in the past, and do so still, grant that my spear may reach its mark: let there be no mistake!' The god granted his prophet's prayer as far as possible, for Mopsus struck the boar, but failed to wound it. As the weapon flew through the air, Diana had stolen away its iron tip, and only the wooden shaft, robbed of its point, reached its destination. But the boar's fury was roused, and blazed up as fiercely as the fire of a thunderbolt. Sparks flashed from its eyes, and it breathed out flames from its breast. Then, with unswerving attack, the murderous brute charged straight down on the band of young warriors, just as a massive rock, shot from the sling of a catapult, goes hurtling through the air towards enemy walls, or towers packed with soldiers. Eupalamus and Pelagon, who were keeping guard on the right, were flung to the ground, but their friends snatched them up from where they lay. Enaesimus, the son of Hippocoon, was not so lucky: he did not escape the boar's deadly tusks. Trembling with fear, he was preparing to run away, when the sinews behind his knees were slashed, and his muscles gave way beneath him. Nestor of Pylos, too, might well have perished before the time of the Trojan war, had he not used his spear as a vaulting pole, and leaped into the branches of a nearby tree, whence he looked down, from a safe height, on the foe he had escaped. The boar fiercely sharpened its tusks on the bark of an oak: then, confident in its newly whetted weapons, returned to its disastrous attacks, ripping open the thigh of the warrior Hippasus with its curved teeth. But now the twin brothers, Castor and Pollux, not yet raised to be stars in the heavens, rode up together, a striking pair on their horses whiter than snow, and both together sent their sharp javelins quivering through the air. They would have wounded the bristling brute, had it not retreated into the dark woods, where neither horse nor javelin could penetrate. Telamon went after it but, in his eagerness, he was careless of where he was going, tripped over the root of a tree, and fell headlong. While Peleus was helping him to his feet, the girl from Tegea fitted an arrow to her bowstring: then, bending the bow, she sent the shaft speeding through the air. It grazed the top of the boar's back, and stuck just below its ear, staining the bristles with a thin trickle of blood. Meleager was as pleased at the girl's success as she was herself. He was the first, so it is thought, to see the blood and, having seen it, was the first to point it out to his friends. 'You will be honoured for your prowess as you deserve,' he told Atalanta.

The men flushed with shame, and urged each other on, shouting words of encouragement, and hurling their weapons without any concerted plan of attack. But just because they were so numerous, the missiles were rendered ineffective and prevented from reaching their mark. Then the Arcadian Ancaeus, armed with his two-headed axe, rushed furiously upon his fate, crying: 'See how far superior to a woman's weapons are those of a man! Make way for me! Even though Leto's daughter herself protect this boar with her own arrows, none the less, in spite of Diana, my hand will destroy it.' With these proud and boastful words, he raised his two-headed axe in both hands, and stood on tip-toe, bending forward, poised to strike. The boar charged down upon this daring foe and, aiming its tusks at the upper part of his loins, gored him in that most vital spot. Ancaeus collapsed: his inner organs slipped and trailed from his body in a mass of blood – the earth was soaked with the crimson stream. Pirithous, Ixion's son, rushed against the brute, brandishing his spears in his strong hand. But Theseus, son of Aegeus, called to him: 'Heart of my heart, dearer than myself to me, stop at a safe distance! We can show our courage from afar: his hot-headed valour did Ancaeus no good!' As he spoke, he hurled his cornel spear with its heavy bronze tip: but though it was well thrown and would have reached its mark, it was stopped by the leafy branch of an oak. Jason, too, threw his javelin; but by bad luck his aim swerved, and the weapon killed an innocent hound, passing through its thighs, and pinning it to the ground. Meleager, son of Oeneus, threw two spears, with very different effect: for the first stuck in the ground, but the other lodged right in the middle of the boar's back. Without loss of time, while the beast was furiously twisting its body round and round, its jaws slavering with a mixture of foam and fresh blood, the hero who had dealt the wound came up close to the animal, and roused his foe to fury, before finally burying his shining spear in its shoulder. His friends cheered with delight, and made a rush to shake the victor by the hand. They gazed with wonder at the huge beast that covered so much ground as it lay and, convinced that it was still unsafe to go near, each one of them stained his own weapon in the blood of the boar.

Meleager himself set his foot on its monstrous head: then, turning to Atalanta, 'Take the spoil I have secured, lady of Nonacris,' he said, 'and let me share my glory with you.' Thereupon he gave her as a trophy the bristling hide, and the boar's head, with its magnificent tusks. She was as pleased with the giver of the gift as with the gift itself: but the others were jealous, and a murmur ran through the whole company. Then the two sons of Thestius shook their fists and shouted: 'Come now, put down these spoils, woman, and do not interfere with our claims to honour! Do not let confidence in your beauty mislead you, either, in case your love-sick benefactor should prove unable to help you.' Then they took away the spoils from Atalanta, and deprived Meleager of the right to present them to her. The son of Mars could not endure this; bursting with rage, gnashing his teeth, he cried: 'You robbers, stealing another man's glory! I shall teach you the difference between threats and action!' and he ran his sword through the heart of Plexippus who was standing by, all unsuspecting. It was an abominable deed. Toxeus hesitated as to what he should do, for he wished to avenge his brother, but at the same time was afraid of sharing his fate: Meleager did not suffer him to hesitate for long, for he plunged his weapon, still reeking with the murder of one brother, into the warm blood of the other.

Althaea had been told of her son's victory, and was already carrying offerings to the temple of the gods, when she saw her brothers being brought home dead. The city was filled with her wailing, as she gave vent to her clamorous grief: she beat her breast, and changed the gold-embroidered robes she wore for black clothing. However, when she heard who had killed her brothers, she forgot her grief, and turned from tears to concentrate on revenge.

There was a log, which the three sister goddesses had placed on the fire, at the time when this Althaea, Thestius' daughter, was lying in bed with her baby newly born. As they spun the threads of destiny, holding them firmly under their thumbs, they said: 'To the log and to the new-born child we assign the same span of years.' As soon as the goddesses had recited their verses and left the house, the mother snatched the blazing log from the fire, and flung cold water on it. For long it had been hidden away in the depths of the house, and its preservation had kept the young hero safe too. Now his mother brought it out, called for chips of pine wood and shavings, and when these had been piled up, kindled the flames that were to be her son's undoing. Then four times she tried to throw the log on the flames, and four times she stopped herself. Her affection for her son fought against her feelings for her brothers, and divided loyalty tore her heart in opposite directions. Often her face grew pale with fear at the thought of such a crime, often blazing anger made her eyes sparkle with fire. At times her expression was cruel and threatening, at others it could have been thought to be full of compassion. The heat of her fierce rage dried up her tears, yet still the tears welled up, and like a ship which feels the double pull as wind and tides draw it in different directions, as it sways uncertainly with both, so Thestius' daughter was swayed by her shifting emotions, and her anger alternately died away and flared up again. However, her sisterly affection began to get the better of her feelings as a mother, and in order to satisfy her brothers' ghosts with blood, by a guilty deed she saved herself from guilt. When the deadly flames were burning steadily: 'Let this funeral pyre consume the child I bore!' she cried. Then, taking the fateful log in her murderous hands, the wretched woman stood before the funeral altars and prayed: 'Goddesses three, who preside over punishments, Furies, behold this unnatural sacrifice, by which I am at once avenging and committing crime. Death must atone for death, wickedness be piled on wickedness, slaughter upon slaughter, till this accursed household perish under its accumulation of woe. Shall Oeneus continue to enjoy the company of his victorious son, while Thestius is deprived of his? Better that both should have cause to mourn! Only do you, my brothers, ghosts but recently descended to the shades, recognize my devotion, and welcome this offering provided at such a cost, the child of my womb, born to my sorrow!

'Alas, where do I rush so fast? O my brothers, forgive a mother! My hands cannot carry out their purpose: I confess my son has deserved to die, but I cannot bear that I should be the author of his death. Will he then go unpunished? Will he live, a victorious hero, exulting in this very exploit, ruling the kingdom of Calydon, while you lie dead, nothing but chill ghosts and a few ashes? No, that I cannot endure. Let the guilty wretch perish too, and carry with him to the grave his father's hopes, his kingdom, and his ruined country. But where is the affection a mother should feel for her son? Where are the loving ties that ought to bind parents to their children. Where the anguish I endured through ten long months? O my son, how much better had I allowed you to burn in those flames, when you were a baby! You received your life from my hands, but now you will die the death you have deserved! Accept the reward for what you have done: give me back the life I have twice bestowed on you, once when you were born, and again when I snatched the log from the fire. Either that, or send me to join my brothers in the tomb!

'I want to, yet I cannot! What am I to do? At one moment I see before my eyes my brothers' wounds, and a vision of their dreadful murder: the next, my love for my son, the name of mother, break my resolution. Poor wretch that I am! It will be an evil thing, my brothers, if you triumph – yet triumph, none the less, provided that I too may follow you to the shades, you and the son I sacrifice to solace you!' With these words she flung the fatal log, with unsteady hands, into the heart of the flames, turning her face away as she did so. The very wood groaned, or seemed to groan, as it was kindled and set alight by the unwilling fire.

Meleager, though he knew nothing of what was happening, and was not even present, was scorched by that flame, and felt a hidden fire consuming his vitals. He endured his agony with indomitable courage; but still, he grieved that he should meet so inglorious an end, that his death involved no bloodshed, and declared Ancaeus lucky to have suffered the wounds he did. For the last time he called upon his aged father, his brothers and loving sisters, cried out his wife's name, groaning as he did so, and perhaps his mother's too. As the fire blazed up, so did his agony: then both died down again, and were extinguished together. Gradually his breath dispersed into the thin air, as the white ash gradually settled over the glowing embers.

The highlands of Calydon were prostrate with grief. Young men and old were in mourning, the common people and the leaders of the country all lamented. The women who dwelt by Evenus' stream tore their hair and beat their breasts. Meleager's father lay prone upon the ground, his white hair and age-worn face begrimed with dust, complaining bitterly that he had lived too long. As for his mother, knowing full well the dreadful thing she had done, with her own guilty hand she exacted punishment from herself, driving a sword through her own body.

Though the gods had given me a hundred mouths and a hundred tongues, poetic genius and all Helicon for my province, still I could not adequately express the sad laments of Meleager's unhappy sisters. Heedless of what was seemly, they beat their bruised breasts and, while their brother's body remained, fondled and cherished it, kissing the poor corpse, and the bier on which it lay. When his limbs had been reduced to ashes, they gathered these together, and clasped them to their breasts: then they flung themselves on the ground by his grave and, embracing the tombstone, bathed the name inscribed there with their tears. At last Diana was content with the disasters which had befallen the house of Parthaon; she raised the girls into the air, all except Gorge and great Alcmene's daughter-in-law, causing feathers to sprout from their bodies, and stretching wings along their arms. She gave them horny beaks and, when she had so changed them, dispatched them into the sky.

Meanwhile Theseus, having played his part in the joint enterprise, was making his way back to Athena's city where Erechtheus once ruled, when Achelous, swollen with rain, blocked his path, and forced him to delay. 'Come into my house, great Athenian,' said the river god, 'and do not trust yourself to my greedy flood. These waters, as they roar in their slanting channel, are wont to sweep away massive tree trunks, and hurl rocks along. I have seen great stables, cattle and all, swept from their sites upon my banks: and then the oxen could make no use of their sturdy strength, nor could the horses use their speed. Many a young man, too, has been drowned in these turbulent waters, when melting snows from the mountains have swollen my torrent. It is safer to wait quietly, till my river runs within its usual limits and, reduced to a slender stream, is contained in its own channel.' Aegeus' son agreed with the river, and replied: 'I shall take your advice, Achelous, and seek shelter in your home.' He did as he said, and entered the caves built of porous pumice and rough tufa stone. The ground was damp with soft moss, the ceiling roofed with alternate bands of conch shells and shells of purple fish.

Now the sun had travelled two thirds of the way across the sky, when Theseus and his companions took their places on the couches. On one side of Theseus was the son of Ixion, on the other the hero Lelex from Troezen, whose hair was already streaked with white at the temples. Others too, were there, whom the Acarnanian river god had deemed worthy of sharing the honour of Theseus' company, for Achelous was highly delighted to have so distinguished a guest. The nymphs, bare-footed, at once set out the tables and loaded them with good things: afterwards, when the banquet had been cleared away, they served wine in jewelled cups. Then Theseus, bravest of heroes, looked out over the waters that stretched before his eyes, and pointing with his finger, said: 'Tell me, what place is that? What is the name of that island? Though it looks like more than one.' 'What you see is not one island,' answered the river. 'There are five there, but the distance prevents your seeing that they are separate. Do not be too astonished at what Diana did to Calydon when she was scorned: for these used to be naiads! But on one occasion, after they had made a sacrifice of ten bullocks, they invited all the other rural deities to their festival, and proceeded with their festival dances, quite forgetting me! I swelled with rage, till my waters were as full as they are when at their fullest. Then, with heart and flood equally ruthless, I tore apart forest from forest, field from field, and in my swirling tide swept down to the sea the nymphs and their dancing floor. Then, at last, too late, did they remember me. My waves and those of the ocean split that piece of land apart and divided it into as many portions as you see islands, dotted over the ocean. They are called the Echinades. But there is one, look, which you see for yourself lies far apart from the others, and it is dear to me. The sailors call it Perimele. I fell in love with that girl, and robbed her of her maidenhood, a thing which outraged her father Hippodamas so much that he hurled his daughter from a cliff into the sea, intending to kill her. But I caught her up, and supported her as she swam. As I did so, I prayed to Neptune: 'You to whose lot has fallen the kingdom of the restless sea, next in importance to that of heaven, lend us your aid, great god of the trident, and grant a place, I pray you, to one drowned by her father's cruelty: or else let her become herself a place.' While I was still speaking land, newly formed, embraced her floating limbs, and a massive island materialized on top of her changed body.'

His story finished, the river god fell silent. The whole company was stirred by the miracle he had related, but Ixion's son laughed at them for believing the tale. Arrogant and contemptuous of the gods as he was, he challenged his host. 'Your story is pure invention, Achelous,' he said. 'You put too much faith in the power of the gods, if you think they can give and take away the shapes of things.' All were dumbfounded, and disapproved of such words, but before anyone else could speak Lelex, ripe in years and wisdom, broke in: 'The power of heaven is measureless, and knows no bounds; whatever the gods wish is at once achieved. Here is a story which will convince you.

'In the hill-country of Phrygia there is an oak, growing close beside a linden tree, and a low wall surrounds them both. I have seen the spot myself, for Pittheus sent me on a mission to that land, where his father Pelops once was king. Not far off is a stagnant pool: once it was habitable country, but now it has become a stretch of water, haunted by marsh birds, divers and coots. Jupiter visited this place, disguised as a mortal, and Mercury, the god who carries the magic wand, laid aside his wings and accompanied his father. The two gods went to a thousand homes, looking for somewhere to rest, and found a thousand homes bolted and barred against them. However, one house took them in: it was, indeed, a humble dwelling roofed with thatch and reeds from the marsh, but a good-hearted old woman, Baucis by name, and her husband Philemon, who was the same age as his wife, had been married in that cottage in their youth, and had grown grey in it together. By confessing their poverty and accepting it contentedly, they had eased the hardship of their lot. It made no difference in that house whether you asked for master or servant – the two of them were the entire household: the same people gave the orders and carried them out. So, when the heaven-dwellers reached this humble home and, stooping down, entered its low doorway, the old man set chairs for them, and invited them to rest their weary limbs; Baucis bustled up anxiously to throw a rough piece of cloth over the chairs, and stirred up the warm ashes on the hearth, fanning the remains of yesterday's fire, feeding it with leaves and chips of dried bark, and blowing on it till it burst into flames. Then the old woman took down finely split sticks and dry twigs which were hanging from the roof, broke them into small pieces, and pushed them under her little pot. Her husband had brought in some vegetables from his carefully-watered garden, and these she stripped of their outer leaves. Philemon took a two-pronged fork and lifted down a side of smoked bacon that was hanging from the blackened rafters; then he cut off a small piece of their long-cherished meat, and boiled it till it was tender in the bubbling water. Meanwhile the old couple chattered on, to pass the time, and kept their guests from noticing the delay. There was a beech-wood bowl there, hanging from a nail by its curved handle, which was filled with warm water, and the visitors washed in this, to refresh themselves. On a couch with frame and legs of willow-wood lay a mattress, stuffed with soft sedge grass. Baucis and Philemon covered this with the cloths which they used to put out only on solemn holidays – even so, the stuff was old and cheap, a good match for the willow couch. Then the gods took their places for the meal. Old Baucis tucked up her dress and, with shaky hands, set the table down in front of them. One of its three legs was shorter than the others, but she pushed a tile in below, to make it the same height. When she had inserted this, and so levelled the sloping surface, she wiped over the table with some stalks of fresh mint. Then she placed upon the board the mottled berry which honest Minerva loves, wild cherries picked in the autumn and preserved in lees of wine, endives and radishes and a piece of cheese, and eggs lightly roasted in ashes not too hot; all these were set out in clay dishes and, after they had been served, a flagon with a raised pattern, just as much silver as their dinner service, was set on the table, and beech-wood cups, lined inside with yellow wax. After a short while, the hearth provided them with food piping hot and the wine, which was of no great age, was sent round again. Then it was set aside for a little, to make way for dessert, which consisted of nuts, a mixture of figs and wrinkled dates, plums and fragrant apples in shallow baskets, and black grapes, just gathered. A shining honey-comb was set in the midst of these good things and, above all, there was cheerful company, and bustling hospitality, far beyond their means.

'As the dinner went on, the old man and woman saw that the flagon, as often as it was emptied, refilled itself of its own accord, and that the wine was automatically replenished. At the sight of this miracle, Baucis and Philemon were awed and afraid. Timidly stretching out their hands in prayer, they begged the gods' indulgence for a poor meal, without any elaborate preparations. They had a single goose, which acted as guardian of their little croft: in honour of their divine visitors, they were making ready to kill the bird, but with the help of its swift wings it eluded its owners for a long time, and tired them out, for age made them slow. At last it seemed to take refuge with the gods themselves, who declared that it should not be killed. "We are gods," they said, "and this wicked neighbourhood is going to be punished as it richly deserves; but you will be allowed to escape this disaster. All you have to do is to leave your home, and climb up the steep mountainside with us." The two old people both did as they were told and, leaning on their sticks, struggled up the long slope.

'When they were a bowshot distant from the top, they looked round and saw all the rest of their country drowned in marshy waters, only their own home left standing. As they gazed in astonishment, and wept for the fate of their people, their old cottage, which had been small, even for two, was changed into a temple: marble columns took the place of its wooden supports, the thatch grew yellow, till the roof seemed to be made of gold, the doors appeared magnificently adorned with carvings, and marble paved the earthen floor. Then Saturn's son spoke in majestic tones: "Tell me, my good old man, and you, who are a worthy wife for your good husband, what would you like from me?" Philemon and Baucis consulted together for a little, and then the old man told the gods what they both wished. "We ask to be your priests, to serve your shrine; and since we have lived in happy companionship all our lives, we pray that death may carry us off together at the same instant, so that I may never see my wife's funeral, and she may never have to bury me." Their prayer was granted. They looked after the temple as long as they lived.

'Then, one day, bowed down with their weight of years, they were standing before the sacred steps, talking of all that had happened there, when Baucis saw Philemon beginning to put forth leaves, and old Philemon saw Baucis growing leafy too. When the tree-tops were already growing over their two faces, they exchanged their last words while they could, and cried simultaneously: "Good-bye, my dear one!" As they spoke, the bark grew over and concealed their lips. The Bithynian peasant still points out the trees growing there side by side, trees that were once two bodies. This tale was told me by responsible old men, who had nothing to gain by deceiving me. Indeed, I myself have seen the wreaths hanging on the branches, and have hung up fresh ones, saying: "Whom the gods love are gods themselves, and those who have worshipped should be worshipped too."'

That was the end of his story. Both the story-teller and the tale he told excited the whole company, but Theseus most of all. As he was clamouring to hear more of the wonderful deeds of the gods, the river god of Calydon raised himself on his elbow, and addressed the hero in these words: 'There are some, bravest Theseus, whose shape has been changed just once, and has then remained permanently altered. Others again have power to change into several forms. Take, for instance, Proteus, the god who dwells in the sea that encircles the earth. People have seen him at one time in the shape of a young man, at another transformed into a lion; sometimes he used to appear to them as a raging wild boar, or again as a snake, which they shrank from touching; or else horns transformed him into a bull. Often he could be seen as a stone, or a tree, sometimes he presented the appearance of running water, and became a river, sometimes he was the very opposite, when he turned into fire.

'The wife of Autolycus, who was Erysichthon's daughter, had the same power. Her father was a man who scorned the gods, and never made any offering of incense on the altars. He is even reported to have used his sacrilegious axe on the trees of Ceres' grove, violating the ancient woodlands with its blade. Among these trees there stood a huge oak, which had grown sturdy and strong in the course of years, a forest in itself, hung round with wreaths and garlands and votive tablets, tributes for prayers that had been granted. Under this tree the dryads often held their festive dances, often they joined hands in a circle and embraced its trunk, whose circumference measured fifteen cubits. In height, too, it towered above the other trees, as much as they did above the grassy sward. Yet this did not deter Erysichthon from wielding his axe against it. He ordered his servants to cut down the sacred tree and, when he saw them hesitate to carry out his commands, the scoundrel snatched an axe from one of the men, and shouted: "Should this tree be itself a goddess, and not just a tree the goddess loves, still its leafy top will be brought down to earth!" As he uttered these words, he held his weapon poised, ready to strike the trunk obliquely. The oak tree of Ceres trembled and groaned: at the same time, the leaves and acorns began to turn white, and the long branches lost their colour. Then, when his impious hand had made a gash in its trunk, blood flowed out where the bark was split open, just as it pours from the severed neck of some mighty bull, slain before the altars as an offering. Everyone stood still in horrified amazement: out of all the company, one man dared to try to prevent the sacrilege, to stop the cruel axe. Thessalian Erysichthon glared at him: "Take that as a reward for your pious thoughts!" he stormed, and swung his axe against the man instead of the tree, lopping off his head. Then he turned again to the oak, and dealt it blow after blow.

'Meanwhile, from the heart of the tree, a voice was heard saying: "I who dwell within this tree am a nymph, whom Ceres dearly loves. I warn you with my dying breath, that punishment for your wickedness is at hand: that thought comforts me in death." But Erysichthon persisted in his criminal action. When the tree had at length been weakened by innumerable blows, ropes were attached to the trunk, and it was brought crashing down, creating havoc in the wood as it fell, by reason of its great weight. All her sister dryads, sorely distressed at the loss which the grove and they themselves had suffered, dressed themselves in black garments, and mournfully approached

Ceres, begging that Erysichthon should be punished. That most
beautiful goddess consented; nodding her head, she made the fields,
laden with heavy harvests, tremble, as she devised a punishment
which would have made its victim an object of pity indeed, if he had
not forfeited all men's pity by his deeds. She planned to torment him
with deadly Hunger.

'Since destiny does not allow Ceres and Hunger to meet, she could
not approach this creature herself, but she gave orders to a rustic
oread, one of the mountain spirits. "There is a place," she said, "which
lies far off, in the icy land of Scythia, a gloomy barren spot where the
earth knows nothing of crops or trees. It is the home of sluggish
Chill, of Pallor and Ague, and ravening Hunger lives there too. Go,
then, bid Hunger bury herself in the wicked stomach of this impious
wretch: tell her to fight and overcome my powers of nourishment,
and to let no amount of food defeat her. Do not be frightened at the
length of the journey; take my chariot and my dragons and drive
them through the air." Ceres then handed over her car, and the oread
was borne through the skies in the borrowed chariot.

'She alighted in Scythia, and there unyoked her dragons on the
summit of a rocky mountain, which the inhabitants call Caucasus.
She went to look for Hunger, whom she found in a stony field, tear-
ing up a few scant grasses with her nails and her teeth. The creature's
face was colourless, hollow-eyed, her hair uncared for, her lips
bleached and cracked. Scabrous sores encrusted her throat, her skin
was hard and transparent, revealing her inner organs. The brittle
bones stuck out beneath her hollow loins, and instead of a stomach she
had only a place for one. Her breast, hanging loose, looked as if it
were held in position only by the framework of her spine. Her joints
seemed large in contrast to her skinny limbs, the curve of her knees
made a real swelling, and her ankle-bones formed protuberances that
were out of all proportion. When the oread saw her, she did not ven-
ture to go up close, but delivered the goddess's orders from a distance
and, in a very short time, though she had only just come, and though
she remained a good way off, she seemed herself to feel the pangs of
hunger. Turning her team, she drove the dragons back through the
air to Haemonia.

'Although she is always opposed to Ceres' activities, Hunger
obeyed the goddess's instructions. The wind carried her through the

air till she came to the house she had been told to visit. Immediately she entered the bedroom of the scoundrel Erysichthon. Finding him sound asleep (for it was night-time) she flung both her arms around him, insinuated herself into her victim, breathing into his lips, his throat, his heart, and spread famishing hunger through his hollow veins. When she had carried out her orders, she left the fertile world again, and returned to her poverty-stricken home and her accustomed haunts.

'Erysichthon was still slumbering peacefully, soothed by the wings of the gentle god of sleep, but he dreamed that he was feasting, and chewed uselessly at nothing, grinding his teeth together, and cheating himself by swallowing a mere pretence of food. Instead of a banquet he gulped down insubstantial air, all to no purpose. When he awoke, he was furiously hungry: his famished jaws and burning stomach were utterly at the mercy of his craving. Without delay, he gave orders for all the foodstuffs that earth and air and sea provide to be brought to him, complained of hunger when the laden tables were set before him, and in the midst of feasting sought still more feasts. Supplies which would have satisfied whole cities or an entire nation were not enough for him, and the more he ate, the more he desired. As the sea receives rivers from all over the earth and yet has always room for more, and drinks up the waters from distant lands, or as greedy flames never refuse nourishment, but burn up countless faggots, made hungrier by the very abundance of supplies and requiring more, the more they are given: so the jaws of the scoundrel Erysichthon welcomed all the provisions that were offered, and at the same time asked for more. All the food he consumed only excited his desire for food, and by eating he continually produced an aching void.

'Now, thanks to this hunger, to the bottomless pit that was his stomach, his family fortunes had dwindled away: but still his dreadful hunger remained, not diminished in the slightest. His burning appetite was unabated. At length, when he had eaten up all his wealth, he was left with only his daughter, a girl who deserved to have had a better parent. In his penniless state, he sold her too: but she was a girl of spirit, and rebelled against having a master. Stretching out her hands over the nearby waters, she cried: "You who robbed me of my maidenhood, and have your reward, rescue me from slavery!" Neptune was the one who had the reward of which she spoke, and he did not scorn her prayer. Although her owner, coming along behind, had seen the girl only a moment before, the god changed her shape, gave her the face of a man, and dressed her in fisherman's clothes. Her master came up and, looking straight at her, said: "You there, concealing your dangling hooks with tiny bits of bait, you with the rod in your hands, I wish you a calm sea, and gullible fishes that never notice the hook till they are caught, if you will tell me where the girl is, who was standing on the shore just now, with her hair all disordered, dressed in cheap clothes. I saw her on the sands: but tell me, where is she? For her footprints go no further."

'The other, realizing that what the god had done for her had been successful, was delighted that she herself should be asked where she was. In reply to her master's question, she said: "Excuse me, whoever you are. I have never taken my eyes off this pool, and have been entirely occupied with my fishing. To remove any doubts you may have, I swear, so may the god of the sea assist me in my livelihood, that no one but myself has been on this shore for a long time, and no woman has set foot here." The man believed her and, turning round, walked away over the sand, cheated of his slave. Then the girl's true shape was restored to her.

'Her father, when he perceived that his daughter could undergo such transformations, often sold her to different masters, and she escaped in the form of a horse, or a bird, or again as an ox or a stag, thus obtaining provisions, dishonestly, for her gluttonous father. However, when in the violence of his malady he had consumed all that was offered and had thus merely aggravated his grievous sickness, the wretch began to bite and gnaw at his own limbs, and fed his body by eating it away.

'But why do I waste time over tales of other people? I myself, my young friend, have the power to alter my body, though the number of shapes I can assume is limited. Sometimes I appear as you see me now, sometimes I change into a snake, or again I become a bull, the leader of the herd, whose strength lies in his horns – horns, I say, for I had two while I could. But now, as you see for yourself, one side of my forehead has lost its weapon' . . . and his words gave place to groans.

BOOK IX

❀

THEN Neptune's son, brave Theseus, asked Achelous why he was groaning, and how his forehead had come by this injury. The river of Calydon, who wore a circlet of reeds on his tangled locks, answered him in these words: 'It is a painful thing you ask of me: who would want to speak of battles in which he had been defeated? However, I shall tell you what happened: for the glory of having fought is greater than the disgrace of having been beaten, and I am much consoled in my defeat by the thought that my opponent was so great a hero.

'Perhaps you have heard tell of Deianira? She was a most lovely girl who, in days gone by, roused jealous hopes in the hearts of many suitors and I, along with the rest, went to the house of the man I hoped would be my father-in-law. "Son of Parthaon," I said, "take me as your daughter's husband." My words were echoed by Hercules, whereupon the other suitors left the field to us two. My rival declared that he would give his bride Jupiter as a father-in-law, and called to mind his own famous Labours, and the fact that he had succeeded in carrying out his stepmother's commands. I countered his claims, saying: "It is disgraceful that a god should yield place to a mortal." – for in those days Hercules was not yet a god – "In me you see the king of the waters which flow through your country in their slanting channels. As a son-in-law I shall not be a stranger, sent from foreign shores, but one of your own people, and a part of your kingdom. Only do not hold it against me that Juno, queen of heaven, does not hate me, that I have never been punished by having labours imposed upon me!

'"As to your other point, son of Alcmene, Jupiter whom you boastfully declare to be your father, is either not your father at all, or if he is, it was guilt that made him so! When you claim him as father, you convict your mother of adultery. Choose whether you prefer to say that Jove is not really your father, or to admit that you were born as a result of a piece of disgraceful behaviour."

'Hercules had long been glowering at me as I spoke. Instead of controlling his flaring rage, as a hero should, he retorted: "I am better with my hands than with my tongue: provided I can defeat you in the fight, you can have your verbal victory!" and he rushed fiercely upon me. I was ashamed to draw back, after my recent boasting. Flinging off my garments, I raised my arms, held them crooked before my chest in a position of defence, and prepared myself to fight. My opponent sprinkled me with dust that he had gathered in his cupped palms, and in his turn was covered with yellow sand, till he was all golden. Then he clutched at my neck, and again at my rapidly shifting legs, or seemed to clutch, attacking me from every angle. But my weight was my salvation. I was impervious to his assaults, just as a massive rock, besieged by the roaring waves, stands fast and is kept safe by its very bulk.

'We drew a little apart, and then rushed to join battle again, each holding his ground, determined not to yield, foot pressed against foot. Leaning forward from the waist, I thrust my fingers against his fingers, my head against his head. I have seen sturdy bulls rush upon one another, in just the same way, when they are fighting to win the sleekest cow in all the meadows for their prize. The herds look on, trembling, not knowing which will be the victor, and gain such mastery. Three times Hercules tried, without avail, to thrust away my breast that was locked against his own; at the fourth attempt he shook off my grip, and loosened my straining arms. Then, striking me a blow that whirled me about (for I am resolved to tell the truth), he flung himself, with all his weight, upon my back, and clung there. Believe me, I am not just trying to enhance your respect for me – it is no exaggeration to say that I really seemed to be crushed down by a mountain on top of me. However, I barely managed to insert my arms, streaming with sweat, beneath his body, and so with difficulty was able to loosen his cruel grip on my breast. Still he pressed me hard, and prevented me, panting and breathless as I was, from recovering my strength. In this way he got control of my neck and then, at last, I was forced to my knees, and bit the dust.

'Proved inferior to him in valour, I had resort to stratagems, and slipped from the hero's grasp by turning myself into a long snake. But when I had coiled my body into sinuous spirals, and was flickering my forked tongue, hissing fiercely, Hercules of Tiryns laughed, and mocked my tricks. "I was defeating snakes in my cradle!" he cried, "and though you may be more terrible than any other, Achelous, yet you are only one solitary serpent, and how small a part of the Lernaean hydra that will be! The hydra throve on its wounds, and none of its hundred heads could be cut off with impunity, without being replaced by two new ones which made its neck stronger than ever. Yet, in spite of its branching snakes, reborn as they were cut down, in spite of the strength it derived from attempts to harm it, still I got the upper hand of the hydra, vanquished the monster, and ripped its body open. Imagine, then, what will happen to you, who have changed yourself into a mere semblance of a snake, employing weapons that are not natural to you, and concealing yourself under a borrowed shape!" With these words, he fastened his fingers tightly round the upper part of my throat. I was being throttled, as if my neck were caught in a vice, and struggled to wrest my jaws out of the grip of his thumbs.

'So he overcame me in this guise too; but there remained my third shape, that of a fierce bull. I therefore transformed myself into a bull, and as such renewed the fight. My adversary, attacking from the left, flung his arms round the bulging muscles of my neck. As I charged away, he followed close beside me, dragging at my head, till he forced my horns into the hard ground, and laid me prostrate in the deep dust. Nor was this enough: as he grasped my stiff horn in his cruel hand, he broke and tore it off, mutilating my brow. But the naiads filled it with fruits and fragrant flowers, and sanctified it, and now my horn enriches the Goddess of Plenty.' When he had finished speaking, one of his attendants, a nymph dressed in the style of Diana, came forward, her hair streaming over her shoulders, and brought all autumn's harvest in the rich horn, with delicious apples for their dessert.

Dawn came, and when the first rays of the sun struck the mountain-tops, the young men went on their way; for they did not wait till the river was flowing peacefully and smoothly, nor even till all the floods had subsided. Achelous hid his rustic features and the head that had lost its horn in the depths of his waters.

However, the loss of this adornment, taken from him by Hercules, was the only humiliation Achelous suffered: in all other respects he was unhurt, and he concealed his loss by wearing on his head a wreath of willow leaves, or of reeds. Fierce Nessus, on the other hand, was utterly destroyed by his love for that same Deianira, when Hercules' swift arrow pierced him in the back.

Jove's son, Hercules, was returning with his new bride to his native city, when he came to the raging waters of Evenus. The river was fuller than usual, increased by winter's rains, and it was impossible to cross the flood, with its swirling eddies. Hercules had no fear for himself, but he was troubled about his wife: then Nessus came up, strong of limb, and well acquainted with the fords. 'I shall carry your wife across, and set her on the further bank,' he told Hercules. 'You keep your strength for swimming!' So the Boeotian hero trusted the centaur with his Calydonian princess, though she was pale with fear, equally afraid of the river and of Nessus. Hercules himself threw his club and his curved bow across the river; then, just as he was, weighed down by his quiver and his lion skin, he shouted: 'Let me complete the conquest of the rivers, already begun!' Without hesitation, without seeking to find where the flood was least fierce, he leaped into the stream, scorning to be carried across by the help of the current. He had reached the bank, and was picking up the bow he had thrown across, when he heard his wife's cries, and realized that Nessus was preparing to betray his trust. 'You scoundrel!' cried Hercules. 'Where are you off to, you fool, trusting in your speed of foot? You, Nessus the centaur, it is to you I am speaking! Pay heed, and do not come between me and mine. If you have no respect for me, surely the wheel on which your father is tormented should prevent you from alliances that are forbidden? Still, you will not escape, confident though you are in your horses' hooves: for I shall overtake you, not on foot, but with my deadly weapons!' His actions made good his last words, for the arrow which he shot pierced the fleeing Nessus in the back. Its barbed tip protruded from his breast. When the shaft was pulled out of the centaur's body, blood gushed out from both wounds, blood tainted with the horrible poison of the Lernaean hydra. Nessus did not let it flow away: 'I shall not die unavenged,' he muttered and, dipping his shirt in the warm blood, presented it to the bride he had stolen, pretending that it was a charm for inspiring love.

A long time passed, and the whole world had heard of the deeds of mighty Hercules, and of his stepmother's hatred. It was after he had conquered Oechalia, and was preparing to offer sacrifices to Jupiter at Cenaeum, that gossiping Rumour, who loves to mingle false with true and, nourished by her own lies, grows steadily from small beginnings, outstripped him on his homeward way and brought to Deianira's ears the tale that her husband, the son of Amphitryon, was in love with Iole. The devoted wife believed the story. At first, stricken by the report of her husband's new attachment, she burst into tears, and gave vent to her grief in piteous sobbing. But then she exclaimed: 'Why do I cry? My rival will rejoice to see me weep. She will soon be here, so I must hurry and think out some plan while I have the chance, before another takes my place as his wife. Should I reproach him, or keep silent? Go back to Calydon, or stay here? Shall I leave this house, or make myself a source of annoyance to them, if I can do nothing more? What if I were to remember that I am your sister, Meleager, make ready for some daring deed and show, by killing my rival, to what lengths a woman can be driven, by the grief and pain of being slighted?'

She pondered the various courses open to her and, of them all, chose to send the shirt, impregnated with Nessus' blood, to strengthen anew her husband's dying love. Knowing no more than he did what she was giving him, the unhappy woman handed Lichas the garment that was to be the cause of her own sorrow and, with persuasive words, bade him carry her present to her husband. Hercules, all unsuspecting, took the gift and wrapped around his shoulders the poison of the Lernaean hydra.

The first fires had been kindled, and the hero was making offerings of incense, reciting prayers to the gods, and pouring a libation of wine from his goblet over the marble altars. Meanwhile the violence of the poison, heated and melted by the fire, coursed right through his limbs, to their furthest parts. With his customary courage, he suppressed his groans as long as he could, but when his suffering was beyond endurance, he flung over the altars, and filled wooded Oeta with his cries. He tried to tear off the deadly garment with all speed. But wherever the cloth was dragged away, it dragged his skin with it and, horrible to tell, either clung to his limbs, resisting all attempts to pull it off, or left lacerated flesh, revealing his massive bones. His blood, saturated by the burning poison, hissed and boiled, like white hot iron plunged into icy water. There was no limit to his agony: greedy flames sucked in his heart, dark perspiration poured from his whole frame, his scorched sinews crackled, and the hidden pestilence melted his bones. Raising his hands to the stars, he cried: 'O Juno, daughter of Saturn, feast your eyes on my disasters: look down from on high upon my torment, and gaze your fill, till your barbarous heart is satisfied. Or, if I am so wretched an object that even an enemy, even you, must pity me, then take away this cruelly tortured, hateful soul, that was born for toil! This will be your gift to me – a fitting one for a stepmother to bestow. Was it for this that I quelled Busiris, the king who defiled his temples with the blood of strangers? For this that I denied cruel Antaeus access to his parent earth, from whom he drew his strength? For this that I faced, unflinching, these triple-bodied monsters, the Spanish herdsman and the dog Cerberus? Are these the hands that forced down the horns of the mighty bull, lent their aid to Elis, to the waters of Stymphalus and to Parthenius' woods, thanks to whose strength I brought home the Amazon's sword-belt of wrought gold, and the apples which the unsleeping dragon guarded closely? The centaurs could not resist me, nor yet the boar that ravaged Arcadia; nor did it profit the hydra that its losses gave it new strength, and redoubled its powers. Again, there was the time when I saw the Thracian horses, fattened on human blood, their stalls full of mangled bodies, and no sooner saw them than I destroyed them, despatching them, and their master too. The huge lion of Nemea lies dead, throttled by these hands: I have borne the sky upon these shoulders. Implacable Juno grew tired of issuing orders ere I was tired of carrying them out.

'But now a new plague is upon me, which no amount of courage can withstand, no weapons of war overcome. Consuming fire steals into the depths of my lungs, feeding on all my limbs, and that while my enemy, King Eurystheus, is strong and well! And there are men who can believe in gods!'

Such were the cries of the wounded warrior as he made his way over the heights of Oeta, like some wild bull carrying a hunting spear fixed in his body, when the huntsman has wounded him and fled. Often he could be seen, groaning and gnashing his teeth, trying to rip the whole garment to pieces, bringing trees crashing down, venting his wrath on the mountains, or stretching up his arms to the heavens that were his father's home.

Suddenly he caught sight of the terrified Lichas, who was hiding in a hollow cave. Pain had roused him to the pitch of madness. 'Was it you, Lichas,' he cried, 'who gave me this fatal gift? Are you responsible for my death?' Lichas trembled and grew pale with fear, as he timorously sought to excuse himself. But while he was still speaking, and was trying to put his hands round the hero's knees, Hercules seized him and, swinging him round three times, four times, flung him into the waters of the Euboean, more violently than if he had been hurled from a sling. His body, as it went soaring through the air, hardened into stone: just as rain, they say, is frozen into snow by chilling winds and as the softly whirling snow, too, is packed and rounded into thick hail-stones, so the men of old declared that when Lichas was flung through the air by Hercules' strong arms, fear drained away his blood and all his moisture, and he was turned into hard, flinty rock. Even now, there is a little reef in the Euboean sea that juts out of the waves and keeps traces of human shape. Sailors are afraid to set foot on it, as if it would feel their weight, and they call it Lichas.

Then Hercules, the renowned son of Jupiter, cut down the trees which grew on lofty Oeta and built them up into a pyre. He told Philoctetes, the son of Poeas, to take his bow, his huge quiver, and the arrows that were destined to see Troy a second time: then, with the help of his friend, he kindled the pyre and, while the greedy flames were taking hold on the pile, laid the skin of the Nemean lion on top of the heap of tree-trunks and lay down, his neck resting on his club, and on his face an expression no different from that of a guest, reclining among the winecups, with garlands on his head.

Now the flames had gained strength, and were roaring as they spread in all directions, attacking limbs that heeded them not at all, and a hero who despised them. The gods were afraid for earth's champion, till Jupiter, perceiving their anxiety, addressed them in these welcome words: 'The fear which you display pleases me, and with my whole heart I freely congratulate myself that I am called ruler and father of a people who do not forget their benefactors. I am glad that my son is protected by your good will as well as mine. For, though you pay this tribute to his mighty exploits, the honour you do him reflects honour on me too. But indeed, you must not let your faithful hearts be filled with groundless fears; do not be dismayed by the flames, blazing on Oeta's heights. Hercules, who conquers all, will conquer the fire you see there: only the human part, which he owes to his mother, will feel Vulcan's power. What he derives from me is eternal, beyond the reach of death, and not to be overcome by any flames. When that part has fulfilled its time on earth, I shall receive it into the realms of heaven, confident that my action will be a source of rejoicing to all the gods. If there is anyone, however, who is likely to be annoyed at Hercules' becoming a god, and grudges him the reward he has been given, even such a one will learn that Hercules has deserved the gift, and will approve it, in spite of private feelings.'

The gods applauded; even Jupiter's royal wife was seen to listen to the rest of his speech without any harsh looks, though she did frown at his last words, resenting the reference to herself. Meanwhile Vulcan had stripped Hercules of whatever fire could ravage, and the form of the hero was left, quite unrecognizable, retaining none of his likeness to his mother, but only the signs of his descent from Jove. Just as a serpent renews its youth, sloughing its old age with its skin, and is left fresh and shining with its new scales, so when the Tirynthian hero had put off his mortal shape, the better part of him grew vigorous, and he began to appear greater than before, a majestic figure of august dignity. Then the omnipotent father swept him up through the hollow clouds in his four-horse chariot, and set him among the glittering stars. Atlas felt the added weight.

Meanwhile the anger of Eurystheus, son of Sthenele, had not yet been appeased, and he was visiting upon Hercules' children the fierce hatred he felt for their father. Alcmene of Argolis was worn out with long-continued anxiety: but she had Iole as her confidante, to whom she could pour out the laments of an old woman, and relate her own misfortunes and the exploits of her son, to which the whole world bore witness. At Hercules' request, Hyllus had taken Iole into his home, and to his heart, and she was carrying in her womb the noble child which he had given her, when Alcmene began: 'I pray that to you, at least, the gods may be kind, and hurry things on when, in the fullness of time, you call on Lucina, the goddess who watches over us weak women in childbirth, who, thanks to Juno's influence, was so harsh to me. For when the sun had reached the tenth of the heavenly signs and the time drew near for the birth of my son Hercules, who was to endure such labours, the weight of the baby stretched my womb, and the burden I carried was such that one could tell Jove was responsible for what was hidden there. I could not bear my pains any longer. Why, even as I speak to you now, a cold shudder runs through my limbs, and it hurts me to remember. For seven nights and as many days, tortured and worn out with agony, I stretched my arms to the sky, and cried aloud to Lucina and her helpers, the Gods of Birth. Lucina came, it is true, but she had been bribed beforehand, and was prepared to surrender my life to cruel Juno. Though she heard my moans, she sat herself by the altar, in front of the door. Crouching there, with her right leg crossed over her left, and fingers intertwined, she prevented the baby's birth. She murmured spells, too, in a low voice, which held back the child when it had begun to be born. I struggled and, in my frenzy, heaped abuse on Jupiter for his ingratitude. But it was all to no purpose. Lamenting in words that would have moved flinty stones, I prayed to die. The women of Thebes, who were present, echoed my prayers, and comforted my distress.

'One of my servant maids was with me, a golden-haired girl called Galanthis, who was humbly born, but assiduous in carrying out my orders, and dear to me for the services she performed. She realized that cruel Juno was up to some mischief. As she was constantly passing in and out of the house, she noticed the goddess Lucina sitting by the altar, her arms crossed upon her knees. She spoke to her and said: "Whoever you are, send your congratulations to my mistress! Alcmene of Argolis has had her prayers answered, and is newly delivered of her child." The goddess of birth leaped to her feet in consternation, loosening her clasped hands, and as soon as these bonds were slackened, I myself was delivered of my baby.

'The story goes that Galanthis laughed at the goddess whom she had deceived: but as she laughed, the cruel goddess seized her by the hair, dragged her down to the ground and, when the girl attempted to raise herself, prevented her from doing so. Then she turned Galanthis' arms into forelegs and altered her shape though her hair kept its original colour. She was changed into a weasel and, because falsehoods issuing from her lips had helped a woman to give birth to her child, her young ones, too, are born by way of her mouth. But she is

211

as active and energetic as ever and still haunts my house, as she did before.'

Alcmene sighed as she spoke, moved by the memory of her former servant. Her daughter-in-law comforted her, as she grieved, saying: 'After all, mother, the girl whose loss of human shape causes you such distress, was not one of our own family. What would you say, I wonder, if I told you of the strange calamity which befell my sister? Though it upsets me so much that it is difficult for me to speak of it, and my tears almost prevent me from telling you the story.

'This girl, whose name was Dryope, was her mother's only child – I was my father's daughter by another wife – and of all the women of Oechalia she was the loveliest. She was assaulted by the god who rules Delphi and Delos and then, though she was no longer a virgin, Andraemon took her in, and was considered lucky to have her as his wife.

'Now there is a lake, with banks gently shelving, so that it looks like the seashore, where myrtle groves encircle the water's edge. Dryope, in ignorance of fate's intent, had come to this spot; and, to make you more indignant at what happened, her purpose in coming was to offer garlands to the nymphs. At her breast she carried a precious burden, her son, not yet a year old, whom she was suckling with her warm milk. Near the lake the water lotus was flowering, bright as Tyrian purple, giving promise of fruits to come. Dryope had plucked some blossoms from the tree, to offer them as playthings to her son. I was there too, and was on the point of doing as my sister had done, when I saw drops of blood falling from the flowers, and a shudder running through the branches. The reason for this, as the peasants told us when it was too late, was that the nymph Lotis, fleeing from the obscenities of Priapus, had been turned into the lotus tree, changing her appearance, but keeping her own name.

'My sister had known nothing of this, and was completely terrified. She wanted to retreat, to depart from the spot, after offering prayers to the nymphs. But her feet were held fast by a root and, when she struggled to tear them free, she could move only the upper part of her body. Pliant bark, growing up from the ground, gradually gripped the whole length of her thighs. When she saw this, she made to tear her hair, but filled her hand with leaves – leaves covered all her head. The boy Amphissos (for such was the name that his grandfather

Eurytus had given him) felt his mother's breasts hardening, and the milky fluid refused to come when he sucked. I stood there, and watched this cruel stroke of fate, and yet I could not help you, my sister. Still, as far as I was able, I delayed the growth of the tree, throwing my arms round the rising trunk and branches, wishing, you may be sure, that I might be buried beneath that same bark.

'Then Dryope's husband, Andraemon, and her unhappy father too, arrived to look for her. When they asked me where she was, I showed them the lotus. They kissed the warm wood and, flinging themselves down, clung to the roots of the tree that was theirs. Nothing now remained of my dear sister, except her face: all the rest was tree. Tears sprinkled the leaves that were growing from her wretched body, and while she could, while her lips afforded a passage for her voice, she poured out her misery in such laments as these: "If there is any truth in the words of the wretched, I swear by the gods that I have not deserved this wicked treatment. I am being punished without having committed any crime. My life was blameless – if my words are false, may I lose the leaves I bear, wither away, and be chopped down and burned. Take, then, this baby from his mother's branches, give him to a nurse, and let him often drink his milk and play beneath my boughs. When he can talk, let him greet his mother, and sadly say, 'My mother is hidden inside this tree-trunk.' Let him beware of pools, and not pick flowers from trees, but believe that all fruitful shrubs are the bodies of goddesses! Dear husband, farewell, and you, my sister, and my father. I pray you, as you love me, preserve me from the blows of the sharp axe, and save my leaves from grazing cattle. Now, since I may not bend down to you, stretch your arms here to me, reach up to my lips while they can be kissed, and lift up my little son. I can say no more: for now the soft bark is creeping over my white neck, and I am being enclosed by the tree-top. Take your hands from my eyes! Without any tribute from you, let the spreading wood shroud my dying gaze." As her lips stopped speaking, they ceased to be, but long after her body was transformed, the new-made branches kept their warmth.'

While Iole, daughter of Eurytus, was recounting this miracle, and Alcmene, though there were tears in her own eyes, was gently wiping away those of her daughter-in-law, a new wonder arrested their sobs. There in the lofty doorway stood Iolaus, almost a boy again, with the first down of manhood covering his cheeks, and his features restored to their youthful appearance. Hebe, Juno's daughter, had been induced by the prayers of her husband, Hercules, to grant him this boon.

She was about to swear that she would never again bestow such a gift on any other, but Themis stopped her, and explained why she did so. 'Thebes,' she said, 'is even now entering upon a civil war, a conflict in which none but Jupiter will be able to conquer Capaneus: two brothers will die, each by the other's hand: and the prophet Amphiaraus, while still alive, will see his own ghost, as the ground yawns open to receive him. Then his son, avenging one parent by slaying the other, will by one and the same deed free himself from guilt and involve himself in crime. Distraught by his troubles, driven out of his mind and from his home, he will be harried by the sight of the Furies' faces, and by his mother's shade: till his wife Callirhoe, Achelous' daughter, demands the fatal golden necklace, and thereby brings about his death. For the sword of Phegeus, his first wife's father, driven deep into his side, will drain his lifeblood. After all this, Callirhoe will humbly beg great Jupiter to increase the age of her infant sons, and bring them to their prime, that there may be no delay in avenging her victorious husband's death. Jupiter, moved by her pleas, will obtain for her in advance this boon which you, his stepdaughter and sister-in-law, bestow, and will turn the boys into men before their age is ripe for manhood.'

When Themis, the goddess who foresees what is to come, had uttered these prophecies, the gods muttered together, voicing various complaints, and murmuring to know why others should not be permitted to grant those same gifts. Aurora, daughter of the Titan Pallas, complained because her husband was so old: gentle Ceres lamented that Iasion was growing grey, Vulcan demanded that Erichthonius should have his youth renewed, and Venus too, anxious about the future, wanted to make a bargain for restoring Anchises to his prime. Every god had someone in whom he was interested, and the disorderly tumult provoked by their favouritism was increasing, till Jupiter opened his lips and spoke: 'If you have any respect for me at all,' he said, 'tell me, where are you heading? Does any one of you think himself so powerful as to prevail even over the fates? It was by fate that the youth which Iolaus had lost was restored to him, it is by fate's decree that Callirhoe's sons are to grow up before their time, not because of bribery or force. You too are ruled by fate and, that you may bear your lot more cheerfully, even I am beneath its sway. If I had the power to change the fates, my dear Aeacus would not be bowed down by advancing years, Rhadamanthus would always enjoy the flower of youth, and so would my Minos, who is now scorned because of his bitter burden of age, and no longer controls things as he did before.' Jove's words moved the hearts of the gods and, when they saw Rhadamanthus, Aeacus, and Minos worn out with years, no one of them pursued his own complaints.

When Minos was in his prime, his very name had terrified great nations: but now he was weak, and very much afraid of Miletus, the son of Deione and Apollo; for the latter was young and strong, and proud of being Phoebus' son. Minos believed that Miletus was plotting an insurrection against his kingdom, but he did not dare to banish him from his native land. However, Miletus fled of his own accord; he crossed the waters of the Aegean in his swift ship and built a walled city in the land of Asia, that still bears the name of its founder.

There dwelt Cyanee, the lovely daughter of the river Maeander, whose course winds back so often upon itself. While she was wandering by the curving banks of her father's stream, she became known to Miletus, and bore him twins, Byblis and Caunus. Byblis, who was seized with passionate love for her own brother, Apollo's grandson, affords a warning to other girls to love only what is permitted. Not as a sister loves a brother did she love Caunus, not as she should have done. At first, indeed, she did not understand her desire at all, and thought that there was nothing wrong in exchanging frequent kisses, or throwing her arms round her brother's neck. For long she deceived herself with the false pretence that this was family affection: but gradually her love strayed from the normal course, and when she was likely to see her brother, she came in her best attire, over-anxious to look beautiful, and jealous of anyone there who was lovelier than herself. She still did not realize what was wrong with her, and at that stage in her affection did not put her feelings into words: but none the less desire was seething inwardly. Already she called Caunus 'lord', and shunned the names that showed they were related, preferring that he should call her Byblis, rather than 'sister'. While she was awake she did not dare to admit such impure desires into her mind: but when she was peacefully relaxed in slumber, she often saw the one she loved, imagined that she lay in her brother's embrace, and blushed although she was asleep. Waking, she lay still for a long time, seeking to recall the vision of her dream, and in her confusion exclaimed: 'Unhappy creature that I am! What is the meaning of that dream? How I hope it will not come true! Why do I see these visions? My brother is handsome, it is true, in all men's eyes, however prejudiced they may be: I admire him, and if he were not my brother, I could love him. He would make me a suitable husband: but it is my misfortune that I am his sister. Still, provided that I do not try to do anything like this in my waking moments, I pray that sleep may often bring me such dreams. No one can witness dreams, and the pleasure we seem to enjoy does no harm. O Venus, O Cupid, winged son of that tender mother, what joys I have experienced! What unconcealed desire took possession of me as I lay, melting with passion to my very marrow! What joy in the remembrance, even though my pleasure was short-lived – for night hurried on its way, jealous of my doings.

'Oh, if I could only change my name, and marry you, what a good daughter-in-law could I be to your father, Caunus, what a good son-in-law you could be to mine! If only the gods would let us share all things, except our family! There I would wish you were of nobler birth than I. But now you, who are so handsome, will make someone else the mother of your children, while to me, since an evil fate allotted us the same parents, you will be only a brother. The one thing we shall have in common is the thing which keeps us apart. But what, then, is the meaning of my dreams? What importance do they have? Or can even dreams be important? The gods forbid!

'Yet surely gods have married their sisters? Saturn was wedded to Ops, though she was related to him by birth, Oceanus married Tethys, and the ruler of Olympus took Juno for his wife. But the gods have their own laws: what is the use of trying to relate human conduct to the ways of heaven, when they are governed by different rules? I shall drive this forbidden passion from my heart or else, if I cannot do so, I pray that I may die before I yield. As I lie dead upon my bier, let my brother give his kisses to my corpse!

'In any case, the thing I long for requires our mutual consent – grant that it pleases me, in my brother's eyes it will be a crime. And yet the sons of Aeolus did not shrink from marriage with their sisters: but

216

how did I come to know of them? Why have I these examples
ready? Where am I heading? Away, away with such unclean desires.
Let me not love my brother except as a sister should. All the same, if
he had fallen in love with me first, perhaps I might have yielded to his
mad passion: should I then seek the favours which I would not refuse,
were they asked of me? Can you speak out, Byblis? Can you confess
the truth? Yes! Love will force me to it. I will be able! Or, if modesty
closes my lips, a secret message will reveal my hidden love.'

This was her resolve, and this decision prevailed over her doubts.
She raised herself on her side, leaning on her left arm, and said: 'Let
him decide for himself. I shall confess my mad desire! Alas, where am
I drifting? What flame has set my heart on fire?' Then she composed
her letter, and proceeded to write it down, with trembling fingers.
She grasped her pen in her right hand, the other held blank writing-
tablets. She began, and hesitated: wrote, and found fault with what
she had written, set down a word and then erased it, changed what
she had said, blamed it or praised it, alternately laid aside the tablets,
and picked them up again. She did not know what she wanted, and
became displeased with whatever she was about to do. On her face
was an expression of mingled shame and boldness. She had written
the words 'Your sister', but decided to scratch them out and, smooth-
ing the wax, wrote as follows: 'One who loves you sends you this,
wishing you the happiness that she will never have, unless you give it
her. I am ashamed, ashamed indeed, to reveal my name, but if you ask
what I require of you, I should like to plead my cause without mention
of my name, and not be known as Byblis until I am sure of having my
prayers granted. You can have evidence of my wounded heart by
looking at my pale cheeks, my thinness, the expression of my face, my
eyes, so often wet with tears. My sighs, that have no apparent cause,
tell the same tale, my frequent embraces, and my kisses which as
perhaps you have noticed, can be felt to be different from those of a
sister. Yet, though my heart is so deeply affected, though the flame
of mad desire burns within me, still, as the gods are my witnesses, I
have done everything to bring myself at length to my senses, and have
long fought miserably to escape Cupid's violent attacks. I have under-
gone more suffering than you would think it possible for a girl to
endure: now I am compelled to confess myself beaten and make timid
overtures begging for your help. You alone can save or destroy the

one who loves you. Choose which you will do. It is no enemy who makes this prayer to you, but a girl who, most nearly related, seeks to be related more nearly still, and would fain be bound to you by closer ties. Let old men know the laws, and inquire into what they allow, what may be done and what may not, observing all the niceties of the statutes. A love that scorns prudence is in keeping with our years. What the law permits, as yet we do not know, but believe all things legitimate, following the example of the mighty gods. No harsh father, no regard for reputation or fear of scandal will impede us. Even if there were reason to fear, we shall conceal the sweets of stolen love under the names of brother and sister. I am free to speak with you in private, and we embrace and kiss in public. Is the one thing still lacking so important? Pity one who confesses her love, and would not have done so, had she not been driven to it by the extremity of her passion. Do not earn the distinction of having your name carved on my tomb, as the one responsible for my death!'

Tracing out this message, doomed to disappointment, she filled the tablets and, when there was no more space, added the last line in the margin. Then she immediately sealed the story of her guilt with the impress of her jewelled signet, moistening it with tears, for her tongue was dry. Shamefacedly she called one of her servants and, in coaxing and anxious tones, made her request. 'My faithful servant,' she said, 'take this message to my – ' and after a long pause, she finished: 'brother.' As she was handing over the tablets, they slipped and fell from her hands, an omen which distressed her: but she sent them none the less.

The servant approached her brother and, when a suitable opportunity offered, handed over Byblis' secret confession. Maeander's grandson took the tablets but, after reading only a part, threw them from him, in a sudden burst of dismayed anger. He was scarcely able to keep his hands from the throat of the trembling messenger. 'You rogue!' he cried, 'to sponsor this incestuous affair! Flee while you can! If your death would not bring me dishonour, I would have killed you!' The messenger fled in terror, and reported to his mistress the fierce words which Caunus had spoken.

When Byblis heard that she had been scorned, she grew pale and shivered, in the grip of an icy chill. Still, as her senses returned, her mad passion revived too; in a feeble voice, scarcely more than a whisper, she said: 'It is just what I deserved! Why did I rashly inform him of my wounded heart? Why was I in such a hurry to set down hastily, in a letter, thoughts which should have been hidden? I should first have found out his feelings, by talking to him in a way that committed me to nothing: I should have tested the wind, with close-reefed sail, in case it should prove unfavourable, and then have voyaged safely over the sea, instead of allowing winds still untried to fill my canvas, as I have done now, with the result that I am being carried upon the rocks, overwhelmed and drowned beneath the entire ocean, and there is no way of reversing my course.

'Was I not warned by unmistakable signs not to indulge my love, when the tablets fell from my hands as I was giving orders for their delivery, showing me that my hopes, too, would come tumbling down? Should I not have changed either the day for carrying out my scheme, or the scheme itself – but preferably only the day? The god himself gave me warning, offered me clear signs of what would happen, had I not been out of my senses. I should have spoken to my brother myself, and revealed my passion to him in person, instead of committing my words to a letter. He would have seen my tears, seen the love in my face, and I could have said more than letters can contain. I could have thrown my arms round his neck, even though he was reluctant and, if rejected, could have pretended to be on the point of death, clasped his feet, and flung myself prostrate before him, begging for my life. I should have done everything possible and, if my pleas taken singly failed to move him, yet all combined might have touched his hard heart.

'The messenger I sent may have been at fault: he did not approach my brother in the right way, or did not choose a suitable time: did not wait, perhaps, for a moment when he would be free to listen. Those are the reasons for my failure! For indeed, Caunus is not the son of a tigress, the heart in his breast is not flinty stone or solid iron or adamant, he was not suckled on a lioness's milk. He shall be won! I must approach him again. Never, as long as breath remains, will I grow weary of trying. If I could undo what I have done, it would be best never to have begun this plan: but the next best thing is to carry it out by force. Were I to abandon my prayers, still he could not help but remember all the time what I had dared to do, and the mere fact that I gave up would make it seem that my love was only a whim, or

219

even that I was testing him, and trying to make him fall into a trap: or at any rate, he would think me the slave, not of this god who weighs upon me so heavily and scorches my heart, but merely of lust. In short, I cannot now be innocent of wrong-doing, I have written to him, and importuned him, and my wish has been dishonourable. Even though I do no more, I cannot be called guiltless. The future can do much to fulfil my hopes, but can add little to my wickedness.'

Such were her words. Her mind was so unsettled and so much at war with itself that, though she was ashamed of having approached her brother, she took pleasure in approaching him again, surpassing all the bounds of decency in her unhappiness, and laying herself open to constant rebuffs. Finally, when there was no end to the business Caunus fled from such shamelessness, left the country, and built himself a new city in a foreign land.

Men say that, when this happened, grief drove Miletus' daughter completely out of her mind. She tore the garments from her breast, and beat her arms in frenzy. Now she openly revealed her mania to everyone, and admitted her hopes of indulging her forbidden passion. When these hopes were frustrated, she left her country, and the home she loathed, and followed in the tracks of her fleeing brother. The women of Bubassus saw her as she passed through their broad lands, howling like one of the Thracian bacchants who, roused to frenzy by Bacchus' thyrsus, celebrate his rites every three years, when his festival comes round. Leaving these regions, she wandered through the country of the Carians, and of the armed Leleges. She made her way through Lycia, and beyond Cragos and Limyre, beyond the waters of Xanthus and the ridge which was the home of the Chimaera, that monster with a lion's head and chest, the tail of a snake, and a body all aflame.

The woods were thinning when, weary with her pursuit, Byblis collapsed and lay where she fell, her hair spread out upon the hard ground, and her face pressed into the fallen leaves. Often the Lelegeian nymphs tried to raise her in their soft arms; often they urged her to find a cure for her love, and tried to comfort her, but she was deaf to them. She uttered not a word, but lay digging her nails into the green grass, watering the meadow with a river of tears. They say that the nymphs fashioned a channel for these tears, which could never run dry: what greater gift could they offer? After that, just as resin oozes from a gash in a pine tree's bark, or sticky bitumen from heavy soil, as water, frozen by winter's chill, melts under the warmth of the sun, when Zephyr's gentle breath returns, so Byblis, Phoebus' grandchild, was consumed by her own tears and changed into a fountain, which even now wells up in that valley, beneath a dark ilex tree, and still bears the name of its mistress.

The report of this new miracle might well have filled the hundred cities of Crete with talk, had not the island recently experienced a miracle nearer home, in the transformation of Iphis. On the borders of the territory of Knossos, in the land of Phaestus, there lived a man, Ligdus by name, of humble family and undistinguished, but free born. His wealth was on a par with his rank, but his life and his loyalty were beyond reproach. His wife Telethusa was about to have a child and, when it was almost time for the baby to be born, he advised her as follows: 'I am praying for two things, that you should be delivered with the least possible pain, and that you may have a boy. A girl is more of a burden, and fortune has not given me the means to support one. So, though I pray it may not happen, if a girl is born, she must be put to death. It is not that I want to order this: I know what is due to family affection and pray to be forgiven.' As he spoke, both he and his wife burst into floods of tears. Though he had given these instructions, he wept no less bitterly than she to whom they had been given. None the less, it was in vain that his wife begged and prayed Ligdus not to narrow down her hopes so: her husband had made up his mind.

Now when Telethusa could scarcely carry the full-grown burden which weighed down her womb, Inachus' daughter, Io, appeared to her in her dreams, in the middle of the night, and stood, or seemed to stand, before her bed, accompanied by a retinue of divinities. Crescent horns adorned the goddess' brow, which was wreathed with yellow corn ears, wrought from shining gold, and she was decked in royal splendour. With her was the dog Anubis, holy Bubastis, Apis with his dappled skin, and the god who never speaks but, finger to his lips, advises silence. The sacred rattles were there to see, and Osiris for whom Io is never finished searching, as well as the foreign serpent, full of drowsy poisons. Then the goddess spoke to Telethusa, as if she had been awakened from sleep, and were really seeing all this.

'Telethusa, you who are one of my own company, forget your bitter anxiety, and deceive your husband in regard to this command.

Do not hesitate to rear your child, when Lucina has delivered you, whatever it may be. I am a helpful goddess, and bring my aid to those who ask it in their prayers; you will not complain that you have worshipped a deity who shows no gratitude.' When she had given this advice, Io left the room. The Cretan Telethusa rose joyfully from her bed and, stretching her innocent hands to the stars, humbly prayed that her dreams might come true.

As her pains increased, and the burden that she carried forced itself of its own accord into life, a female child was born, without its father's knowledge. The mother pretended that it was a boy, and ordered it to be reared. Her word was not doubted, and no one but the nurse knew of the deception. The child's father made good his vows, and called the baby Iphis, after its grandfather. The mother was pleased with the name, because it was used both for boys and for girls, and in this respect she was not deceiving anyone. From that time on, the deceit she had practised was kept hidden by various pretences, well justified in the sight of heaven: the child was dressed as a boy, and its features, whether they were supposed to be those of boy or girl, would have been accounted handsome in either.

Now, when Iphis reached the age of thirteen, her father arranged a marriage between her and Ianthe, the fair-haired daughter of the Cretan Telestes, of all the women of Phaestus the most richly endowed with beauty. She and Iphis were alike in age, equally good-looking, and had received the first elements of their education from the same masters. As a result love had touched their innocent hearts, and wounded both alike: but their beliefs about what lay in store for them were very different. Ianthe was looking forward to marriage, longing for the time when the wedding that had been arranged would take place: for she believed that the one whom she thought to be a man would then be her husband. Iphis loved a girl whom she despaired of ever being able to enjoy, and this very frustration increased her ardour. A girl herself, she was in love with one of her own kind, and could scarcely keep back her tears, as she said:

'What is to be the end of this for me, caught as I am in the snare of a strange and unnatural kind of love, which none has known before? If the gods wished to spare my life, they should have spared it: if not, if they wished to destroy me, they might at least have visited me with some ordinary misfortune, of the sort to which mankind is prone.

Cows do not burn with love for cows, nor mares for mares. It is the ram which excites the ewe, the hind follows the stag, birds too mate in the same way, and never among all the animals does one female fall in love with another. How I wish that I had never been born! That no monstrosity might be lacking in Crete, the daughter of the sun fell in love with a bull – but at least she was a woman, he a male! If the truth be told, my love is more crazy than hers, for she at least pursued a desire that offered some hope of fulfilment: by her tricks, and with the help of an image of a cow, she induced the bull to mount her, and the creature she deceived was a male lover. But though all the world's talent were concentrated here, though Daedalus himself were to fly back on his waxen wings, what could he do? Could all his magic arts change me from girl to boy? Could he change you, Ianthe? No! Pull yourself together, Iphis, be firm, and shake off this foolish, useless emotion. Consider what you were born, unless you are deceiving yourself, as well as everyone else; seek what is permitted to you, and fasten your affections on what a woman should love. It is hope which conceives and nourishes desire: and your case denies you hope. No guardian, no precautions on the part of an anxious husband, no stern father keeps you from the embraces which you long to enjoy; the one you love does not refuse her favours when you ask. Still, she cannot be yours, nor can you be happy, whatever happens, though gods and men should strive for you. Even now, none of my prayers go unanswered: the gods are kind, and have given me all they could. My father, my sweetheart herself, and her father too, all wish the same as I. But Nature is unwilling. She alone stands in my way, but she is more powerful than all the rest. See, the time for which I prayed has come! My wedding day is at hand, and now Ianthe will be mine: yet she will not be. I shall thirst in the midst of the waters. Why do you, Juno, matron of honour, or you, Hymen, come to this ceremony, at which there is no bridegroom, where two brides are being wed?' After that, Iphis fell silent.

Ianthe's love was as passionate as the other's, and she prayed that Hymen should come quickly. But Telethusa, fearing what Ianthe prayed for, kept postponing the occasion, now inventing an illness to cause delay, and constantly putting forward bad omens or dreams as an excuse for waiting. At last there came a time when she had used up all the pretexts she could find, and the delayed marriage ceremony was at hand: only one day remained. Telethusa tore the ribbons from her daughter's head, and from her own: with hair all dishevelled, she clasped the altar and cried: 'O Isis, you who dwell in Paraetonium and in the lands of Mareotis, in Pharos and by the Nile with its seven horns, bring me your aid, and heal my distress. Once upon a time, goddess, I beheld you, and these, your ornaments, and recognized them all, your retinue and the torches and the noise of your rattles. I listened to your behests and stored them in my memory. The fact that my daughter lives, and that I am not punished for it, is due to your counsel and your bounty. Pity us both, and grant me your help!' Her tears flowed as she finished speaking. The goddess seemed to make her altars move – she did indeed move them – and the doors of the temple trembled: her horns shone like those of the moon, and the piercing rattle shrilled. Not entirely reassured, but gladdened by the good omen, the mother left the temple. Iphis accompanied her as she walked along, and moved with a longer stride than usual. Her face lost its fair complexion, her hair looked shorter, plain and simple in style, her features sharpened, and her strength increased. She showed more energy than a woman has – for she who had lately been a woman had become a man! Carry your gifts to the temples, happy pair, and rejoice, confident and unafraid! They bore their gifts to the temples, and set up an inscription as well, which consisted of a short verse:

> The tributes Iphis promised, as a maid,
> By Iphis, now a man, are duly paid.

The rays of the next day's dawn had revealed the wide world, when Venus, Juno, and Hymen too, assembled for the wedding ceremony, and the boy Iphis gained his own Ianthe.

BOOK X

❋

FROM there Hymen, clad in his saffron robes, was summoned by Orpheus, and made his way across the vast reaches of the sky to the shores of the Cicones. But Orpheus' invitation to the god to attend his marriage was of no avail, for though he was certainly present, he did not bring good luck. His expression was gloomy, and he did not sing his accustomed refrain. Even the torch he carried sputtered and smoked, bringing tears to the eyes, and no amount of tossing could make it burn. The outcome was even worse than the omens foretold: for while the new bride was wandering in the meadows, with her band of naiads, a serpent bit her ankle, and she sank lifeless to the ground. The Thracian poet mourned her loss; when he had wept for her to the full in the upper world, he made so bold as to descend through the gate of Taenarus to the Styx, to try to rouse the sympathy of the shades as well. There he passed among the thin ghosts, the wraiths of the dead, till he reached Persephone and her lord, who holds sway over these dismal regions, the king of the shades. Then, accompanying his words with the music of his lyre, he said:

'Deities of this lower world, to which all we of mortal birth descend, if I have your permission to dispense with rambling insincerities and speak the simple truth, I did not come here to see the dim haunts of Tartarus, nor yet to chain Medusa's monstrous dog, with its three heads and snaky ruff. I came because of my wife, cut off before she reached her prime when she trod on a serpent and it poured its poison into her veins. I wished to be strong enough to endure my grief, and I will not deny that I tried to do so: but Love was too much for me. He is a god well-known in the world above; whether he may be so here too, I do not know, but I imagine that he is familiar to you also and, if there is any truth in the story of that rape of long ago, then you yourselves were brought together by Love. I beg you, by these awful regions, by this boundless chaos, and by the silence of your vast realms, weave again Eurydice's destiny, brought too swiftly to a close. We mortals and all that is ours are fated to fall to you, and after a little time, sooner or later, we hasten to this one abode. We are all on our way here, this is our final home, and yours the most lasting sway over the human race. My wife, like the rest, when she has completed her proper span of years will, in the fullness of time, come within your power. I ask as a gift from you only the enjoyment of her; but if the fates refuse her a reprieve, I have made up my mind that I do not wish to return either. You may exult in my death as well as hers!'

As he sang these words to the music of his lyre, the bloodless ghosts were in tears: Tantalus made no effort to reach the waters that ever shrank away, Ixion's wheel stood still in wonder, the vultures ceased to gnaw Tityus' liver, the daughters of Danaus rested from their pitchers, and Sisyphus sat idle on his rock. Then for the first time, they say, the cheeks of the Furies were wet with tears, for they were overcome by his singing. The king and queen of the underworld could not bear to refuse his pleas. They called Eurydice. She was among the ghosts who had but newly come, and walked slowly because of her injury. Thracian Orpheus received her, but on condition that he must not look back until he had emerged from the valleys of Avernus or else the gift he had been given would be taken from him.

Up the sloping path, through the mute silence they made their way, up the steep dark track, wrapped in impenetrable gloom, till they had almost reached the surface of the earth. Here, anxious in case his wife's strength be failing and eager to see her, the lover looked behind him, and straightway Eurydice slipped back into the depths. Orpheus stretched out his arms, straining to clasp her and be clasped; but the hapless man touched nothing but yielding air. Eurydice, dying now a second time, uttered no complaint against her husband. What was there to complain of, but that she had been loved? With a last farewell which scarcely reached his ears, she fell back again into the same place from which she had come.

At his wife's second death, Orpheus was completely stunned. He was like that timid fellow who, when he saw three-headed Cerberus led along, chained by the middle one of his three necks, was turned to stone in every limb, and lost his fear only when he lost his original nature too: or like Olenus and hapless Lethaea, once fond lovers, now stones set on well-watered Ida, all because Lethaea was too confident in her beauty, while Olenus sought to take her guilt upon his own shoulders, and wished to be considered the culprit. In vain did the poet long to cross the Styx a second time, and prayed that he might do so. The ferryman thrust him aside. For seven days, unkempt and neglected, he sat on the river bank, without tasting food: grief, anxiety and tears were his nourishment. Then he retired to lofty Rhodope and windswept Haemus, complaining of the cruelty of the gods of Erebus.

Three times the sun had reached the watery sign of Pisces, that brings the year to a close. Throughout this time Orpheus had shrunk from loving any woman, either because of his unhappy experience, or because he had pledged himself not to do so. In spite of this there were many who were fired with a desire to marry the poet, many were indignant to find themselves repulsed. However, Orpheus preferred to centre his affections on boys of tender years, and to enjoy the brief spring and early flowering of their youth: he was the first to introduce this custom among the people of Thrace.

On the top of a certain hill was a level stretch of open ground, covered with green turf. There was no shelter from the sun, but when the divinely-born poet seated himself there and struck his melodious strings, shady trees moved to the spot. The oak tree of Chaonia and poplars, Phaethon's sisters, crowded round, along with Jupiter's great oak, with its lofty branches, and soft lime trees and beeches, and the virgin laurel, brittle hazels, and ash trees, that are used for spear shafts, smooth firs and the holm oak, bowed down with acorns, the genial sycamore, and the variegated maple, willows that grow by the rivers and the water-loving lotus, evergreen box, slender tamarisks, myrtles double-hued, and viburnum with its dark blue berries. There was ivy too, trailing its tendrils, and leafy vines, vine-clad elms and mountain ash, pitchpine and wild strawberry, laden with rosy fruit, waving palms, the victor's prize, and the pine, its leaves gathered up into a shaggy crest, the favourite tree of Cybele, the mother of the gods: for her priest Attis exchanged his human shape for this, and hardened into its trunk.

With the rest of the throng came the cypress, shaped like the cones that mark the turning point on the race-course: though now a tree, it was once a boy, dearly loved by the god who strings both lyre and bow.

This is the story. There was once a magnificent stag, sacred to the nymphs who live in the fields of Carthaea, whose branching antlers cast deep shade over its head. These antlers gleamed with gold and a necklace of precious stones, encircling the animal's silky neck, hung down over its shoulders. On its forehead swayed a silver charm, kept in place by fine leather straps, which it had worn since it was born, and pearls glistened in either ear, close by its hollow temples. This stag was quite without fear and, its natural timidity forgotten, used to visit people's houses and hold out its neck, even to strangers, to be stroked. But the person who was most attached to it was Cyparissus, the handsomest of the Cean boys. He used to lead it to fresh grazing, or to the waters of some crystal spring, and wove wreaths of different kinds of flowers to hang upon its horns. Sometimes he sat on its back, like a horseman on his horse, and gleefully guided the animal's soft mouth this way and that, by means of scarlet reins.

One summer day, at noon, when the curving arms of the shore-loving Crab were being scorched by the heat of the sun, the stag was tired, and lay down to rest on the grassy ground, finding coolness in the shade of the trees. There Cyparissus unwittingly pierced it with his keen javelin. When he saw his friend cruelly wounded and dying, the boy resolved to die himself. Phoebus said all he could to comfort him, chiding him and telling him that his grief should be moderate, in proportion to its cause. Still the boy groaned and begged, as a last gift from the gods, that he should be allowed to go on mourning for ever. Now, as his blood drained away, by reason of his endless weeping, his limbs began to change to a greenish hue, and the hair which lately curled over his snowy brow bristled and stiffened, pointing upwards in a graceful crest towards the starry sky. Sadly the god Apollo sighed: 'I shall mourn for you,' he said, 'while you yourself will mourn for others, and be the constant companion of those in distress.'

Such was the grove which Orpheus had drawn round him, and now he sat in the midst of a gathering of wild creatures, and a host of birds. He tested the chords of his lyre, striking them with his thumb, till his ear was satisfied that the notes they played, though different, were all in tune. Then he began to sing: 'Since all things bow before Jove's might, begin my song with Jove, O Muse, my mother! Often ere now I have told of Jove's power: in loftier strains I have sung of the giants and those victorious thunderbolts which were hurled down upon the plain of Phlegra, but now I need a lighter refrain to tell of boys whom the gods have loved, and of girls who, seized with unlawful passion, have paid the penalty for their amorous desires.

'The king of the gods was once fired with love for Phrygian Ganymede, and when that happened Jupiter found another shape preferable to his own. Wishing to turn himself into a bird, he none the less scorned to change into any save that which can carry his thunderbolts. Then without delay, beating the air on borrowed pinions, he snatched away the shepherd of Ilium, who even now mixes the winecups, and supplies Jove with nectar, to the annoyance of Juno.

'Hyacinthus too, the boy from Amyclae, would have been given a place in heaven by Phoebus, had cruel destiny allowed the god time to set him there. Still, he was made immortal in such fashion as was possible, and whenever spring drives winter off, and the Ram succeeds the watery sign of Pisces, every year he comes to life again, and grows as a flower in the green turf. My father, Phoebus, loved Hyacinthus beyond all other mortals, and Delphi, the centre of the earth, lost its presiding deity, while the god haunted Eurotas and Sparta's unwalled city, neglecting his harp and his arrows. Heedless of his old habits, Apollo was willing to carry hunting nets, or direct a pack of hounds, as he accompanied Hyacinthus over the rough mountain ridges and, by constant companionship, added fuel to the fire of his love.

'One day, when the sun was halfway between the night that was over and the night that was to come, equally far from both, the god and the boy stripped off their garments, rubbed their bodies, till they gleamed, with rich olive oil, and began to compete with one another in throwing the broad discus. Phoebus threw first: he poised the discus, then flung it through the air. Its weight scattered the clouds in its path and then, after a long time, it fell back again to its natural element, the earth. It was a throw which showed skill and strength combined. Immediately the young Spartan, in his eagerness for the game, ran forward without stopping to think, in a hurry to pick up the discus, but it bounced back off the hard ground, and rose into the air, striking him full in the face. The god grew as pale as the boy himself: he caught up Hyacinthus' limp frame, and tried to staunch the grim wound, rubbing warmth into the limbs, and applying herbs to stay the fleeting spirit. But Apollo's art was of no avail – the wound was beyond any cure. Just as violets in a garden, or stiff poppies or lilies with clustering yellow stamens, once their stems are broken, no longer stand erect but, drooping, let their withered tops hang down and, with lowered heads, gaze upon the ground, so did the head of the dying Hyacinthus droop. His neck, drained of its strength, was a burden to itself, and sank down upon his shoulders. "You are slipping away from me, Hyacinthus, robbed of the flower of your youth," said Phoebus. "Here before my eyes I see the wound that killed you and reproaches me. You are the cause of my grief, as of my guilt, for your death must be ascribed to my hand. I am responsible for killing you. Yet how was I at fault, unless taking part in a game can be called a fault, unless I can be blamed for loving you? I wish that I might give my life in exchange for yours, as you so well deserve, or die along with you! But, since I am bound by the laws of fate, that cannot be. Still you will always be with me, your name constantly upon my lips, never forgotten. When I strike the chords of my lyre, and when I sing, my songs and music will tell of you. You will be changed into a new kind of flower and will show markings that imitate my sobs. Further, a time will come when the bravest of heroes will be connected with this flower, and his name will be read on these same petals."

'While Apollo, who cannot lie, was uttering these words, the blood which had flowed to the ground, and stained the grass, ceased to be blood, and a flower brighter than Tyrian purple grew up and took on the shape of a lily: but it was purple in colour, where lilies are silvery white. Phoebus was responsible for so honouring Hyacinthus, by changing him into a flower; not content with that, he himself inscribed his own grief upon the petals, and the hyacinth bears the mournful letters AI AI marked upon it. Nor was Sparta ashamed of having produced Hyacinthus, for he is honoured there to this very day, and every year the Hyacinthian games are celebrated with festive displays, in accordance with ancient usage.

'But if, by chance, you were to ask the rich mining district of Amathus whether it was through any wish of its own that it produced the Propoetides, it would deny the suggestion as resolutely as it would have denied any wish to produce the men who once earned the name of Cerastae from having a pair of horns on their foreheads. Before the doors of those Cerastae stood an altar to Jupiter, god of hospitality. If any stranger who did not know of their crimes had seen this blood-stained altar, he would have thought that the sacrifices offered there were suckling calves or young sheep of Amathis. But it was their guests they slew! Venus was so sickened by their unspeakable offerings that the gentle goddess was preparing to abandon her cities, and to leave the district of Ophiusia. But she hesitated: "What crime have my cities committed," she said, "or those regions which I love? What fault have I to find with them? Rather let these wicked people be punished either by exile or by death, or by something intermedi-ate between the two: and what could that be, except to be trans-formed into something other than they are?" While she was debating what transformation they should undergo her eyes fell upon their horns, and she bethought herself that these could be left to them: so she changed them into sturdy bullocks.

'As for the loathsome Propoetides, they dared to deny the divinity of Venus. The story goes that as a result of this, they were visited by the wrath of the goddess, and were the first women to lose their good names by prostituting themselves in public. Then, as all sense of shame left them, the blood hardened in their cheeks, and it required only a slight alteration to transform them into stony flints.

'When Pygmalion saw these women, living such wicked lives, he was revolted by the many faults which nature has implanted in the female sex, and long lived a bachelor existence, without any wife to share his home. But meanwhile, with marvellous artistry, he skilfully carved a snowy ivory statue. He made it lovelier than any woman born, and fell in love with his own creation. The statue had all the appearance of a real girl, so that it seemed to be alive, to want to move, did not modesty forbid. So cleverly did his art conceal its art. Pygmalion gazed in wonder, and in his heart there rose a passionate love for this image of a human form. Often he ran his hands over the work, feeling it to see whether it was flesh or ivory, and would not yet admit that ivory was all it was. He kissed the statue, and imagined that it kissed him back, spoke to it and embraced it, and thought he felt his fingers sink into the limbs he touched, so that he was afraid lest a bruise appear where he had pressed the flesh. Some-times he addressed it in flattering speeches, sometimes brought the kind of presents that girls enjoy: shells and polished pebbles, little birds and flowers of a thousand hues, lilies and painted balls, and drops of amber which fall from the trees that were once Phaethon's sisters. He dressed the limbs of his statue in woman's robes, and put rings on its fingers, long necklaces round its neck. Pearls hung from its ears, and chains were looped upon its breast. All this finery became the image well, but it was no less lovely unadorned. Pygmalion then placed the statue on a couch that was covered with cloths of Tyrian purple, laid its head to rest on soft down pillows, as if it could appreciate them, and called it his bedfellow.

'The festival of Venus, which is celebrated with the greatest pomp all through Cyprus, was now in progress, and heifers, their crooked horns gilded for the occasion, had fallen at the altar as the axe struck their snowy necks. Smoke was rising from the incense, when Pygmalion, having made his offering, stood by the altar and timidly prayed, saying: "If you gods can give all things, may I have as my wife, I pray – " he did not dare to say: "the ivory maiden," but finished: "one like the ivory maid." However, golden Venus, present at her festival in person, understood what his prayers meant, and as a sign that the gods were kindly disposed, the flames burned up three times, shooting a tongue of fire into the air. When Pygmalion returned home, he made straight for the statue of the girl he loved, leaned over the couch, and kissed her. She seemed warm: he laid his lips on hers again, and touched her breast with his hands – at his touch the ivory lost its hardness, and grew soft: his fingers made an imprint on the yielding surface, just as wax of Hymettus melts in the sun and, worked by men's fingers, is fashioned into many different shapes, and made fit for use by being used. The lover stood, amazed, afraid of being mistaken, his joy tempered with doubt, and again and again stroked the object of his prayers. It was indeed a human body! The veins throbbed as he pressed them with his thumb. Then Pygmalion of Paphos was eloquent in his thanks to Venus. At long last, he pressed his lips upon living lips, and the girl felt the kisses he gave her, and blushed. Timidly raising her eyes, she saw her lover and the light of day together. The goddess Venus was present at the marriage she had arranged and, when the moon's horns had nine times been rounded into a full circle, Pygmalion's bride bore a child, Paphos, from whom the island takes its name.

'Paphos in turn had a son Cinyras, who might have been considered one of fortune's favourites, if only he had not had a family. The story I am going to tell is a horrible one: I beg that daughters and fathers should hold themselves aloof, while I sing, or if they find my songs enchanting, let them refuse to believe this part of my tale, and suppose that it never happened: or else, if they believe that it did happen, they must believe also in the punishment that followed.

'If then nature allowed such a crime to occur, I congratulate the people of Ismarus and our part of the world, and count this country happy to be so far from regions which produced such wickedness. The land of Panchaia may be rich in balsam, bear cinnamon and ze-doary, and many kinds of flowers, and exude incense from its trees, but it is not to be envied while it grows myrrh with the rest. A new tree was not worth so great a price. Even Cupid denies that it was his bow which wounded Myrrha, and defends his torches against so grievous a charge. One of the three sisters, armed with firebrands from the Styx and swollen snakes, breathed a blight upon her. It is a crime to hate one's father, but Myrrha's love was a crime worse than any hate.

'Suitors had gathered from all directions to seek her hand, and the youth of all the Eastern world had come to vie with one another for the privilege of marrying her. Choose anyone of all their company, Myrrha, provided that one man be excluded from their number!

'The girl realized what was happening to her, and fought against her horrible desire. "What am I thinking of, what am I scheming?" she said to herself. "I pray to the gods in heaven, to the holy ties of love and duty that bind children to their parents, that they may put a stop to this wickedness, and prevent me from crime – if indeed it is a crime. But is it? No fault can be found with this kind of love on the grounds that such affection is unnatural, for other animals mate without any discrimination; there is no shame for a heifer in having her father mount her, a horse takes his own daughter to wife, goats mate with the she-goats they have sired, and birds conceive from one who was himself their father. Happy creatures, who are permitted such conduct! Human interference has imposed spiteful laws, so that jealous regulations forbid what nature itself allows. Yet there are said to be nations where sons wed their mothers, fathers their daughters, to enhance their devotion by doubling the bonds of love. Alas, that I had not the good fortune to be born there, that I have to suffer for the accident of my birthplace! But why do I keep harping back to this

theme? Away with forbidden hopes! Cinyras deserves my love, but
as my father! So then, if I were not the daughter of that great king, I
could be his bride: as it is, because he is already mine, can I not have
him? Is my very closeness to him my misfortune? Would I be able to
do more, were I a stranger? Gladly would I go far away, and leave
my country, provided I could escape my guilt, but loving Cinyras as
I do, I am kept here by my wicked infatuation, so that I may be with
him, look at him, speak to him and touch and kiss him, if I may do
nothing more. Wretched girl, can you look forward to anything else?
Do you realize the confusion you are creating in names and relation-
ships? Will you be your mother's rival, your father's mistress? Will
you be called sister to your son, and mother to your brother? Have
you no fear of the Furies with their black and snaky tresses, the sisters
whom those with guilty hearts perceive, brandishing cruel torches at
their eyes and faces? Take heed, and while you are free from actual sin,
do not nurse sinful thoughts, or trespass against mighty nature's laws,
by seeking an unlawful union. Granted that you wish for this, your
position makes it impossible: your father is a good man, who observes
what is right – and oh, how I wish he were in love with me!"

'Cinyras, meanwhile, when faced with such a throng of eligible
suitors, did not know what to do: so he told the princess their names
and asked her whom she wished to marry. At first she remained
silent, gazing at her father, her mind in a turmoil, and her eyes filled
with warm tears. Cinyras put this down to girlish modesty: drying
her cheeks and kissing her, he told her not to cry. Myrrha delighted all
too keenly in the kisses he gave her. She sighed when he asked her
what kind of husband she wanted, and said: "One like you!" Not
understanding what she meant, he praised her choice, and said: "See
that you are always as devoted to me!" At the word "devoted", the
girl hung her head, conscious of her guilt.

'It was midnight, and mortal men lay relaxed in sleep, their cares
forgotten. But Cinyras' daughter was awake, consumed by a fire she
could not quench. She renewed her frenzied prayers, now despairing,
now ready to test her father's feelings, at once ashamed of her desires
and eager to fulfil them. She did not know what to do, but just as a
huge tree sways, uncertain which way to fall, watched anxiously
from every side, as it waits for the last blow of the axe which has al-
ready almost severed its trunk, so Myrrha's resolution, weakened by

renewed attacks, veered unsteadily, this way and that, and inclined in both directions. She could see no end for her love but death, no other respite from it: so she determined to die. She got up, intending to strangle herself with a noose. Binding her girdle to the top of the door-post, "Good-bye, dear Cinyras," she whispered. "Understand the reason for my death!" Then she fastened the cord around her neck, which was already drained of blood.

'Her murmured words, they say, reached the ears of the faithful nurse, who was keeping guard at the threshold of the girl's bedroom. The old woman rose and unbarred the door. When she saw Myrrha's preparations for suicide, she shrieked aloud, and all at one and the same instant beat her breast, tore her garments, and loosed her mistress' neck, tearing the noose apart. Only then had she time to weep, to throw her arms round the girl, and ask why she had tried to hang herself. Myrrha remained mute and silent. She kept her eyes fixed upon the ground, and grieved that she had been too slow, and had been discovered in her attempt to put an end to her life.

'The old nurse insisted: uncovering her white hairs, and baring her empty breasts, she begged the girl by the cradle of her infancy, by the first nourishment she had known, to tell whatever it was that was worrying her. But Myrrha turned away from her questions with a groan. The nurse was determined to find out the truth, and promised to do more than merely guard the secret safely. "Tell me," she said, "and let me help you. I am old, but not useless. If it is some spasm of madness that has upset you, I know someone who can cure that, with charms and herbs: or if someone has laid a spell on you, you will be cleansed by magic ritual. Again, if the anger of the gods is distressing you, their anger can be appeased by offerings. What else can I suppose to be the matter? Assuredly, your home and its fortunes are safe and prospering, your father and mother are alive and well."

'When Myrrha heard the name "father", she sighed, from the bottom of her heart. But even then her nurse had no suspicion of her guilty secret, though she guessed it was some love affair. Stubbornly resolved to have her own way, whatever the trouble was, she begged her mistress to tell her about it. She held the weeping girl to her wrinkled breast, clasping her closely in trembling arms. "I know what it is," she said, "you are in love! Don't be afraid, you will find me always ready to help you. Your father will never know anything about it."

'At this, Myrrha, utterly distraught, tore herself from her nurse's embrace, and flung herself on the bed, burying her face in the cushions. "Go away!" she cried. "Please go away, and spare my wretched modesty!" When the nurse pressed her further, "Go away," she screamed, "or else stop asking what is upsetting me. It is sheer wickedness, the secret you are so anxious to know." The old woman shuddered. She stretched out her hands, trembling as much from fear as from age, and threw herself at Myrrha's feet, now coaxing, now frightening her as to what she would do if she were not allowed into the secret, threatening to tell the king about his daughter's attempt to strangle herself. But if she were told about the love affair, she promised to lend her assistance.

'Myrrha lifted her head: the tears, welling from her eyes, rained down upon the nurse's breast. Often the girl tried to confess her shame, but each time she checked herself, and hid her face, in confusion, in her robes. All she would say was: "Lucky indeed is my mother, to have such a husband!" and then she sighed. A cold shudder ran over the nurse's limbs, and shook her to the very marrow: for she guessed the truth. Her white hair bristled and stood on end all over her head, and she proceeded to admonish the girl at length, to rid her, if she could, of a love so disastrous: but the other, though she knew that her nurse's warnings were right, was yet resolved to die, if she might not satisfy her love. "No!" said her nurse. "Go on living. You shall have your—" not daring to utter the word "father" she fell silent, and sealed her promises by calling heaven to be her witness.

'Now the time was come when all married women were duly celebrating the annual festival of Ceres, at which, dressed in garments of snowy white, they offer her garlands made of corn ears, the first fruits of the crops, and for nine nights hold love and all male contact in the category of forbidden things. The king's wife, Cenchreis, was there with the rest, taking part in the secret rites. So, while the king's bed was empty of its lawful occupant, the nurse, with misguided eagerness, waiting till Cinyras was drowsy with wine, told him of the girl who was in love with him, altering nothing but her name, and praised her beauty. Asked how old the girl was, "The same age as Myrrha," she said. Then the king bade her bring the girl to him. The nurse went home, and cried to Myrrha: "Rejoice, my darling, we have won!" The joy felt by the unhappy princess was not wholehearted, for she had a presentiment of evil that made her uneasy: still, her mind was so much at variance with itself that she did feel joy as well.

'It was the time when all things are silent, and Bootes had guided his waggon, by means of its slanting pole, in between the Bears. Myrrha set out to perform her guilty deed. The golden moon fled from the sky, black clouds concealed the stars as they shrank from sight. Night was robbed of its starry fires, Icarus being the first to cover up his face, and Erigone, raised to heaven by her devoted love for her father. Three times an unlucky stumble checked Myrrha's steps, three times the funereal screech-owl gave its ominous warning, with fatal croaking, but still she went on, and the darkness and shadows of the night lessened her feeling of shame. With her left hand she clung to her nurse, with the other she groped her way along a road she could not see. Now she reached the threshold of Cinyras' bed-chamber, now she opened the door, and was led inside. Her trembling knees refused to support her, the colour left her face, as the blood drained from her cheeks; her senses were reeling as she went. The nearer she came to the scene of her crime, the more horrified she was, repentant of her rash behaviour, and anxious to be able to go back while she was still unrecognized. As she hesitated, the old nurse took her by the hand, and led her close up to the king's high couch. Handing the girl over to him, "Take her, Cinyras," she said, "she is yours." And she left the doomed pair together. The father welcomed his own flesh and blood into that bed of horror, soothed her girlish fears, and encouraged her when she was afraid. It may well be that he used the name appropriate to her age, and called her "daughter", while she called him "father", so that even the names were not wanting to complete their wickedness.

'When she had been filled with her father's seed, Myrrha left his room, bearing in her disgusting womb a sinful burden, the child she had criminally conceived. The next night they repeated their wickedness, nor was that the end of it: till at length Cinyras, anxious to know the mistress with whom he had lain so often, brought in a lamp, recognized his daughter, and realized his guilt. Filled with anger too great for words, he snatched his gleaming sword from the sheath where it hung. Myrrha fled. In the darkness and concealment which night offered, she was saved from death. This way and that she roamed across the broad lands of her father's kingdom, till she left the palm trees of Arabia and Panchaia's fields behind her.

'For nine months she wandered and at length, tired out, rested in the land of Sabaea. By this time she was scarcely able to support the burden she carried in her womb. Afraid of death, yet sick of life, not knowing what to pray for, she had recourse to these petitions: "O gods, if such there be, who listen to a penitent, I have deserved grievous punishment, nor do I shrink from it: but, in case I should contaminate the living by my presence if I live, or the dead if I die, banish me from the realms of both, and deny me life and death, by changing me into some other form."

'There is a deity who hears the prayers of penitents, for certainly her last prayer did not fall on deaf ears. Earth heaped itself round her legs as she spoke and roots, breaking out through her toe-nails, stretched sideways, forming foundations for a tall trunk. Her bones were changed into hard wood and through the marrow, which survived in their interior, flowed sap instead of blood. Her arms became large branches, her fingers smaller ones, and her skin hardened into bark. The growing tree had already encased her laden womb, had spread over her breast, and was about to cover up her neck. Impatient of delay, she sank down to meet the wood as it rose, and buried her face in the bark. Though she lost her former feelings when she lost her body, yet she still weeps, and warm drops flow from the tree. Even her tears are renowned, and the myrrh that drips from her trunk retains its mistress' name. Men will speak of it to all eternity.

'The infant that Myrrha had conceived in sin had grown inside the tree, and was now seeking some way by which it might leave its mother, and thrust itself into the outer world. Within the tree trunk, Myrrha's womb was swollen and distended with the burden she carried, but her agony found no expression in words, nor could she, in her labour, summon Lucina by her cries. Yet she had all the appearance of a woman struggling to be delivered: the tree bent over, uttered constant moans, and was moist with falling tears. Gentle Lucina stood by the suffering branches and, laying her hand upon them, spoke the words of deliverance. At this, the trunk split open and, through the fissure in the bark, gave up its living burden. The wailing cry of a baby boy was heard. The nymphs laid him on the soft turf, and washed him in his mother's tears. Even Jealousy personified

would have praised his beauty, for he looked like one of the naked
Cupids painted in pictures, differing from them only in his attire:
for to make them alike, the one would have to be given a light quiver,
or the others would have to relinquish theirs.

'The fleeting years glide on unnoticed, and nothing is swifter than
time. This baby, offspring of his sister and his grandfather, so recently
enclosed in the tree-trunk, born but yesterday, soon grew into a
lovely child, soon became a young man, and then a man full-grown,
surpassing even himself in handsomeness. He now became the darling
of Venus, and avenged the passion which had assailed his mother.
For, while her son Cupid was kissing Venus, with his quiver on his
shoulders, he unwittingly grazed her breast with an arrow which
was projecting from the sheath. The injured goddess pushed her son
away. The wound was deeper than it seemed, deeper than she herself
at first realized. The goddess of Cythera, captivated by the beauty of
a mortal, cared no more for her sea shores, ceased to visit seagirt
Paphos, Cnidos rich in fishes, or Amathis with its valuable ores. She
even stayed away from heaven, preferring Adonis to the sky.

'She used to hold him in her arms, and became his constant com-
panion. Though she had always before been accustomed to idle in the
shade, devoting all her attention to enhancing her beauty, now she
roamed the ridges and woods and tree-clad rocks, her garments
caught up as high as her knees, just as Diana wears hers, shouting
encouragement to the dogs, and pursuing such animals as it is safe to
hunt – fleeing hares, deer, or stags with lofty antlers. She kept clear of
sturdy wild boars, and did not risk any encounter with thieving
wolves, bears armed with claws, or lions that glut themselves on slain
cattle. Hoping that her warnings might be of some avail, she advised
Adonis, too, to beware of such creatures. "Show yourself bold when
your quarry flees," she told him. "It is not safe to be daring when the
animal you are hunting is daring too. Do not be rash, dear boy, when
I may be the one to suffer. Do not provoke wild animals which nature
has armed against you, lest your desire for glory should cost me dear.
Your youth and beauty, and the charms which make Venus love you,
have no effect upon lions or bristling boars, or on the eyes and minds
of other wild beasts. The fierce boar deals a blow with his fangs, as
swift as a lightning flash, and tawny lions, filled with boundless rage,
are ever ready to attack – I hate their whole tribe!"

'The boy asked the reason for her hatred. "I shall tell you," she said, "and you will be amazed at this strange tale of wickedness that happened long ago. But my unwonted exertions have tired me. See, this poplar here spreads welcome shade, just where we want it, and the turf provides us with a couch. I should like to rest here with you, on the ground." She sat down as she spoke and, reclining on the grass, leaned against Adonis, and rested her head on his breast. Then she told him this story, interspersing her words with kisses:

'"Perhaps you have heard of a girl who used to race against men and defeat even the fastest runners? That story is no idle tale, for Atalanta did indeed surpass all men, and it would be impossible to say whether she received higher praise for her fleetness of foot, or for her beauty. Now she consulted the god Apollo on the subject of a husband, and he gave her this reply: 'You have no need of a husband, Atalanta. You should avoid any experience of one. But assuredly, you will not escape marriage and then, though still alive, yet you will lose your own self.' Atalanta was frightened by the god's oracle, and lived unwed in the shady woodlands, ridding herself of her insistent suitors by imposing harsh terms upon them. 'No man may have me,' she said, 'unless he first defeats me in a race. Compete against me, and the one who is swift of foot will have my hand in marriage as his prize; but death will be the reward of those who are left behind. Let us race on those conditions.'

'"Cruel though she was, the power of her beauty was so great that a host of suitors rashly came forward, even on those terms. Hippomenes had taken his seat to watch the unequal contest. 'Would any man seek a wife at such risk to himself?' he scoffed, blaming the young men for allowing their infatuation to carry them too far. But when he saw Atalanta's face, and her figure, when she stripped off her outer garments for the race – a figure such as my own, or such as yours would be, Adonis, were you a woman – he was overcome with wonder and, raising his hands to heaven, exclaimed: 'Forgive me, you whom I blamed just now! I did not then know the prize you were seeking to win.'

'"As he praised Atalanta, he began to fall in love with her and, jealousy making him afraid, prayed that none of the young men should run faster than she. 'Why should not I, too, try my fortune in the race?' he said. 'The gods help those who show themselves bold.'

"'While Hippomenes was asking himself this, the girl darted off on winged feet. She seemed to the Boeotian youth to speed on her way like a Scythian arrow, but that only made him admire her beauty all the more. Indeed, she did make a lovely picture, as she raced: the wind blew back her long robes, as she held them up out of the way of her swift feet, her hair floated over her ivory shoulders, and the garters with embroidered edges which bound her legs streamed out in the breeze. The girlish whiteness of her skin was flushed, as when a scarlet awning, drawn over gleaming marble halls, stains them with a colour not their own. While the stranger was remarking all this, the last lap was run, and Atalanta crowned with the wreath of victory. The men she had defeated groaned, and paid the penalty, in accordance with their agreement. However, the young Hippomenes was not deterred by their fate. Stepping forward he stood in the centre of the group and, fastening his eyes upon the girl, said: 'Why seek a title you can easily win, defeating opponents who are slow and out of training? Race against me, and if fortune gives me the victory, you will feel no shame in being beaten by a man of such distinction – for my father was the Megarian Onchestius, and his grandfather was Neptune: so that I am the great-grandson of the king of the ocean, and my courage is in no way inferior to my birth. On the other hand, if I am defeated, your name will be renowned and remembered, for having beaten Hippomenes.'

"'As he spoke, Schoeneus' daughter looked at him tenderly, not sure whether she would rather win or lose, and said to herself: 'What god, hostile to a handsome face, wants to destroy this youth, and so induces him to seek my hand, at the risk of his precious life? It seems to me that I am not worth the risk. It is not his fine presence which appeals to me (though I could be touched by that, as well) but the fact that he is still a boy. His youth, not the boy himself, stirs my pity. Then he has courage too, and a heart that is not afraid to die, and he is fourth in descent from the lord of the sea. On top of that, he loves me, and thinks it worth while to risk death in order to marry me – for death is the price, if cruel fate deny me to him. No, stranger, go while you may, leave my home, stained as it is with the blood of men who sought me as a bride. The conditions for marrying me are too cruel. No other girl will refuse to wed you: a sensible one might well pray for the chance.

241

""'Yet why should I be troubled for you, when so many before
you have already been killed? He must look after himself – let him
die, since he has not taken warning from the death of so many suitors,
but is still driven to show himself tired of living.

""'Will he then die, because he wanted to live with me? Will he
suffer a death he has not deserved in return for his love? If that hap-
pens, my victory will rouse intolerable hatred. But it is not my fault!
If only you would agree to give up the contest, or if only you were
faster, since you are so completely mad! How handsome are his boyish
features, just like those of a girl! Poor Hippomenes – I wish you had
never set eyes on me. You deserved to go on living. If I were luckier,
if cruel fate did not deny me a husband, you would be the only one
with whom I could wish to share my bed!' Inexperienced as she was,
touched by the first stirrings of passion, Atalanta did not know what
she was doing, but loved without realizing that she was in love.

"'Now the citizens and her father were demanding that the usual
race be held, when Neptune's descendant, Hippomenes, invoked my
aid, praying anxiously: 'O lady of Cythera, I beg you to assist me in
my daring venture, and foster the fire of love which you yourself
have kindled!' The kindly breeze brought me his persuasive plead-
ings; I was moved, I confess, and lent him my aid without delay.
There is a field which the islanders call Tamasus, the best part of the
island of Cyprus, which the elders of the people consecrated to me
long ago, bidding me accept it as a gift, in addition to my temple. In
the centre of this field is a gleaming tree, with golden leaves, and
tinkling golden branches. It so happened that I was coming from there,
carrying in my hand three golden apples I had picked: so I went up to
Hippomenes, invisible to all save the youth himself, gave him the
apples, and told him what to do with them.

"'Then the trumpets gave the signal, and both runners shot for-
ward from the starting line, and flew swiftly over the surface of the
sand. They looked as if they could skim the surface of the seas dry
shod, or race over white fields of standing corn. The shouts and the
enthusiasm of the spectators encouraged the young man, for they
cried: 'Now is the time to press on! Run, Hippomenes! Put forth all
your strength! Be quick, and you will win!' It is hard to say whether
the hero from Megara or Schoeneus' daughter was more delighted
by their cries. How often, when she could have passed him, did

Atalanta slow down, and gaze at him for long, before reluctantly leaving him behind.

'"Hippomenes' breath came panting from his dry lips, and the goal lay far ahead. Then, at last, he rolled forward one of the three apples from the tree. The girl stood still in astonishment, and in her eagerness to secure the gleaming fruit, ran out of her course, and picked up the golden ball. Hippomenes passed her, and the benches rang with the spectators' applause. But Atalanta, putting on a spurt, made up for her delay and for the time she had lost, and once again left the young man behind.

'"He held her back a second time, by throwing another apple, but again she overtook and passed him. There remained the last lap of the race. 'O goddess,' he prayed, 'you who gave me the gift, be present now to help me!' And with all his youthful strength he threw the shining golden apple sideways, to the edge of the course, so that it would take Atalanta longer to get back. The girl was seen to hesitate, wondering whether she should go after the apple, but I, Venus, compelled her to pick it up and, when she had done so, I made the apple heavier, hindering her as much by the weight of the fruit as by the time she had lost. Not to make my story longer than the race itself, Atalanta was beaten, and the victor led away his prize.

'"Surely I deserved thanks, Adonis, and an offering of incense? But the thoughtless man expressed no gratitude to me, nor did he give me any such honour. My feelings suddenly changed to anger: indignant at being so scorned, I took good care to make an example of them, so that no one would despise me in future, and roused myself to punish them both.

'"There is a temple, hidden away in the depths of the woods, which the famous Echion once erected to the Mother of the gods, in fulfilment of a vow. Atalanta and Hippomenes were passing this place and, since they had come a long way, they felt inclined to rest. There, by my divine power, I roused in Hippomenes an untimely desire to make love to his wife. Near the temple was a dim recess, like a cave, roofed over with natural rock, which had long been regarded as a holy place. In it, the priest had gathered together a large number of wooden statues of ancient gods. Hippomenes entered this holy spot and, by gratifying his forbidden desire, defiled the sanctuary. The sacred images turned away their eyes, and the Mother of the gods,

with her turreted crown, was on the point of plunging the guilty
pair beneath the waters of the Styx. But she hesitated, for it seemed too
slight a punishment. So, instead of that, tawny manes covered their
necks, which were lately so smooth, their fingers curved round into
claws, their shoulders became those of animals, all their weight was
concentrated in their breasts, and their tails swept the surface of the
sand. There was an expression of rage on their faces, and they growled
instead of speaking. Now they haunt the woods, the forest is their
only home. Changed into lions, they strike terror into the hearts of
others, but have themselves been tamed by Cybele, and their mouths
champ the harness of her car. You must avoid them, my dear one,
and with them every kind of wild beast which does not turn tail and
flee, but faces up to battle. Otherwise your valour may be the ruin of
us both."

'With these words, she yoked her swans, and drove off through the
air. But, though she had warned Adonis, his natural courage ran con-
trary to her advice. By chance, his hounds came upon a well-marked
trail and, following the scent, roused a wild boar from its lair. As it
was about to emerge from the woods, the young grandson of Cinyras
pierced its side with a slanting blow. Immediately the fierce boar dis-
lodged the bloodstained spear, with the help of its crooked snout, and
then pursued the panic-stricken huntsman, as he was making for
safety. It sank its teeth deep in his groin, bringing him down, mortally
wounded, on the yellow sand.

'Venus, as she drove through the air in her light chariot drawn by
winged swans, had not yet reached Cyprus. She recognized the groans
of the dying Adonis from afar, and turned her white birds in his dir-
ection. As she looked down from on high she saw him, lying lifeless,
his limbs still writhing in his own blood. Leaping down from her
car, she tore at her bosom and at her hair, beat her breast with hands
never meant for such a use, and reproached the fates. "But still," she
cried, "you will not have everything under your absolute sway! There
will be an everlasting token of my grief, Adonis. Every year, the scene
of your death will be staged anew, and lamented with wailing cries,
in imitation of those cries of mine. But your blood will be changed
into a flower. Persephone was once allowed to change a woman's
body into fragrant mint, and shall I be grudged the right to transform
Cinyras' brave grandson?"

'With these words, she sprinkled Adonis' blood with sweet-smelling nectar, and, at the touch of the liquid, the blood swelled up, just as clear bubbles rise in yellow mud. Within an hour, a flower sprang up, the colour of blood, and in appearance like that of the pomegranate, the fruit which conceals its seeds under a leathery skin. But the enjoyment of this flower is of brief duration: for it is so fragile, its petals so lightly attached, that it quickly falls, shaken from its stem by those same winds that give it its name, anemone.'

BOOK XI

✿

BY such songs as these the Thracian poet was drawing the woods and rocks to follow him, charming the creatures of the wild, when suddenly the Ciconian women caught sight of him. Looking down from the crest of a hill, these maddened creatures, with animal skins slung across their breasts, saw Orpheus as he was singing and accompanying himself on the lyre. One of them, tossing her hair till it streamed in the light breeze, cried out: 'See! Look here! Here is the man who scorns us!' and flung her spear at the poet Apollo loved, at the lips which produced such melodies. Her weapon, tipped with leaves, left its mark, but did not wound him. Another picked up a stone, and hurled it at Orpheus: but even as it flew through the air it was charmed by the blending harmonies of voice and lyre, and fell at his feet, as if to ask pardon for so daring an assault. None the less, the women's rash attack increased in violence, till all restraint was lost, and maniac fury had them under its sway. All their weapons would have been rendered harmless by the charm of Orpheus' songs, but clamorous shouting, Phrygian flutes with curving horns, tambourines, the beating of breasts, and Bacchic howlings, drowned the music of the lyre. Then at last the stones grew crimson with the blood of the poet, whose voice they did not hear.

The first victims were the countless birds, still spellbound by the voice of the singer, the snakes and the throng of wild animals, the audience which had brought Orpheus such renown. The frenzied women began by seizing upon these; then, with bloodstained hands, they turned on Orpheus himself, flocking together just as birds do, if they see the bird of night abroad by day. It was like the scene in an amphitheatre when, for a morning's entertainment in the arena, a doomed stag is hunted down by dogs. Hurling their leaf-decked

246

thyrsi, made for a far different purpose, the women launched their attack on the poet. Some threw sods of earth, others tore branches from the trees, others again flung stones. To provide real weapons for their mad intent, it happened that there were oxen ploughing in the fields, and not far off sturdy farmers were digging the hard ground, toiling and sweating to secure their harvest. When the farmers saw the horde of women, they fled, leaving their implements behind, so that hoes and heavy rakes and long mattocks lay scattered about the deserted fields. Savagely the women seized hold of these, tore apart the oxen which threatened them with their horns, and rushed once more to the destruction of the poet. He stretched out his hands towards his assailants, but now, for the first time, his words had no effect, and he failed to move them in any way by his voice. Dead to all reverence, they tore him apart and, through those lips to which rocks had listened, which wild beasts had understood, his last breath slipped away and vanished in the wind.

The grief-stricken birds, the host of wild creatures, the flinty rocks and the woods that had so often followed his songs, all wept for Orpheus. The trees shed their leaves and, with bared heads, mourned his loss. Men say that the rivers too were swollen with their own tears, and naiads and dryads tore their hair, and pulled on black garments, over their fine robes. The poet's limbs were scattered in different places, but the waters of the Hebrus received his head and lyre. Wonderful to relate, as they floated down in midstream, the lyre uttered a plaintive melody and the lifeless tongue made a piteous murmur, while the river banks lamented in reply. Carried down to the sea, they left their native river, and were washed up on the shore of Lesbos, near Methymna. Here, as the head lay exposed on that foreign shore, its hair dripping with beads of foam, it was attacked by a savage snake: but Phoebus at last appeared, and checked the snake in the very act of biting, turning its open mouth to stone, and petrifying its gaping jaws. The ghost of Orpheus passed beneath the earth; he recognized all the places he had seen before and, searching through the fields of the blessed, found his Eurydice, and clasped her in eager arms. There they stroll together, side by side: or sometimes Orpheus follows, while his wife goes before, sometimes he leads the way and looks back, as he can do safely now, at his Eurydice.

However, Bacchus did not allow this crime to go unpunished. He was distressed at losing the poet who had sung his mysteries, and immediately all the Thracian women who had watched the wicked scene were fastened to the ground, there in the woods, by means of gnarled roots. The god drew out their toes, as far as each had followed Orpheus, and thrust the tips down into the solid earth. Just as a bird, finding its legs caught in the hidden snare of some cunning fowler, beats its wings when it feels itself held, and tightens the bonds by frightened fluttering, so each of the women, as she became rooted to the spot, went mad with fear, and vainly tried to flee, while the tough root held her fast, preventing her attempts to pull herself away. Each one of them, as she looked for her toes, her feet and nails, saw wood spreading up her shapely legs: when she tried to smite her thighs, in token of her grief, she struck against the bark of an oak tree. Their breasts, too, and likewise their shoulders turned to oak; their arms appeared to have been changed into long branches, as indeed they were – it was no illusion.

Even this was not enough for Bacchus. He abandoned the very fields of Thrace and, with a band of more seemly revellers, betook himself to the vineyards of his beloved Tmolus, and to the river Pactolus, though it was not then rich in gold, or envied for its precious sands. He was attended by his usual throng, satyrs and bacchants, but Silenus was not there. For Phrygian peasants had captured him, as he tottered along on feet made unsteady by age and wine. They had bound him with chains of flowers, and taken him to their king Midas, who had once been instructed in the Bacchic mysteries by Orpheus from Thrace, and by the Athenian Eumolpus. When Midas recognized him as one who was the god's companion and partner in his mysteries, he celebrated the arrival of such a guest with continuous festivities for ten days and nights on end. On the eleventh day, when Lucifer had shepherded away the flock of stars on high, the king came to Lydia, in great good humour, and restored Silenus to his young ward.

The god was glad to have his tutor back, and in return gave Midas the right to choose himself a gift – a privilege which Midas welcomed, but one which did him little good, for he was fated to make poor use of the opportunity he was given. He said to the god: 'Grant that whatever my person touches be turned to yellow gold.' Bacchus, though sorry that Midas had not asked for something better, granted his request, and presented him with this baneful gift. The Phrygian king went off cheerfully, delighted with the misfortune which had befallen him. He tested the good faith of Bacchus' promise by touching this and that, and could scarcely believe his own senses when he broke a green twig from a low-growing branch of oak, and the twig turned to gold. He lifted a stone from the ground and the stone, likewise, gleamed pale gold. He touched a sod of earth and the earth, by the power of his touch, became a lump of ore. The dry ears of corn which he gathered were a harvest of golden metal, and when he plucked an apple from a tree and held it in his hand, you would have thought that the Hesperides had given it him. If he laid his finger on the pillars of his lofty doorways, they were seen to shine and glitter, and even when he washed his hands in clear water, the trickles that flowed over his palms might have served to deceive Danae. He dreamed of everything turned to gold, and his hopes soared beyond the limits of his imagination.

So he exulted in his good fortune, while servants set before him tables piled high with meats, and with bread in abundance. But then, when he touched a piece of bread, it grew stiff and hard: if he hungrily tried to bite into the meat, a sheet of gold encased the food, as soon as his teeth came in contact with it. He took some wine, itself the discovery of the god who had endowed him with his power, and adding clear water, mixed himself a drink: the liquid could be seen turning to molten gold as it passed his lips.

Wretched in spite of his riches, dismayed by the strange disaster which had befallen him, Midas prayed for a way of escape from his wealth, loathing what he had lately desired. No amount of food could relieve his hunger, parching thirst burned his throat, and he was tortured, as he deserved, by the gold he now hated. Raising his shining arms, he stretched his hands to heaven and cried: 'Forgive me, father Bacchus! I have sinned, yet pity me, I pray, and save me speedily from this disaster that promised so fair!' The gods are kind: when Midas confessed his fault, Bacchus restored him to his former state, cancelling the gift which, in fulfilment of his promise, he had given the king. 'And now,' he said, 'to rid yourself of the remaining traces of that gold which you so foolishly desired, go to the river close by the great city of Sardis. Then make your way along the Lydian ridge, travelling upstream till you come to the water's source. There, where the foaming spring bubbles up in great abundance, plunge your head and body in the water and, at the same time, wash away your crime.' The king went to the spring as he was bidden: his power to change things into gold passed from his person into the stream, and coloured its waters. Even to-day, though the vein of ore is now so ancient, the soil of the fields is hardened by the grains it receives, and gleams with gold where the water from the river moistens its sods.

Midas, hating riches, made his home in the country, in the woods, and worshipped Pan, the god who always dwells in mountain caves: but he remained a foolish person, and his own stupidity was to injure its owner again, as it had done before.

There is a mountain, Tmolus, that rises steep and sheer, looking out over a wide prospect of sea, and sloping away on either side, to Sardis on the one hand, and to little Hypaepae on the other. There Pan was boasting to the gentle nymphs, singing them his songs, and playing some trivial tune on the reeds, joined by wax, that formed his pipes. As he did so, he had the audacity to speak slightingly of Apollo's music, compared with his own, and entered into unequal competition with the god, in a contest to be decided by Tmolus. The elderly judge took his seat on his own mountain-side, and shook his ears free of trees, until only an oak wreath encircled his dark hair, with bunches of acorns hanging at his hollow temples. He looked at the god of the flocks, and said: 'The judge is ready.' Pan struck up an air on his rustic pipes and, with his wild strains, charmed Midas, who happened to be near at hand when he was playing. After hearing Pan, the worshipful Tmolus swung round his head to face Phoebus, and as his gaze moved round, his forests followed. Apollo had wreathed his golden hair with laurel from Parnassus, his flowing robes, dyed with Tyrian purple, swept the ground; in his left hand he held his lyre, inlaid with jewels and Indian ivory, his plectrum was in his right. His very stance was that of a musician. Then he plucked the strings with skilful fingers till Tmolus, enchanted by the sweetness of the melody, bade Pan admit his pipes inferior to the lyre.

Everyone else agreed with the verdict of the venerable mountain, but not Midas. He objected to the decision, declaring it to be unjust. The Delian god would not allow ears so foolish to retain their human shape; he lengthened them, filled them with bristling grey hairs, and made them movable, at the point where they joined the king's head,

so that they could twitch. The rest of Midas' shape remained human,
for he was condemned to lose only this one part: but he was made to
assume the ears of a lumbering ass.

Now the king himself, ashamed of his disfigurement, was anxious
to conceal it, and tried to do so by wrapping his head in a purple
turban. But the barber who used to trim his long hair saw what had
happened. Eager though he was to tell what he had seen, he did not
dare to reveal the shameful secret, and yet he could not keep quiet
about it. So he went off, and dug a hole in the ground: then he
whispered softly to the earth he had dug out what kind of ears he had
seen on his master's head. Throwing the earth back again, he buried
the information he had given and, after filling in the trench, went
quietly away. But a thick carpet of trembling reeds began to push up
on the spot and, at the end of the year, when they were full grown, the
reeds betrayed their gardener: for, when stirred by the gentle South
wind, they uttered the words that had been buried, and revealed the
truth about his master's ears.

Apollo, when he had taken his revenge, left Tmolus and journeyed
through the clear air, but stopped short of the narrow strait of Helle,
Nephele's daughter, and alighted on the plains of Troy. There, on
the right of the Sigean promontory, and to the left of the Rhoetean,
stood an ancient altar, sacred to the Thunderer of Panomphe; and
from there the god saw Laomedon, beginning to raise up the walls of
his new city, Troy. He saw, too, that the great task the king had under-
taken demanded no small resources, and that it was proceeding with
much toil and difficulty. So, along with the god who bears the trident,
the father of the swelling seas, Apollo disguised himself as a mortal
and, on receiving a promise of gold in return for the city's defences,
built the walls of Troy for the Phrygian tyrant. The work stood com-
plete: the king, however, refused the gods their price and, as a crown-
ing piece of treachery, falsely swore that he had made no such promise.
'You will be sorry for this!' cried the king of the ocean, and
directed all his seas to the shores of miserly Troy, flooding the earth
till it was indistinguishable from the waters, sweeping away the
farmers' possessions, and overwhelming the fields with his waves.
Nor was this punishment sufficient. He further demanded the king's
daughter, Hesione, as an offering for a sea-monster, and the princess
had already been chained to the hard rocks, when Hercules rescued

her. He had been promised horses as a reward, but when he asked for them, in spite of the fact that he had performed so great a service, he was refused his prize. He therefore vanquished Troy, and captured the walls of the city that had been proved false a second time.

Telamon, who had joined Hercules in this campaign, did not leave the district without due honour, for Hesione was given into his possession. Peleus, who had also helped, was already distinguished by having a goddess for his wife, and was no less proud to claim Jupiter as his father-in-law than as his grandfather; for he was not the only man who had the good fortune to be Jove's grandson, but he was the only one to have a goddess for a wife. It happened in this way.

Aged Proteus had said to Thetis: 'Goddess of the waters, conceive a child! You will be the mother of a young hero who, when he has grown to manhood, will surpass his father's deeds, and will be called greater than he!' Because of this, in case the world should own anything greater than himself, Jupiter had avoided any intimacy with the ocean goddess, even though he had felt the flame of passion burning hotly in his heart. He ordered his grandson Peleus, the son of Aeacus, to become her lover in his stead, and enjoy the embraces of the sea-maiden.

There is a bay in Haemonia, curved like a sickle, and enclosed by jutting arms, where there would be a harbour, if the water were deeper: but the waves just cover the surface of the sand. It has a firm shore, free from seaweed, where the sand retains no footprints, and yet does not clog one's steps. A grove of myrtles grows close by, thick with variegated berries, and in its midst there is a cave, whether made by nature or by man is hard to tell, but it is more like man's handiwork. Thetis used often to come there, unclad, seated on a bridled dolphin, and there Peleus found her, as she lay sound asleep. When he had tried to win her by his pleas, and been rejected, he wound both his arms round her neck, and prepared to use force. Had the goddess not had recourse to her wonted tricks, repeatedly changing her shape, he would have achieved his daring purpose: as it was, he held on to her firmly when she changed herself into a bird, and when she became a stout tree, he clung to the tree-trunk; but the third shape she adopted was that of a spotted tigress and, terrified by this, the son of Aeacus relaxed his grip upon her body.

Then he poured offerings of wine on the waters and, with entrails of sheep and fumes of incense, ceaselessly entreated the gods of the sea, until the Carpathian seer spoke from the depths of his pool, saying: 'Son of Aeacus, you will gain the bride you seek, if you catch her in your snares and bind her fast, while she lies sound asleep in the rocky cave, knowing nothing of what is happening. Do not let her trick you, though she assume a hundred false shapes: whatever she may be, hold her tightly until she returns again to what she was at first.' When he had said this, Proteus submerged his head in the sea, letting the waters close over his final words.

The sun was sinking and, with chariot slanting down the sky, was close to the Western sea, when the fair Nereid again made her way to the rocky cave, and lay down on her usual couch. Then Peleus seized the nymph's limbs in a firm grip; scarcely had he done so, when she began altering her shape, until she realized that her body was securely clasped, her arms stretched wide on either side. Then at last she gave a deep sigh: 'It is not without heaven's aid that you have beaten me!' she said, and revealed herself as Thetis. When she confessed her true self, the hero embraced her, obtained his desire, and filled her with child; her son was the mighty Achilles.

Happy in his wife and happy in his son was Peleus, a man whose life had been all prosperity, apart from his wicked murder of Phocus. But, because he was guilty of shedding his brother's blood, he was driven from his father's house. The land of Trachis took him in, a kingdom which was then being ruled peaceably and without bloodshed by Ceyx, the son of Lucifer. The king's face retained the shining brightness of his father's countenance, but at that time he was sad and unlike himself, since he was mourning the loss of his brother. When Aeacus' son arrived in this land, worn out with travelling and troubles, he entered the city with a few companions, leaving the flocks and herds which he had with him in a shady valley not far from the walls. As soon as he was given a chance to approach the king he went forward, holding out in supplication an olive branch, draped with fillets and explained who he was, and from what family he came. The only thing he concealed was the crime he had committed: he lied about the reason for his exile, but asked the king to give him refuge either in his town or in his country. The ruler of Trachis answered him kindly, and said: 'It is open, even to ordinary people, to enjoy the opportunities my country has to offer, Peleus. The kingdom I rule is not unfriendly to strangers. Such being our normal attitude, you give us further good reasons to welcome you, for you bear a distinguished name, and have Jupiter as a grandfather. Do not waste time in entreaties. You will receive all that you ask; call whatever you see here your own – I only wish you might see something better!' – and he burst into tears.

When Peleus and his friends inquired what occasioned such violent grief he replied: 'You know the hawk, which lives on what it can plunder, and terrifies all other birds? You may perhaps think that it always had wings, but in fact it was once a man, Daedalion by name: he too was all fierceness, for character never changes, ferocious in war, and ready for violence. We were both sons of the star who summons Dawn, and is the last to leave the sky: but I honoured peace, and my thoughts were centred on preserving it, and upon my wife, whereas my brother found his delight in cruel warfare. He subdued kings and nations by his valour, that valour which now, in a different shape, sets Thisbe's doves a-flutter. Daedalion had a daughter, Chione, a girl of fourteen who, being ripe for marriage and endowed with rare beauty, had a thousand suitors. Now Phoebus and Maia's son, Mercury, chanced to be returning, the one from his beloved Delphi, and the other from the summit of Cyllene. They both saw the girl at the same moment and both, at the same moment, fell in love. Apollo deferred his hopes of enjoying her love till night-time, but Mercury, impatient of delay, touched the girl's face with his rod that brings slumber. At that potent touch, she lay still, and suffered the god's violent embrace. Then, when night had scattered the heavens with stars, Phoebus, disguised as an old woman, enjoyed the pleasure which another had had before him. In the fullness of time, Chione bore twins: to the wing-footed god an artful child, Autolycus, who was up to all manner of tricks, accustomed to turn black to white and white to black, a true son of his crafty father, and to Phoebus, a son Philammon, renowned for his singing and his playing of the lyre.

'Yet what good did it do her to have borne two children, to have found favour with two gods, to be the daughter of a brave father, or the grand-daughter of a shining star? Or is it, in fact, a curse to be distinguished? It has done harm to many, and it certainly harmed her! She had the boldness to prefer herself to Diana, and criticized the goddess' looks, whereupon Diana, roused to fierce wrath, took her revenge. "You will find no fault with my actions!" she cried; and without delay bent her bow, shot an arrow from the string, and pierced with her shaft the tongue which had so well deserved it. That tongue fell silent – no sound, none of the words she attempted to form, issued from the girl's lips. As she was trying to speak, life and blood drained from her together.

'Sadly I gathered her into my arms, with all a father's grief in my own heart, and spoke comforting words to my dear brother. But the bereaved father heeded them as much as reefs heed the murmurings of the sea, as he bitterly lamented the daughter he had lost. When he saw her body ablaze on the pyre, four times he tried to rush into the heart of the flames, four times he was driven back. Then he dashed off in frenzied flight; like a bullock whose neck, rubbed tender by the plough, is tormented by stinging hornets, he charged away where there was no path. Even then he seemed to me to run faster than a man, and you would have thought that his feet had wings. So he fled from us all, made swift by his desire for death, till he reached the summit of Parnassus. There Apollo took pity on him and, when Daedalion threw himself from a towering rock, turned him into a bird and bore him up, to hover on the wings which he had suddenly acquired. The god gave him a hooked beak, and curving crooked talons, but left him his onetime courage, and strength greater than his body. Now as a hawk, showing mercy to none, he exercises his cruelty against all other birds and, suffering himself, is become the cause of suffering to others.'

As the son of Lucifer was relating this strange tale about his brother, the Phocian Onetor, who was Peleus' herdsman, came racing up in panting haste, and cried: 'Peleus, Peleus, I come with news of a great disaster!' Peleus bade him tell whatever news he brought, and even the Trachinian king himself waited in suspense, with a look of fear on his face. The herdsman told his story: 'When the sun was at his zenith, midway on his course, seeing as much sky behind him as still lay in front, I had driven your weary cattle down to the curving shore. Some of the oxen had sunk to their knees on the yellow sand, and were lying looking out over the broad stretch of ocean. Some were still wandering slowly up and down, while others were swimming or standing in the sea, with only their necks raised above the water. Close by the water's edge stands a temple, not bright with gold and marble, but built of heavy timbers, and shaded by ancient trees. Nereus and his daughters live there – a sailor who was drying his nets on the shore told me that these were the gods of that sea. Near the temple is a marsh, formed by sea-water left behind in a stagnant pool, and the swampy ground is thickly overgrown with willows. From this spot the sound of heavy crashing struck terror into all the neighbourhood. Then there emerged a huge beast, a wolf, all streaked with slime from the marsh, its swiftly snapping jaws flecked with blood and foam, a red gleam in its eyes. Its fury was due to hunger and savagery both, but of the two its savagery was the greater – for it was not content to find something to eat, and satisfy its grim hunger with the oxen it had killed; instead, it slashed the whole herd, and fiercely felled them all. Even some of us herdsmen were killed or wounded by its murderous jaws while we were trying to keep the brute away. The shore and the edge of the waves were red with blood, and so were the marshes that echoed with the cattle's bellowing. But delay costs us dear – our plight leaves no time for hesitation. While something yet remains, let us all go together and armed with weapons, yes, weapons in hand, make a combined attack on the brute!'

The peasant finished speaking. Peleus did not care about his losses but, remembering the crime he had committed, he realized that the Nereid whose son he had killed was inflicting these calamities upon him to provide a sacrificial offering for her dead Phocus. Meanwhile, the Oetaean king ordered his men to arm themselves, and to take up their weapons for an attack. At the same time, he was making ready to go with them himself, when his wife Alcyone, roused by the commotion, burst in on the company. She tore at her hair, which she had not taken time to arrange properly, and flung herself on her husband's neck, begging him only to send help, not to go himself, and beseeching him with prayers and tears to save both their lives by saving his own. But it was Peleus, the son of Aeacus, who answered her: 'These fears become you well, O queen, and accord with your affection for your husband. But put them aside. I am deeply grateful for your promise of help, but I have no wish that an armed attack be made upon this strange monster. What I must do is to pray to the goddess of the sea.'

There was a high tower on top of the citadel, a beacon that served as a welcome landmark to weary ships. They climbed up there, and looked with groans of distress at the oxen, lying dead on the shore, and the wild beast that had savaged them, its mouth dripping with blood and its long-haired coat stained with gore. Then Peleus, stretching his hands towards the shores of the open sea, prayed the sea-goddess Psamathe to put an end to her anger, and bring him her aid. The goddess was unmoved by his pleas, but Thetis by her prayers obtained for her husband the pardon he sought. However, although the wolf was called off from its savage killing, it had been maddened by the sweet taste of blood, and persisted in slaughter until, as it was fastening its teeth in the torn neck of a heifer, the goddess changed it to marble. The body preserved its original appearance in every respect, except as regards its colour; the whiteness of the stone showed that it was no longer a wolf, and need not be feared any more. But the fates did not allow the fugitive Peleus to settle in this land either: he wandered on, an exile still, to the Magnetes, and there was absolved of the crime of murder, by the Thessalian Acastus.

Meanwhile King Ceyx, much disturbed at heart both by his brother's fate and by the portents that had happened since, was preparing to go to the god of Claros, to consult the sacred oracle which comforts men in their distress. It was impossible to go to the temple at Delphi, for wicked Phorbas and his Phlegyans barred the way. However, before Ceyx set out, he told his faithful Alcyone of his intention. Immediately she was chilled with fear to the very marrow of her bones, her face grew pale as boxwood, and her eyes were wet with streaming tears. Three times, as she tried to speak, the tears coursed down her cheeks and sobs choked her loving reproaches, as she pleaded: 'What fault of mine has altered your feelings, my dearest one? Where is that care for me, that used to come before everything else? Can you now depart, without a qualm, leaving Alcyone behind? Are you now resolved to journey far away? Am I now dearer to you when I am not there? I suppose you will tell me that you are travelling by land, that my troubled thoughts will not be tinged with dread, and I shall only mourn your absence, not fear for you as well? No, no, it is the sea that terrifies me, the dismal ocean. Recently I saw wrecked timbers on the shore, and I have often read names on tombs where no body lay. Do not let any false confidence buoy up your spirits at the thought that Aeolus is your father-in-law, the god

257

who imprisons the strong winds and calms the sea at will. When once the winds have been let out and have laid hold upon the ocean, nothing is forbidden them. Every land and all the waters are at their mercy, and they even harry the clouds in heaven, striking out fiery lightning flashes by their fierce collisions. The more I know them (for I do know them, and often saw them, when I was a little girl in my father's home) the more I think they are to be feared. But if no prayers can alter your resolution, my dear husband, if you are all too determined to go, take me along with you. Then, at any rate, we shall be storm-tossed together, and I shall fear only the perils I myself shall share. Together we shall endure whatever happens, and together sail over the wide seas.'

Her husband, the son of the bright star, was touched by such words, and by the tears that Aeolus' daughter shed: for in his own heart the fire of love burned no less than in hers. But he would not give up his proposed voyage, nor yet was he willing to include Alcyone in a dangerous enterprise. So he answered her at length, trying to soothe her fears: for all that, he did not gain her approval. Then he added this further consolation, the only one that carried any weight with his loving wife: 'Any separation, indeed, is long for us, but I swear to you by my father's light that, provided the fates allow it, I shall return before the moon has twice completed her circle.'

When he had made this promise, raising her hopes of his speedy return, he immediately ordered his ship to be drawn down from the dock, to be launched and fitted with its rigging. When Alcyone saw it, once again, as if she knew beforehand what was to come, she shuddered and the tears started from her eyes. She embraced her husband and at last, most wretchedly, bade him a sad farewell: then she collapsed completely. Ceyx sought excuses for delay, but his youthful crew, seated in a double row, drew back their oars against their stout chests, and cleft the waves with regular strokes. Alcyone raised her moist eyes: at first she could see her husband standing on the curved stern, and returned his salute as he waved her good-bye. As the ship drew further away and her eyes could not distinguish his features, her gaze still followed the departing vessel as long as possible. Then, when even the ship was too far away to be clearly seen, she still watched the sails billowing out from the masthead. Finally not even the sails were visible, and she sought her empty couch where she lay down with a heavy heart. Her bed and her surroundings made her weep afresh, reminding her what part of herself she had lost.

The voyagers had left the harbour, and the breeze had set the sail-ropes quivering. The captain shipped the oars, set the yards at the top of the mast, and unfurled all canvas, to catch the coming winds. Less than half the voyage had been accomplished, or at any rate not more than half, and the ship was far distant from either land, when, about nightfall, the sea began to whiten with rising waves, and the driving East wind to blow more strongly. 'Quick, down with the yards from the top of the mast!' cried the captain. 'Reef in all canvas!' But though he gave the orders, the storm winds blowing in his face prevented them from reaching the crew, and the crashing of the water did not allow any words to be heard. All the same, some sailors hastened of their own accord to draw the oars inboard, others to strengthen the ship's defences, others to reef the sails. One baled out the water, and flung it back into the sea, another hastily secured the spars. While these things were being done, without any kind of order, the storm increased in violence, and winds from every direction fought fiercely, throwing the angry sea into a turmoil. The captain himself was terrified, and admitted that he did not know how matters stood, what he should order, what forbid: so overwhelming was the danger, so much greater than his skill. Men were shouting, ropes creaking, the sea was a tumult of crashing waves, and rolling thunder filled the air. Mountainous seas seemed to reach the heavens, and sprinkle the brooding clouds with spray. Sometimes they were yellow as the sand they churned up from ocean's bed, sometimes blacker than the waters of the Styx, or again they spread out in hissing sheets of white foam. The Trachinian ship was likewise tossed alternately up and down: at one time, perched high as if on a mountain-top, it seemed to look down into the valleys and depths of Acheron, at another it sank down, shut in by arching waves, and looked up as if from some pool of the underworld, at the heavens high above. Often, as a wave struck its side, the ship gave a mighty crash, and groaned under a buffeting no less severe than when on occasion an iron battering-ram or engine of war shakes a shattered citadel. As stout-hearted lions gather their strength, and come rushing upon the arms and weapons directed against them, so the waves, letting themselves go before the risen fury of the winds, flung themselves on the defences of the ship, and towered above it. Now the wedges were slipping from their places, seams gaped apart, with the wax that had covered them washed away, affording a passage to the deadly sea. Suddenly the clouds opened, and rain came lashing down – it was as if the whole heavens were descending into the seas, the whole swelling ocean rising up to the sky. The sails were soaked with the deluge, and the waters of the sea united with those falling from the heavens above. The sky was empty of stars, and the darkness of the storm further intensified the blackness of the night. But lightning flashes dispelled the gloom and lit up the scene; the waters glowed red beneath their fire.

And now the waves came with a bound into the hollow hull of the ship. Just as one soldier, more spirited than all the rest, tries time and again to scale a beleaguered city's ramparts, till at last he attains his goal and, inflamed with a desire for glory, alone among a thousand men takes possession of the wall: so, when the waves had nine times pounded the steep sides of the vessel a tenth, rising yet more hugely, came rushing to the attack, and did not abandon its onslaught on the weary ship till it descended, as if inside its captured walls. Part of the sea, then, was still trying to invade the ship, part was already inside. All were in a state of confused terror, like the panic in a city when enemy soldiers are undermining the walls from the outside, while its own men strive to hold them within. Their seamanship deserted the sailors, their spirits sank, and a separate death seemed to be rushing upon them with each oncoming wave, breaking through their defences. Some could not restrain their tears, one stood dazed, another called those men happy for whom there was proper burial in store, another begged and prayed for heaven's help, vainly stretching out his arms towards the sky he could not see. Some thought of their fathers and brothers, some of their homes and children, and whatever they had left behind. It was the thought of Alcyone that distressed Ceyx: Alcyone and nothing else was on his lips. She was his one desire, and yet he was glad she was not there. He would have liked, too, to look back at the shores of his country, and turn his eyes for a last time in the direction of his home, but indeed he did not know where it lay, amid the boiling and swirling of the sea, and the curtain of pitch-black clouds that concealed the sky, redoubling the darkness of the night. The mast was broken by the onrush of the tempestuous whirlwind, the rudder shattered. Then, like a victor triumphing in his spoils, one last wave arched itself on high, looking down on all the other waves. As violently as if Athos and Pindus were torn from their foundations and hurled in their entirety into the open sea, it crashed sheer down and, by its weight and the force of the blow combined, submerged the ship in the depths of the ocean. Many of the crew sank with the vessel, and were swallowed up in the sea, to die without rising to the surface again. Others clung to spars and broken fragments of the ship. Ceyx himself, with the hand that once wielded a sceptre, held fast to a piece of wreckage and called, alas in vain, upon his father and his father-in-law. But as he swam, the name most often on his lips was that of his wife, Alcyone. He thought of her, spoke of her, prayed that the waves might wash his body up where she would see it, and that in death he might be buried by her loving hands. While he kept himself afloat, whenever the waves let him open his lips, he called to Alcyone, far away, and even when the seas closed over him, still he murmured her name. Suddenly an arching mass of black waters came crashing down over the midst of the seething ocean, and Ceyx sank and drowned beneath the breaking wave. On that day Lucifer was dim and unrecognizable: since he could not leave the sky, he shrouded his face in thick clouds.

Meanwhile Alcyone, knowing nothing of the disaster, was counting the nights, vainly promising herself her husband's return, and hurrying on the making of garments, some for his use, and others which she herself would wear when he came back. To all the gods she made dutiful offerings of incense, but first and foremost she worshipped in Juno's temple, visiting the altars of the goddess on behalf of one who was no more, praying that her husband might be brought safely back to her, and that he might prefer no other woman to herself: of all her many prayers, this was the only one that could be granted.

The goddess could not endure any further petitions for a man who was already dead. So, to remove those ill-fated hands from her altars, she said to Iris: 'Most faithful bearer of my messages, go quickly to the drowsy home of Sleep, and bid him send Alcyone a dream, in the shape of the dead Ceyx, to tell her the true state of affairs.' At her behest Iris put on her trailing robe of a thousand colours and, tracing a curved arc across the heavens, sought the cloud-wrapped palace of the king she had been told to visit.

Near the Cimmerian country is a cave, deeply recessed, a hollow mountainside, the secret dwelling-place of languid Sleep, where the sun's rays can never reach, whether at his rising or at noon or at his setting. Dark mists are breathed out from the ground, and the half-light of evening's gloom. No crested cock summons the dawn with wakeful crowings, no anxious dogs break the silence, or geese, shrewder still than dogs. No wild beasts are heard, no cattle, nor is there any sound of branches swaying in the wind, or harsh quarrelling of human tongues. Voiceless quiet dwells there: but from the depths of the rocky cave flows the river of Lethe whose waters invite slumber as they glide, murmuring over whispering pebbles. Before the doors of the house poppies bloom in abundance and countless herbs from whose juices dewy Night gathers drowsiness and sprinkles it over the dark earth. There is not a door in the whole house, lest some turning hinge should creak, nor is there any watchman at the threshold. In the midst of the cavern stands a lofty couch of ebon wood, dark in colour, covered with black draperies, feather-soft, where the god himself lies, his limbs relaxed in luxurious weariness. Around him lie empty dreams, made to resemble different shapes, as many as the corn ears in the harvest, as leaves on the woodland trees, or sands scattered on the shore.

The goddess entered, and brushed aside with her hands the dreams that stood in her way. Immediately the god's dwelling was filled with the shining gleam of her bright raiment, and Sleep himself struggled to lift his eyes, languid and heavy with slumber. Again and again he fell back and, as his head drooped, his chin nodded against his breast. At length however he roused himself and, leaning on his elbow, recognized Iris and asked her why she had come. She replied: 'O Sleep, in whom all things find rest, most peaceful of the gods, you who calm the mind, put cares to flight, soothe limbs wearied by harsh tasks and refresh them for their toil, bid your dreams, which are indistinguishable from the real shapes they imitate, put on the appearance of King Ceyx, and go to Alcyone in the city of Trachis, which Hercules made famous. There let them conjure up a vision of the shipwreck, for this is Juno's command.' Her mission over, Iris departed, for she could no longer bear the compelling influence of Sleep. As she felt his drowsiness stealing into her limbs, she escaped and traversed once more the arched path by which she had lately come.

Now from his host of sons, a thousand strong, the father woke up Morpheus, who was skilled in imitating human shapes. None was cleverer than he at reproducing a way of walking, an expression, the sound of a voice. In addition, he used the words and wore the clothes most typical of each person. Morpheus specialized in imitating men, whereas a second son, called Icelos by the gods and Phobetor by mortals, used to change himself into beast or bird or lengthy serpent. A third son, Phantasos, was possessed of yet another kind of skill, and assumed the deceptive appearance of earth, rock, water, trees, or anything inanimate. These were the dreams which would show themselves by night to kings and generals, while others strayed among the ranks of common folk. So the aged god passed by the rest, and from all the brothers chose Morpheus alone to carry out the commands of Thaumas' daughter. Then he relaxed again, in soft slumber, and his drooping head sank down into the pillows of his lofty couch.

Morpheus flew through the darkness, his wings making no sound, and soon reached the Haemonian city. There he laid aside his wings, and changed himself to look like Ceyx. When he had assumed the appearance of the king, pale as death, his clothing gone, he stood before the bed of the unhappy wife, Alcyone. His beard was seen dripping wet, and drops of water splashed heavily from his sodden hair, as he leaned over the bed, tears streaming down his cheeks, and said: 'My poor unhappy wife, do you recognize your Ceyx, or has death changed my appearance? Look up, and you will know me: you will find your husband's ghost in place of his true self. O Alcyone, your prayers for me were of no avail. I am dead. Indulge no false hopes of my return. A South wind, blowing from a sky heavy with clouds, overtook our ship in the Aegean, and flung it about with tempestuous buffetings, till the vessel was wrecked, and the waves washed over my lips, as they vainly called your name. No unreliable messenger brings you this news, nor do you glean it from vague rumours. I myself, who suffered shipwreck, am here to tell you of my fate. Come now, rise up, shed tears for me, and put on mourning garb. Do not send me unwept into the void of Tartarus.'

As he spoke, Morpheus seemed to Alcyone to be weeping real tears: moreover, she could easily believe that the voice was that of her husband, and he had Ceyx' gestures too. She moaned and began to cry in her sleep, raising her arms and trying to touch his body – but she embraced only empty air. 'Wait!' she cried. 'Whither away so fast? We shall go together!'

Roused by the vision of her husband and her own cries, the queen started up from sleep, and first of all looked about her, to see if the man who had just appeared to her was indeed there: for her servants, wakened by her voice, had brought in a lamp. When she did not find him anywhere, with her own hand she struck her cheeks, ripped the garments from her breast, beat her breasts too, and tore down her hair without stopping to undo it. To her nurse who sought to know the reason for her grief, she cried; 'Alcyone is no more – she is nothing! She died together with her Ceyx. Do not try to console me; he has perished in a shipwreck. I saw him, recognized him, stretched out my hands as he left me, and tried to hold him back. He was a ghost, but even so, clearly and plainly the ghost of my husband. If you ask me what he looked like, his features were not as they used to be, his face did not shine brightly as before. Naked and pale, his hair still sodden with water – poor wretch, that was how I saw him. Look, he was standing on this very spot, a pitiful sight!' – and she looked to see if any trace of him remained. 'This was the reason, this was what made me apprehensive and afraid, when I begged you not to run away from me, not to follow where the winds bore you. If you were going to your death, I wish you had at least taken me too. It would have been better far for me to go with you, for then none of my life would have been spent away from you, and we should not have been separated in our death. Now, though I was not there, I perished none the less, I too was tempest-tossed, though I was left behind, and though the sea does not have me, still it holds me in its depths. My heart would be more unfeeling than the waters themselves, were I to strive to live any longer, to struggle to survive such grief. No, I shall not fight against my sorrow: I shall not desert you, my poor husband. Now, at least, I shall join you and, though our ashes may not lie in the same urn, one inscription will unite us in a single tomb. If my bones may not mingle with yours, yet our names will be ever linked.' Her grief prevented her from saying more: sobs interrupted every word she spoke, and groans that came from the depths of her stricken heart.

It was morning. She left her home and went to the shore, sadly seeking again the spot from which she had watched Ceyx departing. She lingered there, murmuring: 'Here he untied the mooring ropes, here on the shore he kissed me as he went.' As she recalled his actions, remembering each by the place where it happened, she looked out to sea and descried, far off in the water, a shape like a human form; but at first it was difficult to say what it was. When the waves had brought it a little nearer, it was evident, though it was still some distance off, that it was indeed a body. Alcyone, moved by this omen of a shipwrecked man, but still not knowing who it was, spoke as if shedding tears for a stranger. 'Alas, for your fate, whoever you are, poor soul,' she cried, 'and for your wife, if you have one.' The body was washed in nearer by the waves, and the more she gazed, the less and less could she control herself till, in agony, she saw it brought close in to the shore, near enough to be recognized. It was her husband! 'It is he!' she cried, and at one and the same time rent her clothes, her cheeks, her hair. Then, stretching her trembling hands towards Ceyx, she sobbed: 'O my dear, dear husband, it is thus that you come back to me, so piteously?'

Adjoining the water's edge was an artificial breakwater which, receiving the first onslaught of the waves as they came in from the sea, broke and weakened their force. Alcyone leaped upon this – it was a miracle that she was able to do so. Then she found herself flying, beating the air with wings newly-formed. Changed into a sorrowing bird, she skimmed the surface of the waves. As she flew, a plaintive sound, like the lament of someone stricken with grief, came harshly from the slender beak that was her mouth. When she reached the silent lifeless corpse, she embraced the dear limbs with her new wings, and all in vain kissed the cold lips with her hard beak. The people doubted whether Ceyx felt her, or whether it was the motion of the the sea that made him seem to raise his head: but surely he had felt her! At last the gods had pity on them, and both were changed into birds. Their love endured, even after they had shared this fate, and their marriage vows were not dissolved when they acquired wings. They still mate and become parents, and for seven days of calm in the winter Alcyone broods on the sea, wings outstretched over her nest: then the waves lie still and Aeolus, keeping guard over the winds, prevents their going out, and so provides a smooth sea for his grandsons.

As the birds were flying side by side across the wide stretch of ocean, an old man who was watching them praised the affection they had maintained for each other, right to the end. Then someone else close by, or perhaps it was the same man, pointed to a long-necked diver, and said: 'That bird too, which you see there, skimming the sea with its slender legs trailing behind, is a descendant of kings. If you trace its pedigree, step by step, you will find that the founder of its race was Ilus; then came Assaracus, Ganymede whom Jupiter snatched to heaven, aged Laomedon, and Priam whose reign, thanks to fate's decree, saw the last days of Troy. That bird was Hector's brother and, had he not met with a strange fate in his early youth, he might have had a name no less renowned than Hector's own, although Hector's mother was Dymas' daughter, Hecuba, whereas Aesacus, as he was called, is said to have been the son of Alexirhoe, the daughter of two-horned Granicus.

'Born in the secret haunts of Ida's shady groves, Aesacus hated cities and lived in retirement in the hills. He led a simple country life, far from the elegance of the court, only occasionally visiting the crowds of Ilium. Yet his was no boorish heart, nor was it proof against love. Often he had tried to catch the nymph Hesperie, pursuing her all through the woods, till one day he saw her on the banks of her father's river, the Cebren, where she was sitting with her hair spread out over her shoulders, drying it in the sun. The nymph, when she was seen, sped off like a deer, fleeing in fright from a tawny wolf, or like a water-duck flying from a hawk, when she has been caught far from her own pool. The Trojan prince ran after her and, with feet made swift by love, pressed close on the heels of one made swift by fear. Suddenly a snake, lurking in the grass, bit her foot as she ran, and left the poison from its fangs in her body. At one stroke it ended her flight, and her life. Madly the lover clasped her lifeless body, crying: "Sorry indeed am I that I followed you! But I never guessed that this would happen – it was not worth such a price to win you! Poor girl, we two have destroyed you between us – for the snake inflicted the wound, but I was the cause of it. I am the one who is more to blame: so, by my death, I shall comfort you for yours."

'As he spoke, he flung himself from a rock whose base had been eaten away by the booming waves, down into the sea. But Tethys pitied him as he fell, and received him gently. As he swam through the waters, she clothed him in feathers, and denied him the chance of death which he desired. The lover was indignant that he should be forced to live against his will, and that his spirit should be prevented from leaving its unhappy abode, as it longed to do. So, when he had acquired his newly-formed wings, he flew up high and then, a second time, dashed his body down on to the sea. His feathers broke his fall and, raging wildly, Aesacus went headlong down into the deep waters, incessantly trying to find a way to die. Love made him thin. He retained his long, jointed legs, and a long neck that kept his head and body far apart. He loves the waters of the sea, and has the name of diver, because he dives down into them.'

BOOK XII

❀

AESACUS' father, Priam, not knowing that his son had acquired wings and was still alive, mourned him as one dead. Hector too, and his other brothers, made offerings at an empty tomb that bore his name. One brother, Paris, was absent from this mournful ceremony, but not long afterwards he returned to his country, bringing with him the wife he had stolen, and in her train a protracted war. A thousand ships, leagued together, sailed in pursuit, carrying on board the whole host of the Greeks. Vengeance would not have been long delayed, had not savage gales made the seas impassable, so that the ships, eager though they were to be on their way, were detained in Boeotia, at Aulis, where the waters teem with fishes.

Here, the Greeks had prepared a sacrifice to Jupiter in accordance with their native custom, and the ancient altar was glowing with kindled flames, when they saw a dark gleaming serpent wriggling into a plane tree near the place where the sacrifice had been begun. There was a nest at the top of the tree, containing eight fledgelings. The serpent seized the little birds, and their mother too, who was hovering round her doomed chicks, and devoured them in its greedy jaws. Everyone stood in stunned silence, but the seer, Thestor's son, divined the truth and cried. 'We shall be victorious! Rejoice, people of Greece, for Troy shall fall: but the end of our struggles will be long postponed!' – and he interpreted the nine birds as nine years of war. The serpent, as it twined itself round the green branches of the tree, was turned to stone, and, as a statue, preserved the appearance of a climbing snake.

Nereus continued to display his wrath amid the Aonian waters, and did not allow the expedition to continue its crossing. Some believed that Neptune was sparing Troy, because he had built the city walls, but the son of Thestor was not one of these. He well knew, and proclaimed aloud, that the anger of the maiden goddess must be appeased by the blood of a maiden. So the claim of the common good prevailed over private affection, and the duty of a king conquered a father's feelings. Surrounded by weeping priests, Iphigenia stood before the altar, to offer her pure blood in sacrifice. The goddess was won over: she cast a veil of cloud over the eyes of the assembled company and, amid the bustle and confusion of the ceremony, and the din of suppliant voices, substituted a stag in place of the princess from Mycenae. Thus, when Diana was appeased by this more fitting victim, the wrath of the sea subsided along with that of the goddess and, after many adventures on the way, the thousand ships, with the winds behind them, reached the Phrygian shore.

In the centre of the world, situated between earth and sky and sea, at the point where the three realms of the universe meet, is a place from which everything the world over can be seen, however far away, and to its listening ears comes every sound. There Rumour lives, in a home she has chosen for herself on a hilltop. Night and day the house lies open, for she has given it a thousand apertures and countless entrances, with never a door to barricade her thresholds. The whole structure is of echoing brass, and is full of noises, repeating words and giving back the sounds it hears. There is no quiet within, no silence in any part, and yet there is no loud din, but only murmured whisperings, like the sound of the sea's waves, heard at a distance, or the last rumbles of thunder when Jupiter has crashed dark clouds together. A whole host inhabits these halls: they come and go, a shadowy throng, and a thousand rumours, false mixed with true, stray this way and that, while confused words flit about. Some of them pour their stories into idle ears, others carry off elsewhere the tales they have been told, the story grows, and each new teller adds something to what he has heard. Here live Credulity, and hot-headed Error, groundless Joy and craven Fears, Sedition newly-born, and Whispers whose origin no one knows. Rumour herself sees everything that goes on in heaven, in earth, and on the sea, and seeks information the world over.

She had made it known that Greek ships, with a strong army on board, were approaching Troy, and so, when the armed enemy appeared, they were not unexpected. The Trojans defended their shore, and tried to prevent the Greeks from landing. By fate's decree, the first to fall was Protesilaus: he was the victim of Hector's spear. The Greeks joined battle, but it cost them dear, and they learned the bravery of Hector's spirit by the losses he inflicted on their ranks. The Trojans too realized, at the cost of much bloodshed, what a Greek right hand could do.

Now the Sigean shore was dyed red with blood. Now Cygnus, Neptune's son, had consigned a thousand men to death, while Achilles, pressing on in his chariot, was bringing down whole columns of soldiers, with the blows of that spear whose shaft had grown on Pelion's slopes. Through the lines he rode, seeking either Cygnus or Hector. His meeting with Hector was deferred till the tenth year of the war but he confronted Cygnus. Then, urging on the horses whose snowy necks were straining at the harness he drove his chariot straight at his enemy, brandishing his quivering weapon, and shouting: 'Whoever you are, young fellow, console yourself in death with the thought that you were slain by Achilles of Thessaly!' Without more ado, he followed up his words with his heavy spear, and the unerring weapon made no mistake: but yet the sharpness of the spear he hurled availed the hero nothing – he merely bruised his adversary's breast, as if he had struck him with a blunted point. Achilles was overcome with amazement, but the other cried out to him: 'O son of a goddess – for I know you already by reputation – why are you surprised that I have not been wounded? It is not for protection that I wear the helmet you see, with its crest of tawny horsehair, or this hollow shield that burdens my left arm. These are for ornament: Mars, too, is accustomed to wear armour, for the same reason. Strip me of their protective services, and still I shall depart unharmed. It is something to be the son, not of a Nereid, but of him who rules Nereus and his daughters, and all the ocean!' As he spoke, he hurled his own weapon, to lodge in the boss of Achilles' shield. It pierced the bronze, and passed through nine of the layers of oxhide that lay beneath, but was stopped by the tenth. The Greek hero shook off this missile, and once again his stout arm hurled a quivering spear: once again Cygnus remained whole and unharmed. Nor did a third spear manage to graze him, though he exposed himself, unprotected. Then Achilles' anger blazed up, just like that of a bull in the open arena when, with his terrible horns, he tries to gore the scarlet cloaks that provoke his wrath, and perceives his attempts to wound constantly mocked. He examined his spear, to see whether perhaps its iron tip had fallen off: but it was attached to the wooden shaft. 'Is my hand then weak?' he cried. 'Has it lost, in the case of this one man, the strength it had before? Certainly it was strong enough when, in the forefront of them all, I flung down the walls of Lyrnessus, when I soaked Tenedos and Eetion's city, Thebes, in the blood of their own inhabitants, and made Caicus flow red with the slaughter of neighbouring peoples, or again when Telephus twice experienced what my spear could do. Here too, where I have slain so many men, piling their bodies in heaps upon the shore, where I see them yet, my right hand has been strong, and is so still!' Such were his words: and, as if he could not believe what had happened previously, he hurled his spear at Menoetes, one of the Lycians. With one blow he pierced his cuirass and the breast that lay beneath it. As his victim beat his dying head upon the solid earth, Achilles drew his weapon out of the warm wound and said: 'This is the hand, this the spear with which I have just been victorious. I shall use these same weapons against this foe, and pray that the result may be the same!' With these words, he attacked Cygnus again. The ashen spear did not swerve from its course, and Cygnus made no attempt to avoid it. It struck his left shoulder with a ringing sound, but rebounded as if from a wall or from solid rock. However, Achilles saw that Cygnus was stained with blood where he had been struck, and was filled with exultation: but his joy was groundless, for there was no wound – the blood was that of Menoetes. Then, wild with rage, he leaped headlong down from his high chariot and, with gleaming sword, attacked his imperturbable foe at close quarters. He saw shield and helmet slashed through by his steel, but the blade itself was actually blunted on Cygnus' unyielding body. Achilles could bear it no longer. Drawing back his shield, three times and again, he battered the face of his foe, beat upon his hollow temples with his sword-hilt and, as Cygnus retreated, followed after him, pressing him hard, harrying the enemy he had routed, allowing him no respite in his amazement and distress. Then fear took hold on Cygnus, a dark mist swam before his eyes. He stepped backwards, but a boulder that lay in the midst of the plain blocked his retreat. Achilles forced him against the rock, till his body was bent back over it, then whirled him round with all his might, and dashed him to the ground. Kneeling hard

upon his enemy's ribs, crushing them in with his shield, the Greek
warrior pulled on the thongs of Cygnus' helmet, drawing them tight
beneath his chin, and so prevented his breathing, and strangled him.
He was making ready to strip his conquered foe, when he saw that
the armour was lying empty. The god of the sea had changed
Cygnus into the white bird whose name he lately bore.

This strenuous battle brought about a respite that lasted for many
days: both sides laid down their arms and rested. While watchful
sentries guarded the Trojan walls on the one side, and the trenches
of the Greeks on the other, there came a feast day on which Achilles,
the conqueror of Cygnus, was propitiating Pallas with the sacrifice of
a cow. When he had placed its entrails on the blazing altar, and the
aroma, dear to the gods, rose up to heaven, a portion of the meat was
reserved for the sacred rites, and the rest was distributed at the tables.
The chieftains reclined on their several couches, and filled themselves
with roasted flesh – their thirst, and likewise their anxieties, they
washed away with wine. Not for that audience was the entertainment
provided by harps, or choruses, or the long flute of perforated wood:
they prolonged the night with conversation. Courage was their
theme. They spoke of battles, the enemy's and their own, and enjoyed
relating in turn the dangers they had encountered and endured. For
what else would Achilles prefer to talk about, what else would others
rather discuss in the presence of great Achilles? Their principal topic
was his recent victory, the defeat of Cygnus. All deemed it a miracle
that the body of the young hero had been impervious to any weapon,
proof against all wounds, blunting the edge of the steel. The grandson
of Aeacus and the other Greeks were expressing their astonishment at
this, when Nestor spoke: 'Cygnus has been the only instance in your
lifetime of a man who could disdain the sword, whose body no stroke
could pierce: but I myself once saw Caeneus of Thessaly enduring a
thousand blows, without any injury to his person. He lived on Mount
Othrys, and was renowned for his exploits. In his case, his invulner-
ability was the more surprising, for he had been born a woman.'
Everyone present was interested in so strange a miracle, and asked
Nestor to tell the story. Among the rest, Achilles said: 'You who
embody the wisdom of our times, ripe in years and rich in eloquence,
come now, sire, for we are all of one mind, to hear your tale. Who
was Caeneus? Why did he change to the opposite sex? On what

expedition or in what battle did he become known to you? Who conquered him, if he was conquered by anybody?'

Then the old man answered thus: 'Though the long years, slowly passing, hamper my memory, and many things that I saw in my early days escape me now, yet I remember more than I have forgotten. Of all the many exploits I have seen in peace and war – and if length of years can enable a man to behold much, I have lived two centuries and am now in my third – of them all, I say, none is more firmly fixed in my mind than this.

'Caenis, the daughter of Elatus, was famous for her beauty. She was the loveliest of all the girls in Thessaly, and roused jealous hopes in the hearts of many suitors throughout all the neighbouring cities, and in those of your own land, Achilles, for she was a countrywoman of yours. Perhaps Peleus, too, would have tried to make her his bride, but already he was either married to your mother, or had the promise of her hand. Caenis refused to marry anyone, but the story spread that, as she was wandering on a lonely part of the shore, she was forcibly subjected to the embraces of the god of the sea. The same report went on to tell how Neptune, when he had enjoyed the pleasures of his new love, said to the girl:"You may pray for anything without fear of being refused. Choose what you want." "The wrong I have suffered," replied Caenis, "evokes the fervent wish that I may never be able to undergo such an injury again. Grant that I be not a woman, and you will have given me all." The last words were uttered in deeper tones: that voice could be taken for the voice of a man, as indeed it was. For already the god of the deep sea had granted Caenis' prayer, bestowing this further boon, that the man Caeneus should be proof against any wound, and should never be slain by the sword. Rejoicing in the god's gift, Caeneus departed, and spent his days in the pastimes which men enjoy, roaming the lands of the Peneus.

'Now Pirithous, bold Ixion's son, on the occasion of his marriage to Hippodame, had invited the fierce cloud-born centaurs to take their places at tables set out in order in a tree-sheltered cave. The princes of Thessaly were present, and I too was there at the palace which, on that festive day, was filled with the noisy confusion of the assembled guests. Now they were singing the marriage hymn, the great hall was thick with smoke from the fires, when the bride appeared, surrounded by her many attendants, young wives and matrons, surpassing them

all in her loveliness. We declared that Pirithous was a lucky man to
have such a bride, and thereby all but brought to nothing the good
fortune we predicted for him: for the sight of the bride, no less than
the wine, inflamed the passions of Eurytus, fiercest of all the fierce
centaurs. Under the sway of drunken frenzy, intensified by lust, he
lost all control of himself. Immediately the wedding feast was
thrown into confusion, as tables were overturned, and the new bride
was violently dragged off by the hair. Eurytus seized Hippodame, and
others carried off whichever girl they fancied, or whichever one they
could. It was like the scene in a captured city – the palace echoed with
women's shrieks. Quickly we all jumped to our feet, but Theseus was
the first to speak: "Eurytus," he cried. "What madness hounds you
on, that you attack Pirithous while I yet live, and so unwittingly out-
rage two men, by injuring one?" In case his words would have no
effect, the hero pushed aside the menacing centaurs, and removed
the girl from her demented captors. Eurytus made no reply, for
actions such as his could not be defended by words, but wantonly
attacked the girl's champion, pummelling Theseus' face and noble
breast with his fists. There happened to be an antique goblet lying
near at hand, its surface roughened by a raised design. The son of
Aegeus lifted the cup and, drawing himself up to his full height, flung
it in his enemy's face. The other fell backwards and lay, drumming
his heels on the sodden ground and vomiting from his shattered
mouth gobbets of blood and wine and brains. His brother centaurs,
blazing with anger at his death, vied with one another, shouting with
one accord: "To arms!" Wine gave them courage. As the battle
began, goblets were hurled and went flying through the air, along
with fragile jugs and curved basins, once the panoply of a feast, but
now employed for war and slaughter.

'Amycus, son of Ophion, was the first who dared to rob the inner
shrine of its offerings: he gave the lead by snatching from the sanctu-
ary a branched candlestick, thickly hung with flaring lamps. Raising
this aloft, as the priest raises the sacrificial axe when he strains to cleave
through the snowy neck of the bull, Amycus dashed it against the
forehead of the Lapith Celadon, and left him with his skull smashed,
his face unrecognizable: for his eyes leaped from their sockets, his
nose, pushed backwards as the bones of his face were shattered, was
driven firmly into the middle of his palate. But Pelates from Pella

brought Amycus to the ground with a table-leg, wrenched from a maplewood table. He drove his enemy's chin down into his breast and, as Amycus was spitting out a mixture of teeth and blood, struck him a second blow that despatched him to the shades of Tartarus.

'Then Gryneus, standing near the smoking altar, eyed it with a grim countenance and said: "Why not make use of that?" Raising the huge altar, fire and all, he flung it into the midst of the Lapiths' ranks, and crushed two of their company, Broteas and Orios. Orios' mother was Mycale, whose spells, so men agreed, had often drawn down the horned moon from heaven despite its struggles. "You will suffer for this, if I can but lay hold on a weapon!" shouted Exadius. Instead of a spear, he seized a set of stag's antlers, which had been hung on a tall pine tree as a votive offering. The two branching horns pierced Gryneus' eyes, and gouged out his eyeballs, part of which clung to the horn, part trickled down on to his beard and hung there, congealed with blood. Then Rhoetus snatched a blazing branch of plumwood from the very heart of the altar and, swinging it to the right, grazed Charaxus' temples with their covering of yellow hair. The hair, set alight by the leaping flames, burned like a dry cornfield, and the blood from his wound, as it was scorched, gave a horrible hissing sound, just like iron, red-hot from the fire, when the blacksmith lifts it in his curving tongs, and plunges it in a vat of water, where it hisses and sizzles on being thrust under the tepid liquid. But Charaxus, wounded as he was, shook the greedy fire from his shaggy hair: tearing up out of the earth the slab that formed the threshold of the door, he raised it on his shoulders. It was a cartload in itself, and its very weight prevented him from hurling it far enough to reach his foe: in fact, the massive stone crushed one of his friends, Cometes, who was standing near him. Rhoetus did not contain his exultation: "May the others in your camp display their bravery with like result!" he cried and, with his half-burned branch, he renewed his assault on his foe, striking him repeatedly: three times, four times with violent blows he smashed the joinings of his skull, till the bones sank into the jellied mass of his brains.

'Then the victor turned his attention to Evagrus, Corythus, and Dryas. Corythus, a young lad whose cheeks were covered with the first downy hairs of manhood, fell before his attack. "What glory is there in routing a boy?" cried Evagrus, but Rhoetus prevented him from saying more by fiercely thrusting the fiery flaming brand into his open mouth, as he spoke, and through his mouth down into his chest. Then, whirling his blazing weapon round his head, he pursued savage Dryas: but in this case, the outcome was different. For as Rhoetus came on, elated by his unbroken success in slaying his enemies, Dryas ran him through with the point of a charred wooden stake, just where his neck joined his shoulders. Rhoetus groaned: with difficulty he wrenched the stake out of the solid bone, and fled off, soaked with his own blood. Orneus fled too, and Lycabas, and Medon who was wounded in the right shoulder. Thaumas ran away, and Pisenor, and Mermeros, who had but recently outstripped all rivals in speed of foot, but now moved more slowly because of the wound he had suffered. Pholus also withdrew, and Melaneus, along with Abas, the wild-boar hunter, and the augur Astylos who had vainly tried to dissuade his people from war. To Nessus, who was afraid of being wounded, Astylos gave encouragement, and said: "Don't run away: you will be kept safe, to be a target for Hercules' bow!" But there was no escape from death for Eurynomus or Lycidas, for Areos or Imbreus: Dryas' right hand struck them all down, as they fought facing him. Crenaeus too was wounded in the front of the body, and that though he had turned his back in flight. For, as he looked back, he received a heavy iron spear between the eyes, just where his nose joined the base of his brow.

'Quite undisturbed amid the general tumult, sunk deep in unending slumber, Aphidas was lying stretched out on the shaggy skin of a bear killed on Mount Ossa, still holding in his limp hand the cup that had been mixed for him. Phorbas, from some distance off, saw him lying there useless, contributing nothing to the fight. He slipped his fingers through the thong of his javelin: "You will drink your wine diluted with the waters of the Styx!" he cried and, without more ado, hurled his weapon at the youth. As it happened, Aphidas was lying with his head fallen backwards, and the ashwood tipped with iron drove its way into his throat. He died without knowing anything about it. From his full throat the black blood flowed out, over the coverlets and into the cups themselves.

'I saw Petraeus struggling to root up from the ground an acorn-laden oak tree. As he put his arms round it, shaking it this way and that, in his endeavour to pull up the trunk he had loosened, Pirithous' spear pierced his ribs, and pinned his writhing chest to the solid wood. Both Lycus and Chromis, so men said, fell victims to Pirithous' courage, but neither of them conferred such glory on the victor as did Dictys and Helops. Helops was transfixed by a javelin which, entering his right temple, penetrated all the way through, from ear to ear; Dictys was fleeing in panic, with Ixion's son hard after him, along a narrow mountain track with a sheer drop on either side when he lost his footing and, crashing downwards, impaled his body on the shattered spikes of a huge mountain ash that had broken under his weight.

'Aphareus was at hand to avenge him. He tore up a rock from the mountainside, and tried to hurl it, but Theseus caught him in the very act and, with a blow from his oaken cudgel, broke the massive bones of his elbow. Then, having neither time nor desire to go further and kill one whom he had rendered harmless, the son of Aegeus leaped up on tall Bienor's back, which was quite unused to supporting anyone but its owner. Pressing his knees into his enemy's ribs, he grasped Bienor's mane with his left hand, and held on tightly, while with his knotted club he smashed in the centaur's face, his solid temples and the mouth that was uttering streams of threats. Then with his club the hero felled Nedymnus and the javelin-thrower Lycopes, Hippasus whose flowing beard protected his chest, Ripheus, who towered above the tree-tops, and Thereus who used to seize bears on the Thessalian mountain slopes, and bring his wrathful captives home alive.

'Demoleon could not endure Theseus' success in battle any longer. With all his strength he wrenched at the sturdy trunk of an old pine tree, trying to tear it up: when this was beyond him, he broke off part of the tree and hurled it at his enemy. But Theseus withdrew well out of the way of the approaching missile, thanks to a warning from Pallas – or so he himself would have us believe. The tree-trunk, how-ever, did not fall without effect, for it struck tall Crantor, severing his left shoulder and breast from his neck. He was your father's armour-bearer, Achilles, given to him as a pledge and guarantee of peace by Amyntor, leader of the Dolopes, after your father had defeated him in war. So when Peleus, who was some distance away, saw Crantor with his body torn apart by that horrible wound, he cried out: "Crantor, dearest of all my young warriors, receive at least this

277

tribute to the dead!" and then, with all the strength of his arm, and with strength of purpose too, he hurled his ashen spear at Demoleon. The weapon broke through his ribcage and stuck quivering in the bones. The centaur dragged out the wooden shaft without its iron tip, for even the shaft would scarcely come away. The point remained fixed in his lungs. His very agony gave him strength – though wounded, he reared up to attack his enemy, and made to trample on the hero with his horse's hooves. Peleus received the blows on his helmet and his echoing shield, defending the upper part of his body by holding his weapons out in front while, with one stroke, he thrust his spear through the centaur's shoulders, piercing his two breasts. Previous to this, however, Peleus had killed Phlegraeus and Hyles, with missiles thrown from a distance and, fighting at close range, had despatched Iphinous and Clanis. To these victims he added Dorylas, who used to wear a wolfskin cap on his head and, in place of a spear, carried a fine pair of crooked horns, taken from an ox, and reddened with quantities of blood. I had called out to Dorylas: "See how far inferior your horns are to my steel!" and, courage lending me strength, had hurled my javelin at him; since the centaur could not avoid the weapon, he put up his right hand to shield his forehead where it was likely to be wounded. His hand was pinned to his brow, and he uttered a great cry. Peleus, who was standing near, saw him fastened there, overcome by the painful wound, and struck him with his sword, full in the stomach. The other leaped fiercely forward, dragging his entrails along the ground, trampling them as he dragged, and bursting them as he trampled, till his legs became entangled and, with abdomen emptied, he collapsed.

'Nor did his beauty save Cyllarus in the fight, if indeed we allow beauty to such a shape as his. The golden down of his beard was just beginning to show, golden hair hung from his shoulders, halfway down his flanks. There was a pleasing liveliness in his expression, and neck and shoulders, hands and breast, and all his human parts were like the sculptured statues that men praise. The horse's body that formed his lower half was likewise flawless, in no way inferior to the man above. Given a head and neck, he would have been a fit mount for Castor, so well-suited was his back for a rider, so well-muscled his lofty chest. His coat shone all over, darker than the blackness of pitch, but his tail was white, and his legs white too. Many females of his own kind made overtures to him, but Hylonome alone won his affections, the comeliest of all the female centaurs who lived in the depths of the woods. She, and only she, held Cyllarus' heart by her endearments, by loving him and confessing her love, and by caring for her appearance, as far as was possible with limbs of that description, so that her hair was smoothly combed and in it she twined sometimes rosemary, sometimes violets or roses, or else she wore shining lilies. Twice every day she bathed her face in the spring that flowed down from the woods on the crest of Pagasae, twice she dipped her body in its waters. Draped over her shoulder and her left side she wore chosen skins of wild beasts, selecting only those which were becoming. Cyllarus and she loved each other equally – they wandered together in the mountains, and returned together to the cave that was their home.

'On this occasion, too, they had come into the Lapith palace side by side, and side by side were fighting fiercely. A javelin, thrown by an unknown hand, came speeding from the left, and pierced Cyllarus just below the place where his neck joined his chest. Though the wound was a small one, his heart was injured and grew numb and cold when the weapon was drawn out, as did the rest of his body too. Without losing an instant, Hylonome gathered his dying limbs into her arms, closed the wound by placing her hand against it and, with her lips on his, tried to prevent the escape of his fleeting breath. When she saw that he was dead, she cried aloud words which the uproar prevented me from hearing, then fell on the weapon which had killed her husband, clasping him still in her dying embrace.

'Another figure, too, which stands before my eyes, is that of Phaeocomes, who had knotted six lion skins together as a protective covering both for his human parts and for his horse's body. Hurling a huge block of wood, which two teams of oxen could scarcely have moved, he struck Tectaphos, the son of Olenus, and broke open his head from on top. The broad dome of his skull was shattered, and soft brain matter oozed out through his mouth, through the hollows of his nostrils and his eyes and ears, just as clotted milk trickles through the woven oak twigs of a basket or as the thick liquid, under the sieve's pressure, oozes through the close holes of the mesh. But, as the centaur was about to strip his fallen victim – your father knows the truth of this – I thrust my sword deep into the thigh of the despoiler.

Chthonius and Teleboas too fell beneath my sword: of these, the former had armed himself with a forked branch of a tree, but the other had a javelin, with which he wounded me. You see the mark here – the old scar from the wound is still visible. Ah, I should have been sent to capture Troy in those days! Then I had the power, if not to overcome, at least to check the arms of mighty Hector, with my own. But at that time Hector was not yet born, or else he was only a boy, and now I have reached an age where my strength is failing.

'What need is there to tell how Periphas overcame the centaur Pyraethus or how Ampyx drove his cornel spear, though it had lost its point, right into the face of his four-legged adversary, Echeclus? Macareus killed Erigdupus, from Pelethron, by ramming a stake into his breast: and I remember too how a hunting spear, thrown by Nessus' hand, buried itself in Cymelus' groin. And there was Mopsus, the son of Ampycus: you must not imagine that he was a prophet and nothing else. It was Mopsus' spear that brought down the centaur Hodites who lay, vainly trying to speak, with his tongue pinned to his chin and his chin to his throat.

'Meanwhile Caeneus had consigned five men to death, Styphelus and Bromus, Antimachus, Elymus, and Pyracmus who was armed with an axe. I do not remember how they were wounded, but I noted their number and their names. Then Latreus, huge of limb and body, and armed with spoils captured when he slew Halesus of Macedon, came flying forward. He was in the prime of life, midway between youth and old age, with the strength of a young man, but streaks of grey at his temples. With his shield and sword and Macedonian lance, he was a conspicuous figure as, clashing his arms and galloping his horse in circles, he faced each company in turn, and arrogantly poured out strings of taunts into the empty air. "And am I to put up with this from you, Caenis? Caenis, I say, for to me you will always be a woman, always Caenis. Does not your birth remind you, does it not occur to you, for what deed you were thus rewarded, at what a price you acquired the appearance of a man, to which you have no right? Consider what you were born or, if you prefer, what you suffered, and go, take up your distaff and baskets of wool, twist the threads with your thumb, and leave war to men!" As he was hurling such abuse, Caeneus flung his spear and, striking the centaur just where horse and man were joined, ploughed a furrow along his flank, which was outstretched in the act of running. Latreus, mad with pain, struck the unprotected face of the Phylleian youth with his lance, but the weapon bounded back, just like hail from a rooftop, or pebbles from a hollow drum. Then he came up close, and strove to thrust his sword into Caeneus' side, but the other's body was so hard that there was no place where the sword could enter. "All the same, you will not escape!" cried Latreus. "The edge of my sword will slay you, since the point is blunt!" and, turning his blade sideways, he reached round Caeneus' thighs, with his long right arm. The blow resounded as if marble had been struck and the sword blade shivered into pieces on that hardened skin. Finally, when Caeneus had exposed himself long enough to his enemy and, to the latter's astonishment, had suffered no harm: "Come now," he exclaimed. "Let us see what your body can do against my steel!" and he plunged his deadly sword up to the hilt in the centaur's flanks, twisting and turning the buried weapon in his inner organs, dealing wounds within wounds. At once the centaurs, mad with rage, raised a tremendous shout, and rushed upon Caeneus, all hurling or thrusting their weapons against one man. The spears fell blunted, and Elatus' son remained unwounded – not a weapon drew blood. The strangeness of this astounded his assailants. "What a disgrace!" cried Monychus. "We, a whole people, are worsted by a single man, and scarcely a man at that! Yet truly he is a man, and we, by our weak efforts, are mere women, such as he used to be. What use are our huge limbs? Of what avail our twofold strength, or the fact that our double nature unites in us the strongest of animals? I cannot think that we are the sons of a goddess or yet of Ixion, so great a hero that he indulged in hopes of winning lofty Juno, as long as we are overcome by an enemy who is only half a man! Roll down rocks and trees, cast whole mountainsides on top of him, and crush out that spirit, so tenacious of life, under the forests you hurl against him. Let trees smother his throat, and their weight will take the place of wounds!" As he spoke, he seized a tree which happened to have been blown down by the furious violence of a Southern gale, and flung it against his unflinching foe. The others followed his example and in a brief space Othrys was bared of its trees, Pelion stripped of its forest shade. Overwhelmed by the vast pile, Caeneus struggled under the weight of trees, supporting the heaped-up

timber on his sturdy shoulders: but when the load rose above his
mouth, higher than his head, he had no air to breathe. Now he found
his strength failing, now he tried in vain to raise himself up into the
air, and throw off the trees that had been tossed upon him, now he
heaved them about, just as if lofty Ida which we see there, look, were
to be shaken by an earthquake. What happened in the end is un-
certain. Some said that his body was thrust down into the void of
Tartarus, under the weight of the trees: but Mopsus declared it was
not so. He saw a bird with tawny wings fly out from the midst of the
pile, and soar into the clear air, and I saw it too – a bird which I have
never seen before or since. When Mopsus saw it circling smoothly
above its own company, uttering loud shrill cries, his eyes and his
thoughts followed it as it went, and he cried: "Hail to you, Caeneus,
glory of the Lapith race, once a most mighty hero, and now a bird
unique!" We believed what he said, because he said it. Grief in-
creased our rage, and we were indignant that one man should have
been overwhelmed by so many foes. Working off our anger by wield-
ing our swords, we did not stop till half the enemy were dead, and
darkness or flight had rid us of the rest.'

As the hero from Pylos was describing these battles between the
Lapiths and the half-human centaurs, Tlepolemus could not contain
his indignation that Hercules should be passed over in silence. 'Sir,' he
exclaimed, 'I am surprised that you have forgotten Hercules' exploits.
I am sure my father often used to tell me that he had defeated those
cloud-born creatures.' 'Why do you force me to remember unhappy
things?' replied Nestor sadly. 'To tear open wounds that time has
healed, and speak of my hatred for your father, and of the wrongs he
did me? It is true, as the gods know, he did things beyond belief, and
filled the world with his benefits – I only wish I could deny it. But we
do not praise Deiphobus, or Polydamas, or even Hector himself:
for who ever praised his enemy? That father of yours once razed the
walls of Messene, destroyed the innocent cities of Elis and Pylos, and
ravaged my home with fire and the sword. I shall say nothing of the
others whom he killed, but of Neleus' twelve sons, and fine young
men we were, all twelve, excepting only myself, were slain by Her-
cules' might. We must accept it that the others could be defeated, but
Periclymenus' death was quite extraordinary. Neptune, the founder
of Neleus' line, had given this boy the power to assume any form

he liked, and put it off again at will. So, to escape from Hercules, he changed into all manner of shapes, but it was of no use. Then he turned himself into that bird which is the favourite of the king of the gods, and carries his thunderbolts in its crooked talons. With an eagle's strength, with its wings, hooked beak and curving claws, he tore at Hercules' face. Against this attack, the hero of Tiryns drew his bow, all too unerring, and as the bird, soaring aloft, hovered amid the clouds, he pierced it where its wing was attached to its side. The wound was not deep, but the severed sinews could not perform their function, and without them the eagle had no power to move, no strength to fly. As his weakened pinions gained no purchase on the air, he fell to the ground and the arrow, where it clung lightly to his wing, was forced inwards by the weight of the body on top, and driven through the upper part of his breast, into the left side of his throat.

'Now do you think that I should sing Hercules' praises, my handsome captain of the fleet from Rhodes? Yet I seek no further vengeance for my brothers, beyond passing over Hercules' brave deeds in silence. We share a firm friendship, you and I.'

With these words, spoken in his pleasant voice, the old man finished his tale. The wine circulated again, and the company rose from their couches. The rest of the night was spent in slumber.

But the god who rules ocean's waves with his trident was sore at heart for the son he had changed into one of Phaethon's swans. He brooded over Cygnus' death, cursing fierce Achilles, and nursing against him a wrath that was excessive. Finally, when the war had dragged on for almost ten years, he spoke to long-haired Apollo as follows: 'Dearest by far of all my brother's children, you who built the walls of Troy with me, all to no purpose, are you distressed at all at seeing this citadel on the point of destruction? Are you grieved at so many thousands slain in the defence of her walls? Not to name them all, does the ghost of Hector, who was dragged round his own Pergamum, ever come before your eyes? And yet that barbarian, responsible for more bloodshed than the war itself, the man who ruined our handiwork – Achilles still lives. Let him present himself to me, and I will show him what I can do, with my three-pronged spear! But since I am not permitted to meet my enemy at close quarters, do you destroy him with your unseen arrow, taking him unawares!' The Delian god agreed, satisfying his own wishes no less than those of his uncle. Concealed in a cloud, he made his way to the Trojan battle-line where, in the midst of the carnage, he saw Paris flinging an occasional weapon at some Greek of no importance. The god revealed himself, and said: 'Why waste your shafts, shedding the blood of common folk? If you have any regard for your own relatives, attack the grandson of Aeacus, and revenge your dead brothers!' As he spoke, Apollo pointed out Achilles, who was mowing down the Trojan warriors with his sword. Then he turned Paris's bow in the direction of the Greek hero; with death-dealing hand he guided the unerring arrow. This was the first occasion since the death of Hector that Priam showed any joy. And so the famous Achilles, after triumphing over such great heroes, was defeated by a coward who had stolen away from Greece another man's wife. If he had to die by a woman's hand, he would far rather have fallen beneath the axe of an Amazon.

Now the hero who had been the terror of the Trojan race, the glorious guardian of the Greeks, their unconquerable leader in war, had been consumed by the flames. The same god who armed him for battle cremated him in death. Now he was reduced to ashes, and of the great Achilles there remained only a little handful, scarcely enough to fill an urn: but his glory lived on, and filled the whole world. The extent of his fame is in keeping with the man himself, and by that fame the son of Peleus is as great as he ever was, and is not conscious of Tartarus' empty void. Yet his very shield stirred up quarrels, so that one might know to whom it had belonged, and the question of who should have his weapons caused an armed conflict. None of the other leaders dared lay claim to them, neither Tydides, nor Ajax, son of Oileus, nor the younger son of Atreus, nor yet the elder son, who was his brother's superior in valour as in years: only Ajax, son of Telamon, and the son of Laertes, Ulysses, had sufficient confidence in themselves to claim such glory. The descendant of Tantalus, Agamemnon, in order to shift from his own shoulders the burden of a decision which was bound to cause ill-feeling, commanded the chieftains of Greece to take their seats in the centre of the camp, and handed over the judgement of the case to the general assembly.

BOOK XIII

❀

THE leaders took their seats, and the common soldiers stood in a circle round them. Ajax, lord of the shield of seven layers of bullhide, rose to address them. He was a quick-tempered fellow and now, as he looked behind him at the shores of the Sigean straits, and the ships lying on the beach, he scowled and shook his fist. 'By Jupiter,' he cried. 'Here we are, pleading our cause in front of the fleet, and Ulysses is being compared with me! A man who had no scruples about running away from Hector's flames, while I withstood them, and drove them back from these vessels. He finds it safer, then, to engage in wordy battles than in armed combat: for his prowess in oratory matches mine in war and strife, but I am not ready with my tongue, any more than he is with his hands. However, I do not think I need tell you Greeks of my deeds; you have seen them for yourselves. Ulysses may tell of his, the feats he accomplished with none to witness them, when only darkness knew what he was doing. The prize I claim is a great one, I admit, but my rival's character robs it of any honour. Ajax has no cause for pride, if he secures a prize, however great, to which Ulysses has aspired. Even now, already, my opponent has his reward – when he is defeated, he will be famous for having matched himself with me!

'As for myself, were there any doubt about my courage, I should still have a powerful claim, on the grounds of noble parentage. I am the son of Telamon who, under the leadership of brave Hercules, conquered the walls of Troy, and penetrated to the shores of Colchis in the ship built at Pagasae. Telamon's father was Aeacus, who dispenses justice among the silent dead, in that realm where the heavy rock torments Sisyphus, son of Aeolus. Jupiter, lord of all, recognizes and confesses Aeacus as his son. So I, Ajax, am third in descent from

Jove. Yet, fellow-Greeks, I would not have those distinguished con-
nexions count in my favour in this case, except that they were shared
by great Achilles. He was my cousin: it is my cousin's property I
claim. And you, Ulysses, who are your father Sisyphus all over again
in thieving and deceit, why are you trying to introduce the name of
an outsider into the affairs of the Aeacidae?

'Or am I to be refused the arms because I came forward to the war
before he did, and needed no informer to compel me to fight? Will
you prefer a man who was the last to take up arms, who evaded mili-
tary service, by pretending to be mad, till another, shrewder than
himself but less aware of his own interests, revealed his cowardly
trick? It was Palamedes, son of Nauplius, who dragged Ulysses to the
war he had avoided. Is he, then, to carry off these magnificent
weapons, because he was reluctant to carry any? Am I to be dis-
honoured and deprived of my kinsman's possessions, because I offered
myself to danger from the start?

'I only wish that that madness of his had been real, or that it had
been accepted as such! If only this scoundrel had never accompanied
us against the Phrygian citadels, with his criminal suggestions! With-
out him, we should never have been guilty of abandoning Philoctetes,
the son of Poeas, in Lemnos where, so they say, he now lives hidden
away in the woodland caves, moving the very rocks with his lamenta-
tions, praying that the son of Laertes may meet with his deserts – no
idle prayers, if there be any gods. That poor wretch, who swore
allegiance to the same cause as ourselves, one of our own leaders,
heir to the arrows of Hercules, is now broken by disease and hunger,
clothed and fed by the birds of the air, at whom he aims the arrows
that ought to be bringing about the destruction of Troy. But still, he
is alive, because he did not sail on, in company with Ulysses. Pala-
medes, luckless man, would have preferred to be left behind too: for
then he would be still alive or at any rate, if he had died, it would
have been without dishonour. But Ulysses, remembering all too
clearly how the other had shamed him by exposing his pretended
madness, trumped up a charge that Palamedes was betraying the
Greek cause and, in proof of the crime he had himself invented,
produced gold which he had previously buried on the spot. So, by
exile or by death, he undermined the strength of the Greeks. This is
the way Ulysses fights, this is what you have to fear from him.

'Nor will he convince me, though he be more eloquent than loyal Nestor himself, that, in deserting Nestor, he did nothing wrong. The old man was exhausted, unable to hurry, because his horse was wounded; yet, when he implored Ulysses' help, he was abandoned by his comrade. Diomede, the son of Tydeus, knows well that I am not inventing these charges: for he repeatedly called Ulysses by name, reproaching his panic-stricken friend, and deploring his flight. But the gods above take a just view of human affairs. For behold, he who gave no help came to need help himself. As he had abandoned another, so he should himself have been abandoned – he had established a precedent for his own case. But Ulysses shouted for his friends. I appeared, and saw him, pale and trembling with fear, quaking at the thought of imminent death. I interposed the bulk of my shield, sheltered him as he cowered to the ground, and saved his craven life – small cause for praise in that! If you persist in competing against me, Ulysses, let us return to that spot: conjure up again your foe, your wound, and your habitual fear, hide behind my shield, and vie with me from underneath its shelter! But when I snatched him out of danger that man, whose wounds had left him too weak to stand, fled away, and no wound slowed his progress!

'Then Hector appeared, bringing his gods to do battle with him. Wherever he attacked, he inspired such fear that he terrified even brave warriors, and not just you, Ulysses. But I laid him low; as he was exulting in the success of his bloodshed and slaughter, I knocked him over backwards with a huge rock, thrown from a distance. When he demanded to meet a champion from the Greek host, I alone withstood him. You prayed, Achaeans, that the lot might fall to me, and your prayers were answered. If you ask the outcome of that battle, at least I was not defeated by Hector. See again, how the Trojans attacked the Greek ships with fire and sword, and Jupiter to aid them. Where, then, was your eloquent Ulysses? It was I, forsooth, with my own breast, who defended the thousand ships, in which lie your hopes of reaching home again. Give me the arms, in return for so many ships.

'But indeed, if I may speak the truth, those arms of Achilles are seeking a greater honour than I am: their glory is bound up with mine, and the arms are claiming Ajax, not Ajax the arms. Let the princeling from Ithaca compare these exploits of mine with his killing of Rhesus, and of Dolon who had no spirit for fighting, his capture of Priam's son Helenus, and his theft of Pallas' holy image. He did nothing in the light of day, nothing without the help of Diomede. Supposing you should bestow those arms as a reward for such trivial services, then divide them, and let the larger part go to Diomede.

'Besides, what use is there in giving them to the Ithacan, who always goes about his business stealthily, unarmed, and deceives the unsuspecting enemy by tricks? The very gleam of the helmet, glittering with bright gold, will betray his hiding-place, and reveal him as he lurks unseen. Anyhow, if Ulysses puts Achilles' helmet on his head, he will not be able to support so great a weight: and the ashwood spear from Mount Pelion is bound to be heavy and cumbersome for that weakling's arms. The shield, too, engraved with a picture of the vast universe, will be no fitting burden for that timid left hand of his whose job is stealing. Miserable man, why seek a gift that will crush you? If some mistake on the part of the Greeks presents the prize to you, it will give the enemy cause to rob you, not to fear! Your speed in retreat, the one thing in which you excel, you coward, will be slowed up, if you drag such burdens with you. Consider, too, that your shield, having experienced battle so rarely, is still in perfect condition: whereas mine, which is gaping in a thousand places from the blows of weapons it has stopped, requires to be replaced by a new one.

'But what is the use of talking? Let us once and for all be seen in action. Throw the arms of our hero into the midst of the enemy's ranks. Bid us seek them there, and deck the one who brings them back with the weapons he has recovered.'

The son of Telamon had finished. After his last words, a murmur of applause was heard from the crowd, until the son of Laertes rose to his feet. He kept his eyes fixed on the ground for a little, then raised them to look at the leaders, and opened his lips for the speech they were expecting. His words were eloquent, and he spoke in an engaging manner.

'If my wishes and yours had prevailed, O Greeks,' he said, 'there would be no vexed question of an heir, to cause such strife. You, Achilles, would still have your own arms, and we should still have you. But, my friends, since the cruel fates have denied us our hero,' – and he pretended to brush the tears from his eyes with his hand – 'who better should succeed the great Achilles than the man through whom Achilles took his place among the Greeks? I only ask you not to favour my opponent because he appears to be a blunt fellow – as indeed he is – or be prejudiced against me because of my cleverness which has always been used to your advantage. Do not let this eloquence of mine, if indeed I have any, give rise to ill-feeling. It pleads now for its master, but has often been used on your behalf. Each man must employ the talents that he has.

'Now, as to race and ancestry, and actions in which we ourselves have had no part, I scarcely call such distinctions our own; but still, since Ajax has brought up the fact that he is the great-grandson of Jupiter, I declare that Jupiter was the founder of my family also, and I am related to him in the same degree as Ajax is. For my father, Laertes, was the son of Arcesius, and Arcesius' father was Jupiter. Moreover, no one in *my* family was ever convicted and sent into exile. Then again, on my mother's side, I have a second claim to noble descent, through my connexion with Mercury. Both my parents number a god among their ancestors. But it is not because I come of better stock than Ajax, on my mother's side, nor yet because my father never shed his brother's blood, that I claim those arms that lie before us. Weigh up the case according to our merits, always provided that Ajax gets no personal credit for the fact that Telamon and Peleus were brothers. In determining the fate of those spoils, consider, not our lineage, but the honour our courage has won for us. Or else, if you are looking for the closest relative, the nearest heir, there is Achilles' father, Peleus, and Pyrrhus, Achilles' son. What place has Ajax? Let the arms be taken to Phthia, or to Scyrus! Teucer, too, is no less Achilles' cousin than that fellow: but does he ask for the weapons? And would he get them if he did? So, since this is a contest of achievement, pure and simple, I have done more than I can readily express, but one exploit will lead me on to the next, in the order in which they happened.

'The Nereid who was Achilles' mother, knowing beforehand the death that was in store for her son, had disguised him in women's clothes, and this trick had deceived everyone, including Ajax. But I, displaying to Achilles such wares as women buy, introduced among them weapons of war, guaranteed to stir a manly heart. Then, even before the hero had thrown aside his girl's dress, while he was holding the shield and spear in his hands, I said: "Son of a goddess,

Troy's doomed citadel reserves itself for you. Why do you hesitate to bring about that mighty city's overthrow?" And I took hold of him, and sent the hero forth to his heroic deeds. Therefore, his exploits are mine. It was I who conquered battling Telephus with my spear and, having vanquished him, healed him again in answer to his prayers. The fall of Thebes was my doing: give me the credit for capturing Lesbos, Tenedos, Chryses, and Cilla, Apollo's cities, and Scyrus, too. Reckon that my right hand shattered the walls of Lyrnessus, and razed them to the ground. To say nothing of Achilles' other victims, assuredly it was I who gave you a warrior able to destroy fierce Hector! It is thanks to me that famous Hector lies dead. In return for those arms which exposed Achilles, I ask his arms now. I gave them to him when he was alive, and now that he is dead I ask them back.

'When Menelaus' grief had become the concern of all the Greeks, a thousand ships filled the harbour of Aulis opposite Euboea. They waited a long time, but no winds came, or those that did were contrary to the fleet. Then the harsh oracle bade Agamemnon sacrifice his innocent daughter to Diana's cruelty. The father refused absolutely. He flew into a passion against the gods themselves, and in the mind of the king a father's feelings prevailed. It was I who, by my words, persuaded the soft-hearted parent to consider the good of the state. It was a difficult case I had, I admit – may Atrides forgive me for the admission! – with the judge biased against me. However the people's good, his brother's cause, and the chief command that was vested in him, induced Agamemnon to consider the killing of his daughter justified by the glory it would bring. Then I was also sent to the girl's mother, who had to be, not encouraged, but cunningly tricked into agreement. Had Ajax gone on that mission, our sails would even yet be deprived of the winds.

'I was sent as an ambassador to the Trojan citadel, too, and boldly looked on the senate house of lofty Troy, and entered it, while it was still packed with members. Undismayed, I pleaded the cause which all Greece had entrusted to me, made my accusation against Paris, demanding the return of Helen and the booty, and stirred Priam's sympathies, and Antenor's too. Paris and his brothers, on the other hand, and those who had participated in the robbery under his leadership, were hard put to it to keep their criminal hands off me.

You know this, Menelaus, for that was the first day when we two shared a common danger.

'It would take a long time to tell all the useful things I have achieved by strategy or force, in the course of this lengthy war. When the first battles were over, the enemy long contained themselves within their city walls, and gave us no chance of open fighting. In the tenth year, and not till then, we fought in the field. What were you doing all that time, Ajax, you who know nothing about anything but battle? What use were you? Whereas, if you ask about my activities, I was laying ambushes for our foes, digging a trench round their fortifications, cheering my companions to endure the boredom of protracted warfare with equanimity, showing how we could be fed and armed, and being sent off wherever occasion demanded.

'Then, behold, at Jupiter's command our king, deceived by a dream, ordered us to give up the war we had begun. Agamemnon could defend his order by quoting its source, but Ajax should have refused to allow this: he should have demanded the destruction of Troy and fought, the one thing he can do! Why did he not stop the soldiers, as they made to depart? Why did he not take arms, and give a lead for the wavering mob to follow? This was not too much to ask of one who never speaks without boasting. Now, what do you make of the fact that he actually fled himself? I saw you: I was ashamed to see you, when you withdrew, and disgraced yourself by preparing to set sail. At once I shouted: "What are you doing? My friends, what madness urges you to let go your hold on conquered Troy? What do you carry home with you after ten years, what save dishonour?" By such words, and others like them, in which grief had made me eloquent, I turned the men from their projected flight, and led them back from the ships. Agamemnon called together his terror-stricken allies, and still the son of Telamon did not dare to open his mouth, though even Thersites had the temerity to attack the leaders with his words – thanks to me, the rogue did not get away with that with impunity! I rose to my feet, and encouraged my frightened countrymen against the enemy, restoring their lost courage by my words. From that time, any brave deed which that fellow there can seem to have done is in fact mine, since I dragged him back from flight.

'Finally, of all the Greeks, Ajax, who either praises you, or seeks your company? Now Diomede shares all he does with me, speaks of

me with approbation, and always trusts Ulysses as his comrade. It is
something to be chosen out of so many thousand Greeks by Diomede
to be his sole companion. And there was no drawing of lots to order
me against the foe: all the same, scorning danger from enemies or
from darkness, I sallied forth and killed the Phrygian Dolon, who
was engaged on the same hazardous enterprise as myself; not, how-
ever, before I had forced him to reveal all he knew, and had learned
what preparations were going on in treacherous Troy. I had dis-
covered everything and, having nothing more to spy out, could have
returned, covered in my promised glory; but, not content with that,
I made for the tents of Rhesus and, in his own camp, killed Rhesus
himself and his companions. And so, victorious, having achieved
all I had prayed for, like a general celebrating a joyous triumph, I
mounted the chariot I had captured. Now refuse me the arms of the
hero Achilles, whose horses my Trojan adversary had demanded in
return for his night's work – let Ajax prove more generous than you!

'Why should I speak of the hosts of the Lycian Sarpedon, laid low
by my sword? Amid much bloodshed I killed Coeranus, Iphitus' son,
Alastor and Chromius, Alcander and Halius, Noemon and Prytanis;
I consigned Thoon to his death, and Chersidamas, Charops and
Ennomus, whom a cruel fate hounded on, as well as others, less cele-
brated, who fell to my hand, beneath the city walls. I, too, have re-
ceived wounds, my friends, honourable wounds, as their position
shows. Do not take my word alone for that, but see!' – and he pulled
down his garment – 'Here is a breast,' he said, 'that has always been
employed in your service. But throughout all these years the son of
Telamon has not shed a drop of blood in the allied cause, there is not a
scar on his body!

'What does it matter if he declares that he fought against the
Trojans, and against Jove himself, in defence of the Greek fleet? I
agree that he did: he bore his arms against them, and it is not my
practice to belittle men's services, in a grudging spirit. But I cannot
have him take to himself credit that he shares with others. He should
give you also some share in the honour. For it was Patroclus, pro-
tected by the fact that the enemy took him for Achilles, who thrust
back the Trojans and their champion from the ships they intended to
burn. Ajax imagines, too, that he alone dared to meet Hector's
challenge, forgetting the king, the other leaders, and myself: for he

was the ninth to volunteer for this duty, though he was preferred by the luck of the draw. But, in any case, what was the result of your combat, my brave hero? Hector departed unhurt, without a single wound.

'And now, alas, with what grief am I forced to recall that day when Achilles fell, the bulwark of the Greeks! But neither tears nor grief nor fear hindered me from gathering up his body from the ground, and bringing it back on high: on these shoulders, these I say, I bore the corpse of Achilles and, at the same time, carried the arms which now, likewise, I am anxious to wear. I have strength sufficient for such burdens, and a mind that will surely appreciate the honour you do me. Was it for this that the sea nymph, Achilles' mother, was so ambitious for her son, that those gifts from heaven, fashioned with such surpassing skill, should be worn by a rough soldier of no intelligence? For Ajax does not understand the engravings on the shield, the ocean, the earth and its scattered cities, the heights of heaven set with stars, the Pleiades, the Hyades, the Bear that has no dealings with the sea, and Orion's shining sword. He demands to receive arms which he does not appreciate.

'Moreover, he accuses me of shirking the harsh duties of warfare, and coming late to a contest others had begun. What, does he not realize that he is thus slandering great-hearted Achilles? If you call it a crime to pretend to be what one is not, then both of us pretended: if delay in coming to the war counts as a fault, I came earlier than Achilles. In my case, an affectionate wife detained me: in his, it was an affectionate mother. The early days of the war we gave to them, but the rest we have given to you. Supposing I cannot defend myself, I do not shrink from a charge which I share with so great a hero. All the same, it was Ulysses' sharpness that discovered Achilles, but Ajax never discovered Ulysses.

'It is not surprising that he should pour abuse upon me, with his stupid tongue, when even about you he says things of which he ought to be ashamed. Or was it shameful of me to bring a false charge against Palamedes, and honourable of you to condemn him? No! The son of Nauplius could not defend an action as manifest as it was monstrous. You did not merely hear charges against him, you saw his guilt with your own eyes: the truth of my accusations was established by his bribe.

'Nor do I deserve to be put on trial because Vulcan's island of

Lesbos still contains Philoctetes, Poeas' son. Defend your own action,
for you all agreed to this! I will not deny that I advised him to with-
draw from the rigours of war and travel, to try to relieve the agony
of his suffering by resting. He took my advice – and he is alive. Not
only was my opinion given in all good faith, though that would have
been sufficient, but it had good results. Now, the soothsayers demand
his presence, in order to destroy the Trojan citadel. Do not entrust me
with that commission: the son of Telamon will be a better ambassa-
dor, he will better soothe with his eloquence the wrath of a sick and
angry man or, by some clever cunning trick, will bring him here! But
Simois will flow backwards, Ida stand leafless, and Greece promise
her aid to Troy, before ever any shrewdness on the part of the dull-
witted Ajax assists the Greeks, should I cease to employ my ingenuity
on your behalf. Though Philoctetes nurses an undying hatred against
the allies, against their king, and against myself, though he calls down
endless curses and imprecations on my head and, in his pain, longs for
a chance to have me in his power, to drain my life-blood, and to dis-
pose of me as I disposed of him, still I shall go to him, and try to bring
him back. With Fortune's aid I shall gain possession of his arrows, just
as I gained possession of the Trojan seer whom I captured, as I
revealed the oracles of the gods and the destiny of Troy, as I snatched
the image of Phrygian Minerva from her temple, in the very midst
of the foe. And does Ajax compare himself with me? You remember,
the fates would not allow the capture of Troy without that image.
Where was brave Ajax then? Where the boasts of the mighty hero?
Why were you afraid at that point? Why was it Ulysses who dared to
make his way through the outposts, to entrust himself to the dark-
ness and, passing among the enemy's fierce swords, to enter not only
the walls of Troy, but her highest citadel, snatch the goddess from her
own temple, and carry his stolen prize through the ranks of the foe?
Had I not done this, in vain would the son of Telamon have bran-
dished on his left arm the hides of seven bulls. On that night, by my
action, we gained the victory over Troy. There and then, I took
Troy's citadels, when I made it possible for them to be taken.

'Stop muttering and nodding in the direction of Diomede, to
bring him to my notice. He has his share of praise for that exploit.
Neither were you alone, when you defended the allied fleet with your
shield. There was a host with you, while I had only one. If he did not

know that a fighting man is of less importance than a wise one, and that rewards are not to be given for indomitable strength alone, he also would be a candidate for these weapons. The other and more modest Ajax would claim them too, and so would fierce Eurypylus, as well as the son of famous Andraemon; yes, and Idomeneus, and his fellow-countryman Meriones, and the younger son of Atreus, Menelaus. But indeed, though strong in might, and my equals in war, they yielded place to my wisdom. Your right hand is useful in battle, Ajax, but you need me to direct your thinking. Whereas you have strength without intelligence, I take heed for the future. You can fight, but it is in consultation with me that the son of Atreus chooses the time to fight. You serve the Greeks with your body only, but I with my mind: the man who steers the ship is superior to the one who rows, the general is greater than the common soldier and, to the same extent, I am superior to you. My intellectual powers are greater than my physical strength – all my vigour is in them.

'Do you, then, leaders of the host, give his reward to one who keeps faithful watch for you, and, in return for my care throughout so many anxious years, grant me this honour, to make up for all my services. Now my task is at an end: I have removed the obstacles of fate, and, by making its capture possible, have captured lofty Troy. By the hope that is now on our side, by the doomed walls of the Trojans, and by the gods I lately carried off from the foe, by anything that still remains to be done, needing wise counsel, if there is anything bold or dangerous still to be attempted, if you think that anything yet remains of Troy's destiny, remember me! If you do not give me the arms, give them to this!' and he pointed to the fateful statue of Minerva.

The assembly of generals was swayed by his words and it was evident from the result what eloquence could do: for the skilful speaker carried off the hero's arms.

Then he who had opposed Hector in single combat and had so often withstood fire and the sword, and even Jove, found anger the one thing he could not withstand. Grief and rage conquered the unconquered Ajax. He snatched out his sword, and cried: 'This, at any rate, is mine! Or does Ulysses demand to have it too? This is what I need, to use it on myself. The blade so often steeped in Trojan blood will now stream with its master's own, that none may conquer Ajax save himself!'

So he spoke and, where there was a vulnerable spot, buried the deadly sword in his breast, till then unwounded. His hands had not the strength to pull away the weapon he had implanted: blood itself forced out the sword. Then the earth, crimsoned with his gore, produced from the green turf that purple flower which had previously sprung up from Hyacinthus' blood. In the heart of its petals letters are traced, which apply to the boy and the hero alike, for they record the sound of the hero's name, and of the boy's cry of distress.

The victorious Ulysses set sail for the country of Hypsipyle and of the renowned Thoas, a land made notorious in the past, when its wives murdered their husbands. His purpose was to fetch the arrows which had been the weapons of Hercules. After he had brought them back to the Greeks, and with them their master, the war that had dragged on so long was at last brought to a close. Troy and Priam fell together. Priam's unhappy wife, when all else had been taken from her, lost even her human shape. Where the long Hellespont narrows into the straits, she filled the air of a foreign land with her barking, a strange and terrifying sound. Here is her story.

Ilium was in flames, its fires still raging, the altar of Jupiter had soaked up the scanty stream of aged Priam's blood, and Phoebus' priestess, dragged forth by the hair, was stretching her hands to heaven in vain appeal. The Trojan women, while they could, embraced the statues of their ancestral gods, and thronged the burning temples, but victorious Greeks dragged them away, enviable spoils of war. Astyanax was hurled down from those towers from which, looking where his mother pointed, he often used to watch his father Hector, fighting on his behalf, and defending the kingdom of his fathers.

Now Boreas was urging the Greeks to begin their journey, and the canvas filled and snapped in the favourable breeze. The sailors urged the army to take advantage of the winds. 'Farewell, Troy!' cried the Trojan women. 'We are being carried off!' They kissed their native soil, and left the smoking roofs of their country. The last to embark, a pitiable sight, was Hecuba, who had been found amongst the tombs of her sons. As she clung to their graves, and tried to kiss their bones, Ulysses dragged her forcibly away: but she gathered up the remains out of one tomb and, rescuing Hector's ashes, bore them with her in her bosom. On Hector's grave she left a lock of grey hair, a humble offering to the dead, her hair and her tears.

Opposite Phrygia, where Troy once stood, was a land inhabited by Thracians, where Polymestor had his luxurious court. To this king, Polydorus had been secretly sent by his father Priam, to be brought up far from the Trojan war. It was a wise plan, had not Priam further given his son a large sum of money, a prize for anyone disposed to crime, and a temptation to a covetous nature. When the Trojan fortunes fell, the wicked Thracian king took his sword, and plunged it in the throat of his ward. Then, as though he could destroy his crime by destroying the evidence, he flung the lifeless body from a cliff, into the waves below.

Agamemnon had moored his fleet on the Thracian shore, until the sea should become calm, and the winds more friendly. Here the earth suddenly split wide open, and the ghost of Achilles emerged, as huge as when he was alive, and on his face a threatening expression, like the one he wore when, fiercely and without justification, he attacked Agamemnon with his sword. 'So!' he cried, 'You Greeks are departing, forgetting me! The gratitude my valour inspired was buried with me! This must not be: that my tomb may have its share of honour, let Polyxena be sacrificed, to appease Achilles' shade.' No sooner had he spoken than his former comrades obeyed the pitiless ghost. The girl Polyxena, almost the sole remaining comfort of Hecuba, was snatched from her mother's arms. Brave in spite of her misery, showing more than a woman's courage, she was led to the tomb, and offered as a sacrifice on that grim pyre. As she stood before the cruel altar, and realized that the barbarous rites were being prepared for her, she did not forget herself. Seeing Neoptolemus standing sword in hand, his eyes fixed on her face, she said: 'Be quick, and shed my noble blood. I do not hinder you. Bury your sword in my throat or in my breast!' And she uncovered her breast and her throat together. 'Assuredly, Polyxena would not wish to be slave to any man! But you will not appease the wrath of any god by such a sacrifice as this. My only wish is that my death could be concealed from my mother: she troubles me, and lessens my delight in dying, though indeed it is not my death but her own life she has to fear. But, if there is justice in my plea, attendants, stand aside, and do not lay male hands upon a maiden's body. Let me go to the Stygian shades a

297

free woman. Whoever it is you seek to placate by slaying me, he will welcome more gladly the blood of one who is free. Yet, if the last words I speak move any of you – it is King Priam's daughter, not a slave, who makes this request – give back my body without ransom to my mother. Let her buy the sad right to bury me, not with gold, but with her tears: when she could, she paid in gold as well.' Polyxena finished speaking. The tears which she herself restrained were shed for her by the people. Even the priest himself was weeping, and with un-willing hands drove home the knife, piercing the breast she offered him. Her knees gave way, and she fell to the ground: but her face retained its look of fearless courage to the end. Even when she was falling, she took care to cover the parts of the body that should be covered, and to preserve what was proper for a modest girl.

The Trojan women lifted up her body, counting the number of Priam's children whom they had mourned, remembering how much bloodshed that one house had suffered. They lamented the fate of the maiden and of her mother, lately styled a king's wife, a royal parent, the epitome of Asia's prosperity, and now most wretched even for a captive. The victorious Ulysses would not have had her for his slave, had she not borne Hector: Hector only just found a master for his mother.

Hecuba embraced her daughter's body, from which so brave a spirit had departed, and shed for her, too, the tears that had so often flowed for husband, sons, and country. She poured the salt drops into the girl's wounds, covered the dead mouth with kisses and, beating her own breast, well-used now to such treatment, trailed her long hair in the congealing blood. She tore at her bosom and, among other lamentations, cried: 'O my daughter, last of your mother's woes – for what remains? – my daughter, you lie dead, and I look on your wound, that is mine as well. See, lest I should lose any of my children without bloodshed, you too have your wound. I thought that you, at least, because you were a woman, were safe from the sword: but even though a woman, you have fallen beneath its blade. That same Achilles who destroyed your many brothers has destroyed you too, the man who ruined Troy, and made me childless. When he fell to the arrows of Paris and Phoebus, I said: "Now, at any rate, there is no need to fear Achilles!" but even then I should have feared him. Though he is in his grave, his very ashes rage against my family, and we have felt his enmity even from the tomb! It was for Aeacus' grandson I bore my children. Great Troy lies low, the disaster our state suffered has ended grievously, but still it has ended. For me alone the citadel of Troy still stands, my grief still runs its course. I who was lately the greatest in the land, a woman of consequence, thanks to my husband and my many children, my many sons-in-law, and daughters-in-law, am now dragged off, an exile, destitute, torn away from the tombs of my family, a gift for Penelope, who will point me out to the women of Ithaca as I spin the wool she gives me, and will say: "That woman is the famous mother of Hector, that is Priam's wife."

'When I had already lost so many, now you, the only one left to comfort your mother's grief, have been sacrificed on the tomb of our enemy. I bore you as an offering for my foe! Hard-hearted woman that I am, why do I yet remain? Why linger here? To what end am I kept alive, old and burdened with years? O cruel gods, why do you postpone the death of an old woman, who has lived too long, unless it be that I may see yet more deaths? Who would think that Priam could be called fortunate, after the destruction of Troy? Yet he is happy in his death! For he did not see you slain, O my daughter, but lost his kingdom and his life together. As a princess, I suppose you will be given a rich funeral, and your body will be laid to rest in the tomb of your fathers? Such is not the fortune of this house. Your mother's tears will be your funeral offerings, and a scattering of foreign sand. We have lost all: yet Polydorus remains, to give me cause to live a short time still, my dearest child, once the youngest of my sons, and now the only one, who was sent off to these shores, to the Thracian king. But meanwhile, why am I wasting time, instead of washing your cruel wounds, and your face spattered with blood so pitilessly shed?'

When she had spoken these words, she made her way to the shore, walking with the tottering steps of an old woman, and tearing her white hair as she went. Intending to draw water from the sea, the unhappy mother had called to the Trojan women: 'Give me a pitcher!' when she caught sight of Polydorus' body, washed up on the beach, and saw the gaping wounds that Thracian weapons had made. The Trojan women cried aloud, but Hecuba was dumb with grief. Her very anguish swallowed up her voice, and dried the tears that welled

within. Motionless as flinty rock she stood, now with her eyes fixed
on the ground, now raising her contorted features to the sky, now
gazing at the face of her son, as he lay there, or again at his wounds –
especially at his wounds, as with mounting anger she prepared herself
for vengeance. Then, when her wrath was fiercely blazing, she
determined on revenge just as if she were still a queen, and concen-
trated all her thoughts on punishment. As a lioness, robbed of her un-
weaned cub, rages round till she finds the footprints of the thief, and
follows the trail of her unseen foe, so Hecuba, in a mixture of grief
and rage, forgot her years but not her courage, and made her way to
Polymestor, the scoundrel who had perpetrated this dreadful murder.
She sought an audience with the king, saying that she wished to show
him a secret store of gold she still had left, so that he might give it to
her son. The Thracian believed her and, since greed for gain had
become a habit, came to her in private. Then he spoke to her with
smooth and cunning words: 'Do not waste time, Hecuba, but hand
over the gift for your son. All that you give, as well as all that you
have given in the past, will be his – by the gods I swear it!' Grimly
she watched him as he spoke and falsely swore, till her seething rage
boiled over. Calling the host of captive women to her aid, she seized
the king and sank her fingers in his treacherous eyes, gouging them
out of their sockets – anger lent her strength. Then, horribly stained
with his guilty blood, she plunged in her hands and dragged out not
his eyes, for he had no eyes left, but the places where his eyes had been.

The people of Thrace, roused by this disaster to their king, began
to attack the Trojan Hecuba, pelting her with stones and weapons,
but with harsh growls she snapped at the rocks they threw and, when
she opened her mouth to try to speak, uttered barks instead of words.
The place where this happened is still in existence, and derives its
name from the event. Hecuba, long remembering her past sufferings,
continued to howl mournfully still, as she roamed the Thracian fields.
The fate of that poor queen moved the pity of her own people, the
Trojans, it moved her enemies, the Greeks, and all the gods as well:
so much so, that even Jove's wife and sister, Juno, declared that
Hecuba had not deserved to meet with such an end.

Aurora, though she had favoured that same Trojan cause, had no
time to be distressed by the disasters and downfall of Troy, or of
Hecuba. A more intimate sorrow troubled the goddess, her own

private grief at the loss of her son: for his saffron-robed mother had seen Memnon die on the Phrygian plains, beneath the spear of Achilles. At that sight, the colour which tints the rosy morning hours grew pale, and the bright daylight was concealed by clouds. When his limbs were placed upon the funeral fires, his mother could not bear to look. With hair dishevelled, just as she was, Aurora was not too proud to fling herself down at Jupiter's feet, weeping and praying: 'I know that I am the least of all the gods whom the golden heavens contain, for I have the fewest temples throughout all the world. Yet still I am a goddess. I have not come to ask you to give me shrines, or altars on which fires may glow, or days set apart for sacrifice: though, if you would consider how much I do for you, woman though I am, when at each new dawn I keep night within its limits, you would think it right to reward me. But that is not Aurora's present care, nor is she in a state to demand the honours due to her. I come because I have lost my Memnon, who took up arms bravely but vainly in his uncle's cause, and was slain in his early youth – for so you willed it – by mighty Achilles. Grant him some honour, I pray you, great ruler of the gods, to make his death less hard to bear, and so soothe a mother's wounded heart!' Jupiter nodded his consent. As Memnon's lofty pyre collapsed, consumed by leaping flames, rolling clouds of black smoke darkened the sky, just as when rivers breathe out the fogs they produce, and prevent the sun from shining through. Then the black ash flew upwards and, packed and compressed into a single body, took on a definite shape: it acquired heat and the vital spark of life from the fire, while the lightness of the substance gave it wings. At first resembling a bird, and then in fact a real bird, it flew on whirring wings and countless sisters too, born from the same source, made the air noisy with their flight. Three times they flew around the pyre, and three times in unison uttered a wailing cry, but, as they circled for the fourth time, the birds drew apart in two separate flocks. Then, swooping from opposite directions, the two companies fought fiercely, giving vent to their anger with beaks and hooked claws, tiring the wings and breasts opposed to their own. Remembering that they owed their origin to a man of valour they fought till they fell as funeral offerings to the buried ashes of the hero who was their kinsman. To these birds, so suddenly created, the man who gave them being gave his name as well, and they were called Memnonides after him. When the sun has travelled through the twelve signs of the zodiac, they fight again and die again in honour of their father's festival. So, while others felt the tragedy of Hecuba's barking like a dog, Aurora was absorbed in her own grief. Even now she weeps affectionate tears, and sprinkles them over the whole world.

However, the fates did not allow Troy's hopes to be utterly overthrown, together with her walls. The hero Aeneas, the son of Venus, carried away upon his shoulders the city's sacred images, and with them another burden, equally sacred, his venerable father. Out of all his great possessions, the good Aeneas chose to bear away this portion, and his son Ascanius. Setting out from Antandros, he was borne across the sea, in his fugitive ships, leaving behind him the guilt-stained homes of Thrace, the land reeking with Polydorus' blood. He sailed before prosperous winds and a following tide, till he came with his friends to Delos, and the city of Apollo. There Anius was king and priest in one, serving his people and Apollo with the same devotion. He received Aeneas into his home and temple, and showed him the city, the famous shrine, and the two trees to which Leto had once clung, when she was giving birth to her children. The Trojans sprinkled incense in the flames, and poured wine upon the incense. When the entrails of slain oxen had been duly burned, they made their way to the palace. Lofty couches were set out, and the visitors took a meal of bread, the gift of Ceres, washed down with draughts of wine.

Then goodly Anchises addressed his host, and said: 'Chosen priest of Phoebus, am I mistaken, or did you have a son, when I first saw those city walls, and four daughters too, if I remember aright?' Shaking his head, which was encircled with snowy fillets, sadly Anius replied: 'Great hero, you are not mistaken. You saw me then, the parent of five children. But now, so fickle is human fortune, you see me practically childless. For of what use to me is my absent son, who lives and rules in his father's stead in the land which is called Andros, after him? The Delian god, Apollo, gave my son the power to foretell the future, and to my daughters Bacchus gave other gifts, beyond anything for which they had hoped or prayed. All that they touched was changed into corn, or into streams of wine or olive oil, so that there was rich profit in the girls. But when the man who plundered your city, Agamemnon son of Atreus, heard of this marvel, he used armed force to drag my children from their father's

302

breast, against their will. So, you see, we too, to some extent, felt the hurricane of disaster that overwhelmed you. He ordered the girls to feed the Greek fleet, by means of their heaven-sent gift, but each of them fled for refuge where she could: two made for Euboea, and two for their brother's kingdom of Andros. Up came the army, and threatened war, unless they were handed over. The king's affection for his sisters was overcome by fear, and he surrendered them to their doom. One can forgive the faint-hearted brother: there was no Aeneas there, to defend Andros, no Hector, thanks to whom you Trojans endured till the tenth year of the war. Fetters were already being prepared for the arms of the captives, but while those arms yet were free, the girls raised them up to heaven, and cried to their patron god: "Father Bacchus, lend us your aid!" The god who had given them their gift brought them his help, if it can be called helping to bring about their miraculous destruction. How they lost their human shape I could not discover, nor can I tell you now, but I do know the final issue of this calamity. My daughters took wings, and were changed into snowy doves, the birds that belong to Venus, your wife.'

With these and other such tales besides, the company whiled away the time as they feasted. Then, when the tables had been removed, they retired to sleep. Rising again at daybreak, they approached the oracle of Phoebus, who bade them seek their ancient mother, and the shores from which their family had sprung.

King Anius escorted them on their way, and presented them with parting gifts, a sceptre for Anchises, a cloak and quiver for Anchises' grandson, while to Aeneas he gave a drinking bowl, which had at one time been sent from Boeotia by his friend Therses, who lived in Thebes. Therses had sent the cup, but it was the work of the Hylean Alcon, who had engraved on its surface a long story in pictures. There was a city, where seven gateways could be discerned, which served instead of a name, and indicated what city it was. In front of the town a scene of mourning was depicted, funeral processions, tombs, flaming pyres, and mothers with streaming hair and naked breasts. Nymphs too were seen, weeping and complaining of their dried-up fountains. A tree stood up starkly, bare and leafless, and goats nibbled at the parched and rocky soil. In the middle of Thebes, the artist had portrayed the daughters of Orion, the one slashing her unprotected throat – no wound for a woman to inflict – and the other stabbing herself clumsily with the point of her shuttle. Each killed herself for the sake of the people. Then their bodies were being borne through the city, in a handsome funeral procession, and cremated amid throngs of mourners. Two young men, who have become famous under the name of the Coroni, rose up from the maidens' ashes, to perpetuate their race, and led the cortège, in honour of their mothers' dust.

The gleaming devices so far described were engraved on the antique bronze, but round the rim of the goblet was a band of gilded acanthus leaves, in high relief. The Trojans in return presented their host with gifts no less valuable than those they had been given: a casket in which the priest could keep his incense, a sacrificial saucer, and a crown bright with gold and jewels.

From there, remembering that they derived their origin from Teucer's line, the Trojans put in at Crete, but could not long endure its climate. So they left the island of a hundred cities, hoping to reach the harbours of Ausonia. A raging storm tossed the heroes on the seas, till they sought refuge in the treacherous port of the Strophades, where they were terrified by the harpy Aello. When they had sailed past the harbours of Dulichium, past Ithaca and Samos, and the houses of Neritos, the kingdom of wily Ulysses, they saw Ambracia over which the gods once quarrelled, and the image of the judge who was turned to stone. The land is famous now because of Actian Apollo. They saw too Dodona with its speaking oaks, and the bays of Chaonia where the sons of the Molossian king soared into the sky on wings, to escape the fires that wicked hands had kindled.

After that, they sailed to the land of the Phaeacians, planted with rich orchards, and from there put in at Buthrotos in Epirus, built to resemble Troy, and ruled by the Trojan seer Helenus, one of Priam's sons. From him they learned their future fortunes and, when all had been faithfully revealed to them by his prophecies, they then moved on to Sicily.

Three promontories run out into the sea from this island, Pachynus facing towards the rainy south, Lilybaeum exposed to the soft west winds, and Pelorus looking towards the north and the stars of the Bear, which never sink into the sea. It was at this point that the Trojans approached the island and their fleet, rowing in with the help of the tide, reached the shores of Zancle at nightfall. Scylla loomed dangerously on their right, and restless Charybdis on their left. The latter seizes ships, and swallows them down into its depths, then vomits them up again. The former has a girdle of fierce dogs round her horrid waist. She has the face of a girl and, unless all the poets' tales are false, she was, in fact, a girl once. Many suitors asked for her hand, but she rejected them. She used to go to the sea nymphs, who loved her dearly, and tell them how she had scorned the young men's love.

One day, the nymph Galatea, as she was allowing Scylla to comb her hair, began to sigh deeply, and addressed these words to her companion: 'At least the men who seek your hand are not ruthless, Scylla, and you can refuse them, as you do, with impunity. But I, the daughter of Nereus and of the sea nymph Doris, though protected by a host of sisters too, could not escape the Cyclops' love, except at the cost of grief and pain.' Tears choked Galatea's voice as she spoke, but Scylla wiped them away with her snowy fingers, and comforted the goddess. 'Dearest one, tell me your story,' she said, 'and do not hide from me the reason for your sorrow – you can trust me.' Then the Nereid answered Crataeis' daughter in these words: 'Acis was the son of Faunus and of the sea nymph Symaethis, dearly loved by his father and mother, but dearer still to me: for he, and only he, held all my affection. He was a handsome boy, with the faint down of manhood just showing on his soft cheeks, for he had celebrated his sixteenth birthday. I sought his company incessantly, while the Cyclops Polyphemus sought mine. I cannot tell, if you ask me, whether my love for Acis or my hatred of the Cyclops was the stronger: both passions were equally violent. O gentle Venus, how powerful is your sway! For that savage creature Polyphemus, an object of terror even to the wild woods, a danger to any stranger who saw him, one who despised great Olympus and the gods as well – even he understood what love means. Seized by violent passion, his heart on fire, he forgot his flocks and his caves. O Polyphemus, it was then you began to care about your appearance, to be anxious to please; you combed your bristling hair with a rake, and happily cut your shaggy beard with a scythe, examining your uncouth features as they were reflected in the water, and composing their expression. Your lust for killing, your savagery and insatiable thirst for blood, were all forgotten, ships came and went unmolested.

'Meanwhile Telemus, the son of Eurymus, who had never been mistaken about any omen, reached Sicily in his travels, and came to Etna. He visited the terrible Polyphemus, and warned him: "The single eye you have in the middle of your forehead will be torn from you by Ulysses." But the giant laughed, and said: "You are wrong, you foolish, foolish prophet, for another, a girl, has stolen it already!" So it was in vain that Telemus gave him true warning. Polyphemus scorned his words, striding heavily away along the shore with huge steps or, when he was tired, returning to the darkness of his cave.

'A wedge-shaped hill juts out into the sea in a long promontory, with the sea's waves flowing round on either side. The fierce Cyclops climbed up there, and sat down on the central ridge, followed by his woolly flocks, with none to shepherd them. When he had laid at his feet the pine tree, large enough to carry a ship's rigging, which served him as a staff, he took up his shepherd's pipe, of a hundred reeds fastened together. Then the whole mountain and the waves below heard the pastoral strains. I was lying in my Acis' arms, hidden by a rock, and my ears caught such words as these – for I marked what I heard – "O Galatea, whiter than the petals of the snowy columbine, a sweeter flower than any in the meadows, more tall and stately that the alder, more radiant than crystal, you are more playful than the tender kid, smoother than shells continually polished by the sea, more delightful than sun in winter or shade in summer, more choice than apples, lovelier to see than tall plane trees, more sparkling than ice, sweeter than ripe grapes, softer than swansdown or creamy cheese and, did you not flee from me, fairer than a well-watered garden.

'"Yet, O Galatea, you are at the same time wilder than an un-broken heifer, harder than aged oak, more treacherous than the sea, tougher than willow twigs or white vines, more immovable than these rocks, more turbulent than a river, prouder than the much-praised peacocks, fiercer than fire, harsher than harrows, grimmer than a mother bear, deafer than ocean, more pitiless than a trampled snake. Above all, and this is what I would chiefly wish to change, you flee, not just more swiftly than a stag, driven on its way by shrill-barking hounds, but swifter even than the winds, and the fleeting breezes.

'"But if you knew me well, you would regret having fled; you would reproach yourself for wasting time, and would try hard to hold me. For I have caves, part of the mountainside, arched over with living stone, in which the heat of the midsummer sun is never felt, nor yet winter's chill. I have fruit that weighs down the branches, and on the trailing vines bunches of grapes like gold, and purple ones as well. I am keeping both kinds for you. With your own hands you will pick luscious strawberries in the woodland shade, cherries in the autumn and plums too, not just the juicy blueblack kind, but also fine yellow ones, that look like new wax. When I am your husband, you will have chestnuts in plenty, and arbute berries too: every tree will be at your service.

'"All these sheep are mine, and I have many more, roaming the valleys. Many are sheltering in the woods, and many penned in the caves at home. Were you to ask, I could not tell you how many there are. It is the mark of a poor man, to count his flocks. You need not take my word for their excellence: you can see for yourself, here, how they can hardly walk for their swollen udders. There are lambs, too, in my warm sheepfolds, the younger offspring of the flock, and kids, the same age as the lambs, are kept in other pens. I have a constant supply of snowy milk, some of which is kept for drinking while some has rennet added, to make it into curds.

'"As for pets, you will have those too; and I won't give you just the usual ones, that are easily caught, such as deer or hares or goats, or a pair of doves, or nestlings from the tree-tops. On the summit of the mountain I found twin cubs, belonging to a shaggy bear, so like each other, you can hardly tell them apart. They can play with you. When I found them, I said: 'I shall keep these for my mistress.'

'"Do just raise your shining head from the deep blue sea. Come to me now, Galatea, do not scorn my gifts. Assuredly I know what I look like; quite recently I saw my reflection in the clear water, and I liked what I saw. See how big I am! You speak of some Jupiter or other, who rules in heaven, but Jupiter is no bigger than I. Luxuriant locks hang over my rugged features, and shade my shoulders like a grove. And you must not think me ugly because my body is covered with thick bristling hair: a tree is ugly without leaves, a horse un-sightly unless a tawny mane covers its flanks, birds have their feathers, and sheep are handsome because of their fleece. It is right for men to have a beard, and bristling hairs on their body. I have but one eye, in

307

the middle of my forehead, but it is the size of a huge shield. Think, does not the great sun in heaven see all this world of ours? And yet the sun has just one eye.

'"Consider, too, that my father is king of the sea, in which you live. I make him your father-in-law. Only have pity on me, and hear a suppliant's prayers! For I kneel to you alone. I who despise Jupiter and heaven and the piercing thunderbolt, am awed by you, fair Nereid, and your anger is more terrible than the lightning flash. Even if you scorn me, I could bear it better if you shunned everyone: but why, after rejecting the Cyclops, do you bestow your affections on Acis, and prefer his embraces to mine? Still, he may feel pleased with himself, and even please you, Galatea, though I wish he did not – but just let me get at him! Then he will realize that my strength is as great as my stature. I shall drag his innards out, while he is still alive, tear his limbs apart, and scatter them over the fields and over your waves. In that way, he can unite himself with you! For I am burning with love, and its flame scorches me more fiercely when I am spurned. I feel as if I were carrying Etna, flames and all, within my breast, and you, Galatea, do not care at all!"'

'After these vain laments, Polyphemus rose to his feet (for I was watching all this) just as a bull, maddened by the loss of its cow, cannot stand still, but wanders through the woods and its known haunts. Then he saw me, lying with Acis, oblivious of his coming, never suspecting any such thing. Wildly he cried: "I see you there! I shall make sure this is your last embrace!" His voice was as loud as that of an angry Cyclops ought to be: Etna shuddered at the din, and I, in terror, plunged beneath the neighbouring waters. My hero Acis, Symaethis' son, turned and fled, crying: "Galatea, your help, I pray! O parents, help me, and let me in to your kingdom, or I am doomed to die!" The Cyclops pursued him and, tearing a huge lump out of the mountainside, hurled it forward. Although only the extreme tip of the rock struck Acis, it crushed him completely. Still, I did the one thing the fates allowed, and enabled him to assume the powers that belonged to his family of old. The crimson blood that trickled from under the massive rock began, in a brief space, to lose its redness, taking on at first the hue of a river discoloured by rain, but gradually clearing. Then the rock that Polyphemus had thrown split open and, through the gash, a tall sturdy reed pushed upwards. From the gaping crevasse roared leaping waters, and then a miracle happened. Suddenly a young man, wearing a garland of waving rushes round his newly-grown horns, rose out of the fissure, as far as his waist. Except that he was larger, and his face all a deep blue, it was Acis. Even in this form, he was Acis still, but Acis changed into a river, whose waters retain his original name.'

Galatea stopped speaking, and the group of Nereids dispersed, swimming away over the peaceful waters. But Scylla returned to the shore, for she did not dare trust herself out in the open sea. She wandered, unclad, on the thirsty sand, or when she was tired, sought out some secluded cove, where she bathed her limbs in the cool sheltered waters. Suddenly shrill cries echoed across the sea, and Glaucus appeared. He had only recently become an inhabitant of the deep, after his body had undergone a transformation at Anthedon, opposite Euboea. When he saw the girl, he stopped short, filled with a desire to have her, and called to her, saying anything he thought might stop her running away. But still she fled, made swift by fear, till she reached the top of a mountain, that rose close by the shore. A great expanse of sea lay before her, for the wooded summit, towering up into a single peak, leaned far out over the waters. Here the girl stopped and, from her safe position, not knowing whether Glaucus was a monster or a god, looked with wonder at his colouring, the hair that covered his shoulders and streamed down his back, and the lower part of his body, ending in a writhing fish. He felt her scrutiny and, leaning on a rock, which stood nearby, spoke to her, and said:

'I am no monster, maiden, nor a fierce beast, but a god of the sea. In the realm of ocean, neither Proteus nor Triton is more powerful than I, nor yet Palaemon, Athamas' son. In the past, however, I was a mortal. Being passionately attached to the sea, I occupied myself entirely with its business. Sometimes I sat on a rock and fished with rod and line, sometimes I hauled in the nets, drawing with them a load of fishes.

'Now there is a stretch of shore, bordered by a green meadow, with the sea on one side, and on the other a grassy sward, which has never been harmed by the grazing of horned cattle, or cropped by peaceful sheep or shaggy goats. No bees have ever gathered its flowers or carried them off in their busy search for honey, no garlands have ever come from there, to wreathe the heads of banqueters, no one has

ever mown it, scythe in hand. I was the first to sit on that turf, drying
my dripping lines. To count the fish that I had taken, I laid them all in
order on the grass, those which chance had directed into my nets, and
those which had fastened themselves, all unsuspecting, on my barbed
hooks. What happened next sounds like pure invention, but what
good would it do me to invent this? As my catch came in contact
with the grass, the fish began to stir and turn over, and to move across
the earth as if they were in the sea. Then, while I hesitated, filled with
astonishment, the whole collection slipped away into the waves to
which they belonged, leaving the shore and their new master. Utterly
amazed, I stood stock still, seeking some explanation, and wondering
for a long time whether it was a god, or some juice in the grass, which
had caused this phenomenon. "Now what properties does this grass
possess?" I asked myself. Plucking some blades, I bit and chewed them.
Scarcely had the strange juices passed down my throat, than suddenly
I felt my heart beating fast within me, seized with a passionate desire
for this other element, the sea. I could not linger. Crying: "Good-bye
to earth, which I must never visit more!" I plunged beneath the
waters. The gods of the sea received me, and deemed me worthy to
join their company. They therefore asked Oceanus and Tethys to re-
move whatever mortal elements there were in my nature. I was puri-
fied by these two gods, and when I had recited a charm, nine times
over, to cleanse myself of sin, was told to immerse myself in a hundred
rivers. Straightway streams came flowing down from different
directions, and all their waters churned over my head. So much can I
tell you of the wonderful things that were done, so much do I remem-
ber: but of the rest my mind knew nothing. When my senses were
restored, I found myself, in mind and body, quite different from
before. Then for the first time I saw this beard of rusty green, the hair
which I sweep through the vast seas, these huge shoulders, dark blue
arms, and my legs curving away at the end into a fish complete with
fins. And yet, what pleasure is there in this appearance of mine, in
having found favour with the gods of the sea, and being one myself,
if you are not interested in these things?'

As the god was still speaking, and intending to say more, Scylla
left him. Glaucus, furiously angry at being rejected, made his way to
the marvellous home of Circe, daughter of the sun.

BOOK XIV

✸

ALREADY Etna lay behind him, the mountain piled on top of a giant's jaws, and the fields of the Cyclopes too, whose harvests owed nothing to teams of oxen, where the use of plough or harrow was unknown. He had passed by Zancle, and the walls of Rhegium lying on the opposite coast, and come through the strait that separates Italy from Sicily, where many a ship has been wrecked in the narrow channel between the two shores. From there, swimming strongly across the Etruscan sea, the god whose home is in the surging waters of Euboea approached the domain of Circe, daughter of the sun, her herb-covered hillsides and her palace thronged with the victims she had transformed into beasts. As soon as Glaucus saw the goddess and had exchanged greetings with her, he burst out:

'Goddess, I implore you, take pity on a god! For you alone can relieve this love of mine, if only you think me deserving of your help. No one knows better than I, daughter of Titan, how potent herbs can be, for they transformed me. But in case you do not know the reason for my frenzy, I shall tell you what has happened.

'On the Italian shore, opposite the walls of Messana, I caught sight of Scylla. I am ashamed to tell you of the promises and prayers I made, the endearments I uttered, only to have her treat them all with scorn. But now, if spells have any power, pronounce a spell with those sacred lips of yours: or, if herbs are more effective, employ the tested virtues of some potent herb on my behalf. I do not ask you to cure me, or to heal these wounds of mine. There is no need to put an end to my love, only let her share my burning passion.'

Now whether it was due to her own nature, or to Venus, in her anger at the tales Circe's father had told, no one had a heart more susceptible to love than Circe. Accordingly she said to Glaucus in reply: 'You would do better to pursue someone whose wishes and desires are the same as your own, one held captive by a love that matches yours. You deserved to be the one who was courted: you certainly could have been and indeed, if you hold out any hope, believe me, you will be yet. Look, to dispel any doubts you may have, and give you confidence in your appearance, I myself, though a goddess, daughter of the shining sun, so powerful with herbs and charms, pray to be yours. Scorn the girl who scorns you, pursue in your turn the one who pursues, and so by a single act repay us both as we deserve.' But, though she tried to persuade him in this way, Glaucus replied: 'Sooner will leaves grow in the sea, and seaweed on the mountain-tops, than my love for Scylla change, while she still lives.'

The goddess was indignant. She could not harm Glaucus himself, and would not have wished to do so, since she loved him; but she was angry with the girl he had preferred to herself. In her rage at finding her love rejected, she straightway ground together certain evil herbs, whose juices contained horrid powers and, when she had reduced them to powder, mixed them with spells that Hecate had taught her. Then, wrapping herself in a dark cloak, she proceeded out of the depths of the palace, through the host of fawning beasts. She made her way to Rhegium, which lies opposite rocky Zancle, walking over waves that boiled with currents, treading upon them as if on dry land, and skimming dryshod over the surface of the sea.

There was a little bay that curved round in a smooth crescent, where Scylla loved to rest. When the sun, halfway on his course, was at his strongest, shining from the heights of heaven and reducing shade to a minimum, she used to retreat there, away from the heat of sea and sky. In anticipation of her coming, the goddess tainted this pool with her wonder-working poisons. When she had poured them into its depths, she sprinkled the waters with a baneful root and thrice nine times, with magic utterance, muttered a mysterious spell, in strange and riddling words. Scylla arrived, and had descended into the water up to her waist, when she saw her loins disfigured by barking monsters. At first, not believing that they were part of her own person, she tried to shrink away and drive them off, for she was afraid of the dogs' cruel jaws. But she dragged along with her the beasts she sought to escape, and when she looked for her thighs, her legs, her feet, she found, instead of her own limbs, gaping mouths like those of Cerberus. She was standing upon a pack of wild dogs and, with truncated thighs and womb emerging from the mass, rested heavily on the backs of the wild beasts that supported her from below.

Her lover Glaucus wept her fate, and fled from the embraces of Circe, who had made too cruel a use of the powers of her herbs. Scylla remained where she was and, as soon as she had a chance, gave vent to her hatred of Circe by robbing Ulysses of his friends. In later times she would likewise have sunk the Trojan ships, had she not first been changed into a reef, whose rocks still jut above the sea: and sailors still keep clear of her, even as a rock.

When the Trojan ships, having rowed safely past this obstacle and past greedy Charybdis, were now close to the Italian shore, the wind bore them back to the coast of Libya. There Sidonian Dido received Aeneas into her home, and took him to her heart. But she was not destined to bear the parting well, when her Phrygian husband left her. On the pretext of making sacrifice, she built a pyre, and there fell on a sword, deceiving all in her intention, as she had been herself deceived. Aeneas, a fugitive once more, left the walls of the new city, built on its sandy shore, and was carried back to the land of Eryx, and to faithful Acestes. There he offered sacrifice, and paid the honours that were due to his father's tomb. When this was done, he set sail in the ships which Iris, Juno's messenger, had almost burned. Leaving behind him the kingdom of Hippotades and the land of steaming sulphur pools, he passed the rocky islands where lived the Sirens, Achelous' daughters. Then his ship lost its pilot, but he coasted on, by Inarime, by Prochyte and Pithecusae, perched on its barren hillside. This place derives its name from its inhabitants. Once upon a time, the father of the gods, utterly disgusted by the lying tongues of the Cercopes, and by the sins of that treacherous people, changed the men into a kind of mis-shapen animal, so that they appeared at once like, and yet unlike, human beings. He caused their limbs to shrivel, gave them snub turned-up noses, and scored their cheeks with the wrinkles of old age. Then he covered their bodies all over with bristling yellow hair, and sent them to this home: but first of all he deprived them of speech, and of the tongues to which such horrid perjury came naturally. He left them the power to complain only in raucous shrieks.

When Aeneas had passed these places, and left behind him on the right the walls of Parthenope, and on the left the tomb of the trumpeter Misenus, Aeolus' son, he came to the shores of Cumae, with its water-logged marshes. Entering the cave of the aged Sibyl, he prayed that he might make his way through the underworld, to visit his father's ghost. The Sibyl, however, for a long time kept her face fixed on the ground: at length, inspired by the presence of the god within her, she looked up, and replied: 'O hero, most renowned for your achievements, whose right hand has been tried by the sword, whose devotion by the flames, it is a great boon you ask. But have no fear, Trojan, you will obtain your request and, with me as your guide, will behold the homes of Elysium, the ultimate kingdoms of the universe, and the ghost of your beloved father. There is no path that virtue cannot tread.' As she spoke, she pointed to a gleaming golden branch in the grove sacred to Juno of Avernus, and told the hero to break it off from the trunk. Aeneas obeyed, and visited the realms of awe-inspiring Orcus, where he saw his own ancestors, and the shade of his aged father, great-hearted Anchises. He learned, too, the laws that govern those places, and the dangers he would have to undergo in wars that were yet to come.

Then, as he was retracing his steps wearily up the sloping path, he lightened the hardships of the way by conversing with his guide from Cumae. As he made the fearsome journey through the thick darkness, he said: 'Whether you be a goddess in your own right, or simply a mortal dearly beloved by the gods, you will always be equal to a goddess in my sight, and I shall confess I owe my life to you, since you have allowed me to visit the regions of death and, having seen them, to return again. In gratitude for these services, when I reach the upper air, I shall set up a temple in your honour, and pay tribute of incense.' The Sibyl looked back at him and, with a deep sigh, replied: 'I am no goddess, and you must not think any human being worthy of the honour of holy incense. Lest you should err in ignorance, I shall tell you my story.

'When I was still an innocent young girl, I was offered endless, eternal life, if I would yield myself to Phoebus, who was in love with me. While the god hoped for my consent, he was eager to bribe me with gifts, and said: "Maiden of Cumae, choose what you wish, and you will have your desire!" I pointed to a heap of dust which had been swept together, and foolishly asked that I might have as many birthdays as there were grains of dust: but I forgot to ask for perpetual youth as well. Yet Phoebus offered me all those years, and eternal youth too, if I would suffer his love. I scorned his gift, and remained unwed. Now the happier time of life is fled, and with shaky steps comes sick old age, which I must long endure. For, as you see me now, I have lived through seven generations; in order to equal the number of grains of dust, it remains for me to see three hundred harvests, three hundred vintages. A time will come when I shall shrink from my present fine stature into a tiny creature, thanks to my length of days, and my limbs, shrivelled with age, will be reduced to a mere handful. No one will think that I was ever loved, or that I pleased a god, and perhaps even Phoebus himself will fail to recognize me, or else deny that he ever had any affection for me. So changed shall I be, and invisible to anyone. But still, the fates will leave me my voice, and by my voice I shall be known.'

Such was the tale the Sibyl told, as Trojan Aeneas mounted up the sloping path, and emerged from the Stygian realms, into the Euboean colony of Cumae. When he had duly offered sacrifice, the hero made his way to the shore, which at a later date was called after his nurse, Caieta. Here too a Greek had found a home, Macareus from Neritos, who had settled there, after long and weary wanderings in the train of patient Ulysses. He recognized Achaemenides, abandoned long ago among the rocks of Etna and, marvelling to find him unexpectedly alive, exclaimed: 'What chance or what god saved you, Achaemenides? Why does a ship belonging to the barbarous Trojans carry a Greek on board? For what land is your vessel bound?' Achaemenides, no longer clad in ragged garments held together by thorns, but now entirely master of himself, answered the other's questions in these words:

'May I behold Polyphemus again, and that gaping mouth of his, streaming with human blood, if my home and Ithaca are more to me than this ship, if I honour Aeneas less than my own father. I shall never be able to be sufficiently grateful to him, though I give him my all. Can I forget or be ungrateful for the fact that I live and breathe, and see the heavens and the light of the sun? Aeneas made it possible for me to escape the Cyclops' jaws and now, supposing I should die today, I should be buried in a proper grave, or at any rate not in that monster's belly. What were my feelings (except that fear destroyed all sense and feeling) when I saw you sailing out to sea, and was myself left behind? I wanted to call out, but was afraid of betraying myself to the enemy. Even you, in your ship, almost came to grief, thanks to Ulysses' cries. I was watching when the Cyclops tore a great crag from the mountainside, and hurled it into the midst of the waves. I watched him again when, with all the strength of his gigantic arms, he hurled vast boulders that flew through the air as if they had been launched from some powerful catapult. Forgetting that I was no longer on board, I was afraid lest the wind or the waves might sink the ship.

'But when flight had saved you from certain death, then Polyphemus roamed all over Etna, groaning aloud, groping among the trees. Robbed of his sight, he stumbled against the rocks and, stretching his bloodstained arms out to sea, cursed the Achaean race, saying: "Oh, if some chance could bring Ulysses back to me, or one of his comrades, on whom I could vent my wrath, someone whose vitals I could devour, whose living limbs I might tear apart with my hands, pouring his blood down my throat, and chewing up his quivering flesh between my teeth! How trivial a loss, if a loss at all, would the blinding of my eye be then!"

'Fiercely he flung out this, and more besides, while I shivered and grew pale as I looked at his face, still dripping with the blood of murdered men, his cruel hands, his empty eye-socket, his limbs and beard crusted with human gore. Death stared me in the face, but that was the least of my troubles. I imagined that at any moment he would seize me and swallow down my body into his own. In my mind persisted a picture of the time when I saw the bodies of two of my companions dashed to the ground three times, four times, while the Cyclops, lying over his victims like a shaggy lion over its prey, crammed their flesh and their vital organs into his greedy stomach, their bones full of white marrow, and their limbs still half alive. A fit of trembling shook me. The blood drained from my face as I stood, watching in utter dismay, while he chewed and spat out his gory feast, vomiting up bits of flesh mixed with wine. Wretchedly I imagined that such was the fate in store for me, and for many days lay in hiding, trembling at every sound, afraid of death, yet eager to die, warding off the pangs of hunger with acorns and a mixture of leaves and grasses. I was all alone, without hope or resources, abandoned to a frightful death. After a long time, I spied this ship in the distance. Running to the shore, I gesticulated wildly, begging for a chance to escape. Their pity was roused. A Trojan ship received a Greek on board!

'And now, my dearest comrade, tell me your adventures too, and what happened to your leader Ulysses, and those who entrusted themselves to the sea, along with you.'

Macareus then explained how the leader from Ithaca had received the winds, enclosed in an oxhide bag, as a most precious gift from Aeolus, the son of Hippotes. For Aeolus was ruler of the Tuscan sea, and responsible for keeping the winds imprisoned. For nine days Ulysses and his crew had sailed before a favouring breeze, and had spied the land that was their goal. But when dawn broke on the tenth day, Ulysses' companions were overcome by jealousy, and a greedy desire to share his spoil. Thinking that the bag contained gold, they loosed the strings that bound the winds. Then the ship was carried backwards by the gales, over the waves it had recently crossed, till it sailed again into the harbour of King Aeolus. 'From there,' said Macareus, 'we came to Laestrygonia, to the ancient city that Lamus built, where Antiphates was ruling as king. Along with two others, I was sent into his presence, and only just managed to save myself and one of my comrades by flight. The third member of our company was devoured by the Laestrygonians – his lifeblood stained those accursed jaws. As we fled, Antiphates followed on our heels, calling to his people to attack us. They came rushing together, hurled rocks and tree-trunks at our ships, and sank them, crews and all. However, one vessel escaped, with Ulysses and ourselves on board.

'Mourning our lost comrades, and bitterly lamenting, we then approached that land which you see over there, in the distance. Believe me, I found that island was best seen from a distance! And I warn you too, Aeneas, you who are the son of a goddess and the most upright of the Trojans – for now that the war is over, you are no longer to be called an enemy – shun Circe's shores!

'When we had moored our ship on the beach, we too refused to go up and enter a house about which we knew nothing: for we remembered Antiphates, and the cruel Cyclops. However, we drew lots to determine who should be sent, and the luck of the draw despatched me to Circe's walls, in company with faithful Polites, Eurylochus, Elpenor who was too fond of his cups, and eighteen others. We had no sooner arrived, and were standing at the entrance to the house, when we were frightened by a horde of wild animals, a thousand strong, wolves and bears and lionesses, rushing to meet us. But there was no need to be afraid of them, for none wanted to injure us in any way. On the contrary, they even wagged their tails affectionately and fawned upon us, as they escorted us along, until we were received by servant girls, who led us through marble-roofed halls to their mistress.

'Circe was sitting in a handsome private apartment, raised on a majestic throne, with a gold-embroidered cloak wrapped round her, over her gleaming robes. Nereids and nymphs were with her, but they were not working fleeces with nimble fingers, or spinning long threads. Instead, they were arranging their mistress' herbs, separating into baskets the flowers and variegated grasses, that lay scattered about in no proper order. Circe herself directed them as they worked, for she knew the virtues of each leaf, and what kinds mixed well together. Carefully she watched and weighed the herbs she measured out.

'When she saw us, and received our greetings, she bade us welcome, and her smiling face seemed to augur well for the success of our plans. Immediately she gave orders for a concoction of toasted barley, honey, strong wine, and cheese to be prepared, and to these ingredients she added juices whose taste would be concealed by the sweetness of the rest. We took from the goddess' hand the cups she gave us, and drained them greedily, for we were parched. As soon as we had done so, the dread goddess touched our hair lightly with her wand and at that – ashamed though I am, I shall tell you – my body began to bristle with stiff hairs, and I was no longer able to speak, but uttered harsh grunts instead of words. My body bent forward and down, until my face looked straight at the ground, and I felt my mouth hardening into a turned-up snout, my neck swelling with muscles. My hands, which had lately held the goblet, now left prints, like feet, upon the ground.

'With the others, who had suffered the same fate (such is the power of magic drugs!) I was shut up in a sty, and then we saw that Eurylochus was the only one who had not been turned into a pig. He alone had avoided the cup that was offered him. Had he not done so,

I should still, to this day, be one of that bristling herd, for Ulysses would never have learned from him of the disaster that had overtaken us, and come to Circe for revenge.

'Mercury, bringer of peace, had given Ulysses a white flower, that grows from a black root, and is called by the gods "moly". With this and heaven's warnings to defend him, he entered Circe's home, and was invited to drink the treacherous cup. But when she tried to stroke his hair with her wand, he thrust her back, and frightened off the terrified goddess with drawn sword. Then they took each other's right hands, as a pledge of good faith, and Ulysses, received into Circe's chamber as her husband, requested as a wedding gift from his wife that his companions be restored to their true shape. We were sprinkled with the juices of some mysterious herb, possessing more wholesome properties than the last: then Circe tapped our heads with wand reversed, and chanted spells to counteract her previous charms. The more she recited, the more we raised ourselves erect, lifting ourselves up from the ground. Our bristles fell out, the split disappeared from our cloven hooves, shoulders, upper arms, and forearms, were restored to their proper shape. With tears of joy we embraced Ulysses, who was himself in tears, and the first words we uttered were expressions of gratitude.

'For a year we lingered there, and during so long a time there was much that I saw with my own eyes, and much that I heard. Among many other tales, this one was told me in private by one of the four servant girls employed in such sacred rites as were practised there. While Circe was spending her time along with my leader, this girl showed me a statue of a young man, carved in snowy marble, with a woodpecker on his head. It stood in a temple, and was decked with numerous wreaths. I was curious to know who he was, why he was worshipped in a temple, and why he carried this bird. In reply to my questions, the girl said: "Listen, Macareus, pay attention to what I say, and learn from this story, too, what power my mistress has.

'"Picus once ruled as king in the land of Ausonia. He was one of Saturn's sons, and his chief interest was in horses, trained for use in war. His appearance was such as you see there: you can perceive for yourself how handsome he was and, from his statue, imagine his actual beauty. His courage, too, was in keeping with his looks. At the time of which we are speaking, he was not yet old enough to have paid four visits to the Greek games which are held at Elis, every five years.

'"His handsome features attracted the attention of the dryads who belonged to Latium's hills, the nymphs of the springs sought him out, and the naiads too: those whom the river Albula bore, and the spirits of Numicius' stream, the daughters of the Anio, and of the Almo, whose course is so short, the nymphs of the rushing Nar, of deeply shaded Farfarus, and those who haunt the wooded pool of Scythian Diana, and the nearby lakes. However, Picus scorned them all, and devoted himself to one nymph only. She was reputed to be the daughter of Venilia, and of two-headed Janus, born on the Palatine hill. When this girl grew up and was old enough to be married, Picus of Laurentum was preferred to all other suitors, and she became his bride. She was of rare beauty, but her gifts as a singer were rarer still, and so she was called 'Canens'. She attracted trees and rocks by her voice, soothed wild beasts, detained the roving birds, and stayed long rivers in their courses.

'"One day, while she was singing in her clear treble, Picus left the house for the fields of Laurentum, intending to hunt the wild boars that were found there. Mounted on a mettlesome horse, he wore a purple cloak, fastened by a golden brooch, and carried two hunting spears in his left hand. Meanwhile the daughter of the sun had left the Circaean country that takes its name from hers, and had come into these very woods to gather fresh herbs on the fertile hills. From the cover of the thickets she saw the young king. As soon as she did so, she stood rooted to the spot. The herbs she had gathered fell from her hand, and a flame seemed to go scorching all through the very marrow of her bones. When she had recovered from this violent surge of emotion, she would have confessed at once what she desired: but the speed of Picus' horse, and his companions crowding round, prevented her from reaching him. 'Though the wind itself carry you off, still you shall not escape!' she cried. 'At least if I know my own self, if my herbs have not lost all their powers, and my spells do not deceive me.'

'"As she spoke, she conjured up a phantom boar, that had no real substance, and bade it run across in front of the king's eyes, and seem to vanish into the densely planted forest, where the trees grew closest, so that no horse could pass through. No time was wasted. Picus, not knowing the truth, immediately chased after his shadowy prey. Quickly he leaped from his foam-flecked horse and, in pursuit of an empty hope, went wandering on foot in the depths of the wood. Then Circe turned to prayer and supplication, worshipping her mysterious gods with incantations equally mysterious by means of which she used to dim the face of the snowy moon, and draw a veil of thirsty clouds across her father's orb. On this occasion too, as she chanted the spell, the heavens darkened and the earth breathed out mists, so that the king's comrades wandered blindly about the paths, and he was deprived of their protection. Having thus secured her opportunity, the goddess addressed herself to Picus. 'By those eyes of yours which have captivated mine,' she said, 'and by your beauty, most handsome youth, which makes me, a goddess, beg your favour, be kind to one who loves you, and accept the sun, who sees all things, as your father-in-law. Do not be hard-hearted and scorn Circe, the Titan's daughter!'

"'So she finished speaking. But Picus wildly rejected the goddess and her prayers, crying: 'Whoever you are, I am not for you. Another holds me captive, and I pray that she may do so for long years to come. Never let me break the vows that bind us, by indulging in an affair with anyone else, as long as the fates keep safe my Canens, Janus' daughter!' Again and again Circe renewed her entreaties, but in vain. 'You will suffer for this!' she cried. 'You will learn how one who has been injured, how a lover and a woman can repay! Never will you be restored to Canens!' Then, turning twice to the east, and twice to the west, she touched the young man three times with her wand, and recited three spells. He fled, but marvelled to find himself running more swiftly than his wont. Then he saw feathers covering his body and, indignant that he should be thus summarily added to the birds in Latium's woods, pecked at the rough oak trees with his horny beak, and angrily scarred their long branches. His feathers took on the purple hue of his cloak, while the golden brooch which had pinned his garment became part of his plumage, so that his neck was encircled by a ring of gold. Nothing remained to Picus of his old self, except his name.

"'Meanwhile his comrades had called him repeatedly all over the countryside, and had not found him anywhere: but they did come upon Circe. For she had now brightened the air, and allowed the clouds to be dispersed by sun and wind. They overwhelmed her with

321

accusations that were all too true, demanded to have back their king, threatened to use force, and were preparing to attack her with their fierce weapons. But she sprinkled her noxious drugs and poisonous juices round, summoned Night and the gods of Night from Erebus and Chaos, and prayed to Hecate in long-drawn howling cries. Then from the ground there sprang up a miraculous grove, the earth gave a groan, and the neighbouring trees grew pale. The grass which Circe had sprinkled was wet with drops like blood, the stones seemed to utter hoarse rumblings, dogs barked, the earth crawled with black snakes, and shadowy ghosts flitted noiselessly here and there. The band of huntsmen, dismayed by these horrors, trembled with fear. Then, as they gaped in wonder and terror, Circe touched their faces with her magic wand, and at its touch the young men were transformed into wild beasts of various kinds. Not one of them retained his own form.

'"The rays of the setting sun had bathed Tartessus' shore, but Canens waited in vain for her husband, watching and longing for his return. The servants and townspeople hurried this way and that, all through the woods, carrying lamps to meet him. The nymph herself was not content to weep or tear her hair or beat her breast, though she did all these things, but flung herself out of doors, and roamed distractedly through Latium's fields. Six nights went by, six times daylight returned, and saw her wandering without sleep or food, across mountains and valleys, wherever chance led her. The river Tiber was the last to see her, as she laid herself down, worn out with grief and journeying, on the banks of his lengthy stream. There she wept and softly mourned, pouring out words which, even in her grief, were musical, just as the swan on the point of death sometimes sings its own funeral song. At last the tender marrow of her bones was dissolved by her sorrows; she gradually wasted away, and vanished into thin air. But her story has been preserved by the spot, which the ancient Muses fittingly called Canens, after the nymph."

'Many such tales was I told, and many such things did I see, in the course of a long year. But when we had lost the habit of moving from place to place, and had become slow and settled, we were ordered to take to the sea again, to set sail once more. Circe, the Titan's daughter, had told us of the dangerous voyagings, the long, long journey and the perils of the cruel sea, that remained for us to

endure. I confess that I was thoroughly frightened at the prospect
and, having reached this shore, firmly remained here.'

That was the end of Macareus' story. Then Aeneas' nurse was
buried in a marble urn, and received this brief inscription on her
tomb:

> He whom I nursed, whose goodness men admire,
> Saved me, Caieta, from the Grecian fire,
> Here to cremate me on a fitting pyre.

The mooring cables were untied from the grassy shore, and the
ships of Aeneas, leaving far behind them that treacherous island and
the home of the ill-famed goddess, headed for the groves where the
deep-shaded Tiber, turgid with yellow sand, pours out into the sea.
Their leader Aeneas gained possession of this kingdom, and of the
daughter of Latinus, Faunus' son, though not without a struggle. He
undertook a war with a spirited people, and Turnus fought with fury
for his promised bride. All Etruria clashed in conflict with Latium, and
long did they fight, hard and anxiously, for victory.

Each side sought to increase its own strength by recruiting help
from without, and many peoples fought in support of the Rutulians,
many in defence of the Trojan camp. Aeneas went to Evander's city,
and his journey was not made in vain, but the Rutulian Venulus had
no success when he visited the town of the exiled Diomede. Under
the protection of Iapygian Daunus, Diomede was ruling a tract of
land, given him as a marriage gift, and had founded there a mighty
city. But when Venulus, acting under Turnus' orders, asked for his
help, the Aetolian hero refused, putting forward his lack of resources
as an excuse. He did not wish to involve himself or his father-in-law's
people in war, and had no citizens of his own to arm. 'In case you
should think that I am making up excuses,' he said, 'I shall steel my-
self to tell you my story, though the mere mention of it wakes again
my bitter grief.

'When lofty Ilium had been reduced to ashes and its citadel had
fed the flames kindled by the Greeks, when Locrian Ajax had
offended the maiden goddess by snatching a maiden from her pro-
tection, and brought upon us all the punishment he alone deserved,
we Greeks were scattered and, scudding before the winds across hostile
seas, endured thunderbolts, darkness like that of night, rainstorms, the

fury of sea and sky and, as a final disaster, the perils of Cape Capareus.

'I shall not detain you by describing in detail our dire misfortunes, but Greece could then have seemed deserving of pity, even to Priam himself. However, the warrior goddess Minerva, watching over me with care, kept me safe, and rescued me from the waves. But then, once more, I was driven out of my native Argos, for gentle Venus, remembering the wound I had once dealt her, exacted punishment from me. I experienced such hardships on the high seas, and in warfare on land, that I often called those men happy who had been drowned in the storm we all suffered, or in the relentless waters of Capareus, and wished that I had been among their number. As for my comrades, when they had endured the utmost miseries both in war and at sea, their resolution weakened, and they asked me to put an end to their wanderings.

'But Acmon, hot-spirited by nature, and now further incensed by our disasters, cried out: "What more remains, my friends, that you who have endured so much would refuse to bear? What more can Venus do, suppose she wishes? As long as men fear something worse, they are vulnerable: but when their lot is as bad as it can be, fear is trampled underfoot, and the worst evils trouble us not at all. Though the goddess herself should hear me, though she hate all Diomede's men, as in fact she does, yet we all of us scorn her hatred, and at great cost have purchased this great ascendancy."

'By such provocative words, Acmon of Pleuron goaded Venus to fresh rage, and roused her wrath again. Few approved of what he said, and most of us told our friend Acmon what we thought of him. He tried to reply, but his voice grew thin and his throat too, his hair turned to feathers, his newly-formed neck, his breast and back were covered with plumage, his arms were clothed in larger feathers, and his elbows curved round to form swift wings. His feet spread up over most of his toes, and his mouth hardened and stiffened into a sharply-pointed beak. Lycus stared at him in amazement, as did Idas and Nycteus, and Rhexenor too, and Abas. As they marvelled, they underwent the same transformation. Most of the crew flew up into the air, where they hovered around the rowers on beating wings. Should you inquire the shape of these birds, if birds they can be called, their bodies were very nearly, though not quite, like those of snowy swans.

'As for myself, with a tiny remnant of my people I barely manage to maintain this home and these parched acres, which I received from Daunus of Iapygia when I became his son-in-law.'

That was all that Diomede had to say. Venulus therefore left the kingdom that took its name from Calydon, returning home by way of the Peucetian bays, and the fields of Messapia, where he saw a cave, hidden among slender reeds and shaded by thick trees. It was at that time occupied by the goat-god Pan, but used previously to be a haunt of the nymphs.

Once a shepherd from Apulia filled these nymphs with sudden panic, and sent them at first fleeing in terror from the spot. However, when they recovered their self-possession, and realized with contempt who was pursuing them, they returned to their choral dancing, matching their steps to the rhythm of the song. The shepherd mocked them, leaping clumsily about in imitation, hurling coarse insults as well, and abusing them in foul language. Nothing silenced him, till finally a tree trunk imprisoned his throat: for he became a wild olive, in the taste of whose fruit one can still recognize the character of the man. In its bitter berries the tree reveals traces of his tongue, and the harshness of his language has passed into the olives.

So the embassy returned from their mission, bringing the news that the Aetolians refused to help. Without their aid, the Rutulians carried on the war they had begun, and much blood was shed on either side.

Then Turnus attacked the pinewood ships, carrying his hungry torches against them, and the timbers which the waves had spared shrank from his flames. Already the fire was consuming pitch and wax, and the other fuel that fed its hunger, the flames were climbing up the high mast to the canvas, and the benches across the hollow hull were smouldering, when the sacred Mother of the gods, remembering that these pines were cut on Ida's summit, filled the air with the clash of beating cymbals and the shrilling of pipes. Drawn through the thin air by her tamed lions, she cried aloud: 'It is useless, Turnus, to hurl those firebrands from your impious hands, for I shall save the ships. Never shall I allow consuming flames to burn wood that once grew in my groves, and was part of my forests.' There was a roll of thunder as the goddess spoke, and after the thunder came heavy rain and leaping hail. The winds, Astraea's brothers, flung sky and swelling sea into wild confusion by their sudden conflict, as they rushed together to do battle. The benign mother made use of one of these strong winds to break the ropes that moored the Trojan fleet, to sweep the ships away head-foremost, and plunge them beneath the sea. Their wood grew soft, and was changed into flesh, their curved sterns became heads and faces, the oars turned into fingers and legs that swam through the waters. What had been the side of the ship was now the side of a person: the keel which ran along the middle of the vessel became a spine, the rigging turned into soft tresses, and the yards into arms. Their colour remained a dark bluish-green, as before. Then, playing and sporting as girls love to do, they splashed about in the waters they had feared before: for though they had been born on the rough hillside, they were now nymphs of the sea, and haunted the yielding waves, untroubled by any thought of their origin. However, they had not forgotten how many dangers they frequently endured upon the ocean, and so they often laid helping hands beneath storm-tossed ships, unless the vessels carried Greeks on board. Ever mindful of Phrygia's downfall, they hated the Greeks, and watched with beaming faces the wreck of Ulysses' ship, with beaming faces saw Alcinous' vessel harden into stone as rock spread up over its timbers.

There was some hope that when the fleet was thus changed into living sea nymphs, the Rutulian might be frightened by the miracle into abandoning the war. But Turnus persisted. Each army had gods on its side, and each had courage, which counts for as much as gods. They were no longer fighting to win a kingdom as a dowry, a king's sceptre from their father-in-law, or Lavinia as a bride. They sought only to be victor, and carried on the war because they were ashamed to give it up: till at length Venus saw her son's arms victorious, and Turnus fell.

Ardea fell too, a city renowned for its strength while Turnus was alive. But now the foreign sword razed it to the ground, and its houses were hidden beneath red-hot ashes. From the midst of the ruin and confusion a bird of a kind never seen before flew up into the air, shaking off the cinders from its beating wings. It retained the leanness and the pallor, the mournful cries, and all the other character-istics of a captured town. Even the name of the city survived in that of the bird, and Ardea, changed into a heron, beats itself with its own wings, and bemoans its fate.

The courage of Aeneas had forced all the gods, including even Juno, to put an end to their long-standing anger, and now that the fortunes of his growing son Julus were firmly established, it was time for the hero whom Venus bore to enter heaven. Venus herself, when she had gone round all the gods, threw her arms about the neck of her father Jupiter, and said: 'You have never, at any time, been harsh to me, father, and now I want you to be kinder than ever, and grant some measure of divinity, however small, to my Aeneas – for he made you a grandfather, and has my blood in his veins. It is enough that he has once seen the unlovely kingdom of the underworld, once crossed the river Styx.' The gods gave their approval, and even the royal consort was not unmoved: she nodded her consent, and showed by her expression that she had been appeased. Then the father of the gods said: 'My daughter, you deserve this gift from heaven, both you who ask, and he for whom you ask it. Have your desire!'

When he said this, Venus delightedly thanked her father. Then, drawn through the thin air by her team of doves, she approached the shores of Laurentum, where the reedy waters of the river Numicius wind to the neighbouring sea. She bade this stream wash away all parts of Aeneas that death could harm, and bear them in its silent waters down to ocean's depths. The horned river carried out the goddess' requests and, with its waters, sprinkled and cleansed away all that was mortal in Aeneas: but the best part of him remained. When his body was purified, his mother anointed it with a divine perfume, touched his lips with a mixture of sweet nectar and ambrosia, and made him a god whom the Roman people welcomed with a temple and altars, giving him the name Indiges.

After that, Alba and the Latin kingdom were under the sway of Ascanius, Aeneas' son, who rejoiced in two names. His successor was Silvius, whose son Latinus inherited the name as well as the sceptre of his ancestor, the ancient king. The renowned Alba followed Latinus, and next in succession was Epytus. After him came first Capys, and then Capetus, and Tiberinus took over the kingdom from them. He gave his name to the river of Tuscany, when he was drowned in its waters. His sons were Remulus and the warrior Acrota. The elder, Remulus, was killed by a lightning flash, while he was himself trying to imitate lightning. Acrota, less daring than his brother, handed on his sceptre to the hero Aventinus, who lies buried on the same hill where he reigned, and has given his name to the district. After him, Proca held sway over the Palatine race.

It was under this king that Pomona lived. No other Latin wood nymph could tend a garden more skilfully than she, none was more devoted to the cultivation of the fruit trees from which she derived her name. She did not care for woods or rivers, but loved the country-side, and branches, loaded with luscious apples. Instead of weighing down her hands with heavy javelins, she used to carry a curved knife, with which at one time she would cut away growth that was too luxurious, and prune back branches that were spreading in different directions, at another she would slit open the bark of a tree, and insert a cutting, supplying nourishing sap to a nursling from a different stock. Her plants were never allowed to feel thirsty, for she brought water in trickling streams for the twining root-fibres to drink. Her garden was her passion and her love, and even Venus herself had no attraction for her. But she was afraid of being violently attacked by some rustic wooer, and so she fenced herself inside her orchards, to prevent the men she shunned from reaching her. The satyrs, who were young men and of an age for dancing, did everything to get possession of her, as did the Pans, who wore wreaths of pine leaves on their horns, and Silenus too, always younger than his years, and Priapus, the god who terrifies thieves with his sickle and his girth.

Vertumnus loved her even more than these, but he was not any luckier in his love. How often, disguised as a rough harvester, he used to carry ears of corn in his basket, the very image of a real harvester! Often he could be seen, with wisps of fresh hay tied round his brow, tossing the new-mown hay. Often he carried ox-goads in stiffened hands, so that one would swear that he had just unyoked his bullocks. Sometimes, knife in hand, he was a vineyard worker, prun-ing leaves and vines, or he took a ladder on his shoulder, so that you would think he was intending to pick fruit. He armed himself with a sword, and became a soldier, or again a fisher, carrying his fishing rod. In short, thanks to the many disguises he adopted, he often found some way of approaching his love, in order to enjoy the sight of her beauty. Then, one day, he even turned his hair grey at the temples, put an embroidered cap on his head, and pretended to be an old woman. Leaning on a stick, he entered the well-kept gardens, and admired Pomona's fruit. 'It makes you all the more desirable,' he said, and with these words of praise, kissed her several times, in a way in which a real old woman never would have done. Then, huddled and bent, he sat down on the grass, and looked up at the branches drooping under the weight of their autumn fruit.

There was an elm tree opposite, a lovely sight to see, with its bunches of shining grapes, and this the god praised, and its companion vine no less. 'But,' he said, 'if this tree trunk stood by itself, and was not wedded to the vine, it would be of no interest to anybody, except for its leaves. Moreover, the vine is supported by the elm to which it has been united, whereas if it had not been so married, it would lie trailing on the ground. And yet you are unmoved by the example of this tree! You shun marriage, and do not care to wed. I only wish you would! More suitors would seek your hand than ever troubled Helen, or Hippodame for whom the Lapiths fought, or the wife of Ulysses, a brave hero when faced with timid foes! Even now, when you shun them and turn away from their wooing, a thousand men desire you, as well as gods and demigods, and all the divine spirits that haunt the Alban hills. But if you are wise, if you want to make a good marriage, and are willing to listen to an old woman who loves you more than all of them, more than you think, then reject all ordinary offers, and choose Vertumnus to share your couch. You have my word, as well as his own, to guarantee his worth, for I know him as well as he knows himself. He does not go roaming about, all over the world, but cultivates these wide acres here. Nor does he fall in love with a girl he has only just seen, as the majority of your lovers do: you are his first and last love, and to you alone he will dedicate his life.

'Consider, too, that he is young, that nature has given him a handsome appearance, and that he can readily adopt any and every shape: you can order him to become all things in turn, and he will change into whatever you command.

'Besides, you like the same things. He is the first to have the apples that you grow, and enjoys holding your gifts in his hands. But he no longer desires fruits plucked from the trees, or savoury garden herbs, or anything except yourself. Pity his burning passion, and imagine that he is here in person, speaking through my lips, begging for what he wants. Beware of the gods who wreak vengeance, of Venus who hates hard hearts, and of the anger of Nemesis, whose memory is long. To make you fear them more, I shall tell you a story, the best-known in all Cyprus: for my long life has acquainted me with many tales. It may soften your heart, and make you ready to listen to persuasion.

'Once upon a time, a man of humble birth, called Iphis, caught sight of the princess Anaxarete, who was descended from the ancient line of Teucer. As soon as he saw her, he felt the fire of passion scorching through all his bones. He fought against it for a long time, but when reason could not conquer his mad desire, he came as a suppliant to the threshold of his beloved. Here he confessed his unhappy love to the girl's nurse, appealing to her by the hopes she had for the princess in her charge, not to be hard on him: at other times he coaxed each of the many attendants, anxiously seeking their interest and favour. Often he gave them letters with flattering messages to carry to their mistress, sometimes he hung on her doorposts garlands bedewed with tears, and laid himself on her doorstep, his soft flesh against the hard stone, abusing the stern bolt that held the door.

'But Anaxarete was more cruel than the sea that surges up when the stars of the Kids are setting, harder than iron tempered in the forges of Noricum, or living rock, still fast embedded in the ground. She scorned and mocked him, and in addition to her unkind actions, spoke arrogant words that cruelly deprived her lover even of hope.

'Iphis could not bear the torture of this long-drawn agony, and cried these last words before her door: "You win, Anaxarete! You will no longer have to bear my importunities! Celebrate your joyous triumph, sing your paean of victory, and wreathe your brow with shining laurel. For you are victor, and I gladly die. Come, iron-hearted girl, rejoice! Assuredly, you will be forced to praise something in my love, find something pleasing, and confess my worth! But remember that I never ceased to care for you, as long as I lived, and that for me the light of life and love must be extinguished together. No mere rumour will bring you the news of my death: I myself, be in no doubt of that, shall be here in person for you to see, so that you may feast your cruel eyes on my lifeless body. Yet, O gods above, if you see mortal deeds, remember me – my tongue can pray no more – and see to it that this story of mine is told in ages yet to come. Add to my fame the years that you have taken from my life!"

'As he spoke, he looked up, his eyes wet with tears, at the doorposts he had so often wreathed with flowers. Raising his pallid arms, he fastened a noose to the lintel of the door, and cried: "Here is a garland that will please you, O cruel and wicked heart!" With that, he thrust his head into the noose. Even then, as he hung there piteously, heavy and inert, his life choked out, he turned towards her.

'As his swaying heels struck against the door, it seemed to give a groan, like someone lamenting bitterly and, swinging half-open, revealed what had happened. The servants exclaimed aloud, and lifted him up, but in vain. Then they carried him to his widowed mother's house. She received her son in her arms and, gathering the cold corpse in her embrace, uttered such words as mourning parents use, and did the things that mourning mothers do. Weeping as she went, she headed his funeral procession as it passed through the city, carrying his wan corpse on the bier on which it was to be cremated.

'It so happened that Anaxarete's house was near the road along which the sad cortège made its way, and the sounds of lamentation came to the ears of the hard-hearted girl, who was already being hounded by the god of vengeance. In spite of her callous nature, she was moved to pity: "Let me see this unhappy funeral," she said, and went up to a room at the top of the house, whose windows were open wide. Scarcely had she looked out, and gained a clear view of Iphis, lying on his bier, when her eyes grew fixed, and a lifeless pallor spread over her body, as the warm blood drained away. When she tried to draw back, she was rooted to the spot, and though she made an effort to turn her face away, she could not do that either. Gradually the stone that had long since lain in her hard heart took possession of her limbs. Lest you imagine that this is only a story, Salamis still preserves a statue in the shape of the princess, and she has a temple too, under the name of Venus Prospiciens, the goddess who looks out.

'Remember this tale, my nymph, put away the pride that makes you slow to yield, and give yourself to your lover. So may no frosts nip your budding fruits in spring, no gales shake down your flowers.'

So the god, disguised as an old woman, pleaded with Pomona, but it was all to no purpose. Then he returned to his own shape, revealing himself as a young man. Stripping off the trappings of age, he appeared to the girl in all his glory, as when the sun's brilliant orb conquers the clouds that veil his face, and shines forth undimmed. He was preparing to use force, but there was no need for that. The nymph, entranced by the god's beauty, was smitten with a passion equal to his own.

Next to govern the Ausonian kingdom was the wicked Amulius, who gained the throne by means of his soldiers. But the sceptre which aged Numitor had lost was restored to him as a gift by his grandson and, at the festival of the Palilia, the walls of the city of Rome were founded.

Tatius and the Sabine fathers waged war against the new city and Tarpeia, who had opened up a way into the citadel for them, was punished as she deserved, crushed to death by the weapons they heaped upon her. Then the men from Cures, with voices hushed, like silent wolves, attacked the Roman guards, as they lay asleep, and marched upon the city gates which Ilia's son Romulus had closed and firmly barred. But Juno herself opened one gate: it turned on its hinges without a sound, and only Venus realized that its bars had fallen. She would have closed it, but no god is ever allowed to reverse the actions of another.

Near at hand, close by Janus' temple, in a spot moist with spray from a cool spring, lived the Ausonian water nymphs. Venus sought their aid, and the nymphs could not refuse to help the goddess, for she asked only what was just. They called up the rivers and streams that fed their fountains, but even then the gateway of Janus was not made impassable: it still lay open and the waters had not blocked the way. Then the nymphs put yellow sulphur in the depths of the bubbling spring, and kindled its underground channels with smoking bitumen. Thanks to the potency of these and other substances, the heat penetrated to the very depths of the fountain, and the waters, which had lately dared to challenge Alpine cold, became as hot as fire itself. The posts on either side of the entrance smoked with this fiery spray, and the gate that had promised the stern Sabines a way into the citadel was rendered useless, being defended by this new fountain, until the soldiers of Mars could fit on their weapons.

Then Romulus took the offensive, and the Roman earth was strewn with Sabine bodies, as well as with those of Rome's own citizens. The blood of father-in-law and son-in-law, shed by impious swords, flowed in a mingled stream. However, it was resolved not to fight to the death, but that peace should put an end to war, and Tatius share the Roman throne.

Now Tatius was dead, and Romulus held equal sway over both peoples, when Mars, laying aside his helmet, addressed the father of gods and men in these words: 'The time is at hand, sire, now that Rome's fortunes are securely founded and no longer depend on one champion alone, to award the prize you promised, both to me and to your grandson who has well deserved it. Take Romulus from earth, and set him in heaven. Once, in a council of the gods, you said to me (for I remember your gracious words, and marked them carefully): "One there will be, whom you will raise to the azure vaults of heaven." Now let your words come true!'

Almighty Jupiter nodded his consent and, curtaining the air with a pall of dark clouds, terrified the world with thunder and lightning. Mars realized that these portents warranted his carrying off his son, in accordance with Jupiter's promise. Vaulting up with the help of his spear, he fearlessly mounted his chariot, the horses straining beneath the bloodstained pole. With a touch of his whip he urged them forward and, racing through the air with all speed, came to rest on the summit of the wooded Palatine where Romulus, son of Ilia, was delivering humane judgement to his people. Mars swept him from their midst. The mortal body of the king dispersed into thin air, just as a bullet of lead melts in the sky, when hurled from the broad thong of a catapult. In its place, he acquired a handsome presence, more suited to the couches of the gods on high, an appearance like that of Quirinus, clad in ceremonial robes.

Romulus' wife, Hersilie, was mourning him as lost, when royal Juno ordered Iris to descend along her curved path, and bear these commands to the widow. 'O queen, you who are the chief glory of the Latin and the Sabine race, in the past you well deserved to be the wife of so great a hero, and well deserve to be Quirinus' consort now. If you would see your husband, dry your tears and follow me to the green grove on the Quirinal, that shades the temple of Rome's king.'

Iris obeyed and, gliding to earth down the gaily coloured rainbow, spoke to Hersilie as she had been commanded: the queen replied modestly, scarcely raising her eyes: 'O goddess – for it is not easy for me to tell who you are, but it is clear that you are a goddess – take me, take me and show me my husband's face. If the fates will only permit me to look upon it once, I shall declare myself in heaven!' Immediately, in company with the maiden daughter of Thaumas, she made her way to Romulus' hill. There a star fell from the bright sky, down to earth, and set Hersilie's hair alight. Then, with the star, she departed into heaven. The founder of the Roman city received her in the embrace she knew so well, and at one and the same time altered her appearance and the name she used to bear. He called her Hora, and now she is a goddess, consort of Quirinus.

BOOK XV

✾

MEANWHILE, men on earth were looking for a ruler who could bear such a burden of responsibility, and succeed so great a king: till Fame, a true prophet of the future, marked out the illustrious Numa for the crown. Being a man of able intellect, Numa was not content with learning the rites of the Sabine race, but conceived a grander project, to inquire into the nature of the universe. His enthusiasm for this study made him leave his native town of Cures, and visit the city of Crotona, where Hercules once found hospitality. When Numa inquired who had first founded a Greek city in Italian territory, one of the older inhabitants, versed in stories of the past, told him this tale.

'Hercules, the son of Jupiter, was returning from the ocean, so the story goes, with a rich spoil of Spanish cattle. After a prosperous voyage, he came to the shores of Lacinium and, while his cattle wandered over the tender grass, he himself entered the hospitable home of great Croton, where he rested to recover from his long toils. As he was leaving, he said: "In the days of our grandsons, this will be the site of a city." And his promise came true. For Alemon of Argos had a son, one Myscelus, whom the gods loved above all those of his generation. As he was lying in a deep sleep, the god who bears the club bent over him, and said: "Come now, leave your father's home, and seek the pebbly stream of distant Aesar!" Then, threatening the young man with many fearful disasters if he did not obey, the god departed, and at the same time Alemon's son awoke. He rose and, silently pondering his recent vision, waged a long battle with himself: the god bade him go, but the laws prevented his leaving the country, and death was the penalty, if he tried to move to another. When the shining sun had hidden his bright face in the ocean, and night, thickset with stars, had raised her head, the same god seemed to appear to the prince again, gave the same warnings, and threatened more and worse sufferings, if he did not do as he was told. Myscelus was afraid, and at once began to make preparations to move the possessions he had inherited from his father to a new home.

'There was murmuring in the city, and Alemon's son was brought to trial for showing contempt of the law. The case for the prosecution was heard first, and when it was completed his guilt was obvious, proved without need of witnesses. Then the prisoner, presenting a wretched sight, raised his face to heaven and, stretching up his hands, cried aloud: "O Hercules, whose twelve labours gave you the right to a place in the sky, bring me your aid, I pray! You are responsible for my sin!"

'It was the practice, in days of old, to condemn prisoners with black pebbles, to acquit them with white. On this occasion, the stern verdict was given in the usual way, and every pebble put into the cruel urn was black. But when the jar, turned upside down, poured out the pebbles to be counted, they all changed from black to white. Thanks to Hercules' divine power, the verdict was made favourable to Myscelus, and he was acquitted. He gave thanks to his patron, Amphitryon's son, and then, sped by the winds, sailed across the Ionian sea. Passing by Neretum, the city of the Sallentines, by Sybaris and the Spartan colony of Tarentum, he travelled on beyond the bay of Siris, beyond Crimisa and the land of Iapygia. Scarcely had he steered his wandering course past the lands which border on this shore, when he found the mouth of the Aesar, as destiny had intended, and a mound of earth nearby, which covered the venerable bones of Croton. There he founded his city, in the land where he had been ordered to build its walls, and named it after the buried hero.' Such was the origin of the place, according to the accepted tradition, and such the reason for the building of this city in Italian territory.

There was a man in this town, Pythagoras, who was by birth a Samian: but he had left Samos, fleeing at once the island and its tyrannical government, and in his hatred of despotism had gone into voluntary exile. In his thoughts he drew near to the gods, far removed though they were in their heavenly homes, and with the eyes of the mind he gazed upon those things which nature has denied to human sight. When unremitting care and thought had made everything clear to him, he imparted his knowledge for all to learn, and taught the silent wondering crowds about the origin of the great universe, the reasons for things, what Nature is, and what the gods, whence come the snows, the lightning flash, whether it is Jupiter who thunders, or the winds, splitting the clouds apart, what causes earthquakes, the laws that govern the movement of the stars, and all that is hidden from man's knowledge. He was the first to ban the serving of animal food at our tables, first to express himself in such words as these – wise words, indeed, but powerless to convince his hearers:

'O my fellow-men, do not defile your bodies with sinful foods. We have corn, we have apples, bending down the branches with their weight, and grapes swelling on the vines. There are sweet-flavoured herbs, and vegetables which can be cooked and softened over the fire, nor are you denied milk, or thyme-scented honey. The earth affords a lavish supply of riches, of innocent foods, and offers you banquets that involve no bloodshed or slaughter; only beasts satisfy their hunger with flesh, and not even all of those, for horses, cattle, and sheep live on grass. But creatures whose nature is wild and fierce, Armenian tigers and raging lions, bears and wolves delight in butchered food. Alas, what wickedness to swallow flesh into our own flesh, to fatten our greedy bodies by cramming in other bodies, to have one living creature fed by the death of another! In the midst of such wealth as earth, the best of mothers, provides, nothing forsooth satisfies you, but to behave like the Cyclopes, inflicting sorry wounds with cruel teeth! You cannot appease the hungry cravings of your wicked gluttonous stomachs, except by destroying some other life!

'But that ancient age, to which we have given the name of golden, was blessed with fruits plucked from the trees, and crops the earth put forth. Its people did not defile their lips with blood. Then birds flew through the air in safety, the hare wandered fearlessly in the open fields, no fish was hooked because of its own credulity. There were no snares, no fear of treachery, but everywhere peace in full measure. Then someone, setting an unprofitable example, whoever he was, envied the lions their diet and, by swallowing down a meal of flesh into his greedy stomach, took the first steps on the road to crime. It may be that originally the reeking swords were stained with blood from killing wild animals, and I admit that creatures trying to kill us

may be killed, without involving us in guilt. But that should have
been enough. It was as wrong to eat them as it was right to slay.

'Then wickedness went further. The pig is thought to have been the
first victim to meet a well-deserved fate, because it rooted out seeds
with its turned-up snout, and destroyed the hope of harvest. Then the
goat, they say, was sacrificed at Bacchus' altars, as a punishment for
having gnawed his vines. Both had themselves to blame. But what
did sheep do, to merit such a fate, peaceful flocks, born for the service
of man, who bring us sweet milk in their full udders, whose wool
provides us with soft garments, who do more for us alive than dead?
What have oxen done, animals quite innocent of guile or treachery,
harmless and simple, born to toil? Thankless indeed was he, and un-
deserving of the gift of corn, who first had the heart to lift the weight
of the curved plough from his beast's neck, and slay the ox who had
tilled his fields, bringing down his axe on the work-worn necks of
the cattle with whose help he had so often broken up the hard earth
and planted so many crops.

'Not content with committing such crimes, men have enrolled the
very gods as their partners in wickedness, and suppose that the
divinities in heaven take pleasure in the slaying of patient bullocks!
A victim of outstanding beauty, free from any blemish, whose
pleasing looks are its undoing, is set before the altars, decked with
garlands and with gold. There it hears, without understanding, the
prayers of the priest, and sees the corn it has cultivated sprinkled on
its forehead, between its horns. It is struck down, and stains with its
blood the knives which it may well have seen beforehand, reflected
in the clear water. At once the lungs are torn from its still living
breast, that the priest may examine them, and search out the purpose
of the gods, revealed therein. And then, so great is man's hunger for
forbidden food, you mortals dare to eat that flesh! I beg you, heed
my warnings, and abstain! Know and understand that when you put
the meat of slaughtered oxen in your mouth, the flesh you eat is that
of your own labourers.

'Now, since a god directs my speech, I shall duly follow him who
guides, reveal the secrets of my beloved Delphi and of the heavens
themselves, and unlock the oracles of a majestic mind. I shall speak of
things of great import, never studied by previous intellects, which
have long lain hid. I joy to journey among the stars, high above, to

leave the earth and this dull abode, to ride on the clouds and stand on stout Atlas' shoulders, looking down from afar on men as they wander aimlessly, devoid of any guiding principle, to unroll for them the scroll of fate, and cheer their panic and their fear of death, saying: "You people, dismayed by the fear of icy death, why are you terrified by the Styx, by shadows and empty names, the stuff of poet's tales, by the dangers of a world that does not exist? Our bodies, whether destroyed by the flames of the funeral pyre, or by slow decay, do not feel any suffering – you must not think so. Our souls are immortal, and are ever received into new homes, where they live and dwell, when they have left their previous abode. I myself at the time of the Trojan war – for I remember it well – was Panthous' son, Euphorbus, who once received full in the breast the heavy spear of Menelaus, Atreus' younger son. Quite recently, in the temple of Juno at Argos, Abas' city, I recognized the shield I used to carry on my left arm. All things change, but nothing dies: the spirit wanders hither and thither, taking possession of what limbs it pleases, passing from beasts into human bodies, or again our human spirit passes into beasts, but never at any time does it perish. Like pliant wax which, stamped with new designs, does not remain as it was, or keep the same shape, but yet is still itself, so I tell you that the soul is always the same, but incorporates itself in different forms. Therefore, in case family feeling prove less strong than greedy appetite, I warn you, do not drive souls that are akin to yours out of their homes by impious killings, do not nourish blood with blood.

'Since I have set sail upon a wide ocean, and spread my canvas to the wind, let me continue further. Nothing is constant in the whole world. Everything is in a state of flux, and comes into being as a transient appearance. Time itself flows on with constant motion, just like a river: for no more than a river can the fleeting hour stand still. As wave is driven on by wave, and, itself pursued, pursues the one before, so the moments of time at once flee and follow, and are ever new. What was before is left behind, that which was not comes to be, and every minute gives place to another. You see the nights, completed, pass into day, the shining rays of morning succeed the darkness of the night: the colour of the sky is not the same, when all things lie wearily in the still midnight, as when bright Lucifer emerges on his white steed. It changes again when Aurora, forerunner of the day, gilds the sky she must hand on to Phoebus. The orb of the sun-god himself, red in the morning when he rises from beneath the earth, red when he sinks below, shines white in the heights of heaven, because the air is better there, far removed from earth's contagion. Nor can the moon by night retain one and the same shape all the time: she is smaller to-day than she will be to-morrow, if she is waxing, and greater if she wanes.

'Or again, don't you see the year passing through a succession of four seasons, thus imitating our own life? In the early spring, it is tender and full of sap, like the age of childhood. Then the crops, in shining trim but still delicate, shoot up in the fields and, though they are not yet stout and strong, fill the farmers with joyous hopes. Everything is in flower, the fertile earth gay with brightly-coloured blossoms, but there is as yet no sturdiness in the leaves. Spring past, the year grows more robust and, moving on into summer, becomes like a strong young man. There is no time hardier than this, none richer, none so hot and fiery. Autumn takes over when the ardour of youth is gone, a season ripe and mellow, in temper midway between youth and age, with a sprinkling of grey hairs at its temples. Then aged winter comes shivering in, with tottering steps, its hair all gone, or what it has turned white.

'In the same way, our own bodies are always ceaselessly changing, and what we have been, or now are, we shall not be to-morrow. There was a day when we lived in our mother's womb, mere seeds that held the first promise of a man. To these nature applied her hands, skilfully fashioning them. Then, unwilling that our bodies should lie tightly cramped and buried inside our mother's swollen shape, she sent us out from our home, into the empty air. The baby, first born into the light of day, lies weak and helpless: after that he crawls on all fours, moving his limbs as animals do, and gradually, on legs as yet trembling and unsteady, stands upright, supporting himself by some convenient prop. Then he becomes strong and swift of foot, passing through the stage of youth till, having lived through the years of middle age also, he slips down the incline of old age, towards life's setting. Age undermines and destroys the strength of former years. Milon, grown old, weeps to see those arms hanging limp and thin, whose massive knotted muscles once rivalled those of Hercules. Helen weeps too, when she sees herself in the glass, wrinkled with age, and asks herself why she was twice carried off. Time, the devourer, and the jealous years that pass, destroy all things and, nibbling them away, consume them gradually in a lingering death.

'Even the things which we call elements do not remain constant. Consider the changes that they undergo: for I shall instruct you. The everlasting universe contains four elements that give rise to bodies. Two of these, earth and water, are heavy and, by their own weight, sink down, while the other two, air and fire, which is more rarefied than air itself, are weightless, and soar upwards, unless something holds them under. Though these four elements are distinct from each other in space, yet they are all derived from one another, and are resolved back again into themselves. Earth is broken up and refined into liquid water, water becoming still less substantial changes into air and wind, and air too, being already of the finest texture, flashes upwards when it loses weight, into the fiery atmosphere above. Then the process is reversed, and the elements are restored again in the same order: fire condenses and thickens into air, air into water, and water, under pressure, produces earth.

'Nor does anything retain its own appearance permanently. Ever-inventive nature continually produces one shape from another. Nothing in the entire universe ever perishes, believe me, but things vary, and adopt a new form. The phrase "being born" is used for beginning to be something different from what one was before, while "dying" means ceasing to be the same. Though this thing may pass into that, and that into this, yet the sum of things remains unchanged.

'For my part, considering how the generations of men have passed from the age of gold to that of iron, how often the fortunes of different places have been reversed, I should believe that nothing lasts long under the same form. I have seen what once was solid earth now changed into sea, and lands created out of what once was ocean. Seashells lie far away from ocean's waves, and ancient anchors have been found on mountain tops. What was at one time a level plain has become a valley, thanks to the waters flowing down over it, mountains have been washed away by floods, and levelled into plains. Land that once was marshy has become a barren stretch of arid sand, and thirsty deserts are moist with stagnant pools. In one place, nature sends out new springs, in another she blocks existing ones, and rivers may either burst from the ground, disturbed by tremors in the depths of the earth, or they may drain away and sink out of sight. So the Lycus, after being swallowed up in a chasm of the earth, appears again far away, reborn from a new source: the Erasinus too at one point is sucked down, and flows beneath the ground, to return again as a mighty river in the fields of Argos. The Mysus, they say, ashamed of his source and his original bed, now flows elsewhere as the Caicus. In Sicily too the Amenanus sometimes runs full, churning the sands in his waters, but at other times his springs are checked, his channel dry. Formerly the river Anigrus was used for drinking, but now it pours forth waters no one would wish to touch: since the time when, unless we are to discredit the poets completely, the centaurs used its stream to wash the wounds inflicted by the bow of Hercules, the club-bearer. Again, is it not true that the Hypanis, which rises in Scythia's mountains, and was once fresh water, is now tainted with bitter salt?

'Antissa and Pharos, and Tyre too, the city of the Phoenicians, were once surrounded by sea, but not one of them is an island now. In the old days, the inhabitants of Leucas occupied a continuation of the mainland, now the sea encircles them. Zancle, too, is said to have been joined on to Italy till the sea destroyed their common border, and the intervening waves thrust back the lands. If you look for Helice and Buris, once cities of Achaea, you will find them beneath the waters: the sailors still point out the drowned walls of the fallen towns. Near Troezen, where Pittheus ruled, is a mound, rising steeply, bare of trees, which was once an absolutely flat plain, but is now a hill. It is a terrible tale, how the fierce and violent winds, shut up in their hidden caverns, wished to find some exit for their blasts, and struggled in vain to enjoy the wide expanse of the open sky. There was no chink anywhere in their prison, through which their gusts might go. They stretched the earth, and made it swell, just as a man blows up a bladder, or the skin of a horned goat, with his breath. The swelling in the ground remained and now, hardened by the long passage of years, has the appearance of a high hill.

'Many instances occur to me, which I have heard and been told, but I shall mention only a few more. Come now, admit that even water gives and takes new forms. At mid-day the waters of horned Ammon are chill, but at sunset and sunrise they grow warm. It is said that the Athamanians kindle wood by pouring these waters over it, at the season when the moon has dwindled to its smallest crescent.

The Cicones have a river that turns to stone the inner organs of those who drink it, and spreads a marble covering over anything it touches. Crathis and Sybaris too, the latter flowing close to our own country here, give hair the colour of gold or amber. More surprising still, there are some streams which can change not only men's bodies, but their characters as well. Who has not heard of Salmacis' loathsome waters, or the Ethiopian lakes? If anyone drinks of these, he either goes mad, or falls into a deep miraculous sleep. A man who quenches his thirst at Clitorius' spring shuns wine, and soberly enjoys water by itself: perhaps this is because there is some property in these waters incompatible with the warmth of wine, though the inhabitants of the place have another explanation. They say that when Amythaon's son cured Proetus' demented daughters of their madness by means of spells and herbs, he threw the charms which had restored the girls' senses into this spring, so that the waters developed a lasting hatred of wine. The Lyncestian river has the opposite effect: for if anyone drinks too much of it, he reels about, just as if he had been drinking neat wine. There is a place in Arcadia too, which people of old called Pheneus, whose waters are distrusted because of their double nature. Beware of them at night: for if drunk then, they are harmful. But they do no hurt to those who taste them by day. So lakes and rivers have different properties at different seasons.

'There was a time when Ortygia was a floating island, but now it is firmly fixed. The Argo feared the Symplegades, rocks which once clashed together in a cloud of spray from the waves they smashed. Now those crags stand immovable, resistant to the winds. Even Etna, glowing with its sulphurous furnaces, will not always be fiery, nor was it always so. For, if its fires are to be explained by the fact that the earth is a living animal, possessed of many air passages that breathe out flames, then as often as it moves, it can change the channels through which it breathes, putting an end to one set of holes, and opening up another. Or, if swift winds, shut up in the caverns of the mountain, fling together inflammable material, and rock upon rock, till Etna catches fire owing to their friction, then when the winds die down, the caverns will be left cold. Again, if it is bitumen that blazes up, or yellow saffron, that burns with little smoke, then surely when, in the long course of time, earth's stocks are exhausted, she will no longer afford a rich abundance of fuel for the flames: deprived of the sustenance their natural greed demands, they will succumb to hunger and, starved themselves, will starve their fires.

'There is a tale that in Pallene, in the region beyond the North wind, there are men whose bodies, when they have dipped themselves nine times in Minerva's pool, acquire a covering of downy feathers. I do not, myself, believe this, but the Scythian women are said to practise the same magic, achieving their end by sprinkling their limbs with magic drugs.

'However, if I must add further proof of things already proved, you surely see that when bodies decay, either owing to the passage of time, or when heat has reduced them to a pulp, they turn into little animals? Experience has shown that if you select bulls, kill them, and bury them in a trench, from every part of the rotting carcases will come bees, to sip honey from the flowers. Like the beasts from which they spring, the bees frequent the countryside, are devoted to toil, and are ever working in hope of harvest. A war-horse, covered over with earth, produces hornets. If you remove the hollow claws of land crabs and bury the rest in the earth, there will emerge from the buried remains a scorpion, with curved and threatening tail. And the farmers know full well that the worms which spin a cocoon of white threads on the leaves, in country places, change into butterflies, the symbol of death. Mud contains germs that produce green frogs; these have no legs when they are first born, but soon acquire limbs suitable for swimming and, to enable them to make long jumps on land as well, the hind legs are longer than the front. When the bear first gives birth to her young, it is not a cub, but merely a lump of flesh, living and no more. By her licking, the mother fashions limbs out of this bundle, and reduces it to her own shape. Moreover, you see, don't you, that the larvae of the honey-bee, born in the hexagonal cells of the honey-comb, have bodies but no limbs, and only late in life develop feet and wings?

'Consider Juno's bird, which wears stars on its tail, think of the eagle that carries Jove's thunderbolt, and Venus' doves, and the whole race of birds – who would believe that they could come from the inside of an egg, if he did not know that it happened?

'Some people also believe that when a human body is shut up in the tomb, and its backbone rots away, the marrow changes into a snake.

344

'All these creatures, however, derive their origin from something other than themselves. There is one living thing, a bird, which re-produces and regenerates itself, without any outside aid. The Assyrians call it the phoenix. It lives, not on corn or grasses, but on the gum of incense, and the sap of balsam. When it has completed five centuries of life, it straightway builds a nest for itself, working with unsullied beak and claw, in the topmost branches of some swaying palm. Then, when it has laid a foundation of cassia, and smooth spikes of nard, chips of cinnamon bark and yellow myrrh, it places itself on top, and ends its life amid the perfumes.

'Then, they say, a little phoenix is born anew from the father's body, fated to live a like number of years. When the nestling is old enough and strong enough to carry the weight, it lifts the heavy nest from the high branches and, like a dutiful son, carries its father's tomb, its own cradle, through the yielding air, till it reaches the city of the sun, where it lays its burden before the sacred doors, within Hyperion's temple.

'If there is anything strange or wonderful in such novelties, we may well wonder that the hyena can change its sex, the female that lately allowed the male to mount her becoming now a male herself. Then there is the animal which lives on air and wind, and immediately assumes the colour of whatever it touches. Conquered India gave his lynxes to Bacchus, god of the vine-cluster. Men say that whenever these animals empty their bladders, the contents turn to stone, and harden in contact with the air. In the same way coral, too, hardens as soon as air touches it, whereas under the water it was a waving plant.

'The day will end, and Phoebus sink his panting horses in the deep, before I can recount all the things that have been altered to a different shape. So we see times change, and some nations gain strength, while others sink into obscurity. Troy was great in wealth and men, and for ten years could afford to lose so many lives in war: now humbled to the dust, she can but point to her ancient ruins, ancestral tombs are all her wealth. Sparta too was famous once, once the great city of Mycenae flourished, Amphion's citadel prospered once, and that of Cecrops too. Now Sparta is a tract of worthless land, lofty Mycenae has fallen, what but a name is Oedipus' city, Thebes? What remains of Pandion's Athens but a name? Even to-day, rumour has it that a

345

Trojan city, Rome, is rising close to the river Tiber, that flows down from the Appennines, rising on foundations built to support a vast structure. This city, too, alters her form as she grows, and will one day be the capital of the wide world. This, they say, is what the prophets predict, this is foretold by the oracles that reveal the fates. So too, as I remember, when Troy was tottering to her destruction Helenus, son of Priam, comforted Aeneas, who was in tears, and trembling for his safety: "O goddess-born prince, if you note well what I prophesy, Troy will not utterly perish, while you are safe. Fire and the sword will give way to you, and you will journey forth, bearing with you the rescued symbols of Pergamum, till you find a foreign field, more friendly than your own land to you and to your Troy. A city I see there, even now, intended for Troy's descendants, greater than any seen in the past, greater than any that now exists, or ever shall be. Other leaders will raise it to power, through the long years, but one, born of Julus' line, will make it mistress of the world. When the earth has enjoyed his presence, the realms of heaven will enjoy him too, and the sky will be his final destination."

'I remember well that Helenus prophesied such things to Aeneas, as that hero bore the Penates out of Troy, and it gladdens my heart that the walls of this city, descended from Troy, are rising now, that the Greek victory has been a good thing for the Trojans.

'But now, lest I should stray far from my course, and allow my horses to forget that they are making for a goal, I return to my theme. The heavens and everything that lies below them change their shape, as does the earth and all that it contains. We too, who are part of creation, since we are not merely bodies, but winged souls as well, can find a home in the forms of wild beasts, and be lodged in the breasts of cattle. Therefore, let us leave unmolested those bodies, which may contain the souls of our parents or of our brothers, or those of other relatives, or at least the souls of men. Let us not dishonour our kind, or cram our stomachs with feasts like that of Thyestes. What evil habits a man learns, how wickedly does he prepare himself to shed human blood, when he cuts open a calf's throat with his knife, and listens unmoved to its mournful lowing, when he can slay a kid that cries like a child, or feed on the birds which he himself has fed! How little short of full-fledged crimes are acts like these! And to what do they lead?

'Let the ox proceed with his ploughing, or blame his death on advancing years: let the sheep supply us with a defence against the biting North wind, and well-fed goats present their udders to be milked. Away with nets and snares, traps and cunning ruses. Cease to trick birds with limed twigs, to make a sport of hunting stags with feather-decked cords, or hiding barbed hooks beneath your treacherous bait. Destroy creatures that harm you, but even in their case, be content to destroy. Do not let their flesh pass your lips; live on some less barbarous diet.'

When Numa had been instructed in these and other such teachings, he returned, they say, to his native land and, at the people's request, took over the reins of government in Latium. Then, blessed with a nymph as his wife, and with the Muses to guide him, he taught the nation religious rites, and introduced to the arts of peace a race accustomed only to the violence of war. When, at a ripe old age, he came to the end of his kingship and his life, the women of Latium, the people, and the senators mourned for Numa dead. But his wife left the city, and concealed herself in a hiding-place in the deep woods that grow in the valley of Aricia.

There, with her moans and lamentations, she hampered the worship of Diana, which had been introduced into this grove by Orestes. Many a time the nymphs of the grove and of the pool warned her against this, and sought to console her with their words. Time and again Theseus' brave son rebuked her weeping, and said: 'Do restrain yourself: you are not the only one whose fortune calls for complaint. Look at the others who have suffered similar losses. Then you will be more reconciled to your lot. I wish it were only other people's sorrows, not my own, that could serve to comfort your grief: but my story too is a case in point.

'Some mention of Hippolytus may have come to your ears, I fancy, the prince who met his death through the trickery of his accursed stepmother, and his father's credulity? You will be surprised at what I say, and I shall find it difficult to prove, but none the less, I am that same Hippolytus. In days gone by Pasiphae's daughter tried to persuade me to dishonour my father's bed. Finding her efforts vain, she then pretended that I lusted after what she in fact desired herself. Whether in fear, lest I inform against her, or annoyed at being rejected, she turned upon me the charge that she deserved, and had me condemned. Though I was guiltless, my father cast me out of the city, calling down angry curses on my head as I left. I drove off into exile, directing my chariot towards Troezen, the city of Pittheus, and was already crossing the shore of the Corinthian gulf, when the sea rose up, and a huge mass of waters seemed to curl itself into a mountainous shape from which, as its size increased, came bellowing roars. Then the summit seemed to split, and there erupted a horned bull, which burst through the waters, rearing itself into the yielding air, till its chest was clear of the waves, vomiting quantities of sea water from its nostrils and gaping mouth. My companions were terror-stricken, but I, absorbed in thoughts of my own exile, remained unconcerned. Then suddenly my mettlesome horses turned their heads towards the sea, their ears pricked up, trembling all over. In their fright and confusion at the sight of the monster, they hurled the chariot down over the steep rocks. Vainly I struggled to pull on the reins that were flecked with white foam. Bending backwards, I strained at the supple thongs. The horses, maddened though they were, would not have been too much for my strength, had not the tip of the axle round which the wheel revolves struck against a jutting tree stump, so that the wheel itself was shattered and wrenched away. I was flung from the chariot but, my limbs being still entangled in the reins, my living flesh was dragged along, while my muscles were held fast by the stump. Part of my body was pulled away, and part was left impaled. There were ominous cracks from breaking bones, and there you might have seen me, utterly prostrated, breathing out my life, no part of my body recognizable, but all one gaping wound.

'Can you, nymph, or dare you compare your calamity with mine? I have even seen the kingdoms wrapped in night, and bathed my torn body in the waters of Phlegethon, nor would my life have been restored, but for the potent remedies of Apollo's son. Thanks to his powerful herbs, and Paean's aid, I did regain my existence, but it was contrary to the will of Dis. And so, in case the sight of me should increase the bitterness that boon had caused, Diana shrouded me in a dense mist. Then, to keep me safe, and enable me to appear with impunity, she added years to my age, and altered my features till they could not be recognized. For a long time she pondered whether she should let me have Crete, or Delos, as my home: but she decided against both, and set me here. At the same time, she told me to give up a name that might evoke the memory of horses, and said: "You who were Hippolytus, be now Virbius!" From that time I have lived in this grove as one of the minor gods, sheltering under the divine power of my mistress, and my name is coupled with hers.'

However, the sufferings of others had no power to lessen Egeria's grief. Prostrate at the foot of the mountain, she melted away in tears, till Phoebus' sister, moved by the devoted affection of the mourning wife, turned her body into a cool spring, and dissolved her limbs into everlasting waters.

This miracle impressed the nymphs, and filled the Amazon's son with an amazement as deep as that felt by the Etruscan ploughman when, in the midst of his fields, he saw the fateful sod stir and move of its own accord, though no one had disturbed it. Then the lump of earth lost its own form, and acquired that of a man, who opened his new-made lips to reveal the shape of things to come. The natives of the place called him Tages, and he it was who first taught the Etruscan race how to discover the future.

Romulus, too, felt similar surprise when, long ago, he saw his spear, stuck fast in the Palatine hillside, suddenly put forth leaves. It stood there, firmly held, not by the iron point which had driven into the earth, but by newly-formed roots. No longer a spear, but a tough-fibred tree, it afforded unexpected shade to the wondering onlookers.

Equally amazed was Cipus, the Republican general, when he looked at himself in the waters of the river: for he saw horns sprouting from his brow. Thinking it was a trick of reflection, he raised his hands repeatedly to his forehead, and there touched what he saw. No longer could he refuse to believe his eyes. Halting in his triumphant return from the foe he had vanquished, he lifted eyes and hands to the skies, and cried: 'O gods in heaven, whatever is foreshadowed by this portent, if it be good fortune, may it be for my country and for Quirinus' people, but if disaster threatens, let it be for me alone!'

From sods of green turf he constructed a grassy altar, and burned offerings of incense, to appease the gods, pouring libations the while from sacrificial dishes. Then he sought to learn, from the still quivering entrails of slaughtered sheep, what they portended for him. The Etruscan soothsayer, as soon as he saw the entrails, perceived that they foretold happenings of great import, but it was not clear what these events would be. However, when he raised his keen eyes from the organs of the sheep, to behold Cipus' horns, he cried: 'Hail, O king! For to you, Cipus, and to your horns, this place and the citadels of Latium will owe their obedience. Only cut short delay, and hasten to enter the gates standing open to receive you. Such is fate's command: for, once received within the city, you will be king, and will safely gain possession of an everlasting throne.'

Cipus drew back. Turning his rugged features away from the city walls, he answered the priest: 'May the gods avert all such threats, and drive them far away! Far better that I should spend my life in exile, than that the Capitol should see me as its king!' Immediately he had spoken he called together the people, and the reverend senate; but first he wreathed his horns with branches of laurel, the symbol of peace. Then he took his stand on a mound which his warriors had raised and, after praying to the ancient gods in accordance with the usual custom, addressed the people.

'There is one here,' he said, 'who, unless you drive him from the city, will be king! Who he is, I indicate to you, though I shall not name him. He wears horns on his forehead! The priest declares that this man, if he once enters Rome, will impose laws that will make you slaves. He could, indeed, have broken in, through the open gates, but I prevented him, though he is closer kin to me than any other. Do you, citizens, keep this man out of your city. If he deserves it, load him with heavy chains, or else put an end to fear by killing your fated tyrant!'

Like the murmur that comes from high-skirted pine trees, when the violent East wind whistles through, or the noise of the sea-waves heard from afar, there came a murmuring from the people. But, rising above the confused babble of the muttering crowd, one voice rang out: 'Who is he?' Men looked at their foreheads, in search of the horns that had been foretold. Again Cipus spoke to them, and said: 'Here you have the man you seek!' and, removing the wreath from his forehead, though the people sought to stop him, he showed them his temples, conspicuously adorned with twin horns.

All the people groaned, and lowered their eyes. Though no one would have believed it possible, they were unwilling to look at that head, so deservedly renowned. They would not suffer his brow to be without its meed of honour any longer, but set a festive wreath upon his head. Since it was not permissible for him to enter the city walls, the leaders of the people assigned a portion of land to Cipus, as a mark of honour, as much as he could drive round with a team of oxen harnessed to the plough, between sunrise and sunset. Then they engraved horns, that represented the miraculous horns of the hero, on the bronze pillars of the city gate, there to remain for years to come.

O Muses, ever present to assist a poet, now unfold the tale of how Coronis' son was added to the deities worshipped in Romulus' city; tell us whence he came, to dwell in the island round which the deep Tiber flows. You know the story, nor can long intervening years distort your memory.

Once, long ago, a dreadful pestilence tainted the air of Latium, and its pallid inhabitants were ravaged by a sickness that drained away their blood. Weary with funeral processions, when they saw that human efforts were of no avail, and that doctors' remedies could do nothing, they sought the help of heaven. They went to Delphi, the earth's centre, to visit Phoebus' oracle, and prayed him to grant them his aid in their misery, to give them some oracle that would restore their health and put an end to the evils of their great city. The ground, the laurel tree and the quivers which the god himself carries, all trembled together and, from the depths of the shrine, the sacred tripod uttered these words, making the listeners' hearts quake with fear:

'What you seek from me, O Roman, you might have looked for nearer home! Seek it there now. It is not Apollo you need, to alleviate your distress, but Apollo's son. Go with my blessing, and call upon my child.' When the senate in its wisdom heard the god's commands, it made inquiries to find the city where Phoebus' son lived, and sent a deputation to sail before the wind, to Epidaurus' coast. As soon as the ambassadors touched land in their hollow ship, they made their way to the assembly of the Greek elders, and begged them to give the Romans the god who, by his presence, might stop the deaths that were wiping out the Italian race. For so the oracle promised, and it could not be doubted.

Opinion in the assembly was divided, and at variance. Some thought that help should not be refused, but many argued that the god should be retained. They should not send away the source of their own

safety, nor yet hand over their divinities to others. While the question
was still undecided, twilight drove away the last of the daylight.
When darkness had spread its shades over the world, the health-
bringing god appeared to the Roman envoy in his dreams. He stood
by the bed, holding a rustic staff in his left hand, stroking his long
beard with his right, just as he is wont to be seen in his temple. Then
he seemed to speak in gentle tones, and say: 'Forget your fears: I shall
come, and leave a phantom of myself behind. Only look at this
serpent that twines around my staff, and mark it well, so that you may
be able to recognize it. For I shall disguise myself as my serpent, but I
shall be larger, and appear as mighty as gods ought to be, when they
transform themselves.' As soon as his voice ceased, the god dis-
appeared. With him, sleep departed too, and kindly daylight fol-
lowed hard on the heels of sleep.

When the dawning of the next day had put the fiery stars to flight,
the leaders of the people, uncertain what to do, assembled at the sump-
tuous temple of the god whom the Romans were seeking, and prayed
that he would indicate by a sign from heaven where he himself wished
to dwell. Scarcely had they fallen silent when the golden god, dis-
guised as a serpent, with crest raised erect, sent forth a hissing sound to
announce his coming and, by his arrival, shook statue and altars, doors
and marble threshold, and the golden gables. He halted in the midst
of the temple, rearing his breast up from the ground, and his eyes,
flashing fire, travelled round the assembled company. The terror-
stricken crowd was filled with panic but the priest, his holy locks
bound with a white fillet, recognized the divine presence. 'It is the
god, behold, the god! Let all who are present keep silence, and cleanse
their minds of unclean thoughts. And you, O god most beautiful,
let this appearance prove to our advantage, and bless those who
worship at your shrine!'

All who were present adored the god, as they were bidden; all
echoed the words of the priest and, with minds and voices, the
Romans too showed proper devotion. The god bowed his head
towards them and, swaying his crest, gave them assurance of his
favour, hissing repeatedly with flickering tongue. Then he glided
down the shining steps and, turning his head backwards, looked
behind him at the ancient altar he was about to leave. After bidding
farewell to his accustomed home and to the temple where he had

dwelt, the huge serpent slithered along the ground, that was covered
with flowers strewn for him. With snaking coils he made his way
through the heart of the city, to the curving mole that sheltered the
waters of the harbour. There he stopped and, glancing gently round,
seemed to dismiss the crowd that had dutifully followed in his train.
He placed himself in the Italian ship, and it sank lower in the water
when it felt the weight of the god on board.

Aeneas' descendants were filled with joy. After they had slain a bull
on the shore, they unfastened the twisted cables that held their flower-
decked ship, and a light breeze sped the vessel on its way. The god,
towering above the ship, rested his neck heavily on the curving stern,
and looked down into the dark blue waters.

Carried by gentle breezes over the Ionian sea, at dawn on the sixth
day he reached Italy, and sailed along past the shores of Lacinium,
famed for Juno's temple, and past the coast of Scylacium. He left
Iapygia behind him, and was rowed past the rocks of Amphrisia on
the left, the cliffs of Cocinthus on the right. Coasting by Romethium,
by Caulon and Narycia, he sailed through the narrow strait of Sicilian
Pelorus, journeying towards the domain of King Hippotades, the
mines of Temesa, Leucosia and the rose-gardens of sunny Paestum.
From there he skirted Capreae, and the promontory of Minerva, the
hills of Surrentum with their noble vineyards, the city that takes its
name from Hercules, Stabiae and Parthenope, home of idleness, till
he came to Cumae, where the Sibyl has her temple. After that he
went on to the warm springs of Baiae, and to Liternum, the region of
the mastic trees. He reached the Volturnus, which carries down great
quantities of sand in its swirling waters, and Sinuessa where many
snowy doves make their nests, the unhealthy marshes of Minturnae,
and Caieta, called after the nurse who was buried there by her charge.
Past these he went, to the home of Antiphates, and to Trachas, sur-
rounded by swamps, to Circe's land, and Antium's shore with its
firm sand. Here, since the sea was rough, the sailors brought their ship
with its spreading sails to land.

Then the god unwound his coils and, gliding along, fold upon fold,
in vast curves, entered the temple dedicated to his father, that was
situated close to the yellow strand. When the waves were calm again,
the Epidaurian left the altars where he had enjoyed his parent's hos-
pitality and, cleaving a furrow in the sandy shore as he dragged his

rasping scales along, climbed up the rudder into the ship. There he laid his head on the high stern, and remained thus till he came to Castrum, to the venerable city of Lavinium, and the Tiber's mouths.

All the people, men and women alike, had come flocking from every side to this place, to meet him; among the rest, the Vestal virgins, who guard Trojan Vesta's fires, greeted the god with joyful cries. As the swift ship sailed up-river, incense burned with a crackling sound on altars ranged along the banks on either side. Its fumes perfumed the air, while the sacrificial knives reeked with the blood of victims slain.

Now the serpent-god had entered the Roman city, the world's capital. He raised himself upright and, leaning his neck on the top of the mast, turned his head about, looking round for a suitable dwelling. The Tiber divides into two streams and flows round a piece of land which is called 'The Island', the arms of the river stretching out equally on either side, to embrace the land that lies between them. The snake that was Phoebus' son left the Latin ship, and betook himself to this island, where he resumed his divine appearance, put an end to the citizens' distress, and brought health to the city by his coming.

All the same, he was a foreigner, introduced into our temples from without. Caesar is a god in a city that is his own. He excelled in peace and war, but it was not so much the wars he brought to a triumphal conclusion, or his achievements at home, or his majesty swiftly won, but rather his own offspring that caused him to become a new star, a fiery-tailed comet. Among Caesar's exploits, no achievement was greater than this, that he was the father of such a son. He conquered the sea-girt Britons, and sailed a victorious fleet through the seven channels of the papyrus-bearing Nile, he brought the rebellious Numidians under the sway of the Roman people, and Juba too, from the land of the Cinyps, and Pontus that proudly boasts of Mithridates. He earned many triumphs, and celebrated not a few: yet surely none would count this more glorious than to have been the father of one so great. Since Caesar's son became the guardian of the world, the gods have shown abundant favour to the human race. Therefore, so that his descendant might come of more than mortal stock, Caesar had to be made a god.

When the golden goddess who was Aeneas' mother saw this, when she saw too that an armed conspiracy was being formed, and grim death planned for Rome's high priest, she grew pale, and went about crying to every god she met: 'See, what an elaborate plot is being hatched against me, what a treacherous attack is being made on the only one of Trojan Julus' descendants left to me! Shall I always be singled out, to be harassed by anxiety all too well-founded, I who was wounded by the spear of Calydonian Diomede, overwhelmed by Troy's failure to defend her walls, who saw my son driven to wander far, tossed about upon the sea, visiting the abodes of the silent shades, fighting with Turnus or rather, if I am to speak truth, with Juno? Why recall now the sufferings of my family in the past? My present fear does not allow me to remember previous misfortunes. Look there, do you see those guilty weapons being sharpened? Keep them away, I pray you, prevent this wicked deed! Do not let Vesta's flames be extinguished by the blood of her priest!'

It was in vain that Venus anxiously voiced these complaints all over the sky, trying to stir the sympathies of the gods. They could not break the iron decrees of the ancient sisters. However, they gave unmistakable warnings of the grief that was to come. Tales are told of how arms clashed amid black thunderclouds, and terrifying trumpets and battle-horns were heard in the sky, foretelling the guilty deed. The face of the sun, too, was gloomy, and shed a pallid light upon the troubled earth. Firebrands were often seen, blazing among the stars, and drops of blood fell with the rain. The day-star was dark, with spots of rusty black upon its disc, and the chariot of the moon was spattered with blood. In a thousand places the Stygian screech-owl gave its ominous warnings, in a thousand places ivory statues wept, and chants and threatening words are said to have been heard, in the sacred groves. No victim could gain a favourable response; when the entrails were examined, the head of the liver was found to be severed, and the liver itself indicated that civil strife was at hand. In the forum and around the houses and the temples of the gods, dogs howled by night, and the silent shades of the departed roamed abroad, while earthquakes shook the city.

Yet the warnings sent by the gods could not defeat the conspiracy, or stop fate's destined plan. Drawn swords were carried into the sacred building – for of all the places in the city, none but the senate-house sufficed for the foul deed of murder. Then Venus beat her breast, with both hands, and tried to hide Aeneas' descendant in that cloud which had previously cloaked·Paris, when he was snatched away from his enemy, the son of Atreus, the cloud in which Aeneas had escaped the sword of Diomede. But the father of heaven reproached her: 'Are you trying, all by yourself, my daughter, to alter the course of fate, that none can combat? You may go yourself into the house of the three sisters, and there you will see the records of destiny, massive tablets of bronze and solid iron, which have no fear of thunderings in the sky, or of the wrathful lightning, safe and eternal though the heavens fall. You will find there the fate of your descendant engraved in everlasting adamant. I have read it myself, and noted it: now I shall repeat it to you, that you may no longer be ignorant of the future.

'This man for whom you are distressed, my Venus, has finished his allotted span, and completed the number of years he was fated to spend on earth. But he will enter heaven as a god, and be worshipped on earth in temples: for you will bring this about, you and his son who, inheriting his name, will bear alone the burden set upon his shoulders. Yet, in his heroic quest for vengeance for his murdered father, he will have us on his side in war. The walls of Mutina, besieged by an army under his auspices, will be defeated, and will sue for peace. Pharsalia will feel his power, Macedonian Philippi will be soaked in blood a second time. The great name of Pompey will be vanquished on the Sicilian seas, and the Egyptian consort of a Roman general, trusting in that marriage bond to her cost, will be brought low. Her threats to make my Capitol the slave of her Canopus will prove an empty boast. Why should I go through the tale of barbarian lands and races, lying on the shores of ocean, in the east and in the west? All habitable lands on earth will be his, and even the sea will be his slave.

'When the blessing of peace has been bestowed upon the earth, he will turn his attention to the rights of the citizens, and will pass laws, eminently just. By his own example he will direct the people's ways and, looking forward to the future and his remote descendants, will require the son of his hallowed wife to adopt his name, and with it his responsibilities. Only when he is ripe in years, and has lived as long as Nestor of Pylos, will he ascend to our heavenly home, and the stars that are his kin. Meanwhile, snatch up Caesar's soul from his murdered body, and transform it into a star, so that Julius deified may ever look from his lofty seat upon the forum and my Capitol.'

Scarcely had Jupiter finished speaking when gentle Venus stood in the midst of the senate-house, though none could see her, and snatched away from the body of her Caesar the soul that had been newly released. She did not allow it to be dispersed into the air, but bore it up to the stars in heaven. As she carried it, she felt it kindle and catch fire. Released from her bosom, it flew up high beyond the moon and, its fiery tail leaving a wide track behind, flashed forth as a star. Julius the god, looking down upon the good deeds of his son, admits that they are greater than his own, and glories in being surpassed. Though Augustus forbids his own actions to be rated above those of his father, yet the talk of men, free and unrestricted by any edicts, prefers him against his will, and in this alone opposes his commands. Thus did great Atreus yield to Agamemnon's claim to fame, so Theseus was greater than Aegeus, Achilles than Peleus. Lastly, to cite a family as great as Caesar's own, so is his father Saturn less than Jove.

Jupiter controls the palaces of heaven, and the kingdoms of the threefold universe. The earth is under Augustus' sway. Each is a father and a ruler. I pray you, gods who accompanied Aeneas, to whom fire and sword gave way, gods of our own land, and you, Romulus, founder of our city, Mars, the father of unconquered Romulus, and Vesta too, worshipped among Caesar's household gods, and with her you, O Phoebus, who have your home with us, and Jupiter on high, who dwell on the Tarpeian citadel, and all the rest whom it is right and proper for a poet to invoke: may that day be slow to come, postponed beyond our generation, on which Augustus, leaving the world he rules, will make his way to heaven and there grant the prayers which he is no longer present to receive.

My work is complete: a work which neither Jove's anger, nor fire nor sword shall destroy, nor yet the gnawing tooth of time. That day which has power over nothing but my body may, when it pleases, put an end to my uncertain span of years. Yet with my better part I shall soar, undying, far above the stars, and my name will be imperishable. Wherever Roman power extends over the lands Rome has subdued, people will read my verse. If there be any truth in poets' prophecies, I shall live to all eternity, immortalized by fame.

INDEX

READ MORE IN PENGUIN

In every corner of the world, on every subject under the sun, Penguin represents quality and variety – the very best in publishing today.

For complete information about books available from Penguin – including Puffins, Penguin Classics and Arkana – and how to order them, write to us at the appropriate address below. Please note that for copyright reasons the selection of books varies from country to country.

In the United Kingdom: Please write to *Dept. EP, Penguin Books Ltd, Bath Road, Harmondsworth, West Drayton, Middlesex UB7 ODA*

In the United States: Please write to *Consumer Sales, Penguin USA, P.O. Box 999, Dept. 17109, Bergenfield, New Jersey 07621-0120*. VISA and MasterCard holders call 1-800-253-6476 to order Penguin titles

In Canada: Please write to *Penguin Books Canada Ltd, 10 Alcorn Avenue, Suite 300, Toronto, Ontario M4V 3B2*

In Australia: Please write to *Penguin Books Australia Ltd, P.O. Box 257, Ringwood, Victoria 3134*

In New Zealand: Please write to *Penguin Books (NZ) Ltd, Private Bag 102902, North Shore Mail Centre, Auckland 10*

In India: Please write to *Penguin Books India Pvt Ltd, 706 Eros Apartments, 56 Nehru Place, New Delhi 110 019*

In the Netherlands: Please write to *Penguin Books Netherlands bv, Postbus 3507, NL-1001 AH Amsterdam*

In Germany: Please write to *Penguin Books Deutschland GmbH, Metzlerstrasse 26, 60594 Frankfurt am Main*

In Spain: Please write to *Penguin Books S. A., Bravo Murillo 19, 1° B, 28015 Madrid*

In Italy: Please write to *Penguin Italia s.r.l., Via Felice Casati 20, I–20124 Milano*

In France: Please write to *Penguin France S. A., 17 rue Lejeune, F–31000 Toulouse*

In Japan: Please write to *Penguin Books Japan, Ishikiribashi Building, 2–5–4, Suido, Bunkyo-ku, Tokyo 112*

In Greece: Please write to *Penguin Hellas Ltd, Dimocritou 3, GR–106 71 Athens*

In South Africa: Please write to *Longman Penguin Southern Africa (Pty) Ltd, Private Bag X08, Bertsham 2013*

READ MORE IN PENGUIN

A CHOICE OF CLASSICS

Aeschylus	The Oresteian Trilogy
	Prometheus Bound/The Suppliants/Seven Against Thebes/The Persians
Aesop	Fables
Ammianus Marcellinus	The Later Roman Empire (AD 354–378)
Apollonius of Rhodes	The Voyage of Argo
Apuleius	The Golden Ass
Aristophanes	The Knights/Peace/The Birds/The Assemblywomen/Wealth
	Lysistrata/The Acharnians/The Clouds
	The Wasps/The Poet and the Women/The Frogs
Aristotle	The Art of Rhetoric
	The Athenian Constitution
	Ethics
	The Politics
	De Anima
Arrian	The Campaigns of Alexander
St Augustine	City of God
	Confessions
Boethius	The Consolation of Philosophy
Caesar	The Civil War
	The Conquest of Gaul
Catullus	Poems
Cicero	The Murder Trials
	The Nature of the Gods
	On the Good Life
	Selected Letters
	Selected Political Speeches
	Selected Works
Euripides	Alcestis/Iphigenia in Tauris/Hippolytus
	The Bacchae/Ion/The Women of Troy/Helen
	Medea/Hecabe/Electra/Heracles
	Orestes/The Children of Heracles/Andromache/The Suppliant Women/The PhoenicianWomen/Iphigenia in Aulis

READ MORE IN PENGUIN

A CHOICE OF CLASSICS

Hesiod/Theognis	**Theogony** and **Works and Days/ Elegies**
Hippocrates	**Hippocratic Writings**
Homer	**The Iliad**
	The Odyssey
Horace	**Complete Odes and Epodes**
Horace/Persius	**Satires and Epistles**
Juvenal	**Sixteen Satires**
Livy	**The Early History of Rome**
	Rome and Italy
	Rome and the Mediterranean
	The War with Hannibal
Lucretius	**On the Nature of the Universe**
Marcus Aurelius	**Meditations**
Martial	**Epigrams**
Ovid	**The Erotic Poems**
	Heroides
	Metamorphoses
Pausanias	**Guide to Greece** (in two volumes)
Petronius/Seneca	**The Satyricon/The Apocolocyntosis**
Pindar	**The Odes**
Plato	**Early Socratic Dialogues**
	Gorgias
	The Last Days of Socrates (Euthyphro/ The Apology/Crito/Phaedo)
	The Laws
	Phaedrus and **Letters VII and VIII**
	Philebus
	Protagoras and **Meno**
	The Republic
	The Symposium
	Theaetetus
	Timaeus and **Critias**

READ MORE IN PENGUIN

A CHOICE OF CLASSICS

Plautus	**The Pot of Gold/The Prisoners/The Brothers Menaechmus/The Swaggering Soldier/Pseudolus**
	The Rope/Amphitryo/The Ghost/A Three-Dollar Day
Pliny	**The Letters of the Younger Pliny**
Pliny the Elder	**Natural History**
Plotinus	**The Enneads**
Plutarch	**The Age of Alexander** (Nine Greek Lives)
	The Fall of the Roman Republic (Six Lives)
	The Makers of Rome (Nine Lives)
	The Rise and Fall of Athens (Nine Greek Lives)
	Plutarch on Sparta
Polybius	**The Rise of the Roman Empire**
Procopius	**The Secret History**
Propertius	**The Poems**
Quintus Curtius Rufus	**The History of Alexander**
Sallust	**The Jugurthine War** and **The Conspiracy of Cataline**
Seneca	**Four Tragedies** and **Octavia**
	Letters from a Stoic
Sophocles	**Electra/Women of Trachis/Philoctetes/Ajax**
	The Theban Plays
Suetonius	**The Twelve Caesars**
Tacitus	**The Agricola** and **The Germania**
	The Annals of Imperial Rome
	The Histories
Terence	**The Comedies (The Girl from Andros/The Self-Tormentor/TheEunuch/Phormio/The Mother-in-Law/The Brothers)**
Thucydides	**The History of the Peloponnesian War**
Virgil	**The Aeneid**
	The Eclogues
	The Georgics
Xenophon	**Conversations of Socrates**
	A History of My Times
	The Persian Expedition